Presented as a service to medicine by Bayer plc

Ciprofloxacin:
10 years of clinical experience

APR Wilson
RN Grüneberg
Department of Microbiology
University College London Hospitals
Grafton Way
London
WC1E 6DB

With a contribution by:
P Davey
Department of Clinical
Pharmacology and
Infectious Diseases
University of Dundee
Dundee
DD1 9SY

The views expressed in this publication are the views of the authors and not necessarily those of Maxim Medical or of Bayer plc.

Always refer to the manufacturer's Prescribing Information before prescribing drugs cited in this book.

British Library Cataloguing in Publication Data.
A catalogue record for this book is available from the British Library.

ISBN 1 900654 02 4

Published by Maxim Medical
Magdalen Centre, The Oxford Science Park, Oxford OX4 4GA, UK
http://www.maximmed.com/

Designed and typeset by Creative Associates
115 Magdalen Road, Oxford OX4 1RS, UK

Printed in the UK by Butler & Tanner Ltd
The Selwood Printing Works, Caxton Road, Frome, Somerset BA11 1NF, UK

Supported by an unrestricted grant from Bayer AG
Leverkusen, Germany

Dedication

This book is dedicated to JT Smith (1934–1996)

Acknowledgements

We would like to thank Alasdair Geddes for providing the *Preface*, Sherwood Gorbach and Kristin Nelson for preparing the *Foreword*, Peter Davey for contributing the chapter on *Pharmacoeconomics*, Glenn Tillotson and Ian Dorrian of Bayer plc for support, and Rebekah Ponsford and Sarah Tarrant of Maxim Medical for project management and editorial help.

Preface

Alasdair Geddes

From the Department of Infection
University of Birmingham, Birmingham, UK

The second half of the 20th century saw truly remarkable advances in the therapy of bacterial infections. Unfortunately, but predictably, the bacteria began to fight back – developing mechanisms for resisting the action of anti-microbial agents. Particular problems were posed by Gram-negative bacilli and staphylococci which, in the late 1970s and early 1980s, were rapidly becoming resistant to the available antimicrobials.

The development of the fluoroquinolone agents which were active against many of these resistant organisms represented a significant advance in the fight against infection. The fluoroquinolones possessed another important quality – they penetrated well into tissues and cells. They could also be given by mouth, even for serious infections.

In 1983 Bayer released ciprofloxacin, a highly active fluoroquinolone, for preclinical and early clinical studies. I was fortunate to be involved in these studies and was impressed by the efficacy of ciprofloxacin in two infections which, until that time, had been 'difficult to treat' – typhoid fever and chronic deep-seated infections, such as osteomyelitis caused by *Pseudomonas aeruginosa*. Both responded extremely well to ciprofloxacin and I was particularly impressed by the absence of a chronic carrier state following the treatment of typhoid fever. Ciprofloxacin went on to become the agent of choice for infections caused by enteric pathogens. Several of our patients with chronic pseudomonas bone infections unresponsive to other antibiotics have reason to be grateful for cures following prolonged treatment with ciprofloxacin.

Ciprofloxacin's clinical development was led by Peter Schacht and George Arcieri; their energy, vision and fortitude ensured that it gained a product licence within 5 years. The first country to grant a licence was the Philippines in October 1986, followed by the UK and Germany in February 1987.

Peter Wilson and Reuben Grüneberg tell the 'ciprofloxacin story' in this book. The breadth of the chapters is a reflection of the range of indications for ciprofloxacin, which has been prescribed for over 150 million patients in either the hospital or community setting. Sherwood Gorbach and Peter Davey's contributions highlight different perspectives of the ciprofloxacin story.

Considering that more than 15,000 publications relating to ciprofloxacin have been published since the drug's inception, the efforts of the authors are all the more remarkable. They have assembled a cogent and considered clinical account of 10 years of experience with ciprofloxacin. This book represents a state-of-the-art review, and, as such, will assist clinicians throughout the world with essential data on ciprofloxacin. All involved with this drug's development are to be congratulated on its success.

Wilson APR and Grüneberg RN.
Ciprofloxacin: 10 years of clinical experience
© 1997 Maxim Medical, Oxford.

AM Geddes
February 1997

Contents

Foreword

Development of ciprofloxacin: the USA perspective

Sherwood L Gorbach and Kristin W Nelson
From the Departments of Community Health and Medicine
Tufts University School of Medicine, Boston, USA

Ciprofloxacin, developed by Bayer in 1981, has become a remarkable success story in the pharmaceutical industry, not only for being the first oral antimicrobial drug with broad-spectrum activity that can be used to treat serious infections, but also for its penetration into the commercial market place. Within a decade of its release, ciprofloxacin has achieved the first-place position in international sales of anti-infective products. Based on current projections, the drug will sell $US1.5 billion worldwide in 1996. The USA accounts for $US800 million or 54% of total sales. Besides the importance of the USA in sales figures, American investigators also played a seminal role in the scientific development of the drug and in propelling ciprofloxacin to its current place of prominence.

This foreword reviews the story of ciprofloxacin development in the USA since 1983 (Table 1), based on interviews with many of the key figures and references to important papers in the field. While the intrinsic antimicrobial activity and excellent pharmacokinetics were bound to make ciprofloxacin a resounding success, involvement of American investigators in the development process contributed to its popularity in a major way.

In the beginning...

The predecessor to the new class of quinolones was nalidixic acid, an accidental by-product that emerged in the synthesis of the antimalarial compound, chloroquine. Nalidixic acid was a disappointing antimicrobial drug due to its limited spectrum of activity and its poor tissue penetration. With the introduction of the piperazine group and the fluorine atom into the structure, fluoroquinolones were created. Ciprofloxacin was developed in 1981 by Bayer in Germany, and was released for *in vitro* studies the following year.

The medical community first heard about ciprofloxacin at the 1983 annual meeting of the American Society for Microbiology when Harold Neu of Columbia University presented data showing that this drug had activity against both Gram-negative and Gram-positive bacteria, including *Pseudomonas* spp. and *Staphylococcus* spp. There was immediate enthusiasm for this new agent among American microbiologists and infectious diseases physicians, and many were interested in working with this exciting new drug. This abstract was later published.[1]

Planning the research in the USA

At Miles Pharmaceuticals in West Haven, Connecticut (the Bayer subsidiary in the USA),

Wilson APR and Grüneberg RN.
Ciprofloxacin: 10 years of clinical experience
© 1997 Maxim Medical, Oxford.

Table 1. Milestones in the development of ciprofloxacin in the USA.

1983	Abstract presented on the *in vitro* activity of ciprofloxacin by Harold Neu at the Annual Meeting of the American Society for Microbiology.
1984	Compassionate-use programme started with treatment of a patient of George Gee Jackson in Chicago who had *Pseudomonas* bacteraemia; the programme would swell to 1100 patients by 1986.
1986	Meeting of investigators in Florida in which George Arcieri summarised the results of 3981 patients treated in 146 clinical trials, of which 133 were performed in the USA.
1987	Ciprofloxacin approved for use in the oral form by the FDA.
1991	Intravenous ciprofloxacin approved for use by the FDA based on bioequivalence with the oral form.

a team was assembled to develop this new product. George Arcieri and Doug Webb, joined later by Jim Layman, were the major figures in this project. Their combined efforts led to a remarkably rapid and comprehensive programme of basic research, *in vitro* studies, pharmacology, toxicology, animal models and clinical trials, eventually leading to licensing of the oral compound by the FDA in 1987.

The timing of the ciprofloxacin research programme was impeccable. On the one hand, investigators were able to turn their attention to this drug because there was a dearth of new antimicrobial drugs in the pipeline with anti-pseudomonal activity, and virtually no oral products. On the other hand, there was an incipient, but rising, concern about pharmaco-economics and the financial impact of prolonged hospitalisation. The potential advantages of an oral compound that could treat complicated infection outside the hospital was immediately grasped by the infectious diseases community. The prospect of shorter hospital stays, lower acquisition costs and fewer complications than intravenous therapy, made ciprofloxacin a welcome newcomer to the research ranks.

The initial clinical studies focused on urinary tract infections (UTI), mainly because there was considerable scepticism on the part of infectious diseases physicians about the use of an oral agent in the treatment of systemic infections caused by Gram-negative bacteria. After success in UTI, the Miles team organised a protocol that allowed investigators to treat infections outside the urinary tract to build a database on efficacy. Favourable reports from the clinic led to increased confidence in the drug, and protocols were developed in the USA for treatment of infections in skin and soft tissues, bone, and the gastrointestinal and respiratory tracts.

When the Miles group approached investigators with these expanded protocols, the response was overwhelmingly positive. George Arcieri recalled, "From the start, everyone knew that the activity of this drug was a quantum step forward. Once the compound was identified, there were no great surprises. The anti-pseudomonal activity of the drug and the ability to treat infection outside the urinary tract with an oral drug was encouraging."

Doug Webb was responsible for developing protocols and contacting investigators. He reminisced, "The early *in vitro* and animal model studies made people take notice, and by 1985, everyone agreed that this would be a big drug. People were interested in getting involved in the clinical studies."

The 1986 meeting of investigators in Florida

The watershed of research studies on ciprofloxacin was reached in 1986 at the investigators' meeting in Florida organised by Miles and chaired by Harold Neu. Only 3 years after the clinical research effort was initiated, the papers presented at this meeting summarised the results accumulated by hundreds of investigators from various institutions, mostly in the USA. (These papers were published in a supplement to the *American Journal of Medicine* in 1987.)[2]

Hooper, Wolfson and other colleagues at the Massachusetts General Hospital reported their classic studies that showed that the activity of ciprofloxacin correlated with its effect on DNA gyrase A subunit.[3] Resistance occurred as a result of spontaneous single-step mutation at a low frequency. The *in vitro* antimicrobial activity extended to a broad array of micro-organisms, as presented by several laboratories: Enterobacteriaceae, *Pseudomonas aeruginosa* and other non-fermenters among the Gram-negative bacteria; *Streptococcus* spp. and *Staphylococcus* spp., including *Staphylococcus aureus*, coagulase-negative staphylococci, and methicillin-resistant forms, among the Gram-positive forms; and an array of intracellular micro-organisms, including *Chlamydia*, *Mycoplasma*, *Legionella*, *Brucella* and *Mycobacteria* spp.

The big excitement of the meeting was generated by the paper presented by George Arcieri entitled *Ciprofloxacin: an update on clinical experience*.[4] He reported on 146 clinical trials monitored by Miles, of which 133 were conducted in the USA. The number of patients in these combined studies was 3981. Ciprofloxacin was compared to standard therapy in a double-blind, randomised manner in 53 trials. He also presented pharmacokinetic data on oral ciprofloxacin from 26 studies. The infections covered in these trials included those in skin and soft tissues, respiratory tract, bone, and the gastrointestinal tract. An extensive review of adverse events was reviewed on the basis of 2829 patients' reports suitable for analysis and drug safety.

Lowell Young of San Francisco presented data at this meeting that demonstrated the *in vitro* efficacy of ciprofloxacin against *Mycobacterium avium–intracellulare*. He showed that, in association with other agents, ciprofloxacin was effective in an animal model of infection similar to that seen in patients with AIDS.[5]

Studies in other animal models not only corroborated the clinical results, but pointed to new areas of potential therapeutic application. The animal studies were presented by Vincent Andriole of New Haven[6] and Merle Sande of San Francisco.[7] Ciprofloxacin was used to advantage in animal models of respiratory tract infection (RTI), UTI, osteomyelitis, endocarditis and neutropenia.

Harold Neu summarised the conference on an upbeat note, but he also issued a challenge to the medical profession in the clinical application of this new drug.[8] "Oral ciprofloxacin offers an alternative form of therapy to many currently used β-lactams and aminoglycosides... Quinolones such as ciprofloxacin are appearing at a time in medicine when the availability of a highly potent, oral form of therapy that will permit patients to leave the expensive environment of the hospital is critical. In many ways, drugs such as ciprofloxacin are a challenge to the physician and surgeon. Can the medical profession apply the drugs in a rational manner so as to avoid clinical situations in which drug resistance or toxicity will readily occur?"

Compassionate use

At the Florida conference, George Arcieri mentioned in passing the administration of ciprofloxacin to 1100 patients in the USA under an emergency, compassionate-use protocol. The first patient in the programme was enrolled in 1984 by George Gee Jackson in Chicago. The patient was dying of a pseudomonal blood-borne infection that was unresponsive to available therapy. Although he was concerned about using an oral agent to treat such a serious infection, Jackson appealed to Arcieri to release the drug in an effort to save the patient's life. Ciprofloxacin was given in large doses, and it cleared the bloodstream, saving the patient's life. The patient died a few months later of his underlying disease, and *Pseudomonas* was found only in the bowel at autopsy. Although complete data forms were available for this and over 1000 others, Miles did not include them in the database, relying instead on the patients enrolled in their formal trials. Nevertheless, many physicians and their patients were extremely grateful to Miles for their charitable and unqualified assistance in these difficult clinical situations.

Problems along the way

The Miles group did not always walk a garden path littered with roses on the way to marketing ciprofloxacin. There were, in fact, serious issues that threatened to side-track the effort at several junctures in the early development and clinical trials periods. The particular issues were confronted by the team, and the response was "more studies" in an effort to solve each problem.

Arcieri remembered some of these "down moments". The early preparations of ciprofloxacin formed crystals in the urine at low pH. This problem was conquered by more work on formulations. There were concerns about central nervous system toxicity, which were relieved by the low incidence of such adverse effects in humans once the clinical data became available. Genotoxicity became a concern, but additional laboratory work satisfied the team that this was not going to be an issue. Doug Webb recalled that they had problems with convincing investigators to use the appropriate doses. A once-a-day regimen became popular among some investigators, despite the pharmacological data that discouraged such use.

A pharmacologist from Virginia, Ron Polk, was working on theophylline interactions with ciprofloxacin. He was instrumental in conducting several key studies and making the information on drug interactions available for dissemination to physicians and pharmacists.

Layne Gentry of Texas received "an early jolt" in his studies of ciprofloxacin in the treatment of sternal wound infections caused by coagulase-negative staphylococci which were sensitive to the drug. The wound healed and it seemed that the patient was cured; however, the wound later became red and painful. It "popped open" and drained purulent material containing the same organism which was now resistant to ciprofloxacin. It was clear to Gentry that this was a class of bacteria that would present problems for ciprofloxacin.

Despite these disappointments, these contentious issues were faced by Miles and investigators alike in a spirit of honest inquiry, recognising not only the strengths, but also the weaknesses of this drug. In every instance the information was subjected to careful scrutiny and full disclosure.

Co-operation with Bayer

An important element in the success of the Miles team in mobilising American investigators in the studies of ciprofloxacin was the support and co-operation of senior management in the Bayer corporate offices in Germany. The potential for disharmony existed when a vigorous group from an overseas subsidiary wanted to forge ahead on the research front, possibly outpacing the efforts of the home office. Instead of conflict, the enthusiasm of the Miles team and American investigators was met with co-operation and support from Bayer in Germany. Throughout the development of ciprofloxacin, Bayer was willing to provide substantial financial support for the studies in the USA. They also assembled leading investigators from many countries to review and criticise the protocols. The overriding thrust in designing studies was a spirit of co-operation with investigators rather than dictating an approach from central administration. Bayer also did a good job in promoting awareness of quinolones in the physician community by sponsoring symposia and developing educational materials. Overall, in the view of American investigators and the Miles team, Bayer was highly supportive and placed no barriers to developing ciprofloxacin in the USA.

Approval of the intravenous form: a unique event

At the Florida meeting in 1986, several papers were devoted to the use of intravenous ciprofloxacin, the comparison of dose and response of the intravenous and oral forms in particular. The approval of the intravenous form was granted by the FDA in 1991 on the basis of bioequivalence with the oral form. The company agreed to develop new clinical data on the intravenous drug to justify the FDA's confidence, which was subsequently done. The approval based on bioequivalence was a new step for the FDA, which expressed its confidence in ciprofloxacin as an effective anti-infective, but also supported the clinical research effort undertaken by Miles.

The release of the intravenous form of ciprofloxacin allowed physicians to make the transition from treating serious infections initially with an intravenous drug to switching to the same agent in an oral form. Richard Quintiliani and Charles Nightingale of Hartford have referred to this seamless process as "transitional therapy".[9] This procedure, now widely practised in American hospitals, lowers costs, facilitates earlier discharge from the hospital and reduces nosocomial infections associated with intravenous lines and lengthy hospitalisation.

Current developments by American investigators

Clinical research with ciprofloxacin is continuing in the USA, albeit at a reduced level. Recent studies have been directed at serious infections of the respiratory tract and intra-abdominal cavity. A massive multicentre trial of severe pneumonia in hospitalised patients was reported in 1994 by Fink and a cast of 13 other authors and a study group of 60 collaborators, all cited in the publication.[10] (This paper is a serious contender for the award of the most extensive list of authors and supporting spearholders in the medical literature!) Treatment with either intravenous ciprofloxacin or imipenem in 205 evaluable patients showed that ciprofloxacin had significantly superior clinical responses and bacteriological eradication, as well as fewer side-effects. Disappointing results were seen with both drugs as monotherapy in pulmonary infections caused by *Pseudomonas aeruginosa*.

In a trial of complicated intra-abdominal infections by Solomkin *et al.*, intravenous ciprofloxacin and metronidazole was as effective as imipenem.[11] A subset of the patients were converted to follow-up oral therapy with ciprofloxacin and metronidazole, and had outcomes that were therapeutically equivalent to intravenous treatments with the same drugs or imipenem. Based on cost savings and convenience, the intravenous therapy followed by the oral combination of ciprofloxacin–metronidazole should become an attractive alternative to the available intravenous drugs for treating serious intra-abdominal infections.[11]

Based on these studies, the FDA is being asked to extend the indications for treatment with ciprofloxacin in the USA to include intra-abdominal infections and severe pneumonia. Approval for sinusitis and an otic suspension are also pending. Most importantly, based on a large database accumulated by the company over the past decade in compassionate use along with clinical trials, approval is requested for treatment of children with cystic fibrosis who have complicated RTIs.

During the development phase of ciprofloxacin, the focus of studies in the USA was somewhat different from those in Europe and elsewhere. In Europe, early work was related to UTI and diarrhoea, later branching out to RTI. American investigators concentrated on a broader range of indications, including skin and soft tissues, bone and joint, sexually transmitted diseases and pneumonia. Larger doses were used by USA investigators, perhaps explaining the somewhat higher incidence of adverse effects seen in their studies. Animal models were investigated extensively by the USA groups.

The overall impact of the studies by American workers has been significant in the development of ciprofloxacin. The USA investigators have contributed a vast number of clinical and laboratory studies, along with their energy and scientific credibility. While the drug is intrinsically a good product, these studies, along with the important contributions of colleagues in Europe, have shown its excellent clinical efficacy and low toxicity, and increased the awareness of this antibiotic, enabling it to become one of the most widely prescribed drugs on the international market.

References

1. Chin NX, Neu HC. Ciprofloxacin, a new quinolone carboxylic acid compound active against aerobic and anaerobic bacteria. Antimicrob Agents Chemother 1984; 25: 319–26.

2. Neu HC, Percival A, Lode H, editors. Ciprofloxacin: A major advance in quinolone chemotherapy. Am J Med 1987; 82(Suppl 4A): 1–404.

3. Hooper DC, Wolfson JS, Ng EY, Swartz MN. Mechanisms of action of and resistance to ciprofloxacin. Am J Med 1987; 82(Suppl 4A): 12–20.

4. Arcieri G, Griffith E, Gruenwaldt G, Heyd A, O'Brien B, Becker N et al. Ciprofloxacin: an update on clinical experience. Am J Med 1987; 82(Suppl 4A): 381–6.

5. Young LS, Berlin OG, Inderlied CB. Activity of ciprofloxacin and other fluorinated quinolones against mycobacteria. Am J Med 1987; 82(Suppl 4A): 23–6.

6. Andriole VT. Efficacy of ciprofloxacin in animal models of infection. Am J Med 1987; 82(Suppl 4A): 67–70.

7. Sande MA, Brooks-Fournier RA, Gerberding JL. Efficacy of ciprofloxacin in animal models of infection: endocarditis, meningitis, and pneumonia. Am J Med 1987; 82(Suppl 4A): 63–6.

8. Neu HC. Ciprofloxacin: an overview and prospective appraisal. Am J Med 1987; 82(Suppl 4A): 395–404.

9. Quintiliani R, Nightingale C. Transitional antibiotic therapy. Infect Dis Clin Practice 1994; 3(Suppl 3): S161–6.

10. Fink MP, Snydman DR, Niederman MS, Leeper KV, Jr., Johnson RH, Heard SO et al. Treatment of severe pneumonia in hospitalised patients: results of a multicentre, randomised, double-blind trial comparing intravenous ciprofloxacin with imipenem–cilastatin. The Severe Pneumonia Study Group. Antimicrob Agents Chemother 1994; 38: 547–57.

11. Solomkin J, Reinhart H, Dellinger EP, Bohnen JM, Rotstein OD, Vogel SB et al. Results of a randomized trial comparing sequential intravenous/oral treatment with ciprofloxacin plus metronidazole to imipenem/cilastin for intra-abdominal infections. Ann Surg 1996; 223: 303–15.

Chapter 1

Chemistry and mode of action

In 1962, Lescher *et al.* described nalidixic acid, the precursor of the 4-quinolones, which had been discovered during the synthesis of chloroquine.[1] Its clinical usefulness other than in the treatment of urinary infection was limited by its low serum concentrations and high minimum inhibitory concentrations (MIC 4–16 mg/litre). Oxolinic acid and cinoxacin, which became available 10 years later, provided few additional benefits. However, when the fluoroquinolones appeared, their activity was found to be 100 times greater and to have a broader spectrum by virtue of a fluorine atom at C6.[2] The N-1, C-2, C-3 and C-4 positions vary little, if at all, throughout the family of quinolones (Figure 1.1). The 3-carboxylate and 4-carbonyl groups bind DNA gyrase and are essential to antibiotic activity, and the C-7 substituent ensures the correct orientation of the quinolone molecule.[3] At position 7, pyrrolidines improve activity against Gram-positive organisms while piperazines, as in ciprofloxacin, improve activity against Gram-negative organisms.

The first 1-cyclopropyl fluoroquinolone, ciprofloxacin, was synthesised in 1983[4] and was found to have a range of potencies depending on the non-polar aliphatic substituents at N-1 (Table 1.1). The antibiotic was remarkable among the quinolones for its high activity. *In vitro* and in mice, it was at least twice as potent as norfloxacin against the Enterobacteriaceae, *Pseudomonas aeruginosa* and *Staphylococcus*

aureus. The reason for the improved activity with a 1-cyclopropyl substituent is unclear, but ciprofloxacin is considerably more active than the similar isopropyl quinolones. Alkyl substitution on the cyclopropyl group or enlargement of the ring reduces activity.[4] The N-*tert*-butyl analogue, $C(CH_3)_3$, has greater activity against Gram-positive bacteria.[3] Binding of ciprofloxacin is enhanced in the presence of non-steroidal anti-inflammatory drugs, but the clinical effects can not be predicted reliably. Central nervous system side-effects are related to the binding of ciprofloxacin to γ-aminobutyric acid (GABA) receptors, which is a property of all quinolones with unsubstituted piperazine side chains.

The quinolones selectively inhibit bacterial DNA synthesis by acting on the enzyme DNA gyrase. This enzyme is one of a group of topoisomerases, which inserts negative supercoils into DNA (i.e. against the normal direction of the DNA helix).[5] The bacterial chromosome comprises a molecule of DNA which is 1300 µm in length and this is compressed into a cell of 1×2 µm in size. In a DNA molecule of 4 million base pairs, each strand is intertwined 400,000 times (the linking number) and the strands have to be unwound during replication. A topoisomerase alters the linking number without changing the DNA molecule itself. All living cells contain two types of topoisomerase. Type I topoisomerases break one strand of DNA and pass a single strand through the gap, thus removing the negative supertwists from DNA. Type II topoisomerases, which are the target of ciprofloxacin, temporarily cut both

Wilson APR and Grüneberg RN.
Ciprofloxacin: 10 years of clinical experience
© 1997 Maxim Medical, Oxford.

Basic quinolone formula

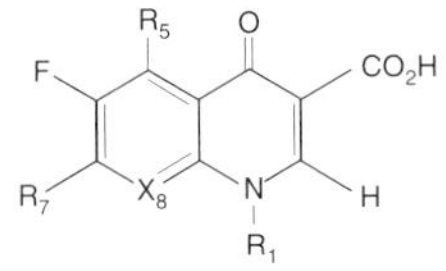

Name/identification	R$_7$	X$_8$	R$_1$	R$_5$
Ciprofloxacin	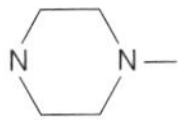 (piperazinyl) N N—	CH	c-C$_3$H$_5$[a]-	H-
Tosufloxacin	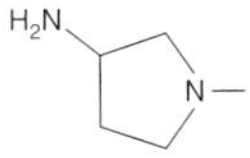 H$_2$N (aminopyrrolidinyl) N—	N	2,4-diFPh[b]-	H-
Lomefloxacin	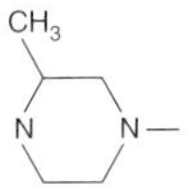 CH$_3$ (methylpiperazinyl) N N—	CF	CH$_3$CH$_2$-	H-
Clinafloxacin (CI-960, AM-1091)	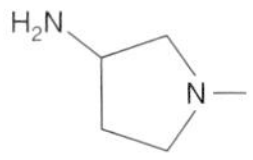 H$_2$N (aminopyrrolidinyl) N—	CCl	c-C$_3$H$_5$-	H-
DU 6859a	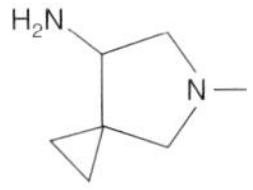 H$_2$N (spiro aminopyrrolidinyl) N—	CCl	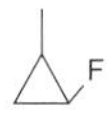 (fluorocyclopropyl) F	H-
Sparfloxacin	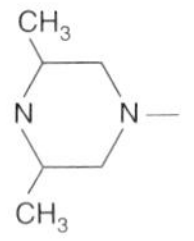 CH$_3$ (dimethylpiperazinyl) N N— CH$_3$	CF	c-C$_3$H$_5$-	NH$_2$
Enoxacin	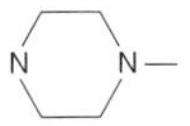 (piperazinyl) N N—	N	CH$_3$CH$_2$-	H-
Norfloxacin	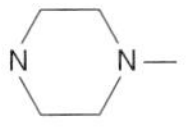 (piperazinyl) N N—	CH	CH$_3$CH$_2$-	H-
Pefloxacin	CH$_3$N (methylpiperazinyl) N—	CH	CH$_3$CH$_2$-	H-

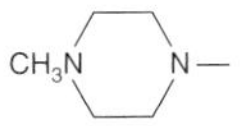

[a]c-C$_3$H$_5$ represents cyclopropyl
[b]2,4-diFPh represents a 2,4-difluorophenyl group

Ofloxacin

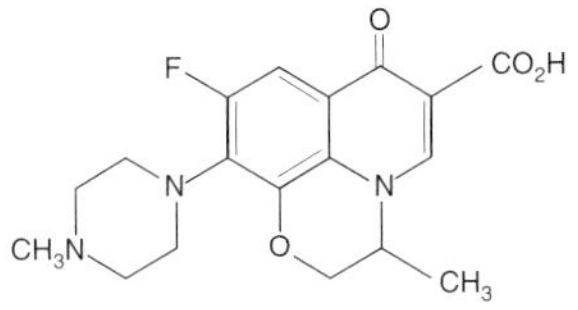

Figure 1.1. Structural formulae of the quinolones.[2]

strands of the DNA and pass another double-helix segment through the break, thereby introducing negative supertwists.[6]

DNA gyrase has four subunits; two A subunits (atomic mass 100 kDa) and two B subunits (atomic mass 90 kDa), derived from the *gyrA* and *gyrB* genes, respectively.[6,7] Supercoiling reduces the size of the molecule by introducing 65 domains with a length of 20 µm, and achieves further compaction by supertwisting (around 400 times).[8] During supercoiling of the domains, the two A subunits produce a staggered cut in the DNA, resulting in DNA termini with free 3′ hydroxyl groups and a 5′ extension.[9] The 5′ termini are covalently bonded to the enzyme, the cut being made at a thymine–guanine dinucleotide on one strand, but at random on the other strand.[9] The

Table 1.1. Susceptibilities of organisms to ciprofloxacin with non-polar aliphatic substituents at N-1.[3]

Substituent	Mean inhibitory concentration (mg/litre)			
	Escherichia coli	*Pseudomonas aeruginosa*	*Staphylococcus aureus*	*Klebsiella pneumoniae*
$CH(CH_2)_2$	0.004–0.05	0.4–0.125	0.25–3.1	–
$CH(CH_3)_2$	0.5	1	1	–
$C(CH_3)_3$	0.06	0.5	0.06	0.13
$CH_2CH(CH_2)_2$	0.5	4	1	–
$CH(CH_2)_3$	0.13	1	0.5	0.13
$C(CH_3)_2CH_2F$	0.016	1	0.13–0.16	0.006
$CCH_3(CH_2F)_2$	0.13	0.5	1–2	0.13

two B subunits then introduce the supercoiling before the A subunits reseal the DNA. DNA gyrase will form and remove knots in a single DNA molecule. The enzyme is needed for initiation, propagation and termination of DNA replication. Energy for these activities is supplied by hydrolysis of ATP and magnesium is required.

Quinolones prevent the A subunits resealing the strands of DNA, the compaction is reversed and the incorporation of precursors into DNA is stopped. They stabilise the double-strand breaks and the binding of DNA gyrase to the exposed 5′ ends.[10] The cells form filaments and the exposed breaks in the DNA promote the activity of exonucleases leading to cell death.[11] RNA and protein synthesis must still be able to continue after DNA replication is affected in order to produce cell death. Rifampicin inhibits this process. Ciprofloxacin has a second bactericidal action that is not inhibited by rifampicin, which may be the result of changed gene expression. Quinolones bind more strongly to denatured and negatively supertwisted DNA than to normal double-strand DNA.

The A subunit and the DNA substrate for the enzyme have been proposed as the prime targets for quinolones including ciprofloxacin.[10,12] Mutations giving rise to quinolone resistance are usually found to arise in the *gyrA* gene, though they may appear in genes coding for outer membrane proteins or in *gyrB*.[13] The mutations occur in the N-terminal domain of the A protein, which controls the DNA cutting and resealing; Ser-83 is the most common site.[13] It is close in linear sequence to Tyr-122, which forms the covalent bonds between DNA and protein. Gyrase is affected via the C-7 group of the quinolone. However, the C-7 group is highly variable in the quinolone family and hydrogen bonding may occur between the 3-carboxy and 4-oxo groups on the antibiotic and hydrogen-bond donors on the enzyme.[13] Shen *et al.* proposed that the exposed single strand regions are the binding sites for quinolones.[14] In contrast, novobiocin and coumermycin act principally on the B subunit and inhibit the ATPase reaction.

The concentrations of quinolones required to inhibit the actions of DNA gyrase on DNA are 10–1000 times greater than those which inhibit bacterial growth. The double-strand breaks can only be detected in the presence of detergent, proteinase K, alkali or other denaturing conditions. Crumplin therefore believes that the question of the binding site for quinolones is unanswered.[10] However, in the living cell, minor changes in DNA behaviour may be sufficient to stop growth and a 10% reduction in supertwisting is observed at concentrations near the MIC.

Ciprofloxacin and other quinolones are bactericidal over a broad range of concentrations and inhibit all the activities of DNA gyrase. In addition to supercoiling, the quinolones relax positively supercoiled DNA, and catenate and decatenate double-stranded DNA circles. These functions may be much more sensitive to quinolones than supercoiling, which may account for the low MICs, but this has not been confirmed.[13] Alternatively, the quinolone–gyrase–DNA complex, which is known to be stable, may block the passage of polymerase and this could occur when only a small proportion of gyrase molecules have been bound. The activity of DNA gyrase *in vitro* is often assessed by using small, easily cloned plasmids, and gyrases from different species are often studied. However, there may be a sequence preference for the insertion sites for supercoiling and the chromosomal DNA sequences from the same species as the gyrase.[10] The chromosome is far more complex than plasmids, and presents many possible binding sites to the enzyme. Removing the *gyrA* gene product from the cell, which is possible by incubating a mutant with a thermolabile enzyme at 42°C, does not cause death, but merely inhibits growth. Removing the *gyrB* product in the same way causes rapid cell death.

DNA gyrase is important in replication when supercoils are not needed, such as in the linear DNA of bacteriophage T7. Nalidixic acid still inhibits replication, but the site of action must be different: quinolones could therefore induce different activities in DNA gyrase. DNA cleavage may be induced at a non-catalytic site of binding of the gyrase to DNA. The cleavage sites found in the presence of quinolones may not then be those normally involved in supercoiling. Crumplin proposed that the sites of action *in vivo* are the binding sites on the chromosome not involved in super-coil insertion and that these are affected by low concentrations of the antibiotics.[10] Nalidixic acid and other quinolones cause the accumulation of segments of single-stranded DNA corresponding to the size of domains produced by supercoiling. The quinolones cause DNA gyrase to cleave once in each domain. It is possible that DNA gyrase acts as a structural protein supporting the radial loops of DNA, as has

been shown in the T4 bacteriophage. If this is the case, the quinolones may prevent replication by altering the structure of the gyrase–DNA complex.

In mammalian cells, the 46 chromosomes are bounded by a nuclear membrane unlike the single bacterial chromosome.[8] Compaction of the DNA is necessary to reduce the total length of DNA (189 cm) to fit in a cell 10 μm in diameter. Although the process is poorly understood, mammalian DNA topoisomerase differs from the bacterial equivalent in that it has only two subunits and does not introduce any negative supercoils.[15,16] The enzyme has similar activity to the topoisomerase of the bacteriophage T4. It is not susceptible to inhibition by quinolones, the agents being 100–1000 times less potent against purified mammalian topoisomerase II than DNA gyrase.[6]

The fluoroquinolones represent a considerable improvement in antibacterial activity over the older hydrophobic quinolones. Ciprofloxacin and other quinolones act by inhibiting the action of bacterial DNA gyrase, but controversy remains as to the discrepancy between the concentrations required for inhibition of DNA synthesis and the MIC. It is likely that the mode of action is considerably more complex than generally recognised.

References

1. Lescher GY, Froelich ED, Gruet MD, Bailey JH, Brundage PR. 1,8-Naphthyridine derivatives. A new class of chemotherapeutic agents. J Med Pharm Chem 1962; 5: 1063–8.
2. Domagala JM. Structure–activity and structure–side-effect relationships for the quinolone antibacterials. J Antimicrob Chemother 1994; 33: 685–706.
3. Mitscher LA, Devasthale P, Zavod R. Structure–activity relationships. In: Hooper DC, Wolfson JS, eds. Quinolone antimicrobial agents. 2nd ed. Washington: American Society for Microbiology, 1993: 3–51.
4. Wentland MP. Structure activity relationships of fluoroquinolones. In: Siporin C, Heifetz CL, Domagala JM, eds. The new generation of quinolones. New York: Marcel Dekker, 1990: 1–43.

5. Norris S, Mandell GL. The quinolones: history and overview. In: Andriole VT, ed. The quinolones. London: Academic Press, 1988: 1–4.

6. Wolfson JS, Hooper DC. Introduction to DNA gyrase, quinolones and quinolone resistance. In: Fernandez PB, ed. Quinolones. Princeton: JR Prous Science Publishers, 1989: 137–57.

7. Higgins NP, Peebles CL, Sugino A, Cozarelli NR. Purification of subunits of *Escherichia coli* DNA gyrase and reconstitution of enzymic activity. Proc Nat Acad Sci USA 1978; 75: 1773–7.

8. Smith JT. The mode of action of 4-quinolones and possible mechanisms of resistance. J Antimicrob Chemother 1986; 18 (Suppl D): 21–9.

9. Morrison A, Cozzarelli NP. Site-specific cleavage of DNA by *E. coli* DNA gyrase. Cell 1979; 17: 175–84.

10. Crumplin GC. Aspects of the mechanism of action of the 4-quinolone antibacterial agents. In: Fernandez PB, ed. Quinolones. Princeton: JR Prous Science Publishers, 1989: 219–33.

11. Gellert M, Mizuuchi K, O'Dea MH, Itoh T, Tomizawa J-I. Nalidixic acid resistance: a second character involved in DNA gyrase activity. Proc Nat Acad Sci USA 1977; 74: 4772–6.

12. Hooper DC, Wolfson JS, Ng EY, Swartz MN. Mechanisms of action of and resistance to ciprofloxacin. Am J Med 1987; 82 (Suppl 4A): 12–20.

13. Maxwell A. The molecular basis of quinolone action. J Antimicrob Chemother 1992; 30: 409–16.

14. Shen LL, Mitscher LA, Sharma PD, O'Donnell TD, Chu DTW, Cooper CS *et al*. Mechanism of inhibition of DNA gyrase by quinolone antibacterials: a cooperative drug-DNA binding model. Biochemistry 1989; 28: 2886–94.

15. Liu U, Rowe TC, Yang L, Tewey KM, Chen GL. Cleavage of DNA by mammalian DNA topoisomerase II. J Biol Chem 1983; 258: 15365–70.

16. Miller KG, Liu LF, Englund PT. A homogenous type II DNA topoisomerase from HeLa cell nuclei. J Biol Chem 1981; 256: 9334–9.

Chapter 2

Antibacterial activity

Ciprofloxacin has a broad spectrum of anti-microbial activity (Table 2.1).[1–32] It is highly active against many Gram-negative species, particularly *Neisseria* spp., *Escherichia coli*, *Salmonella* spp. and *Haemophilus influenzae*. It is considerably more potent against Enterobacteriaceae than the cephalosporins, β-lactams or trimethoprim. Ciprofloxacin is the most active of the quinolones against *Pseudomonas aeruginosa*, but the range of susceptibility is wide. In common with other quinolones, except sparfloxacin, it is less active against Gram-positive than Gram-negative bacteria; it is also less potent than the penicillins against β-haemolytic streptococci, *Streptococcus pneumoniae* and the enterococci. Ciprofloxacin has limited activity against anaerobes, but mycobacteria are often susceptible.

Gram-negative aerobic bacteria

Ciprofloxacin is highly active against Enterobacteriaceae, including salmonellae and shigellae, and *Haemophilus influenzae*, irrespective of ampicillin resistance. It is more potent than gentamicin, the ureidopenicillins, and in many cases, than cefotaxime against the Enterobacteriaceae. More than 85% of Enterobacteriaceae are susceptible, although there are local variations.[10] In a large multicentre study in the USA, the mean inhibitory concentration (MIC) of ciprofloxacin was 1 mg/litre or less for the following: *Citrobacter freundii* (93%; n = 250), *Enterobacter aerogenes* (97%; n = 305), *Enterobacter cloacae* (94%; n = 468), *Escherichia coli* (99%; n = 1398), *Klebsiella pneumoniae* (96%; n = 1021), *Proteus mirabilis* (99%; n = 517), and *Morganella morgagni* (97%; n = 180).[33] *Serratia marcescens* (86%; n = 427) and *Providencia stuartii* (70%; n = 110) are usually susceptible to ciprofloxacin. Ciprofloxacin is also the most active of the quinolones against *Pseudomonas aeruginosa* (84%; n = 798).[33,34] Less than 35% of strains of *Burkholderia cepacia* are sensitive to ciprofloxacin and activity against *Stenotrophomonas maltophilia* (18%; n = 164) and *Acinetobacter calcoaceticus* (63%; n = 109) is variable.[10] However, its activity against *Acinetobacter* spp. is greater than the cephalosporins, aminoglycosides or norfloxacin. Ciprofloxacin is active against almost all strains of *Moraxella catarrhalis* (98%; n = 212), *Haemophilus influenzae* (99%; n = 412) and *Neisseria meningitidis*.[33] Ciprofloxacin is more active than norfloxacin or ofloxacin against *Moraxella catarrhalis* and has greater or similar activity against *Neisseria* spp. than cefotaxime or ceftazidime. Against *Haemophilus* spp. activity is similar to that of cefotaxime, but greater than that of ceftazidime, ureidopenicillins or ampicillin.

Approximately 20% of patients with typhoid fever are infected with *Salmonella typhi* resistant to multiple antibiotics (i.e. chloramphenicol, ampicillin and co-trimoxazole).[35] These isolates are often sensitive to

Wilson APR and Grüneberg RN.
Ciprofloxacin: 10 years of clinical experience
© 1997 Maxim Medical, Oxford.

Table 2.1. *In vitro* susceptibility of bacterial species to ciprofloxacin and other agents. The median mean inhibitory concentrations (MIC) for isolates from a number of studies are given and the comparators are those used in these studies. Ranges of MIC_{50} and MIC_{90} values are given in parentheses.

Species	Number of isolates	Antibiotic	MIC_{50} (mg/litre)	MIC_{90} (mg/litre)	Range MIC (mg/litre)	References
Staphylococcus aureus	2544	Ciprofloxacin	0.5 (0.01–0.5)	1 (0.03–> 8)	0.01–≥32	1–10
	2152	Ofloxacin	0.25	0.5	≤ 0.06–≥32	
	728	Norfloxacin	0.5	1	0.06–≥ 32	
	30	Sparfloxacin	0.03	0.06	0.03–0.06	
	225	Erythromycin	≤ 0.13	8	≤ 0.13–> 256	
	225	Chloramphenicol	8	8	4–128	
	40	Trimethoprim	0.25	0.5	0.03–8	
	135	Co-amoxiclav	0.5	0.5	0.12–16	
	95	Cefuroxime	1	2	≤ 0.5–2	
Methicillin-resistant *Staphylococcus aureus*	2128	Ciprofloxacin	0.25 (0.25–> 16)	1 (1–>16)	≤ 0.06–> 16	2–5, 10
	21	Sparfloxacin	8	8	0.3–8	
	1235	Norfloxacin	1	2	≤ 0.15–16	
	872	Ofloxacin	> 8	> 8	0.12–> 8	
	1203	Erythromycin	> 256	> 256	≤ 0.25–> 256	
	1203	Gentamicin	32	> 64	≤ 0.25–> 64	
	1203	Chloramphenicol	8	128	4–128	
	1203	Fusidic acid	≤ 0.25	≤ 0.25	≤ 0.25–128	
	1203	Rifampicin	≤ 0.25	≤ 0.25	≤ 0.25–16	
	1203	Vancomycin	1	2	1–2	
Coagulase-negative staphylococci	791	Ciprofloxacin	0.25 (0.25–0.5)	1 (0.5–> 8)	≤ 0.06–> 8	1–7, 10
	791	Ofloxacin	0.5	1	≤ 0.06–> 8	
	65	Norfloxacin	0.5	1	0.25–2	

Table 2.1. (continued)

Species	Number of isolates	Antibiotic	MIC$_{50}$ (mg/litre)	MIC$_{90}$ (mg/litre)	Range MIC (mg/litre)	References
Staphylococcus epidermidis	1959	Ciprofloxacin	0.25 (0.25–0.5)	1 (0.25– > 8)	0.03– > 16	2–5, 7, 10
	64	Sparfloxacin	0.06	2	0.03–4	
	165	Norfloxacin	1	2	0.125–1	
	134	Erythromycin	≤ 0.13	> 64	0.13–32	
	134	Chloramphenicol	4	64	≤ 0.13–256	
	20	Trimethoprim	1	> 128	2–128	
	20	Co-amoxiclav	0.25	1	0.12– > 128	
					0.03–8	
Staphylococcus simulans	38	Ciprofloxacin	0.25	0.5 (0.5– > 8)	≤ 0.06– > 8	3, 10
	24	Norfloxacin	0.5	2	0.25–4	
	14	Ofloxacin	0.25	> 8	0.12– > 8	
Staphylococcus capitis	31	Ciprofloxacin	0.125 (0.12–0.25)	0.5	≤ 0.06–1	3
	20	Norfloxacin	0.5	2	0.125–2	10
	11	Ofloxacin	0.5	1	≤ 0.06–1	
Staphylococcus haemolyticus	48	Ciprofloxacin	0.5	> 8	≤ 0.06– > 8	10
	48	Ofloxacin	0.5	> 8	0.12– > 8	
Staphylococcus hominis	31	Ciprofloxacin	0.12	4	≤ 0.06– > 8	10
	31	Ofloxacin	0.25	4	0.12–8	
Staphylococcus warneri	17	Ciprofloxacin	0.25	1	0.12– > 8	10
	17	Ofloxacin	0.5	1	0.25– > 8	

Table 2.1. (continued)

Species	Number of isolates	Antibiotic	MIC$_{50}$ (mg/litre)	MIC$_{90}$ (mg/litre)	Range MIC (mg/litre)	References
Staphylococcus saprophyticus	163	Ciprofloxacin	0.5	1 (0.5–2)	0.12–8	5, 7, 10
	36	Norfloxacin	4	8	0.5–4	
	36	Erythromycin	≤ 0.13	16	≤ 0.13– > 256	
	36	Chloramphenicol	8	8	4–128	
	127	Ofloxacin	1	1	0.25– > 8	
	20	Trimethoprim	0.12	0.25	0.03–0.25	
	20	Co-amoxiclav	0.5	0.5	0.12–0.5	
Micrococcus spp.	50	Ciprofloxacin	0.5	0.5	0.25–1	1
	50	Ofloxacin	1	1	0.5–1	
	50	Norfloxacin	2	4	2–4	
Corynebacterium spp.	100	Ciprofloxacin	8 (0.25–8)	> 16 (8– > 16)	0.03– > 16	2, 10
	64	Sparfloxacin	4	> 16	0.03–>16	
	36	Ofloxacin	0.25	> 8	0.12–>8	
Enterococcus faecalis	1259	Ciprofloxacin	1 (0.5–4)	>8 (1–>16)	≤ 0.06– > 8	1–8, 10
	1155	Ofloxacin	2	4	≤ 0.06– > 8	
	378	Norfloxacin	2	4	0.25–≥32	
	32	Sparfloxacin	1	> 16	0.12– > 16	
	32	Penicillin	2	2	1–4	
Enterococcus faecium	208	Ciprofloxacin	4 (1–4)	> 8 (2– > 8)	0.5–8	3, 4, 10
	35	Norfloxacin	4	8	2–32	
	173	Ofloxacin	4	> 8	0.25– > 8	

Table 2.1. (continued)

Species	Number of isolates	Antibiotic	MIC$_{50}$ (mg/litre)	MIC$_{90}$ (mg/litre)	Range MIC (mg/litre)	References
Enterococcus spp.	354	Ciprofloxacin	1 (1–2)	> 8 (2–> 8)	0.12–> 8	6, 7, 10
	25	Norfloxacin	4	8	2–8	
	354	Ofloxacin	4	> 8	0.12–> 8	
	24	Trimethoprim	0.03	0.5	0.016–32	
	24	Amoxycillin	0.5	8	0.12–16	
Streptococcus group A	928	Ciprofloxacin	0.5	2 (1–2)	≤ 0.06–> 8	3, 5, 10
	21	Norfloxacin	4	8	2–> 64	
	885	Ofloxacin	1	2	≤ 0.06–> 8	
	22	Penicillin	≤ 0.03	≤ 0.03	≤ 0.03	
	22	Cefotaxime	≤ 0.25	≤ 0.25	≤ 0.25	
	22	Erythromycin	≤ 0.13	≤ 0.13	≤ 0.13–8	
Streptococcus group B	696	Ciprofloxacin	1 (0.5–1)	2 (1–2)	≤ 0.06–> 8	1, 3–7, 10
	640	Ofloxacin	2	4	≤ 0.06–> 8	
	106	Norfloxacin	2	4	1–8	
	25	Penicillin	≤ 0.03	≤ 0.03	≤ 0.03	
	25	Cefotaxime	≤ 0.25	≤ 0.25	≤ 0.25	
	25	Erythromycin	≤ 0.13	≤ 0.13	≤ 0.13–2	
	24	Trimethoprim	0.5	0.5	0.12–1	
	24	Amoxycillin	0.03	0.06	0.03–0.06	
Streptococcus group C	34	Ciprofloxacin	0.5 (0.5–1)	2 (1–2)	0.25–2	3, 5
	21	Norfloxacin	4	8	2–8	
	13	Penicillin	≤ 0.03	≤ 0.03	≤ 0.03	
	13	Cefotaxime	≤ 0.25	≤ 0.25	≤ 0.25–2	
	13	Erythromycin	≤ 0.13	≤ 0.13	≤ 0.13	

Table 2.1. (continued)

Species	Number of isolates	Antibiotic	MIC$_{50}$ (mg/litre)	MIC$_{90}$ (mg/litre)	Range MIC (mg/litre)	References
Streptococcus group F	10	Ciprofloxacin	1	4	≤ 0.03–4	10
	10	Ofloxacin	1	4	≤ 0.03–8	
Streptococcus group G	36	Ciprofloxacin	0.25 (0.25–0.5)	1	0.25–2	3, 5
	20	Norfloxacin	2	4	0.5–8	
	16	Penicillin	≤ 0.03	≤ 0.03	≤ 0.03	
	16	Erythromycin	≤ 0.13	4	≤ 0.13–4	
Streptococcus pneumoniae	1105	Ciprofloxacin	1 (0.5–1)	2 (1–4)	≤ 0.008–4	1–7, 9, 10
	843	Ofloxacin	2	2	≤ 0.03–>4	
	151	Norfloxacin	8	16	2–32	
	64	Sparfloxacin	0.25	1	≤ 0.008–2	
	67	Penicillin	≤ 0.03	≤ 0.03	≤ 0.03–0.25	
	67	Cefotaxime	≤ 0.25	≤ 0.25	≤ 0.25– > 64	
	67	Erythromycin	≤ 0.25	≤ 0.25	≤ 0.25– > 64	
	67	Chloramphenicol	2	2	1–16	
	20	Trimethoprim	1	8	0.12–64	
	20	Amoxycillin	0.008	0.016	0.004–1	
	100	Co-amoxiclav	≤ 0.25/0.12	≤ 0.25/0.12	≤ 0.25/0.12	
	100	Cefuroxime	≤ 0.5	≤ 0.5	≤ 0.5	
Streptococcus mitis	20	Ciprofloxacin	1	2	0.5–2	3
	20	Norfloxacin	2	2	1–4	
Streptococcus salivarius	20	Ciprofloxacin	1	2	1–2	3
	20	Norfloxacin	2	2	1–4	
Streptococcus sanguis	20	Ciprofloxacin	0.25	0.25	0.25	3
	20	Norfloxacin	0.5	1	0.5–1	

Table 2.1. (continued)

Species	Number of isolates	Antibiotic	MIC$_{50}$ (mg/litre)	MIC$_{90}$ (mg/litre)	Range MIC (mg/litre)	References
α-haemolytic streptococci	68	Ciprofloxacin	1	2 (2–4)	≤ 0.06–4	6, 7, 10
	20	Norfloxacin	8	16	4–16	
	68	Ofloxacin	2	4	≤ 0.06–4	
	19	Amoxycillin	0.03	0.25	0.016–0.25	
Propionibacterium spp.	36	Ciprofloxacin	0.25	0.25	0.12–0.25	11
	36	Clindamycin	0.03	0.06	0.03–0.12	
	36	Ceftazidime	1	16	0.06–16	
Listeria monocytogenes	32	Ciprofloxacin	0.5 (0.5–1)	2 (0.5–2)	0.25–2 0.5–2	2, 3
	12	Sparfloxacin	2	2	0.25–0.5	
	20	Norfloxacin	2	4	1–4	
Neisseria meningitidis	180	Ciprofloxacin	0.008 (0.008–0.015)	0.008 (0.008–0.015)	0.004–0.015	1, 3
	160	Ofloxacin	0.015	0.015	0.015	
	180	Norfloxacin	0.015	0.03	0.015–0.5	
Neisseria gonorrhoeae	133	Ciprofloxacin	0.002 (≤ 0.015–0.002)	0.004 (≤ 0.015–0.06)	≤ 0.015–0.25	6, 7, 12
	78	Norfloxacin	0.025	0.1	≤ 0.015–0.4	
	133	Ofloxacin	0.016	0.12	0.004–0.5	
	85	Co-amoxiclav	0.12	1	0.03–2	

Table 2.1. (continued)

Species	Number of isolates	Antibiotic	MIC$_{50}$ (mg/litre)	MIC$_{90}$ (mg/litre)	Range MIC (mg/litre)	References
Moraxella catarrhalis	606	Ciprofloxacin	0.015 (0.015–0.03)	0.06 (0.03–0.06)	≤ 0.008– > 4	2, 3, 6, 7, 9, 10
	32	Sparfloxacin	≤ 0.008	≤ 0.008	≤ 0.008	
	40	Norfloxacin	0.5	0.5	0.06–0.5	
	504	Ofloxacin	0.06	0.12	≤ 0.03– > 4	
	20	Trimethoprim	16	32	8–64	
	20	Co-amoxiclav	0.03	0.25	0.008–0.25	
Escherichia coli	2980	Ciprofloxacin	0.016 (≤ 0.008–0.13)	≤ 0.06 (≤ 0.008–0.25)	0.008–32	3–7, 10, 13
	178	Norfloxacin	0.12	0.5	≤ 0.03–4	
	2905	Ofloxacin	0.12	0.12	0.03– > 8	
	58	Ampicillin	4	> 256	0.5– > 256	
	58	Cefotaxime	≤ 0.25	≤ 0.25	≤ 0.25–32	
	58	Gentamicin	1	2	0.5–64	
	40	Trimethoprim	0.12	> 128	0.008– > 128	
	40	Co-amoxiclav	8	32	4–64	
Salmonella typhi	70	Ciprofloxacin	≤ 0.008	0.015 (0.01–0.06)	≤ 0.008–0.12	1, 2, 13
	49	Ofloxacin	0.03	0.06	0.03–0.12	
	25	Norfloxacin	0.03	0.06	0.03–0.06	
	21	Sparfloxacin	≤ 0.008	0.01	≤ 0.008–0.25	
Salmonella spp.	133	Ciprofloxacin	0.015 (0.008–0.03)	0.03 (0.015–0.15)	≤ 0.008–0.25	1, 2, 10, 13
	123	Ofloxacin	0.12	0.12	0.03–1	
	50	Norfloxacin	0.06	0.06	0.03–0.06	
	10	Sparfloxacin	0.06	0.06	0.06	
Salmonella typhimurium	100	Ciprofloxacin	0.06	0.125	0.015–0.25	14

Table 2.1. (continued)

Species	Number of isolates	Antibiotic	MIC_{50} (mg/litre)	MIC_{90} (mg/litre)	Range MIC (mg/litre)	References
Salmonella enteritidis	22	Ciprofloxacin	≤ 0.06	≤ 0.06	≤ 0.06	10
	22	Ofloxacin	0.12	0.25	0.12–0.25	
Salmonella group A	27	Ciprofloxacin	0.125	0.125	0.03–0.25	3
	27	Norfloxacin	0.25	0.5	0.06–0.5	
Salmonella group B	23	Ciprofloxacin	0.06	0.06	0.03–0.125	3
	23	Norfloxacin	0.125	0.5	0.06–0.5	
	37	Ciprofloxacin	≤ 0.06	≤ 0.06	≤ 0.06– > 8	10
	37	Ofloxacin	0.12	0.25	0.12–1	
Salmonella group C	20	Ciprofloxacin	0.06	0.125	0.06–0.25	3
	20	Norfloxacin	0.125	0.5	0.03–1	
Salmonella group D	26	Ciprofloxacin	0.25	0.25	0.125–0.5	3
	26	Norfloxacin	0.25	0.5	0.06–1	
	21	Ciprofloxacin	≤ 0.06	≤ 0.06	≤ 0.06–0.25	10
	21	Ofloxacin	0.25	0.25	0.12–0.25	
Salmonella group E	21	Ciprofloxacin	0.125	0.125	0.06–0.125	3
	21	Norfloxacin	0.25	1	0.125–2	
Shigella spp.	195	Ciprofloxacin	0.008 (≤ 0.008–0.01)	0.015 (≤ 0.008–0.015) 0.12	≤ 0.008–0.03	1, 2, 13, 14
	90	Ofloxacin	0.06	0.06	0.03–0.12	
	50	Norfloxacin	0.03	0.06	0.03–0.12	
	30	Sparfloxacin	0.01	0.01	≤ 0.008–0.06	
Shigella dysenteriae	24	Ciprofloxacin	0.03	0.03	0.015–0.06	3
	24	Norfloxacin	0.03	0.125	0.03–0.25	

Table 2.1. (continued)

Species	Number of isolates	Antibiotic	MIC$_{50}$ (mg/litre)	MIC$_{90}$ (mg/litre)	Range MIC (mg/litre)	References
Shigella flexneri	47	Ciprofloxacin	0.015 (0.015–≤0.06)	0.03 (0.03–≤0.06)	0.015–0.06	3
	21	Norfloxacin	0.125	0.125	0.03–0.125	10
	26	Ofloxacin	≤0.06	0.12	≤0.06–0.5	
Shigella boydii	22	Ciprofloxacin	0.03	0.03	0.015–0.06	3
	22	Norfloxacin	0.125	0.25	0.06–0.5	
Shigella sonnei	91	Ciprofloxacin	0.015 (0.015–≤0.06)	0.015 (0.015–≤0.06)	0.015–>8	3, 10
	20	Norfloxacin	0.125	0.125	0.03–0.125	
	71	Ofloxacin	0.12	0.12	≤0.06–>8	
Klebsiella pneumoniae	2334	Ciprofloxacin	≤0.06 (0.03–0.06)	0.5 (≤0.06–0.5)	0.01–>8	2–5, 9, 10
	156	Norfloxacin	0.13	0.5	0.03–4	
	2146	Ofloxacin	0.25	2	≤0.06–>8	
	68	Ampicillin	128	>256	1–>256	
	68	Cefotaxime	4	64	1–>256	
	68	Gentamicin	0.5	32	≤0.25–>64	
	100	Co-amoxiclav	4/2	>16/8	1/0.5–>16/8	
	100	Cefuroxime	4	32	≤0.5–>32	
Klebsiella oxytoca	612	Ciprofloxacin	0.015 (0.01–≤0.06)	0.12 (0.06–0.12)	≤0.008–>8	2, 3, 10
	612	Sparfloxacin	0.03	0.06	≤0.008–0.12	
	612	Norfloxacin	0.25	1	0.06–2	
	612	Ciprofloxacin	≤0.06	0.12	≤0.06–>8	
	612	Ofloxacin	0.12	0.5	≤0.06–>8	

Table 2.1. (continued)

Species	Number of isolates	Antibiotic	MIC$_{50}$ (mg/litre)	MIC$_{90}$ (mg/litre)	Range MIC (mg/litre)	References
Klebsiella ozaenae	18	Ciprofloxacin	≤ 0.06	1	≤ 0.06– > 8	10
	18	Ofloxacin	0.12	2	≤ 0.06– > 8	
Klebsiella spp.	80	Ciprofloxacin	0.03	0.25	0.008–2	6, 7
	45	Norfloxacin	0.12	1	0.03–2	
	80	Ofloxacin	0.12	1	0.03–4	
	35	Trimethoprim	0.5	> 128	0.03– > 128	
	35	Co-amoxiclav	4	16	1–64	
Hafnia alvei	77	Ciprofloxacin	0.008 (0.008–≤ 0.06)	0.008 (0.008–≤ 0.06)	0.004–1	6, 7, 10
	15	Norfloxacin	0.03	0.06	0.03–0.06	
	77	Ofloxacin	0.12	0.25	0.03–2	
	19	Trimethoprim	0.5	2	0.25–2	
	19	Co-amoxiclav	64	64	0.5–64	
Enterobacter spp.	33	Ciprofloxacin	0.01	0.12	≤ 0.008–2	2
	33	Sparfloxacin	0.01	0.06	≤ 0.008–2	
Enterobacter aerogenes	872	Ciprofloxacin	0.016 (0.016–≤ 0.06)	0.5 (0.03–0.5)	0.008– > 8	3–7, 10
	83	Norfloxacin	0.12	0.12	0.03–2	
	827	Ofloxacin	0.12	1	≤ 0.06– > 8	
	8	Ampicillin	16	> 256	8– > 256	
	8	Cefotaxime	0.25	8	0.25–8	
	8	Gentamicin	0.5	1	0.5–1	
	25	Trimethoprim	1	4	0.12– > 128	
	25	Co-amoxiclav	64	128	2–128	

Table 2.1. (continued)

Species	Number of isolates	Antibiotic	MIC$_{50}$ (mg/litre)	MIC$_{90}$ (mg/litre)	Range MIC (mg/litre)	References
Enterobacter agglomerans	103	Ciprofloxacin	0.03 (0.03–≤ 0.06)	0.125	0.015–0.5	3, 10
	23	Norfloxacin	0.125	0.5	0.03–2	
	80	Ofloxacin	0.12	0.5	≤ 0.06–2	
Enterobacter cloacae	1201	Ciprofloxacin	0.016 (0.015–0.06)	0.25 (0.03–0.25)	0.015–> 8	3–7, 10
	95	Norfloxacin	0.13	0.5	0.03–4	
	1141	Ofloxacin	0.12	1	0.03–> 8	
	35	Ampicillin	32	> 256	8–> 256	
	35	Cefotaxime	0.5	64	≤ 0.25–> 256	
	35	Gentamicin	0.5	8	0.5–> 64	
	36	Trimethoprim	1	> 128	0.03–> 128	
	36	Co-amoxiclav	128	128	2–128	
Enterobacter sakazakii	16	Ciprofloxacin	≤ 0.06	0.25	≤ 0.06–2	10
	16	Ofloxacin	0.12	0.5	≤ 0.06–4	
Enterobacter taylorae	11	Ciprofloxacin	≤ 0.06	≤ 0.06	≤ 0.06–0.12	10
	11	Ofloxacin	0.12	0.25	0.12–0.25	
Proteus mirabilis	1285	Ciprofloxacin	0.03 (0.01–0.06)	0.12 (0.03–0.25)	≤ 0.008–> 8	2–7, 10
	20	Sparfloxacin	0.25	0.5	≤ 0.008–2	
	20	Norfloxacin	0.12	0.12	0.03–8	
	1202	Ofloxacin	0.12	0.25	≤ 0.06–> 8	
	56	Ampicillin	1	> 256	1–> 256	
	56	Cefotaxime	4	16	4–256	
	56	Gentamicin	1	4	0.5–64	
	37	Trimethoprim	0.25	> 128	0.016–> 128	
	37	Co-amoxiclav	2	8	0.5–16	

Table 2.1. (continued)

Species	Number of isolates	Antibiotic	MIC_{50} (mg/litre)	MIC_{90} (mg/litre)	Range MIC (mg/litre)	References
Proteus penneri	20	Ciprofloxacin	≤ 0.06	0.12	≤ 0.06–0.12	10
	20	Ofloxacin	0.12	0.12	≤ 0.06–0.25	
Proteus vulgaris	269	Ciprofloxacin	0.03 (0.015–≤ 0.06)	0.06 (0.03–0.12)	0.004–0.5	2–4, 6, 7, 10
	31	Sparfloxacin	0.25	1	0.06–1	
	55	Norfloxacin	0.06	0.06	0.06–1	
	208	Ofloxacin	0.06	0.25	≤ 0.06–2	
	25	Trimethoprim	1	2	≤ 0.06–0.125	
	25	Co-amoxiclav	2	4	2–8	
Morganella morganii	522	Ciprofloxacin	0.016 (0.015–≤ 0.06)	0.06 (0.03–0.12)	0.008– > 8	2–7, 10
	29	Sparfloxacin	0.25	0.5	0.12–4	
	84	Norfloxacin	0.03	0.06	0.03–0.5	
	460	Ofloxacin	0.12	0.25	0.03– > 8	
	31	Ampicillin	128	256	1– > 256	
	31	Cefotaxime	≤ 0.25	1	≤ 0.25–8	
	31	Gentamicin	1	2	≤ 0.25– > 64	
	19	Trimethoprim	2	> 128	0.25– > 128	
	19	Co-amoxiclav	128	> 128	64– > 128	
Serratia spp.	84	Ciprofloxacin	0.06 (0.06–4)	0.12 (0.12– > 16)	0.03– > 16	2, 6, 7
	34	Sparfloxacin	8	> 16	0.03– > 16	
	25	Norfloxacin	0.12	0.5	0.06–4	
	50	Ofloxacin	0.25	0.5	0.12–1	
	25	Trimethoprim	2	4	0.12– > 128	
	25	Co-amoxiclav	128	128	4– > 128	

Table 2.1. (continued)

Species	Number of isolates	Antibiotic	MIC$_{50}$ (mg/litre)	MIC$_{90}$ (mg/litre)	Range MIC (mg/litre)	References
Serratia marcescens	1000	Ciprofloxacin	0.25 (≤ 0.06–0.25)	2 (0.5–2)	0.03–> 8	3–5, 10
	66	Norfloxacin	0.5	1	≤ 0.06–8	
	959	Ofloxacin	0.5	4	≤ 0.06–> 8	
	959	Ampicillin	256	> 256	16–> 256	
	959	Cefotaxime	1	8	≤ 0.25–> 64	
	959	Gentamicin	1	4	1–64	
Serratia liquefaciens	49	Ciprofloxacin	≤ 0.06	0.12	≤ 0.06–> 8	10
	49	Ofloxacin	0.12	0.5	≤ 0.06–> 8	
Citrobacter spp.	42	Ciprofloxacin	≤ 0.008 (≤ 0.008– ≤ 0.06)	0.06 (0.06–0.5)	≤ 0.008–0.5	2, 10
	31	Sparfloxacin	0.03	0.5	≤ 0.008–0.5	
	11	Ofloxacin	0.25	0.5	≤ 0.06–0.5	
Citrobacter freundii	664	Ciprofloxacin	0.008 (0.008– ≤ 0.06)	0.125 (0.03–1)	0.008–> 8	3–7, 10
	88	Norfloxacin	0.12	0.5	0.03–1	
	614	Ofloxacin	0.25	4	≤ 0.03–> 8	
	18	Ampicillin	8	64	4–64	
	18	Cefotaxime	≤ 0.25	≤ 0.25	≤ 0.25–0.5	
	18	Gentamicin	1	2	0.5–2	
	19	Trimethoprim	0.5	> 128	0.03–> 128	
	19	Co-amoxiclav	64	> 128	1–> 128	

Table 2.1. (continued)

Species	Number of isolates	Antibiotic	MIC$_{50}$ (mg/litre)	MIC$_{90}$ (mg/litre)	Range MIC (mg/litre)	References
Citrobacter diversus	376	Ciprofloxacin	0.015 (0.015–≤ 0.06)	0.03 (≤ 0.03–≤ 0.06)	0.015– > 8	3, 5, 10
	34	Norfloxacin	0.03	0.25	0.008–0.5	
	356	Ofloxacin	0.06	0.25	≤ 0.03– > 8	
	14	Ampicillin	32	> 256	2– > 256	
	14	Cefotaxime	≤ 0.25	0.5	≤ 0.25–0.5	
	14	Gentamicin	1	1	0.5–1	
Citrobacter koseri	40	Ciprofloxacin	0.008	0.016 (0.008–0.016)	0.002–0.06	6, 7
	20	Norfloxacin	0.03	0.06	0.016–0.06	
	40	Ofloxacin	0.06	0.06	0.03–0.25	
	40	Trimethoprim	0.25	4	0.06– > 128	
	40	Co-amoxiclav	4	8	2–16	
Citrobacter amalonaticus	30	Ciprofloxacin	≤ 0.06	≤ 0.06	≤ 0.06–0.5	10
	30	Ofloxacin	0.12	0.25	≤ 0.06–2	
Yersinia enterocolitica	90	Ciprofloxacin	0.015 (0.015–0.06)	0.03 (0.015–0.06)	0.008–0.25	1–3, 10
	37	Ofloxacin	0.06	0.12	≤ 0.06–0.5	
	47	Norfloxacin	0.06	0.06	0.03–1	
	31	Sparfloxacin	0.06	0.12	≤ 0.008–0.12	

Table 2.1. (continued)

Species	Number of isolates	Antibiotic	MIC$_{50}$ (mg/litre)	MIC$_{90}$ (mg/litre)	Range MIC (mg/litre)	References
Pseudomonas aeruginosa	2452	Ciprofloxacin	0.25 (0.06–8)	4 (0.5–>16)	≤0.008–>16	1–7, 8–10
	2248	Ofloxacin	1	8	≤0.06–64	
	658	Norfloxacin	1	1	0.03–>16	
	36	Sparfloxacin	>16	>16	0.25–>16	
	169	Ceftazidime	1	4	≤0.25–8	
	169	Piperacillin	4	16	1–>256	
	169	Imipenem	1	4	≤0.25–16	
	169	Gentamicin	2	4	≤0.25–128	
	100	Co-amoxiclav	>16/8	>16/8	1/0.5–>16/8	
	100	Cefuroxime	32	>32	16–32	
Burkholderia cepacia	78	Ciprofloxacin	4 (1–4)	>8 (2–>16)	0.25–>16	2, 3, 10
	14	Sparfloxacin	1	16	0.25–>16	
	22	Norfloxacin	4	8	1–8	
	42	Ofloxacin	8	>8	1–>8	
Pseudomonas fluorescens	65	Ciprofloxacin	0.12 (0.12–0.25)	1 (1–2)	0.03–>8	3, 10
	65	Norfloxacin	0.5	4	0.25–4	
	65	Ofloxacin	1	8	≤0.06–>8	
Pseudomonas putida	18	Ciprofloxacin	0.5	8	≤0.06–>8	10
	18	Ofloxacin	2	>8	0.25–>8	
Pseudomonas stutzeri	10	Ciprofloxacin	0.25	1	≤0.06–2	10
	10	Ofloxacin	0.25	2	0.12–2	
Pseudomonas putrefaciens	23	Ciprofloxacin	0.125	1	0.03–1	3
	23	Norfloxacin	0.5	4	0.25–8	

Table 2.1. (continued)

Species	Number of isolates	Antibiotic	MIC$_{50}$ (mg/litre)	MIC$_{90}$ (mg/litre)	Range MIC (mg/litre)	References
Comomonas acidovorans	10	Ciprofloxacin	0.12	0.12	0.06–0.12	7
	10	Ofloxacin	0.12	0.25	0.12–0.25	
Pseudomonas spp.	58	Ciprofloxacin	0.12 (0.12–1)	2 (2–8)	≤0.008–>16	2
	23	Sparfloxacin	0.5	8	0.01–>16	
	35	Norfloxacin	1	16	0.03–16	
	35	Ofloxacin	1	2	0.03–2	
Stenotrophomonas maltophilia	477	Ciprofloxacin	4 (0.25–4)	>8 (1–>16)	0.03–>16	2, 3, 5, 7, 10
	35	Sparfloxacin	2	16	0.06–16	
	24	Norfloxacin	1	4	0.125–8	
	20	Ceftazidime	2	32	≤0.25–256	
	20	Piperacillin	32	128	1–256	
	398	Ofloxacin	2	>8	≤0.06–>8	
Acinetobacter spp.	148	Ciprofloxacin	0.5 (0.03–0.5)	1 (0.25–>16)	0.008–128	2, 5–7, 10
	32	Sparfloxacin	0.12	16	0.03–>16	
	116	Ofloxacin	0.12	0.25	0.008–>8	
	60	Norfloxacin	1	8	0.06–32	
	25	Ampicillin	32	128	16–>256	
	25	Cefotaxime	32	64	0.004–1	
	33	Trimethoprim	4	16	0.5–64	
Acinetobacter calcoaceticus	139	Ciprofloxacin	0.5 (0.25–0.5)	>8 (0.5–>8)	≤0.06–>8	3
	25	Norfloxacin	2	8	0.125–16	10
	114	Ofloxacin	0.5	>8	≤0.06–>8	

Table 2.1. (continued)

Species	Number of isolates	Antibiotic	MIC$_{50}$ (mg/litre)	MIC$_{90}$ (mg/litre)	Range MIC (mg/litre)	References
Acinetobacter calcoaceticus var. *anitratus*	450	Ciprofloxacin	0.5	> 8	≤ 0.06– > 8	10
	450	Ofloxacin	0.5	> 8	≤ 0.06– > 8	
Acinetobacter calcoaceticus var. *lwoffi*	66	Ciprofloxacin	0.25	1	≤ 0.06– > 8	10
	66	Ofloxacin	0.25	1	≤ 0.06– > 8	
Acinetobacter baumannii	26	Ciprofloxacin	0.5	> 8	≤ 0.06– > 8	10
	26	Ofloxacin	0.5	> 8	0.12– > 8	
Alcaligenes faecalis	15	Ciprofloxacin	4	> 8	0.25– > 8	10
	15	Ofloxacin	4	> 8	1– > 8	
Alcaligenes xylosoxidans	51	Ciprofloxacin	8	>8	≤ 0.06– > 8	10
	51	Ofloxacin	8	> 8	0.12– > 8	
Providencia rettgeri	158	Ciprofloxacin	0.03 (0.03–0.12)	1 (0.06–1)	0.008– > 8	3, 6, 7, 10
	45	Norfloxacin	0.5	1	0.03–2	
	133	Ofloxacin	0.25	2	0.03– > 8	
	20	Trimethoprim	2	64	0.12– > 128	
	20	Co-amoxiclav	64	128	8– > 128	
	93	Ciprofloxacin	≤ 0.06	1	≤ 0.06– > 8	
Providencia stuartii	294	Ciprofloxacin	0.25 (0.12–2)	> 8 (2– > 8)	0.008– > 8	3, 5–7, 10
	88	Norfloxacin	0.5	8	0.03–16	
	260	Ofloxacin	1	> 8	≤ 0.06– > 8	
	14	Ampicillin	64	> 256	1– > 256	
	14	Cefotaxime	≤ 0.25	1	≤ 0.25–32	
	14	Gentamicin	32	128	2–128	
	37	Trimethoprim	16	> 128	0.5– > 128	
	37	Co-amoxiclav	128	128	1–128	

Table 2.1. (continued)

Species	Number of isolates	Antibiotic	MIC$_{50}$ (mg/litre)	MIC$_{90}$ (mg/litre)	Range MIC (mg/litre)	References
Providencia alcalifaciens	40	Ciprofloxacin	0.03 (0.016–0.03)	0.06	0.004–0.06	3, 6, 7
	30	Norfloxacin	0.06	0.5	0.03–1	
	20	Ofloxacin	0.12	0.5	0.03–0.5	
	10	Trimethoprim	0.25	1	0.06–1	
	10	Co-amoxiclav	32	128	0.25–128	
Vibrio cholerae	34	Ciprofloxacin	0.004 (0.004–≤ 0.008)	0.008	0.004–0.008	1, 13
	34	Ofloxacin	0.015	0.015	≤ 0.008–0.015	
	34	Norfloxacin	0.008	0.015	0.008–0.015	
Vibrio parahaemolyticus	35	Ciprofloxacin	0.06	0.06 (0.06–0.12)	≤ 0.008–0.12	1, 13
	35	Ofloxacin	0.25	0.25	≤ 0.008–0.25	
	10	Norfloxacin	0.03	0.06	0.03–0.06	
	10					
Aeromonas spp.	25	Ciprofloxacin	0.002 (0.002–≤ 0.008)	0.03 (0.004–0.03)	0.001–0.5	2
	15	Sparfloxacin	0.06	0.12	0.03–1	6
	10	Norfloxacin	0.008	0.016	0.008–0.03	
	10	Ofloxacin	0.016	0.016	0.016–0.03	
Aeromonas hydrophila	101	Ciprofloxacin	0.008 (0.004–≤ 0.06)	0.015 (≤ 0.008–≤ 0.06)	0.004–0.12	1, 7, 10, 13
	101	Ofloxacin	0.015	0.03	≤ 0.008–0.12	
	25	Norfloxacin	0.015	0.03	0.008–0.03	
	13	Trimethoprim	0.5	2	0.12–2	
	13	Co-amoxiclav	16	32	4–64	

Table 2.1. (continued)

Species	Number of isolates	Antibiotic	MIC$_{50}$ (mg/litre)	MIC$_{90}$ (mg/litre)	Range MIC (mg/litre)	References
Plesiomonas shigelloides	10	Ciprofloxacin	0.008	0.008	0.008	1
	10	Ofloxacin	0.015	0.015	0.015	
	10	Norfloxacin	0.015	0.015	0.015	
Flavobacterium meningosepticum	10	Ciprofloxacin	8	> 8	1–> 8	10
	10	Ofloxacin	4	> 8	1–> 8	
Campylobacter jejuni	140	Ciprofloxacin	0.06 (0.06–0.25)	0.12 (0.12–0.5)	0.03–0.5	1, 4, 13
	130	Ofloxacin	0.12	0.25	0.03–1	
	110	Norfloxacin	0.25	0.5	0.06–2	
Campylobacter spp.	20	Ciprofloxacin	0.12	0.12	0.06–0.5	7
	20	Ofloxacin	0.12	0.12	0.06–0.5	
	20	Co-amoxiclav	1	2	1–4	
Helicobacter pylori	88	Ciprofloxacin	0.12 (0.12–0.25)	0.25 (0.25–0.5)	0.06–0.5	15, 16
	70	Penicillin	0.015	0.03	0.002–0.06	
	88	Erythromycin	0.06	0.12	0.008–0.5	
	70	Gentamicin	0.12	0.25	0.06–0.5	
	88	Metronidazole	1	8	0.5–16	
	70	Bismuth sodium tartrate	8	16	2–32	
Haemophilus influenzae	1419	Ciprofloxacin	0.008 (0.008–≤ 0.06)	0.06 (0.008–0.06)	0.004–> 4	1, 3, 6, 7, 9, 10
	1293	Ofloxacin	0.03	0.06	0.015–> 4	
	146	Norfloxacin	0.06	0.06	0.03–0.12	
	38	Trimethoprim	0.12	0.25	0.06–0.5	
	138	Co-amoxiclav	0.5/0.25	2/1	≤ 0.12/0.06–> 32/16	
	100	Cefuroxime	≤ 0.5	≤ 0.5	≤ 0.5	

Table 2.1. (continued)

Species	Number of isolates	Antibiotic	MIC$_{50}$ (mg/litre)	MIC$_{90}$ (mg/litre)	Range MIC (mg/litre)	References
Haemophilus ducreyi	269	Ciprofloxacin	≤0.02 (0.004–0.03)	≤0.02 (0.015–0.03)	0.0005–0.03	17, 18, 19
	50	Ofloxacin	0.03	0.03	0.015–0.03	
	50	Norfloxacin	0.12	0.12	0.06–0.12	
	100	Sparfloxacin	≤0.02	≤0.02	≤0.02	
	100	Ceftriaxone	≤0.12	≤0.12	≤0.12	
Gardnerella vaginalis	90	Ciprofloxacin	1	1 (1–2)	0.5–2	1, 6, 7
	90	Ofloxacin	2	2	1–2	
	70	Norfloxacin	8	16	4–32	
	20	Trimethoprim	0.5	2	0.06–2	
	20	Co-amoxiclav	0.03	0.12	0.016–0.25	
Chlamydia trachomatis	20	Ciprofloxacin	1	2 (1–2)	0.5–2	8, 20
	10	Ofloxacin	1	4	1–8	
	10	Norfloxacin	16	16	16	
	10	Doxycycline	0.06	0.06	0.03–0.06	
Chlamydia pneumoniae	3	Ciprofloxacin	1	1	1	21
Ureaplasma urealyticum	42	Ciprofloxacin	16 (1–16)	32 (2–32)	0.5– >64	8, 20
	42	Ofloxacin	4	8	1–16	
	42	Norfloxacin	16	32	8–64	
	42	Doxycycline	0.5	4	0.12–32	
Mycoplasma hominis	22	Ciprofloxacin	2 (0.25–2)	4 (0.5–4)	2–4	20, 22
	12	Ofloxacin	16	64	16–64	
	12	Norfloxacin	8	16	8–16	
	12	Doxycycline	4	4	4	

Table 2.1. (continued)

Species	Number of isolates	Antibiotic	MIC$_{50}$ (mg/litre)	MIC$_{90}$ (mg/litre)	Range MIC (mg/litre)	References
Mycoplasma pneumoniae	30	Ciprofloxacin	4	8	2–8	23
	30	Erythromycin	≤ 0.004	≤ 0.004	≤ 0.004–0.06	
Legionella spp.	53	Ciprofloxacin	0.25 (0.06–0.5)	0.5	0.06–0.5	24, 25
	53	Ofloxacin	0.25	0.25	0.03–0.5	
	53	Norfloxacin	2	2	0.04–4	
	15	Erythromycin	0.5	0.5	0.02–0.5	
	15	Rifampicin	≤ 0.002	0.008	≤ 0.002–0.015	
Brucella melitensis	163	Ciprofloxacin	0.25 (0.25–0.5)	0.5 (0.5–1)	0.12–1	26, 27
	68	Norfloxacin	2	4	0.25–16	
	95	Doxycycline	0.12	0.12	0.06–0.25	
	95	Ceftriaxone	0.25	0.5	0.12–1	
	95	Streptomycin	0.5	0.5	0.12–1	
Bacteroides fragilis	171	Ciprofloxacin	8 (2–16)	32 (4–32)	1–64	1, 2, 6, 7
	140	Ofloxacin	4	8	1– > 32	
	80	Norfloxacin	16	32	4– > 128	
	31	Sparfloxacin	2	8	1–16	
	60	Co-amoxiclav	0.5	4	0.12–8	
	60	Metronidazole	1	1	0.12–2	
Prevotella melaninogenica	124	Ciprofloxacin	1	2 (1–4)	0.06–16	1, 6, 7
	124	Ofloxacin	1	2	0.5–4	
	60	Norfloxacin	4	32	1–64	
	60	Ciprofloxacin	1	4	0.5–16	
	64	Amoxycillin	0.5	16	0.002–64	
	64	Metronidazole	0.5	1	0.03–1	

Table 2.1. (continued)

Species	Number of isolates	Antibiotic	MIC$_{50}$ (mg/litre)	MIC$_{90}$ (mg/litre)	Range MIC (mg/litre)	References
Prevotella bivia	10	Ciprofloxacin	16	16	8–16	1
	10	Ofloxacin	16	32	8–32	
	10	Norfloxacin	64	128	64–128	
Bacteroides thetaiotaomicron	20	Ciprofloxacin	> 16	> 16	16–> 16	2
	20	Sparfloxacin	2	16	2–16	
Bacteroides ureolyticus	20	Ciprofloxacin	0.03	0.06	0.016–0.06	6, 7
	10	Norfloxacin	0.12	0.25	0.06–0.25	
	20	Ofloxacin	0.12	0.12	0.06–0.12	
	10	Amoxycillin	0.06	0.06	0.03–0.12	
	10	Metronidazole	1	2	0.5–2	
Fusobacterium spp.	38	Ciprofloxacin	2 (1–2)	2 (2–4)	0.5–4	1, 6, 7
	38	Ofloxacin	2	4	0.5–8	
	20	Norfloxacin	16	16	4–32	
	18	Amoxycillin	0.06	0.12	0.016–0.12	
	18	Metronidazole	0.06	0.25	0.008–0.25	
Peptostreptococcus spp.	110	Ciprofloxacin	0.5 (0.5–1)	1 (0.5–4)	0.12–8	1, 6, 7
	110	Ofloxacin	0.5	2	0.25–16	
	70	Norfloxacin	8	16	0.5–16	
	40	Amoxycillin	0.12	8	0.008–32	
	40	Metronidazole	0.25	1	0.06–1	
Peptococcus spp.	20	Ciprofloxacin	0.5	0.5	0.25–0.5	6
	20	Norfloxacin	2	8	0.5–16	
	20	Ofloxacin	4	4	0.25–16	

Table 2.1. (continued)

Species	Number of isolates	Antibiotic	MIC$_{50}$ (mg/litre)	MIC$_{90}$ (mg/litre)	Range MIC (mg/litre)	References
Mobiluncus spp.	40	Ciprofloxacin	0.5	1	0.03–1	6, 7
	40	Norfloxacin	4	8	1–8	
	40	Ofloxacin	1	2	0.5–2	
	20	Amoxycillin	0.06	0.12	0.03–25	
	20	Metronidazole	64	>128	4–>128	
Clostridium perfringens	50	Ciprofloxacin	0.25	1	0.12–1	1
	50	Ofloxacin	0.5	1	0.5–1	
	50	Norfloxacin	1	2	0.5–2	
Clostridium difficile	100	Ciprofloxacin	8	16	4–16	1
	100	Ofloxacin	8	16	4–16	
	100	Norfloxacin	64	128	32–128	
Clostridium spp.	49	Ciprofloxacin	8 (4–8)	32	0.12–64	6, 7
	25	Norfloxacin	32	128	0.25–128	
	49	Ofloxacin	8	32	0.25–64	
	24	Amoxycillin	0.25	16	0.008–32	
	24	Metronidazole	0.25	0.5	0.016–1	
Nocardia asteroides	31	Ciprofloxacin	2	16	0.12–16	1
	31	Ofloxacin	4	32	0.25–32	
	31	Norfloxacin	32	64	0.5–128	
Mycobacterium tuberculosis	106	Ciprofloxacin	0.5 (0.5–1)	1 (0.5–1)	0.25–2	28–30
	31	Ofloxacin	1	1	0.5–2	
	21	Norfloxacin	4	8	4–16	

Table 2.1. (continued)

Species	Number of isolates	Antibiotic	MIC$_{50}$ (mg/litre)	MIC$_{90}$ (mg/litre)	Range MIC (mg/litre)	References
Mycobacterium avium	13	Ciprofloxacin	8	32	2–32	30
	13	Norfloxacin	> 32	> 64	8– > 64	
	13	Ofloxacin	16	64	2–64	
Mycobacterium avium–intracellulare complex	14	Ciprofloxacin	1	2	≤ 0.12–4	31
Mycobacterium kansasii	9	Ciprofloxacin	1	1	1	30
	9	Norfloxacin	4	8	2–8	
	9	Ofloxacin	0.5	1	0.5–1	
Mycobacterium xenopi	22	Ciprofloxacin	0.5	1	0.12–2	30
	22	Norfloxacin	2	4	1–8	
	22	Ofloxacin	1	2	0.5–4	
Mycobacterium fortuitum	32	Ciprofloxacin	0.06	0.5	< 0.03–1	30, 32
	32	Norfloxacin	1	8	0.25–8	
	12	Ofloxacin	0.5	1	0.25–2	
Mycobacterium chelonae	20	Ciprofloxacin	4	64	0.12–64	30, 32
	20	Norfloxacin	64	>64	1– > 64	
	14	Ofloxacin	16	32	4–32	

ciprofloxacin,[14,36] which has replaced chloramphenicol in the empirical treatment of typhoid.[35,37] Despite resistance to chloramphenicol, co-trimoxazole and amoxycillin, *Shigella* spp. are consistently susceptible to ciprofloxacin.[14]

Vibrio spp. are susceptible to most quinolones, which differ little in their effectiveness (Table 2.1).[1–32] *Aeromonas hydrophila* and other *Aeromonas* spp. are more susceptible to ciprofloxacin than norfloxacin or the aminoglycosides. *Campylobacter jejuni* is inhibited at much lower concentrations of ciprofloxacin than cefotaxime, ceftazidime or ampicillin. *Helicobacter* spp. are less susceptible to ciprofloxacin than penicillin, but the activity of erythromycin and gentamicin is similar.[15,16] Ciprofloxacin is highly active against *Haemophilus ducreyi*, but has only moderate activity against *Gardnerella vaginalis*, ampicillin, penicillin and tetracycline being more potent (Table 2.1).[1–32] It has more activity against *Chlamydia trachomatis* (MIC 1–2 mg/litre) than norfloxacin or ofloxacin. Ridgway *et al.*[20] reported activity of ciprofloxacin against *Mycoplasma hominis* and *Ureaplasma* spp. (MIC$_{50}$ 1 mg/litre and 0.25 mg/litre). There is little activity against *Mycoplasma pneumoniae*.[23] Against *Brucella melitensis*, ciprofloxacin is as active as tetracycline, streptomycin and ceftriaxone, but is less active than doxycycline.[26,27]

Gram-positive aerobic bacteria

Ciprofloxacin is active against most staphylococci and streptococci, but is less effective against the enterococci.[10,33] Ciprofloxacin has similar activity to ofloxacin against staphylococci and is more potent than norfloxacin. The streptococci are moderately susceptible to ciprofloxacin, but cefotaxime and the ureidopenicillins have greater activity.

Oxacillin-sensitive *Staphylococcus aureus* is usually susceptible (96%; n = 735), but most oxacillin-resistant strains are also resistant to ciprofloxacin.[33] Before the use of quinolones

became widespread, there was no appreciable relationship between oxacillin and ciprofloxacin sensitivity.[10] Coagulase-negative staphylococci show a similar pattern of susceptibility. A total of 96% (n = 405) of oxacillin-sensitive strains of *Staphylococcus epidermidis* are sensitive compared with 68% (n = 349) of oxacillin-resistant isolates.[33] Up to 50% of strains of *Staphylococcus haemolyticus* are resistant. *Streptococcus pyogenes* (90%; n = 380) and *Streptococcus* group B (78%; n = 185) are usually susceptible.[33] Ciprofloxacin is much less active against *Streptococcus pneumoniae* than other respiratory pathogens (58%; n = 307) and concentrations that can be attained in the respiratory tract are only one-third of the MIC.[38] The fluoroquinolones are not particularly active against the enterococci. Beskid found that 63% (n = 400) of strains of *Enterococcus faecalis* were susceptible, compared with only 28% (n = 82) of strains of *Enterococcus faecium*.[33]

Listeria spp. are more susceptible to ciprofloxacin than other quinolones (MIC$_{90}$ 0.4–1.0 mg/litre) (Table 2.1).[1–32] *Nocardia asteroides* has a high MIC (8–16 mg/litre). Some strains of *Corynebacterium* spp. and *Propionibacterium* spp. are susceptible to ciprofloxacin (Table 2.1).[1–32]

Mycobacteria

Ciprofloxacin has significant activity against *Mycobacterium* spp. and, compared with other agents, has the advantage of retaining activity following uptake into macrophages. In a series from New York, USA, all 172 isolates of *Mycobacterium tuberculosis* were susceptible to ciprofloxacin, even though 28% were resistant to isoniazid and 21% were resistant to rifampicin.[39] In another study, 96% (n = 75) of strains were inhibited by ciprofloxacin at a MIC of 2 mg/litre.[29] The *Mycobacterium avium–intracellulare* complex is generally susceptible to ciprofloxacin, but the reproducibility of test results may be poor.[31] Other studies report *Mycobacterium avium* and *Mycobacterium scrofulaceum* to be uniformly resistant.[30] *Mycobacterium xenopi* and *Mycobacterium fortuitum* are susceptible, but only 28% of strains of *Mycobacterium chelonae* are inhibited at therapeutic concentrations.[30,31]

Anaerobic bacteria

Resistance to ciprofloxacin is seen among most strains of *Bacteroides fragilis*, but there is some activity against 80% of strains of *Prevotella melaninogenica* and *Fusobacterium* spp.[6] *Fusobacterium fusiforme* is more susceptible to metronidazole and clindamycin than ciprofloxacin. *Fusobacterium nucleatum* and *Fusobacterium necrophorum* are moderately susceptible.[6] *Bacteroides oralis* and *Bacteroides ureolyticus* are susceptible.[6,40] Ciprofloxacin is active against *Peptococcus magnus* and the peptostreptococci. *Clostridium perfringens* is susceptible to ciprofloxacin, but *Clostridium difficile* and other clostridia are resistant.

Plasmodium falciparum

Of all the quinolones, ciprofloxacin has the greatest activity against *Plasmodium falciparum*. When measured by incorporation of radiolabelled hypoxanthine, ciprofloxacin at 9.5 mg/litre inhibited 50% of activity at 48 hours.[41] After exposure for 72 hours, a concentration of 1.7 mg/litre is sufficient to inhibit 50% of activity.[42] Ciprofloxacin is active against chloroquine-resistant *Plasmodium falciparum* at an MIC of 5.2 mg/litre.[43]

Bactericidal activity

Ciprofloxacin is rapidly bactericidal, but this property is inhibited by agents that block protein synthesis (e.g. chloramphenicol, rifampicin) and by a lack of amino acids. Inhibition of protein or RNA synthesis impedes the action of the exonucleases responsible for cell death. Bactericidal activity is also lost under anaerobic conditions. The bactericidal activity is biphasic in that there is a single concentration, usually 30–60 times the MIC, above and below which bactericidal activity is reduced. At high antibiotic concentrations, inhibition of RNA synthesis may occur resulting in bacteriostasis. Against *Escherichia coli*, ciprofloxacin becomes increasingly bactericidal up to a concentration of 0.15 mg/litre after which it decreases again.

Agents acting on RNA synthesis (e.g. rifampicin), can slow the bactericidal action of ciprofloxacin and ofloxacin, but, unlike most other quinolones, bacterial killing is not abolished.[44] Ciprofloxacin and ofloxacin must have a secondary mechanism of bacterial killing and they are more rapidly bactericidal than other quinolones (19 minutes versus 59 minutes for 90% bacterial killing).[45]

In most studies, the minimum bactericidal concentration (MBC) is within a two-fold dilution of the MIC.[46,47] For some strains of *Pseudomonas aeruginosa* and staphylococci the MBC may be 2–4 times the MIC. Chin and Neu found that 25% of isolates had MBCs more than four-fold the MIC, but no MBC was greater than 1.5 mg/litre.[48] The ratio of MBC to MIC was lower for ciprofloxacin than other quinolones for enterococci, *Streptococcus agalactiae* and the Enterobacteriaceae but higher for staphylococci and *Pseudomonas aeruginosa*.[46] The serum bactericidal activity (SBA) of ciprofloxacin against Enterobacteriaceae is greater than that of piperacillin, but is similar to that of ceftazidime.[49] After intravenous ciprofloxacin, 200 mg, at a serum concentration of 0.6 mg/litre, the SBA was 1/32 to 1/64 for the Enterobacteriaceae.[49] After the same dose, however, the SBA for *Pseudomonas aeruginosa* was only $^1/_3$ and < $^1/_2$ for staphylococci, *Corynebacteria* and *Listeria* spp.[50,51] An oral dose of ciprofloxacin, 500 mg, produced similar results.[52] High SBA titres are obtained against *Salmonella typhi* (1/119–1/388) compared with ofloxacin (1/26–1/84) or other antibiotics.[53]

Bactericidal activity against *Staphylococcus aureus* and *Escherichia coli* is reduced when the inoculum rises from 10^6 cfu/ml to 10^8 cfu/ml.[54] It is likely that hypoxia is the cause as ciprofloxacin has no bactericidal activity under anaerobic conditions. In the treatment of prosthetic joint infections, for example, ciprofloxacin would probably be bacteriostatic. Both MIC and bacterial killing of *Escherichia coli* are affected by pH and the presence of magnesium ions. At an acidic pH, in the presence of magnesium, the MIC is increased 75-fold and the bactericidal effect reduced 60-fold.[55] In early morning urine, the apparent MIC of *Escherichia coli* can be 0.75 mg/litre.[55]

In vitro testing and its problems

In most studies, a rise in inoculum from 10^5 to 10^7 cfu/ml has only a minor effect on MIC,[56–58] although the change produced an eight-fold rise in MIC in one study.[48] Rises in MIC of up to eight-fold have been reported in *Staphylococcus aureus*, *Enterococcus faecalis*, *Escherichia coli*, and *Serratia marcescens*.[59] Comparing inocula of 10^4 and 10^8 cfu/spot, a 1–16-fold increase in MIC was found for *Enterobacter cloacae*, a 4–16-fold increase for *Serratia marcescens* and 2–8-fold increase for other Enterobacteriaceae.[46]

Agar dilution and broth dilution methods usually produce similar results. For methicillin-resistant *Staphylococcus aureus*, the MBC_{90} has been reported as eight-fold higher by broth macrodilution than by microdilution methods (4 versus 0.5 mg/litre). Similarly, the MIC_{90}s for *Escherichia coli* and *Klebsiella pneumoniae* are higher by macrodilution.[56] Others have found agar dilution methods yield an MIC for *Pseudomonas aeruginosa* twice that of a broth microdilution method.[58]

Comparison between two reference centres showed that MICs obtained on different media (Iso-Sensitest and Diagnostic Sensitivity Test agar) were still within one doubling dilution of each other for 627 of 635 isolates.[60] The use of Mueller-Hinton, brain-heart infusion, tryptic soy digest, Columbia or nutrient medium did not affect the MIC for a variety of species.[48] The use of Mueller-Hinton agar rather than broth either has no effect or increases the MIC only two-fold.[56,58] Susceptibilities of anaerobic bacteria were not affected by the choice of medium, except for a rise in MIC for *Bacteroides fragilis* on brucella agar compared with Wilkins Chalgren.[61,62]

The activity of ciprofloxacin is reduced both in urine and at an acidic pH. MICs for *Enterobacter cloacae* were 0.01 mg/litre in broth, 0.04 mg/litre in urine of pH 7.5 and 6.3 mg/litre in urine of pH 5.5.[48] The MIC rises 8–16-fold when the pH of Mueller-Hinton broth is lowered from 7.5 to 5.5.[61,62] For anaerobes, the MIC at pH 5 is four-fold that at pH 8.[61,62] Increased magnesium concentration in the medium also results in smaller zones of inhibition, but this does not occur with zinc or calcium salts.[46,58] Estimation of MIC is little affected by the use of 50% serum in Mueller-Hinton broth.[48]

Comparison of susceptibility testing in 12 UK laboratories using disc methods revealed 46 discrepancies for *Staphylococcus aureus* and *Pseudomonas aeruginosa*, usually when the MIC was close to the break-point. Disc testing may give a spuriously high prevalence of resistance; for example, 6% of *Staphylococcus aureus* and 9% of *Pseudomonas aeruginosa* compared with 2% and 4%, respectively, by MIC (Figure 2.1).[60] Far more discrepancies occurred with disc diffusion (41 of 476) than with break-point methods (4 of 184), but the size of disc and disc method used made little difference. Moderately susceptible enterococci (MIC, 1–8 mg/litre) are classed as resistant if a 1 μg antibiotic disc is used. A 5 μg disc provides better discrimination.[63,64] Agreement between disc testing and MIC was 97% in one study of Enterobacteriaceae and staphylococci, but fell to 88% if enterococci and other species were included.[65] Agar dilution has been recommended for susceptibility testing of *Stenotrophomonas* spp. because the disc method shows a false sensitivity in 12% of cases.[66]

Using the methods recognised by the National Committee for Clinical Laboratory Standards (NCCLS), the relationship between

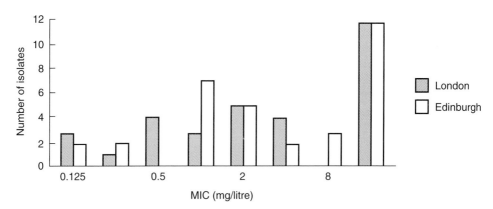

Figure 2.1. Minimum inhibitory concentration (MIC) of *Pseudomonas aeruginosa* and *Staphylococcus aureus*, determined by two reference laboratories, for isolates reported by referring laboratories as ciprofloxacin resistant.[60]

MIC and the zone of inhibition by a disc method becomes weaker when the disc content rises above 5 μg. Using a disc of that size, Grimm recommended a zone of 15 mm or less to be resistant, a zone of 16–20 mm to be intermediate, and a zone of 21 mm or more to be susceptible; the corresponding break-points were susceptible, 1 mg/litre or less, intermediate, 2 mg/litre, and resistant, 4 mg/litre or more.[67]

A 5 μg disc can, however, produce unacceptably large zone sizes (> 40 mm) on disc testing of some highly susceptible strains. Using a 1 μg disc and a cut-off of 18 mm to evaluate 750 strains of Enterobacteriaceae and staphylococci, 17 strains (2.3%) were found to be falsely resistant and 3 (0.4%) to be falsely sensitive.[68] Similarly, of 227 strains of streptococci, 30 (13%) strains were falsely resistant (25 were *Streptococcus pneumoniae*) and 3 (1.3%) were falsely sensitive. It has been difficult to define a resistance break-point for *Neisseria gonorrhoeae*, because of the lack of resistant strains, but an MIC of ≤ 0.06 mg/litre is taken as susceptible.[69] Nalidixic acid has been used for susceptibility testing.

Pathogen susceptibility has been measured in peritoneal dialysate to establish the likely efficacy of ciprofloxacin in treating peritonitis associated with peritoneal dialysis.

Reconstitution of broth with peritoneal dialysis effluent caused the MIC_{50} for coagulase-negative staphylococci to rise four-fold.[70] In fresh dialysis fluid and to a lesser extent in effluent, markedly reduced activity against staphylococci, *Escherichia coli* and *Klebsiella pneumoniae* has also been reported.[71] Others have found that the bactericidal activity of ciprofloxacin against staphylococci, *Pseudomonas aeruginosa* and *Escherichia coli* was not adversely affected by dialysis fluid or effluent.[72]

Post-antibiotic effect

The post-antibiotic effect (PAE) is the delayed regrowth of surviving bacteria following transient exposure to an antibiotic. It is observed with many antibiotics and is used to rationalise dosing intervals. The PAE is species specific and is affected by the antibiotic concentration, the length of exposure, the growth conditions and the bacterial inoculum. After removal of the drug, incorporation of radiolabelled ^{3}H gradually increases in *Staphylococcus aureus* to a level dependent on the duration of the PAE, which may possibly indicate the time needed for DNA repair.[73]

Ciprofloxacin usually has a long PAE (Figure 2.2),[74] but there is considerable variation between and among species.[75] In *Escherichia coli*, exposure to ciprofloxacin results in an immediate fall in DNA synthesis, which persists for more than 4 hours after removal of the antibiotic.[76] No PAE is usually observed in *Enterococcus faecalis*[77] and there is no prolonged effect in *Legionella pneumophila*.[78] In *Burkholderia cepacia*, no PAE may be manifest or it can last as long as 5 hours.[79] The PAE is shorter following repeated exposure, probably as the result of a rising MIC, but can be prolonged by addition of gentamicin.[74,80] As with other antibiotics, pooled human cerebrospinal fluid markedly prolongs the PAE of *Escherichia coli*.[81]

The PAE is greatest at a concentration four times the MIC and reduces once levels exceeding 64 times the MIC are reached. Following exposure to ciprofloxacin at a concentration of 1 mg/litre for 1 hour, the PAE was 250 minutes for *Escherichia coli* (MIC 0.03 mg/litre), 309 minutes for *Klebsiella pneumoniae* (MIC 0.12 mg/litre), 329 minutes for *Enterobacter cloacae* (MIC 0.03 mg/litre), 196 minutes for *Acinetobacter* var. *lwoffi* (MIC 0.25 mg/litre),

167 minutes for *Pseudomonas aeruginosa* (MIC 0.25 mg/litre) and 72 minutes for *Staphylococcus aureus* (MIC 1 mg/litre).[82] At the MIC, the PAEs were 56–124 minutes, 64 minutes, 46 minutes, 126 minutes, 84 minutes and 113 minutes, respectively. At four times the MIC, the PAE was 145–250 minutes for *Escherichia coli*, 196 minutes for *Acinetobacter* spp., 167 minutes for *Pseudomonas aeruginosa* and 107 minutes for *Staphylococcus aureus*. Howard *et al.* reported a PAE of 145 minutes for *Staphylococcus aureus* exposed to four times the MIC for 1 hour, but rapid cell division occurred soon afterwards.[83] The lag was 135 minutes when organisms were exposed to the MIC for 3 hours. Similarly for *Escherichia coli*, the PAE of 120 minutes following exposure to four times the MIC for 1 hour was followed by more rapid replication than in unexposed organisms, suggesting repair of DNA during the lag phase. Under the same conditions, the lag phase for *Streptococcus pyogenes* was 135 minutes.

The duration of PAE is related to the length of exposure. It lasts for more than 30 minutes at eight times the MIC for *Enterococcus faecalis*

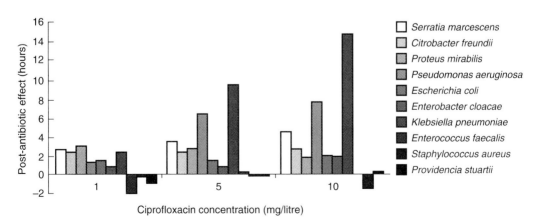

Figure 2.2. Post-antibiotic effect of ciprofloxacin. If the isolate regrows more rapidly than the control, a negative value is shown.[74]

and at twice the MIC for *Pseudomonas aeruginosa* after exposure for 0.5–1 hour.[84] If exposed to ciprofloxacin for just 15 minutes, the required concentrations are twice as high. The PAE for *Pseudomonas aeruginosa* is significantly shorter at acid than at alkaline pH, but for *Staphylococcus aureus* it is longer at pH 5 and pH 8 than at pH 7.[85] The PAE for *Staphylococcus aureus* is also longer in the presence of serum.[86]

Synergy with other agents

Synergy with other antibiotics is usually defined by a reduction in the MIC or MBC of at least four-fold or a fractional inhibitory index of 0.5 or less. There appears to be no appreciable synergy or antagonism between ciprofloxacin and aminoglycosides against the majority of Gram-negative species.[87] However, synergy between ciprofloxacin and amikacin has been reported in 57% of strains of *Serratia marcescens* and in 67% of strains of *Staphylococcus aureus*.[57] The combination of ciprofloxacin and piperacillin/tazobactam shows synergistic killing of *Pseudomonas aeruginosa* and is associated with a reduced likelihood of resistant strains emerging.[88] Ciprofloxacin has also shown synergism with azlocillin *in vitro* against 30–56% of strains of *Pseudomonas aeruginosa*, but others have shown no interaction.[88–90] Ciprofloxacin in combination with imipenem has shown enhanced killing of *Pseudomonas aeruginosa* in 9–42% of strains.[91,92] Synergy between ciprofloxacin and trimethoprim has been demonstrated in 31% of clinical isolates and antagonism in only 1%.[93] There is no interaction between ciprofloxacin and vancomycin against *Staphylococcus aureus*.[51] Ciprofloxacin is synergistic with cefotaxime against 16% of anaerobic strains and with clindamycin against 9–38%.[94,95] Antagonism is rarely reported with any agent.

In vivo activity in animals

The efficacy of ciprofloxacin in various animal models has been documented in more than 46 reports.[96] In neutropenic mice, ciprofloxacin was more effective than enoxacin or ofloxacin in protecting against *Pseudomonas aeruginosa* while, in non-neutropenic animals, efficacy was similar to, or better than, ofloxacin against *Staphylococcus aureus*, *Pseudomonas aeruginosa* and Enterobacteriacae. Implantable extravascular chambers have been widely used to give a controlled assessment of efficacy *in vivo*. Ciprofloxacin was more effective than azlocillin in infections caused by *Pseudomonas aeruginosa*, *Escherichia coli* and *Klebsiella pneumoniae*. In combination with azlocillin, efficacy against enterococci was superior to that of penicillin and gentamicin. However, azlocillin was more effective than ciprofloxacin against *Streptococcus pneumoniae*. In fibrin clots, ciprofloxacin was effective against *Pseudomonas aeruginosa* and *Escherichia coli*, but not enterococci.

Peterson identified 36 studies using animal models to imitate human infections.[96] In the rabbit model of endocarditis, ciprofloxacin was not as effective as penicillin plus gentamicin against enterococci, but showed similar or greater potency against *Staphylococcus aureus* and *Staphylococcus epidermidis* than vancomycin, and against *Pseudomonas aeruginosa* than azlocillin plus tobramycin.[96] At ciprofloxacin doses of 60 and 100 mg/kg/day, improvements were observed in cure and relapse rates, mortality and vegetation titres. Abscess formation in other organs and bacteraemia were reduced. Ciprofloxacin was also more potent than ceftazidime in experimental *Pseudomonas* endocarditis in rats.[96]

In the treatment of *Staphylococcus aureus* endocarditis in rabbits, ciprofloxacin given for 4 days reduced vegetation titres to 10^2 cfu/g compared with 10^3 in animals given nafcillin and 10^8 in controls.[97] Ciprofloxacin when compared with vancomycin achieved similar results in the treatment of methicillin-resistant *Staphylococcus aureus* endocarditis.[97] Others have found ciprofloxacin and vancomycin to produce similar results in *Staphylococcus aureus* endocarditis, but in 12% of animals the strain developed resistance to ciprofloxacin.[98] Tolerance to vancomycin and flucloxacillin in *Staphylococcus aureus* does not affect the reduction in vegetation titres produced by ciprofloxacin.[99]

Ciprofloxacin had efficacy similar to other quinolones and ceftazidime in pneumonia caused by *Pseudomonas aeruginosa* in guinea-pigs. In pneumonia caused by *Klebsiella pneumoniae* in mice, it appeared more effective than ofloxacin, and unlike ceftazidime, could kill inhibited organisms within the lung.[98] In mice with pneumonia due to *Haemophilus influenzae*, ciprofloxacin resulted in a greater survival rate than chloramphenicol or ampicillin.[98] Ciprofloxacin plus rifampicin showed no advantage over ciprofloxacin alone in the survival of guinea-pigs infected with *Legionella pneumophila*.[98] In rabbits, a single dose of ciprofloxacin cleared an empyema due to *Klebsiella pneumoniae*.[100]

In rats and mice, ciprofloxacin was at least as protective as azlocillin or ceftazidime against bacteraemia caused by *Pseudomonas aeruginosa*. Ciprofloxacin plus gentamicin was most effective in treating infection caused by intraperitoneal injection of *Pseudomonas aeruginosa*, followed by ciprofloxacin alone, then ofloxacin plus gentamicin.[100] In the same model, ciprofloxacin was as active as cefoxitin and more active than pefloxacin against *Escherichia coli* and *Bacteroides fragilis*, and a combination of ciprofloxacin plus clindamycin was as effective as perfloxacin plus metronidazole.[100] Ciprofloxacin did not eradicate *Bacteroides fragilis*, but sufficiently reduced numbers of *Escherichia coli* in abdominal abscesses to prevent death.[101]

Ciprofloxacin was more potent than the aminoglycosides in the treatment of rabbit osteomyelitis caused by *Pseudomonas aeruginosa* or *Escherichia coli*.[96] Tobramycin treatment for 4 weeks failed to sterilise tibial infection, whereas ciprofloxacin was successful in 17 of 18 animals.[100] Ciprofloxacin plus rifampicin was effective in methicillin-resistant

Staphylococcus aureus osteomyelitis, but ciprofloxacin alone resulted in little improvement and regrowth later.[102] In septic arthritis due to *Escherichia coli*, ciprofloxacin caused a greater reduction than gentamicin in bacterial numbers in the synovium.[100,103] Ciprofloxacin, 80 mg/kg/day, achieved cure in 16 of 17 animals and significant reduction in bacterial titres in joint fluid and synovium.[103]

In a thigh abscess model, efficacy has been demonstrated in infections caused by *Escherichia coli*, *Klebsiella pneumoniae*, *Pseudomonas aeruginosa*, *Staphylococcus aureus* and *Bacteroides fragilis*.[96] In mice, ciprofloxacin was more effective than norfloxacin, vancomycin, cephalothin or methicillin against *Staphylococcus aureus*.[104] In the rat granuloma pouch model, ciprofloxacin has been shown to be effective against *Escherichia coli* in the stationary phase.[105] Perioperative, but not postoperative, treatment with ciprofloxacin prevented abscess formation on a prosthetic implant following administration of *Staphylococcus epidermidis*.[98] In addition, ciprofloxacin was more effective than cefazolin in preventing abscess formation following injection of *Staphylococcus aureus* into guinea-pigs.[106]

A short course of ciprofloxacin treatment permanently cured chronic campylobacter infection in marmosets.[100] Ciprofloxacin compared with chloramphenicol or ampicillin significantly improved survival of mice injected with *Salmonella typhimurium*.[98,107] Liposomes have been used to deliver ciprofloxacin to mice induced with salmonellosis.[108] All control mice died within 12 days of injection with *Salmonella dublin*. Liposomal ciprofloxacin was significantly more effective than conventional ciprofloxacin when both were administered as single injections, but was equal in efficacy to a 5-day course of ciprofloxacin.[108] In a rat model of prostatitis, ciprofloxacin eradi-cated infection in 80% of cases. In urinary infections in mice, ciprofloxacin was more effective than piperacillin, gentamicin, norfloxacin or ofloxacin.[100] In chronic pyelonephritis in rats, ciprofloxacin has greater efficacy than cefotaxime, which may be due to the longer serum half-life of ciprofloxacin.[109] Ciprofloxacin was significantly more effective than gentamicin or piperacillin in sterilising the kidney in experimental pyelonephritis in rats.[110]

In rabbits, meningitis induced by *Pseudomonas aeruginosa* was treated with an intravenous infusion of ciprofloxacin at a dose of 1–30 mg/kg/hour.[111] Penetration into the cerebrospinal fluid of infected animals reached 18% of serum concentrations compared with 4% in uninfected animals. At a dose of 5 mg/kg/hour, penetration into the cerebrospinal fluid was 0.8 mg/litre and bacterial killing was similar to ceftazidime plus tobramycin.

Less common uses of ciprofloxacin have also been examined in animal models. A combination of ciprofloxacin and isoniazid cured tuberculosis in mice and did so more rapidly than rifampicin plus isoniazid.[112] At high doses (160 mg/kg for 12 hours), ciprofloxacin can produce an 86% reduction in experimentally induced malaria parasitaemia in mice.[113] Topical ciprofloxacin is more effective than tobramycin/polymixin in sterilising the rabbit cornea following injection of $1.2-1.7 \times 10^3$ cfu *Pseudomonas aeruginosa*.[114] It will also significantly reduce the bacterial load of *Mycobacterium fortuitum* or *Mycobacterium chelonae* in a rabbit model of keratitis.[115]

Immunological effects

Ciprofloxacin does not affect phagocytic function or chemotaxis directly, but susceptible bacteria are more readily phagocytosed if they have been previously exposed to subinhibitory concentrations of ciprofloxacin.[116,117] Intracellular penetration of ciprofloxacin is high and can be further increased by exposing polymorphs to opsonized zymosan.[118] Within 30 minutes of exposure, the intracellular concentration is 6–7 times greater than the extracellular concentration.[119] Other antibiotics do not interfere with penetration, but amphotericin B increases the cellular:extracellular ratio. The likely mechanism of ciprofloxacin's penetration is diffusion and, furthermore, it is not

firmly bound within the cell.[116,120] Intracellular bactericidal activity of the quinolones has been demonstrated for *Staphylococcus aureus*, *Legionella* spp., *Mycobacterium fortuitum* and *Salmonella* spp.[120]

High concentrations of ciprofloxacin (50 mg/litre) inhibit lymphocyte proliferation as measured by uptake of radiolabelled thymidine, but at therapeutic concentrations *in vitro*, it has little effect. Some studies have found that incubation with ciprofloxacin for more than 3 days results in an increased uptake.[117] In the mouse, the effects of ciprofloxacin are complex. A 3-day course of intraperitoneal ciprofloxacin given to mice inhibits IgG-forming cells, delayed-type hypersensitivity responses and proliferation of lymphocytes in response to lipopolysaccharide or concanavalin A.[121] The numbers of granulocyte-macrophage colony-forming cells increase, but the white cell count decreases. However, colony-stimulating factor production by cultured mice spleen cells in the presence of pokeweed mitogen is increased three-fold by the addition of ciprofloxacin at a dose of 5–10 mg/litre.[122] The number of myeloid progenitors in the bone marrow and spleen of irradiated mice is also increased by ciprofloxacin, and a higher peripheral white cell count is seen after 4 days. Mice receiving such treatment have a significantly better survival at 4 weeks than those given placebo (5 of 38 versus 20 of 44).[122] Ceftazidime did not have significant effects. In a second experiment, 19 of 76 irradiated mice given bone marrow transplants survived when treated with ciprofloxacin compared with 36 of 55 given ceftazidime or 38 of 76 given placebo.[123] Bone marrow engraftment in mice is suppressed at a dose of 100 mg/kg/day, well above therapeutic levels.[117] These findings may be of importance in the management of human bone marrow recipients.

At concentrations above 25 mg/litre, ciprofloxacin and other quinolones inhibit the production of the cytokines – interleukin 1 (IL-1), IL-6 and tumour necrosis factor (TNF) – by monocytes in response to endotoxin.[124] Ciprofloxacin inhibits production by 70%

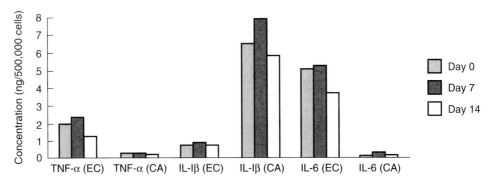

Figure 2.3. The effect of a 1-week course of ciprofloxacin on endotoxin-induced monocyte production of tumour necrosis factor α (TNF-α), interleukin 1α (IL-1α) and IL-6 in volunteers. EC, extracellular; CA, cell associated.[124]

compared with 20% by ofloxacin.[125] At concentrations above 50 mg/litre, ciprofloxacin reduces extracellular IL-1 production,[117] but at a low concentration of 1–2.5 mg/litre, ciprofloxacin increases production.[116] When ciprofloxacin is given at an oral dose of 50 mg/kg/day to volunteers for 1 week, the release of all three cytokines by monocytes in peripheral blood is increased in response to endotoxin (Figure 2.3).[124] Production of IL-2 by stimulated human lymphocytes is increased 50–60-fold in the presence of ciprofloxacin across a wide range of concentrations (5–100 mg/litre).[116,117] The production of interferon-γ by endotoxin-stimulated monocytes is not altered in the presence of ciprofloxacin at a concentration of 5–20 mg/litre, but is increased at concentrations above 50 mg/litre.[116] Ciprofloxacin increases the concentration of mRNA for various interleukins and TNF in human lymphocytes stimulated by mitogenic lectin, exerting its effect at the transcriptional stage.[126]

References

1. Felmingham D, O'Hare MD, Robbins MJ, Wall RA, Cremer AW, Ridgway GL *et al.* Comparative *in vitro* studies with 4-quinolone anti-microbials. Drugs Exp Clin Res 1985; 11: 317–29.

2. García-Rodríguez JA, García Sanchez JE, García García MI, Fresnadillo MJ, Trujillano I, García Sanchez E. *In vitro* activity of four new fluoro-quinolones. J Antimicrob Chemother 1994; 34: 53–64.

3. Cornaglia G, Pompei R, Dainelli B, Satta G. *In vitro* activity of ciprofloxacin against aerobic bacteria isolated in a Southern European hospital. Antimicrob Agents Chemother 1987; 31: 1651–5.

4. Eliopoulos GM, Gardella A, Moellering RC Jr. *In vitro* activity of ciprofloxacin, a new carboxy-quinoline antimicrobial agent. Antimicrob Agents Chemother 1984; 25: 331–5.

5. Fernandes CJ, Ackerman VP. *In vitro* studies of ciprofloxacin and survey of resistance patterns in current isolates. Diagn Microbiol Infect Dis 1990; 13: 79–91.

6. King A , Phillips I. The comparative *in-vitro* activity of eight newer quinolones and nalidixic acid. J Antimicrob Chemother 1986; 18 (Suppl D): 1–20.

7. King A, Bethune L, Phillips I. The *in-vitro* activity of temafloxacin compared with other antimicrobial agents. J Antimicrob Chemother 1991; 27: 769–79.

8. Kresken M, Wiedemann B. Development of resistance to nalidixic acid and the fluoroquinolones after the introduction of norfloxacin and ofloxacin. Antimicrob Agents Chemother 1988; 32: 1285–8.

9. Venezia RA, Yocum DM. The *in vitro* activity of oral ciprofloxacin and beta-lactam antimicrobials against bacteria from the respiratory tract. Curr Ther Res 1991; 50: 282–7.

10. Prosser BLaT, Beskid G. Multicenter *in vitro* comparative study of fluoroquinolones against 25,129 Gram-positive and Gram-negative clinical isolates. Diagn Microbiol Infect Dis 1995; 21: 33–45.

11. Höffler U. In vitro sensitivity of Bacteriodaceae clostridia and propionibacteria to newer antimicrobial agents. J Antimicrob Chemother 1986; 18 (Suppl E): 41–6.

12. Aznar J, Caballero MC, Lozano MC, de Miguel C, Palomares JC, Perea EJ. Activities of new quinolone derivatives against genital pathogens. Antimicrob Agents Chemother 1985; 27: 76–8.

13. Felmingham D, Robbins MJ. *In vitro* activity of lomefloxacin and other antimicrobials against bacterial enteritis pathogens. Diagn Microbiol Infect Dis 1992; 15: 339–43.

14. Karjuki S, Gilks C, Brindle R, Batchelor B, Kimari J, Waiyaki P. Antimicrobial susceptibility and presence of extrachromosomal deoxyribonucleic acid in *Salmonella* and *Shigella* isolates from patients with AIDS. East Afr Med J 1994; 71: 292–6.

15. McNulty CAM, Wise R. Susceptibility of clinical isolates of *Campylobacter pyloridis* to 11 antimicrobial agents. Antimicrob Agents Chemother 1985; 28: 837–8.

16. Loo VG, Sherman P, Matlow AG. *Helicobacter pylori* infection in a pediatric population: in vitro susceptibilities to omeprazole and eight antimicrobial agents. Antimicrob Agents Chemother 1992; 36: 1133–5.

17. Aldridge KE, Cammarata C, Martin DH. Comparison of the *in vitro* activities of various parenteral and oral antimicrobial agents against endemic *Haemophilus ducreyi*. Antimicrob Agents Chemother 1993; 37: 1986–8.

18. Wall RA, Mabey DCW, Bello CSS, Felmingham D. The comparative *in vitro* activity of twelve 4-quinolone antimicrobials against *Haemophilus ducreyi*. J Antimicrob Chemother 1985; 16: 165–8.

19. Naamara W, Plummer FA, Greenblatt SM, D'Costa LJ, Ndinya-Achola JO, Ronald AR. Treatment of chancroid with ciprofloxacin. A prospective randomized trial. Am J Med 1987; 82 (Suppl 4A): 317–20.

20. Ridgway GL, Mumtaz G, Gabriel FG, Oriel JD. The activity of ciprofloxacin and other quinolones against *Chlamydia trachomatis* and Mycoplasmas *in vitro*. Eur J Clin Microbiol 1984; 3: 344–6.

21. Chirgwin K, Roblin PM, Hammerschlag MR. *In vitro* susceptibilities of *Chlamydia pneumoniae* (Chlamydia sp strain TWAR). Antimicrob Agents Chemother 1989; 33: 1634–5.

22. Escalante A, Aznar J, de Miguel C, Perea EJ. Activity of nine antimicrobial agents against *Mycoplasma hominis* and *Ureaplasma urealyticum*. Eur J Sex Transm Dis 1985; 2: 85–7.

23. Cassell GH, Waites KB, Pate MS, Canupp KC, Duffy LB. Comparative susceptibility of *Mycoplasma pneumoniae* to erythromycin, ciprofloxacin and lomefloxacin. Diagn Microbiol Infect Dis 1989; 12: 433–5.

24. Ruckdeschel G, Ehret W, Ahl A. Susceptibility of *Legionella* spp. to quinolone derivatives and related organic acids. Eur J Clin Microbiol 1984; 3: 373.

25. Saito A, Koga H, Shigeno H, Watanabe K, Mori K, Kohno S *et al*. The antimicrobial activity of ciprofloxacin against *Legionella* species and the treatment of experimental *Legionella pneumonia* in guinea pigs. J Antimicrob Chemother 1986; 18: 251–60.

26. Bosch J, Linares J, Lopez de Goiciechea MJ, Ariza J, Cisnal MC, Martin R. *In vitro* activity of ciprofloxacin, ceftriaxone and five other antimicrobial agents against 95 strains of *Brucella melitensis*. J Antimicrob Chemother 1986; 17: 459–61.

27. Gobernado M, Canton E, Santos M. *In vitro* activity of ciprofloxacin against *Brucella melitensis*. Eur J Clin Microbiol 1984; 3: 371.

28. Rastogi N, Goh KS. *In vitro* activity of the new difluorinated quinolone sparfloxacin (AT-4140) against *Mycobacterium tuberculosis* compared with activities of ofloxacin and ciprofloxacin. Antimicrob Agents Chemother 1991; 35: 1933–6.

29. LaBombardi VJ, Cataldo-Caputzal L. Ciprofloxacin susceptibility testing by MIC and disk elution of drug resistant *Mycobacterium tuberculosis* and *Mycobacterium avium* complex. Antimicrob Agents Chemother 1993; 37: 1556–7.

30. Texier-Maugein J, Mormède M, Fourche J, Bébéar C. *In vitro* activity of four fluoroquinolones against eighty-six isolates of mycobacteria. Eur J Clin Microbiol 1987; 6: 584–6.

31. Klopman G, Li J, Wang S, Pearson AJ, Chang K, Jacobs MR *et al*. *In vitro* anti-*Mycobacterium avium* activities of quinolones: predicted active structures and mechanistic considerations. Antimicrob Agents Chemother 1994; 38: 1794–802.

32. Khardori N, Nguyen H, Rosenbaum B, Rolston K, Bodey GP. *In vitro* susceptibilities of rapidly growing mycobacteria to newer antimicrobial agents. Antimicrob Agents Chemother 1994; 38: 134–7.

33. Beskid G, Prosser BLaT. A multicenter study on the comparative *in vitro* activity of fleroxacin and three other quinolones: an interim report from 27 centers. Am J Med 1993; 94 (Suppl 3A): 2–8.

34. Peters G, Schumacher-Perdreau F, Pulverer G. *In vitro* activity of ciprofloxacin, ofloxacin, and pefloxacin against clinical isolates of *Pseudomonas aeruginosa* and staphylococci. Rev Infect Dis 1988; 10 (Suppl 1): S41.

35. Threlfall EJ, Ward LR, Rowe B, Raghupathi S, Chandrasekaran Y, Vandepitte J *et al*. Widespread occurrence of multiple drug-resistant *Salmonella typhi* in India. Eur J Clin Microbiol Infect Dis 1992; 11: 990–3.

36. Dar L, Gupta BL, Rattan A, Bhujwala RA, Shriniwas. Multidrug resistant *Salmonella typhi* in Delhi. Indian J Pediatr 1992; 59: 221–4.

37. Rowe B, Ward LR, Threlfall EJ. Spread of multiresistant *Salmonella typhi*. Lancet 1990; 336: 1065–6.

38. Cherubin CE, Eng RHK, Smith SM, Tan EN. A comparison of antimicrobial activity of ofloxacin, L-ofloxacin, and other oral agents for respiratory pathogens. Diagn Microbiol Infect Dis 1992; 15: 141–4.

39. Weltman AC, Rose DN. Tuberculosis susceptibility patterns, predictors of multidrug resistance and implications for initial therapeutic regimens at a New York City Hospital. Arch Intern Med 1994; 154: 2161–7.

40. Kleitmann W, Focht J, Nosner K. Comparative *in vitro* activity against aerobic and anaerobic bacteria from clinical isolates. Arzneimittel-Forschung 1987; 37: 661–6.

41. Divo AA, Sartorelli AC, Patton CL, Bia FJ. Activity of fluoroquinolone antibiotics against *Plasmodium falciparum in vitro*. Antimicrob Agents Chemother 1988; 32: 1182–6.

42. Krishna S, Davis TME, Chan PCY, Wells RA, Robson KJH. Ciprofloxacin and malaria. Lancet 1988; i: 1231–2.

43. Midgley JM, Keter DW, Phillipson JD, Grant S, Warhurst DC. Quinolones and multiresistant *Plasmodium falciparum*. Lancet 1988; ii: 281.

44. Smith JT, Ratcliffe NT. Ciprofloxacin and ofloxacin possess an extra bactericidal mechanism absent from other 4-quinolone antibacterial agents. 4th Mediterranean Congress of Chemotherapy, Rhodes, Greece 1984: 462–3.

45. Smith JT. Awakening the slumbering potential of the 4-quinolone antibacterials. Pharmaceutical J 1984: 299–305.

46. Auckenthaler R, Michea-Hamzehpour M, Pechere JC. *In vitro* activity of newer quinolones against aerobic activity. J Antimicrob Chemother 1986; 17 (Suppl B): 29–39.

47. Wise R, Andrews JM, Edwards LJ. *In vitro* activity of Bay 09867, a new quinolone derivative, compared with those of other antimicrobial agents. Antimicrob Agents Chemother 1983; 23: 559–64.

48. Chin N, Neu HC. Ciprofloxacin, a quinolone carboxylic acid compound active against aerobic and anaerobic bacteria. Antimicrob Agents Chemother 1984; 25: 319–26.

49. Weiss D, Trautmann M, Wagner J, Borner K, Hahn H. Ciprofloxacin: a comparative evaluation of its bactericidal activity in human serum against four enterobacterial species. Drugs Exp Clin Res 1986; 12: 889–94.

50. Standiford HC, Drusano GL, Forrest A, Tatem B, Plaisance K. Bactericidal activity of ciprofloxacin compared with that of cefotaxime in normal volunteers. Antimicrob Agents Chemother 1987; 31: 1177–82.

51. Van der Auwera P, Klastersky J. Bactericidal activity and killing rate of serum in volunteers receiving ciprofloxacin alone or in combination with vancomycin. Antimicrob Agents Chemother 1986; 30: 892–5.

52. Machka K, Milatovic D. Serum bactericidal activity of ciprofloxacin and ofloxacin in volunteers. Eur J Clin Microbiol 1987; 6: 59–62.

53. Trautmann M, Krause B, Birnbaum D, Wagner J, Lenk V. Serum bactericidal activity of two newer quinolones against *Salmonella typhi* compared with standard therapeutic regimens. Eur J Clin Microbiol 1986; 5: 297–302.

54. Lewin CS, Morrissey I, Smith JT. Role of oxygen in the bactericidal action of the 4-quinolones. Rev Infect Dis 1989; 11 (Suppl 5): 913–14.

55. Ratcliffe NT, Smith JT. Ciprofloxacin's bacterial and inhibitory actions in urine. Chemioterapia 1985; 4 (Suppl 2): 385–6.

56. Gombert ME, Aulicino TM. Comparison of agar dilution, microtitre broth dilution and tube macrodilution susceptibility testing of ciprofloxacin against several pathogens at two different inocula. J Antimicrob Chemother 1985; 16: 709–12.

57. Moody JA, Gerding DN, Peterson LR. Evaluation of ciprofloxacin's synergism with other agents by multiple *in vitro* methods. Am J Med 1987; 82 (Suppl 4A): 44–54.

58. Blaser J, Dudley MN, Gilbert D, Zinner SH. Influence of medium and method on the *in vitro* susceptibility of *Pseudomonas aeruginosa* and other bacteria to ciprofloxacin and enoxacin. Antimicrob Agents Chemother 1986; 29: 927–30.

59. Fass RJ. *In vitro* activity of ciprofloxacin (Bay 09867). Antimicrob Agents Chemother 1983; 24: 568–74.

60. King A, Phillips I, Amyes S, Lewin C, Paton R, Tillotson G. MIC audit for routine ciprofloxacin sensitivity testing. J Antimicrob Chemother 1993; 31: 321–3.

61. Watt B, Brown FV. Is ciprofloxacin active against clinically important anaerobes? J Antimicrob Chemother 1986; 17: 605–13.

62. Borobio MV, Perea EJ. Effect of inoculum, pH and medium on the activity of ciprofloxacin against anaerobic bacteria. Antimicrob Agents Chemother 1984; 25: 342–3.

63. Perry JD, Ford M, Gould FK. Susceptibility of enterococci to ciprofloxacin. J Antimicrob Chemother 1994; 34: 297–8.

64. Paton R, Lewin CS, Hood J, Amyes SGB. Sensitivity testing of enterococci to ciprofloxacin. J Antimicrob Chemother 1989; 24: 265–72.

65. Tilton RC. Ciprofloxacin disc susceptibility tests. 1st International Ciprofloxacin Workshop, Leverkusen, Germany, 1985: 26–9.

66. Hohl P, Frei R, Aubry P. *In vitro* susceptibility of 33 clinical isolates of *Xanthomonas maltophilia*. Inconsistent correlation of agar dilution and of disk diffusion test results. Diagn Microbiol Infect Dis 1991; 14: 447–50.

67. Grimm H. *In vitro* study with ciprofloxacin: interpretive criteria of agar diffusion test according to standards of the NCCLS and DIN. Am J Med 1987; 82 (Suppl 4A): 376–80.

68. Andrews JM, Wise R. Disc sensitivity testing with ciprofloxacin. J Antimicrob Chemother 1989; 23: 156–8.

69. Fuchs PC, Barry AL, Baker C, Murray PR, Washington JA. Proposed interpretative criteria and quality control parameters for testing *in vitro* susceptibility of *Neisseria gonorrhoeae* to ciprofloxacin. J Clin Microbiol 1991; 29: 2111–14.

70. Guay D, Klicker R, Pence T, Peterson P. *In vitro* antistaphylococcal activity of teicoplanin and

ciprofloxacin in peritoneal dialysis effluent. Eur J Clin Microbiol 1986; 5: 661–3.

71. Weisser-Condon C, Engels I, Daschner FD. *In vitro* activity of four new quinolones in Mueller-Hinton broth and peritoneal dialysis fluid. Eur J Clin Microbiol 1987; 6: 324–6.

72. McCormick EM, Echols RM. Effect of peritoneal dialysis fluid and pH on bactericidal activity of ciprofloxacin. Antimicrob Agents Chemother 1987; 31: 657–9.

73. Gottfredsson M, Erlendsdóttir H, Kolka R, Gudmunsson S. Metabolic and ultrastructural effects induced by ciprofloxacin in *Staphylococcus aureus* during the postantibiotic effect (PAE) phase. Scand J Infect Dis 1991; Suppl 74: 124–8.

74. Gould IM, Milne K, Jason C. Concentration-dependent bacterial killing, adaptive resistance and post-antibiotic effect of ciprofloxacin alone and in combination with gentamicin. Drugs Exp Clin Res 1990; XVI: 621–8.

75. Drabu YJ, Blakemore PH. The post-antibiotic effect of teicoplanin: monotherapy and combination studies. J Antimicrob Chemother 1991; 27 (Suppl B): 1–7.

76. Guan L, Blumenthal RM, Burnham JC. Analysis of macromolecular biosynthesis to define the quinolone-induced post antibiotic effect in *Escherichia coli*. Antimicrob Agents Chemother 1992; 36: 2118–24.

77. Chin N-X, Neu HC. Post-antibiotic suppressive effect of ciprofloxacin against Gram-positive and Gram-negative bacteria. Am J Med 1987; 82 (Suppl 4A): 58–62.

78. Rajagopalan-Levasseur P, Douron E, Dameron G, Vilde J, Pocidalo J. Comparative postantibacterial activities of pefloxacin, ciprofloxacin and ofloxacin against intracellular multiplication of *Legionella pneumophila* serogroup 1. Antimicrob Agents Chemother 1990; 34: 1733–8.

79. Kumar A, Hay MB, Maier GA, Dyke JW. Post-antibiotic effect of ceftazidime, ciprofloxacin, imipenem, piperacillin and tobramycin for *Pseudomonas cepacia*. J Antimicrob Chemother 1992; 30: 597–602.

80. Karlowsky JA, Zhanel GC, Davidson RJ, Zieroth SR. *In vitro* postantibiotic effects following multiple exposures of cefotaxime, ciprofloxacin and gentamicin against *Escherichia coli* in pooled human cerebro-spinal fluid and Mueller-Hinton broth. Antimicrob Agents Chemother 1993; 37: 1154–7.

81. Zhanel GC, Karlowsky JA, Davidson RJ, Hoban DJ. Effect of pooled human cerebrospinal fluid on the post-antibiotic effects of cefotaximen ciprofloxacin and gentamicin against *Escherichia coli*. Antimicrob Agents Chemother 1992; 36: 1136–9.

82. Wiedemann B, Kratz B. The postantibiotic effect of ciprofloxacin. In: Garrard C, ed. Ciprofloxacin iv. Defining its role in serious infections. Berlin: Springer Verlag, 1994: 13–19.

83. Howard BMA, Pinney RJ, Smith JT. Contributions of post-antibiotic lag and repair-recovery to the post-antibiotic effects of ciprofloxacin on *Escherichia coli*, *Klebsiella pneumoniae*, *Staphylococcus aureus* and *Streptococcus pyogenes*. Chemotherapy 1993; 39: 22–31.

84. Pastor A, Pemán J, Cantón E. *In-vitro* postantibiotic effect of sparfloxacin and ciprofloxacin against *Pseudomonas aeruginosa* and *Enterococcus faecalis*. J Antimicrob Chemother 1994; 34: 679–85.

85. Gudmundsson A, Erlendsdottir H, Gottfredsson M, Gudmundsson S. Impact of pH and cationic supplementation on *in vitro* postantibiotic effect. Antimicrob Agents Chemother 1991; 35: 2617–24.

86. Davidson RJ, Zhanel GC, Phillips R, Hoban DJ. Human serum enhances the postantibiotic effect of fluoroquinolones against *Staphylococcus aureus*. Antimicrob Agents Chemother 1991; 35: 1261–3.

87. Haller I. Comprehensive evaluation of ciprofloxacin-aminoglycoside combinations against Enterobacteriaceae and *Pseudomonas aeruginosa* strains. Antimicrob Agents Chemother 1985; 28: 663–6.

88. Ainsworth S, Gelfand MS, Stratton CW. *In vitro* assessment of ciprofloxacin in combination with antipseudomonal β-lactam agents against *Pseudomonas aeruginosa*. 7th European Congress of Clinical Microbiology and Infectious Diseases, Vienna, Austria, 1995: Abstract 703.

89. Chin NX, Jules K, Neu HC. Synergy of ciprofloxacin and azlocillin *in vitro* and in a neutropenic mouse model of infection. Eur J Clin Microbiol 1986; 5: 23–8.

90. Overbeek BP, Rozenberg-Arska M, Verhoef J. Interaction between ciprofloxacin and tobramycin or azlocillin against multi-resistant strains of *Acinetobacter anitratum in vitro*. Eur J Clin Microbiol 1985; 4: 140–1.

91. Giamarellou H, Petrikkos G. Ciprofloxacin inter-actions with imipenem and amikacin against multi-resistant *Pseudomonas aeruginosa*. Antimicrob Agents Chemother 1987; 31: 959–61.

92. Chin N-X, Neu HC. Synergy of imipenem – a novel carbapenem, and rifampin and ciprofloxacin against *Pseudomonas aeruginosa*, *Serratia marcescens* and *Enterobacter* spp. Chemotherapy 1987; 33: 183–8.

93. Huovinen P, Wolfson JS, Hooper DC. Synergism of trimethoprim and ciprofloxacin *in vitro* against clinical bacterial isolates. Eur J Clin Microbiol Infect Dis 1992; 11: 255–7.

94. Whiting JL, Cheng N, Chow AW. Interactions of ciprofloxacin with clindamycin, metronidazole, cefox-itin, cefotaxime and mezlocillin against Gram-positive and Gram-negative anaerobic bacteria. Antimicrob Agents Chemother 1987; 31: 1379–82.

95. Esposito S, Gupta A, Thadepalli H. *In vitro* synergy of ciprofloxacin and three other antibiotics against *Bacteroides fragilis*. Drugs Exp Clin Res 1987; XII: 489–92.

96. Peterson LR. Animal models: the *in-vivo* evaluation of ciprofloxacin. J Antimicrob Chemother 1986; 18 (Suppl D): 55–64.

97. Sande MA, Brooks-Fournier RA, Greenberg JL. Efficacy of ciprofloxacin in animal models of

infection: endocarditis, meningitis and pneumonia. Am J Med 1987; 82 (Suppl A): 63–6.

98. Andriole VT. An update on the efficacy of ciprofloxacin in animal models of infection. Am J Med 1989; 87 (Suppl 5A): 32–4.

99. Voorn GP, Thompson J, Goessens WHF, Schmal-Bauer WC, Broeders PHM, Michel MF. Efficacy of ciprofloxacin in treatment and prophylaxis of experimental *Staphylococcus aureus* endocarditis caused by a cloxacillin-tolerant strain and its non-tolerant variant. J Antimicrob Chemother 1994; 33: 785–94.

100. Andriole VT. Efficacy of ciprofloxacin in animal models of infection. Am J Med 1987; 82 (Suppl 4A): 67–70.

101. Fu KP, Vince T, Bloom R, Gregory FJ, Hung PP. Therapeutic efficacy and pharmacokinetic properties of ciprofloxacin in intra-abdominal abscesses caused by *Bacteroides fragilis* and *Escherichia coli*. Drugs Exp Clin Res 1987; XIII: 493–6.

102. Henry NK, Rouse MS, Whitesell AL, McConnell ME, Wilson WR. Treatment of methicillin-resistant *Staphylococcus aureus* experimental osteomyelitis with ciprofloxacin or vancomycin alone or in combination with rifampin. Am J Med 1987; 82 (Suppl 4A): 73–5.

103. Bayer AS, Norman D, Anderson D. Efficacy of ciprofloxacin in experimental arthritis caused by *Escherichia coli* – *in vitro* and *in vivo* correlations. J Infect Dis 1985; 152: 811–16.

104. Rolin O, Huet Y, Bouanchaud DH. Comparative efficacy of pefloxacin and six other antimicrobial agents on *Staphylococcus aureus* experimental abscesses. J Antimicrob Chemother 1986; 17 (Suppl B): 49–52.

105. Zeiler HJ, Voigt WH. Efficacy of ciprofloxacin in stationary-phase bacteria *in vivo*. Am J Med 1987; 82 (Suppl 4A): 87–90.

106. Kernodle DS, Kaiser AB. Comparative prophylactic efficacies of ciprofloxacin, ofloxacin, cefazolin, and vancomycin in experimental model of staphylococcal wound infection. Antimicrob Agents Chemother 1994; 38: 1325–30.

107. Easmon CSF. Protective effects of ciprofloxacin in a murine model of Salmonella infection. Am J Med 1987; 82 (Suppl 4A): 71–2.

108. Magallanes M, Dijkstra J, Fierer J. Liposome-incorporated ciprofloxacin in treatment of murine salmonellosis. Antimicrob Agents Chemother 1993; 37: 2293–7.

109. Tietgen K, Schulz E, Boness J, Marre R. Ciprofloxacin and cefotaxime: pharmacokinetics and therapeutic efficacy in the *E. coli* pyelonephritis in rats. Immun Infekt 1986; 4: 152–5.

110. Peerbooms PGH, MacLaren DM. Comparative activities of five antimicrobial agents in experimental Proteus pyelonephritis in mice. Pharm Weekbl (Sci) (Suppl) 1987; 9: S30–2.

111. Hackbarth CJ, Chambers HF, Stella F, Shibl AM, Sande MA. Ciprofloxacin in experimental *Pseudomonas aeruginosa* meningitis in rabbits. J Antimicrob Chemother 1986; 18 (Suppl D): 65–9.

112. Chadwick M, Nicholson G, Gaya H. Brief report: combination chemotherapy with ciprofloxacin for infection with *Mycobacterium tuberculosis* in mouse models. Am J Med 1989; 87 (Suppl 5A): 35–6.

113. Salmon D, Deloron P, Gaudin C, Malhotra K, Lebras J, Pocidalo JJ. Activities of pefloxacin and ciprofloxacin against experimental malaria in mice. Antimicrob Agents Chemother 1990; 34: 2327–30.

114. Guzek JP, Chacko D, Kettering JD, Wessels IF, Aprecio RM. Comparison of topical ciprofloxacin to conventional antibiotic therapy in the treatment of experimental *Pseudomonas aeruginosa* keratitis. Cornea 1994; 13: 500–4.

115. Lin R, Holland GN, Helm CJ, Elias SJ, Berlin OGO, Bruckner DA. Comparative efficacy of topical ciprofloxacin for treating *Mycobacterium fortuitum* and *Mycobacerium chelonae* keratitis in an animal model. Am J Otolaryngol 1994; 117: 657–62.

116. Rubinstein E, Shalit I. Effects of the quinolones on the immune system. In: Hooper DC, Wolfson JS, eds. Quinolone antimicrobial agents. 2nd ed. Washington DC: American Society for Microbiology, 1993: 519–26.

117. Shalit I. Immunological aspects of new quinolones. Eur J Clin Microbiol Infect Dis 1991; 10: 262–6.

118. García I, Pascual A, Perea EJ. Effect of several antimicrobial agents on ciprofloxacin uptake by human neutrophils. Eur J Clin Microbiol Infect Dis 1992; 11: 260–2.

119. Easmon CSF, Crane JP. Uptake of ciprofloxacin by human neutrophils. J Antimicrob Chemother 1985; 16: 67–73.

120. Easmon CSF, Crane JP, Blowers A. Effect of ciprofloxacin on intracellular organisms: *in vitro* and *in vivo* studies. J Antimicrob Chemother 1986; 18 (Suppl D): 43–8.

121. Jimenez-Valera M, Sampedro A, Moreno E, Ruiz-Bravo A. Modification of immune response in mice by ciprofloxacin. Antimicrob Agents Chemother 1995; 39: 150–4.

122. Kletter Y, Riklis I, Shalit I, Fabian I. Enhanced re-population of murine hematopoietic organs in sublethally irradiated mice after treatment with ciprofloxacin. Blood 1991; 78: 1685–91.

123. Kletter Y, Singer A, Nagler A, Slavin S, Fabian I. Ciprofloxacin enhances hematopoiesis and the peritoneal neutrophil function in lethally irradiated, bone marrow-transplanted mice. Exp Hematol 1994; 22: 360–5.

124. Bailly S, Fay M, Ferrua B, Gougerot-Pocidalo MA. Ciprofloxacin treatment *in vivo* increases the *ex vivo* capacity of lipopolysaccharide-stimulated human monocytes to produce IL-1, IL-6 and tumour necrosis factor-alpha. Clin Exp Immunol 1991; 85: 331–4.

125. Gougerot-Pocidalo MA, Bailly S. Effects of various antibiotics on the production of cytokines by human monocytes. Allergy 1992; 47 (Suppl 12): 351.

126. Riesbeck K, Sigvardsson M, Leanderson T, Forsgren A. Superinduction of cytokine gene transcription by ciprofloxacin. J Immunol 1994; 153: 343–52.

Chapter 3

Resistance

Mechanism

Resistance to ciprofloxacin has not been clearly related to plasmids, drug inactivation or target modification, but has been shown to result from chromosomal mutation, or alterations of the quantity or type of porins in the outer membrane of Gram-negative bacteria. Mutations occur in the *gyrA* and *gyrB* genes that code for the A and B subunits of DNA gyrase, *nfxB*, *norB*, *norC* and *cfxB*, which affect permeability to the quinolones, and a number of other loci which are associated with low-level resistance.

Mutation in *gyrA* produces resistance to all quinolones and has been identified in *Escherichia coli (cfxA, gyrA, nalA, nfxA), Pseudomonas aeruginosa (nalA, cfxA), Haemophilus influenzae, Citrobacter freundii, Staphylococcus aureus* and *Serratia marcescens.*[1] It also occurs in *Enterobacter cloacae, Proteus mirabilis, Morganella morganii, Campylobacter jejuni* and *Neisseria gonorrhoeae.*[2] The mutant *gyrA* gene of *Escherichia coli* causing resistance to ciprofloxacin has been cloned and sequenced (Figure 3.1).[3] The mutations causing resistance were at the N-terminus of the *gyrA* gene. A total of 56 changes were found compared with the wild type, but only three resulted in amino acid changes in the A subunit (Ser-83 → Leu, Asp-87 → Gly and Asp-678 → Glu).

Alteration of Ser-83 itself confers low-level quinolone resistance. Some *gyrA* mutants have resistance to low levels of quinolones, which is antagonised by the presence of *gyrB* mutants.[4] Ciprofloxacin resistance in *Salmonella typhimurium* can be reversed by insertion of wild type *gyrA* into the isolate.[5] Reduced levels of accumulation of quinolones are also found, but there was no relationship to lack of outer-membrane protein factor (*ompF*).

Mutation in *gyrB* causes amino acid changes, which affect the binding of the B subunit to the A subunit. The *nal24* mutation results in exchange of asparagine for aspartic acid and the *nal31* exchanges lysine for glutamic acid.[1] The negative charge of the B subunit is reduced by *nal24* and increased by *nal31*. The latter confers resistance only to quinolones without a C7 piperazine substituent.

Antibiotics cross the outer membrane of the bacterial cell through porins and the hydrophobic pathway, and by a self-promoted route. The aqueous polysaccharide side chains of the lipopolysaccharide are not a barrier for ciprofloxacin, which has a partition coefficient of 0.03; the same is found with ofloxacin, pefloxacin and other quinolones with higher coefficients.[6] Hydrophobic patches can be formed in the outer membrane by chelation of magnesium in the lipopolysaccharide, creating a pathway for some agents. The porin pathway is, however, the most important in *Escherichia coli*, and changes in the outer membrane proteins and reduced uptake of ciprofloxacin or norfloxacin have been demonstrated in resistant strains of Enterobacteriaceae.[6]

Wilson APR and Grüneberg RN.
Ciprofloxacin: 10 years of clinical experience
© 1997 Maxim Medical, Oxford.

67			70					75					80
Ala	Arg	Val	Val	Gly	Asp	Val	Ile	Gly	Lys	Tyr	His	Pro	His
GCC	CGT	GTC	GTT	GGT	GAC	GTA	ATC	GGT	AAA	TAC	CAT	CCC	CAT

			85					90					
Gly	Asp	Ser	Ala	Val	Tyr	Asp	Thr	Ile	Val	Arg	Met	Ala	Gln
GGT	GAC	TCG	GCG	GTC	TAT	GAC	ACG	ATT	GTC	CGC	ATG	GCG	CAG
		T		T		G		C		T			
		Leu				Gly							

95				100						106	
Pro	Phe	Ser	Leu	Arg	Tyr	Met	Leu	Val	Asp	Gly	Gln
CCA	TTC	TCG	CTG	CGT	TAT	ATG	CTG	GTA	GAC	CGT	CAG
				C	T						

Figure 3.1. Mutations in the region determining resistance in the *gyrA* gene of *Escherichia coli* 205096. The DNA sequence of wild-type *Escherichia coli* is shown together with the changes in the resistant mutant. Changes in the amino acid sequence are also shown. Reproduced with permission.[3]

Alterations in the outer membrane protein (*ompF*) by class II mutations give rise to resistance to quinolones and other agents (e.g. β-lactams, chloramphenicol, tetracyclines, trimethoprim).[7] These mutations have been identified in *Escherichia coli* (*nalB*, *nfxB*, *norB*, *cfxB*), *Salmonella*, *Pseudomonas* (*nalB*, *cfxB*, *nfxB*, *qr1*, *qr2*), *Klebsiella* spp. and *Serratia* spp. *Pseudomonas aeruginosa* can become resistant as a result of changes at the *nalA* locus, which affects the A subunit of DNA gyrase, or *nalB*, which affects permeability. The *nfxB*, *cfxB* or *norB* mutations in *Escherichia coli* decrease *ompF* expression despite being distant from the *ompF* gene. The *cfxB* gene is an allele of *marA*, which produces a factor that reduces *ompF* expression.[1] Even if the ciprofloxacin concentration is sufficient to overcome the permeability barrier, DNA synthesis may not be inhibited. The Q2 mutant of *Escherichia coli* was selected in a patient treated for a urinary infection caused by a susceptible Q1 strain. Unusually, it was sensitive to

nalidixic acid and resistant to ciprofloxacin.[8] Uptake was reduced three-fold, but a 500-fold increase in ciprofloxacin concentration was needed to inhibit DNA synthesis.

Membrane proteins other than *ompF* can be affected. The *norC* mutation causes changes in the lipopolysaccharides of the outer membrane causing reduced expression of a second outer membrane protein, *ompC*, and an increased hydrophobicity of the cell surface. *Escherichia coli*, which is 6–18 times less susceptible to quinolones than wild strains, can be selected on agar containing chloramphenicol or tetracycline.[9] The resistance is partly related to decreased amounts of *ompF*, but other outer membrane changes are responsible for at least 50% of the difference in quinolone uptake and susceptibility.[9] In *Pseudomonas aeruginosa*, the *cfxB* and *nalB* mutations involve proteins other than *ompF*, and low-level resistance may be associated with loss of a 31–32 kDa protein or *ompG* plus a related 40 kDa outer membrane protein.[1] Loss of protein F has been demonstrated by gel electrophoresis and using monoclonal antibodies in a strain of *Pseudomonas aeruginosa* that transiently acquired ciprofloxacin resistance during treatment.[10] Lipopolysaccharide was altered allowing an increase in the uptake of hydrophobic molecules of 20–30%. However, the relationship between the mean inhibitory concentration (MIC) and the concentration necessary to produce inhibition of DNA synthesis was similar irrespective of the presence of protein F. The *cfxB5* permeability mutant of *Pseudomonas aeruginosa* is eight times more resistant to ciprofloxacin than the wild type.[11] Accumulation of ciprofloxacin in this mutant is greater in the presence of carbonyl cyanide m-chlorophenyl-hydrazone, an uncoupler, but still only 25% of that in wild-type strains. It is associated with a 51 kDa protein which may be reponsible for reduced permeability. The *nfxB* mutant results in production of a 54 kDa protein, but there is no concomitant resistance to other antibiotics.[1] Other mutants associated with increased production of a 54 kDa protein and resistance to other antibiotics have been described.[1] A mutant strain with reduced susceptibility to ciprofloxacin and resistance to norfloxacin associated with the *nfxC* gene has been reported in *Pseudomonas aeruginosa*.[12] Permeability mutants also occur in *Klebsiella*, *Enterobacter* and *Serratia* spp., but not Gram-positive bacteria.

The steady-state intracellular concentration of ciprofloxacin depends on the rate of entry through porins and the rate of exit through an energy-dependent efflux system. Cell entry does not require energy, is not saturable and is reduced at 4°C compared with 37°C. Quinolones can be washed away from the cell surface for 40–60 minutes after exposure. It is likely, therefore, that entry is by simple diffusion. Liposomes have been used to model the process. Binding of ciprofloxacin to liposomes *in vitro* is greatest in acidic conditions, when quinolones are positively charged and phospholipid is negatively charged. In alkaline conditions when both are negatively charged, binding is greatly reduced.[6] At neutral pH,

quinolones exist as zwitterions and could then pass into phospholipids.

Efflux of quinolones from the cell occurs by diffusion through the membrane and by a saturable energy-requiring process. Studies using everted inner membrane vesicles indicate that the system is carrier mediated and the hydrophilic quinolones will compete with each other for the carrier site.[13] Active efflux also occurs in *ompF* mutants leading to a reduced steady-state uptake of quinolones. An efflux system with a high rate of activity might contribute to resistance in species where uptake is poor (e.g. *Pseudomonas aeruginosa*).[11] The use of radiolabelled norfloxacin has shown that uptake in *cfxB* and *nfxB* mutants of *Escherichia coli* is 4–5 times less than in a wild strain, but blocking of the inner membrane efflux system with carbonyl cyanide m-chlorophenylhydrazone results in drug binding by mutant strains similar to that of the wild type.[14]

Mutation in the DNA gyrase is responsible for resistance in *Staphylococcus aureus*; the changes comprise Ser-84 → Leu and Ser-85 → Pro in *gyrA* protein.[15] In *Staphylococcus epidermidis*, the change is Ser-84 → Phe, but in both species the substitution in *gyrA* is C → T at position 251. No resistance due to reduced permeability is demonstrable in Gram-positive species and uptake is by simple diffusion. There was no significant change in uptake by methicillin-resistant *Staphylococcus aureus* when an ionic uncoupler was added.[16] Efflux systems also contribute to quinolone resistance. The *norA* gene is associated with quinolone resistance in *Staphylococcus aureus* and produces a protein with a similar amino acid sequence to a protein known to be associated with a drug efflux system in *Bacillus subtilis* (the *bmr* protein).[17] Overexpression of the *bmr* protein leads to quinolone resistance in *Bacillus* sp. and it is inhibited by reserpine. When placed in *Bacillus* sp., both genes confer resistance to various unrelated compounds as well as quinolones (Figure 3.2).[18] The *norA* gene confers resistance to hydrophilic, but not hydrophobic, quinolones.[16] When placed into *Escherichia coli*, it is associated with the

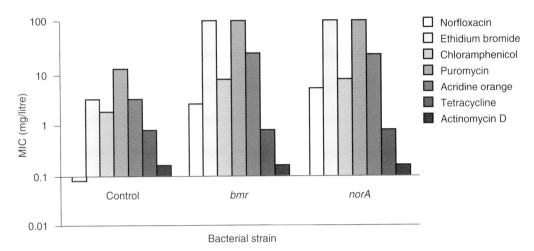

Figure 3.2. Relative susceptibility of control *Bacillus subtilis*, and strains containing *bmr* and *norA* genes to a variety of agents.[18]

production of a hydrophobic membrane protein. A cloned 5.5 kb fragment of staphylococcal DNA raises the MIC of ciprofloxacin in a susceptible *Escherichia coli* from 0.1 mg/litre to 0.4 mg/litre.[19] When this is placed into a susceptible *Staphylococcus aureus*, the MIC rises from 0.2 mg/litre to 12.5 mg/litre. Both *gyrA* and *gyrB* appear to be contained in this fragment.

Resistance mutations are not found on plasmids because of the dominance of the wild-type gene if a cell expresses both wild and mutant *gyrA*. Genes altering the outer membrane protein have delayed expression in wild strains, and quinolones both inhibit plasmid conjugation and can eliminate certain plasmids.[1] Quinolones may select plasmid-free cells or plasmid replication may be more susceptible to quinolones than chromosomal replication. Doubt has been cast on the report of a transmissible 20 MDa plasmid conferring resistance to nalidixic acid in *Shigella dysenteriae* type 1.[20] The resistance gene could not be shown to be successively transferred between several recipient strains and the plasmid did not confer resistance to the recent quinolones. However, ciprofloxacin resistance in these strains may have been more common,

suggesting that the plasmids encouraged chromosomal mutations.[1] Some *Pseudomonas* spp., anaerobes and fungi display intrinsic resistance.

Organisms that have small pores (e.g. *Alcaligenes faecalis*) have poor uptake of ciprofloxacin and DNA synthesis is inhibited at concentrations below the MIC. For *Escherichia coli*, the concentration for inhibition of DNA synthesis is similar to the MIC, suggesting permeability was not a barrier. In *Pseudomonas aeruginosa*, the concentration inhibitory to DNA synthesis is higher than the MIC, because DNA gyrase is less sensitive to quinolones.

Selection of resistant mutants in Enterobacteriaceae is possible only at 2–8 times the MIC and is extremely rare.[7] At five times the MIC, no resistant mutants could be found in 10^{12} bacteria.[21] Highly resistant strains can be isolated after serial passage through increasing drug concentrations, but, in some cases, resistance is lost in the absence of the drug. Mutants are cross-resistant to all quinolones and the mean increase in resistance is greater in ciprofloxacin than norfloxacin or ofloxacin, but less than in nalidixic acid. However, ciprofloxacin remains the most active agent against mutant strains, the maximum MIC being 0.5 mg/litre in one series.[21] Selection of resistance is less difficult at the MIC (1×10^{-6}), which suggests that maintenance of therapeutic serum concentrations is important to prevent emergence of resistance. With the exception of *Enterococcus faecalis*, mutation to resistance is more common in Gram-positive bacteria.[1] Ciprofloxacin resistance in *Legionella pneumophila* is rare; the incidence of mutants is less than 1×10^{-9}. A 16–32-fold reduction in susceptibility is probably related to permeability changes, but the strains also have less ability to infect host cells.[22]

Acquisition and relationship to use

The emergence of resistance to ciprofloxacin during treatment in a range of bacterial species, including those in which *in vitro* selection is difficult, has been reported. Susceptibility often returns after treatment has stopped. However, such reports are necessarily anecdotal and uncontrolled.[1] In early trials with ciprofloxacin, resistance was thought to have developed during treatment in only 5 of 1993 patients.[1] Resistance in the absence of ciprofloxacin use is found in species with a low constitutive susceptibility.

Reduced susceptibility of *Pseudomonas aeruginosa* is detected during treatment in 10% of cases of complicated urinary tract infection and 10–50% of pseudomonal respiratory infection in cystic fibrosis.[23,24] Failure to eradicate *Pseudomonas aeruginosa* in patients with cystic fibrosis appears to be the result of both changes in DNA gyrase and an altered outer membrane protein during treatment with ciprofloxacin;[25] some organisms lose resistance after the treatment and some retain it. A variety of species have developed resistance to quinolones when used to treat infections in intensive care unit patients, particularly *Pseudomonas aeruginosa*, methicillin-resistant *Staphylococcus aureus* and *Staphylococcus epidermidis*. Resistance can emerge during courses as short as 5 days.[26] Ciprofloxacin-

resistant *Pseudomonas aeruginosa* was isolated from the faeces in 6 of 186 samples from patients with leukaemia undergoing selective decontamination.[27]

Ribotyping has shown that ciprofloxacin resistance in *Staphylococcus aureus* emerged in several clones at the same time after the drug was introduced into hospital use.[28] Several mechanisms of resistance may emerge. During treatment of experimental *Staphylococcus aureus* endocarditis in rabbits, two resistant strains were found to have altered DNA gyrase and another to have an energy-dependent efflux system.[29] Resistance has been reported to develop in JK coryneforms during 1 week of treatment with ciprofloxacin.[30]

In the USA and Canada, 3013 respiratory tract isolates were collected and tested for susceptibility to ciprofloxacin (Figure 3.3).[31] *Streptococcus pneumoniae* and *Acinetobacter* spp., *Enterococcus* spp. and β-haemolytic streptococci were the least likely to be susceptible. Of 3449 soft tissue infection isolates, resistance to ciprofloxacin was low with the exception of *Enterococcus faecalis* (7%) and coagulase-negative staphylococci (10%).[31] Among urinary tract pathogens (n = 5360), ciprofloxacin was active against almost all Enterobacteriaceae, but 15% of strains of *Pseudomonas aeruginosa*, 18% of enterococci and 28% of staphylococci were resistant (Figure 3.4). No genital isolates were resistant to ciprofloxacin. In another survey of 67,000 isolates in the USA, most Enterobacteriaceae (99%), staphylococci (98%) and *Pseudomonas aeruginosa* (97%) were susceptible, but only 53% of enterococci and 68% of *Stenotrophomonas* spp. were susceptible.[32]

In a European survey of blood culture isolates (n = 2193), ciprofloxacin resistance amongst Gram-negative bacilli was highest in Southern Europe (8% in France, 6% in Portugal, 3% in Greece) and did not rise above 1% in the UK, Sweden, Denmark or Finland.[33] Resistance was found in 28% of *Pseudomonas* spp. in France and 25% in Portugal, compared with 10% in the UK. For *Staphylococcus aureus*, the rate of resistance ranged from 0%

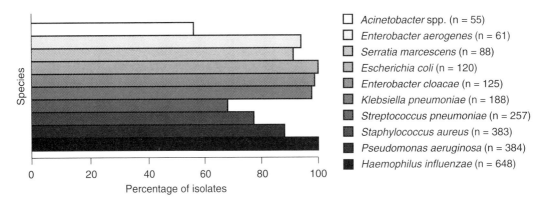

Acinetobacter spp. (n = 55)
Enterobacter aerogenes (n = 61)
Serratia marcescens (n = 88)
Escherichia coli (n = 120)
Enterobacter cloacae (n = 125)
Klebsiella pneumoniae (n = 188)
Streptococcus pneumoniae (n = 257)
Staphylococcus aureus (n = 383)
Pseudomonas aeruginosa (n = 384)
Haemophilus influenzae (n = 648)

Figure 3.3. Susceptibility of 3013 respiratory tract isolates to ciprofloxacin in the USA and Canada.[31]

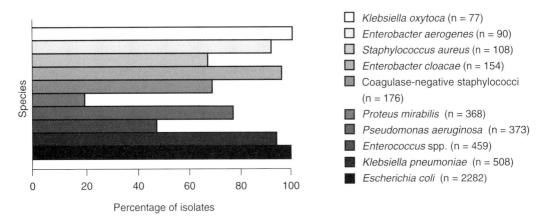

Klebsiella oxytoca (n = 77)
Enterobacter aerogenes (n = 90)
Staphylococcus aureus (n = 108)
Enterobacter cloacae (n = 154)
Coagulase-negative staphylococci (n = 176)
Proteus mirabilis (n = 368)
Pseudomonas aeruginosa (n = 373)
Enterococcus spp. (n = 459)
Klebsiella pneumoniae (n = 508)
Escherichia coli (n = 2282)

Figure 3.4. Susceptibility of 5360 urinary isolates to ciprofloxacin in the USA and Canada.[31]

to 13% and for coagulase-negative staphylococci from 0% to 8%. In Spain, 8% of 973 strains of *Escherichia coli*, 18% of 353 strains of *Pseudomonas aeruginosa* and 66% of *Acinetobacter* spp. were resistant.[34] In the UK in 1987, a survey of 44 hospital laboratories showed 99.8% of 13,068 strains of *Escherichia coli* were susceptible compared with the same percentage of 4622 strains of *Staphylococcus aureus*, 99.7% of 2261 isolates of *Proteus mirabilis* and 98.2% of 1797 isolates of *Pseudomonas aeruginosa*.[35] Others report 0% resistance in *Escherichia coli*, 2% for *Staphylococcus aureus* and 4% for *Pseudomonas aeruginosa*.[36] The differences between the surveys may relate to antibiotic use.

Resistance to ciprofloxacin is commonly associated with resistance to other antibiotics and cross-resistance with other quinolones is usual (see Table 2.1, Chapter 2).[37,38] Although older studies suggest ciprofloxacin is active against methicillin-resistant staphylococci, resistance in methicillin-resistant *Staphylococcus aureus* is now common (17% in one survey).[39–41] Even among methicillin-susceptible *Staphylococcus aureus*, 7% of strains have been found to be resistant, mostly in elderly patients receiving ciprofloxacin to treat catheter-related bacteriuria.[42] Ciprofloxacin is moderately active against penicillin-resistant *Streptococcus pneumoniae* (MIC 0.25–2 mg/litre).[40] Enterobacteriaceae resistant to cephalosporins are susceptible to ciprofloxacin and *Pseudomonas aeruginosa* resistant to aminoglycosides, ceftazidime and penicillins remains moderately susceptible to ciprofloxacin.[41] Treatment with ciprofloxacin can select *Pseudomonas aeruginosa* resistant to quinolones and imipenem, and this effect has been reproduced in the laboratory.[43] In multiresistant *Acinetobacter calcoaceticus*, resistance to ciprofloxacin has increased in one hospital since it went into general use from 10% to 46%; resistance in *Pseudomonas aeruginosa* increased from 1% to 7%. Smaller rises were observed in *Escherichia coli*, *Citrobacter diversus* and *Providencia rettgeri*.

A rising prevalence of resistance in strains of *Enterococcus faecalis* has been observed in Japan, where 10% of strains are resistant to ciprofloxacin at a concentration of 25 mg/litre.[44] Purification showed the DNA gyrase to be similar to that of *Escherichia coli*. Supercoiling was inhibited at 25–50 mg/litre in DNA gyrase from susceptible strains, but was unaffected even by 800 mg/litre in gyrase from resistant strains. Alterations in the A subunit were responsible, because the strains were susceptible to novobiocin, which binds to the B subunit. Differences in drug uptake explained part, but not all, of the resistance.

In a series from Nairobi, ciprofloxacin was the only antibiotic to which all *Salmonella typhimurium* and *Shigella* spp. were susceptible.[45] The difficulty in obtaining ciprofloxacin in Tanzania is thought to be responsible for the continued susceptibility of Enterobacteriaceae, despite a high prevalence of resistance to other oral antibiotics.[46] Ciprofloxacin resistance in *Salmonella* and *Campylobacter* has been related to the use of quinolones in veterinary practice. In 1987, none of 187 strains of *Campylobacter jejuni* were found to be resistant to ciprofloxacin compared with 47 of 154 strains (30%) in 1991.[47] Similar changes were found in *Campylobacter coli* after 1991.

The introduction of enrofloxacin for treatment of animals coincided with this rise in resistance. In Oxford in 1991, 3% of *Campylobacter* spp. were resistant to ciprofloxacin.[48] Two clinical isolates became resistant to ciprofloxacin during treatment, probably as the result of mutation of DNA gyrase.[49]

Longitudinal surveys

Kresken and Wiedemann found no overall increase in nalidixic acid resistance in Germany and Austria, despite the increasing use of quinolones over an 11-year period to 1986.[50] There was a wide variation between species and participating centres with 12% of Enterobacteriaceae (mostly *Klebsiella* spp.) being resistant to quinolones at one centre. Between 1983 and 1986, resistance to ciprofloxacin in *Pseudomonas aeruginosa* increased from 3% to 10%. In contrast, a longitudinal survey of urinary isolates in the UK between 1984 and 1992 showed a decline in susceptibility of community isolates from 94.6% in 1988 to 89.9% in 1992, and in hospital isolates from 89% in 1986 to 79.4% in 1992.[51] *Escherichia coli* remained largely susceptible with 98.7% of community isolates and 98.6% of hospital isolates remaining sensitive in 1992.

Susceptibility testing of *Escherichia coli* in 14 UK laboratories did not show any increase in resistance between 1987 (99.8% of 17,136 versus 99.8% of 52,173).[52] Similar results were obtained for *Klebsiella* spp. (99.7% to 96.8%), and the susceptibility of *Pseudomonas aeruginosa* decreased from 98.6% to 89.4%. At a French hospital, resistance in *Staphylococcus aureus* increased over 5 years from 0.8% to 4.2% and in methicillin-resistant *Staphylococcus aureus* from 5% to 94%.[24] An 18-month survey of an Australian hospital showed appreciable resistance in *Acinetobacter* spp. and *Providencia* spp. (Table 3.1). However, the only marked changes were an increase in resistance of *Streptococcus pneumoniae* from 10% to 67% (at 1 mg/litre) and in *Streptococcus* group B

Table 3.1. Resistance to ciprofloxacin in Australia.[37] Isolates were considered resistant if they grew on media containing ciprofloxacin at a concentration of 2 mg/litre.

Bacterial species (number of routine isolates, number of multi-resistant isolates)	Prevalence of resistance (%)	
	Routine isolates	Multi-resistant
Acinetobacter spp. (25, 50)	10	26
Citrobacter diversus (14, 11)	0	0
Citrobacter freundii (18, 14)	0	0
Enterobacter aerogenes (8, 25)	0	4
Enterobacter cloacae (35, 28)	0	0
Escherichia coli (58, 189)	0	< 1
Klebsiella pneumoniae (68, 167)	0	0
Morganella morganii (31, 36)	0	0
Proteus mirabilis (56, 106)	0	0
Proteus vulgaris (9, 17)	0	0
Providencia stuartii (14, 37)	7	3
Serratia marcescens (25, 41)	4	2
Pseudomonas aeruginosa (169, 112)	1	5
Staphylococcus aureus (225, 1203)	< 1	1

from 0% to 49%.[37] Records of antibiotic susceptibilities over 2 years showed no change in the susceptibility of enterococci and Enterobacteriaceae, but an increase in the resistance of *Pseudomonas aeruginosa* (from 4% to 11%) and staphylococci.[53]

A significant increase in the resistance of *Bacteroides fragilis* following 2 years of ciprofloxacin use has been observed in Japan.[54] In Bangladesh, a high increasing prevalence of co-trimoxazole resistance in *Shigella* spp. resulted in the widespread use of nalidixic acid as empirical treatment. As a result, nalidixic acid resistance in *Shigella* spp. increased from 0.8% in 1986 to 20% in 1990.[55] In isolates of *Shigella dysenteriae* type 1, resistance to nalidixic acid rose from 2% to 58% over the 4 years.

Resistance to ciprofloxacin is still rare with the exception of *Pseudomonas aeruginosa* and MRSA. However, continued surveillance is required and some restriction of use in hospitals may be needed to preserve its usefulness.

References

1. Lewin CS, Allen RA, Amyes SGB. Potential mechanisms of resistance to the modern fluorinated 4-quinolones. J Med Microbiol 1990; 31:153–61.
2. Power EGM, Bellido JLM, Phillips I. Detection of ciprofloxacin resistance in Gram-negative bacteria due to alterations in gyrA. J Antimicrob Chemother 1992; 29: 9–17.
3. Heisig P, Schedletzky H, Falkenstein-Paul H. Mutations in the *gyrA* gene of a highly fluoroquinolone-resistant clinical isolate of *Escherichia coli*. Antimicrob Agents Chemother 1993; 37: 696–701.
4. Aleixandre V, Urios A, Herrera G, Blanco M. New *Escherichia coli* gyrA and gyrB mutations which have a graded effect on DNA supercoiling. Mol Gen Genet 1989; 219: 306–12.
5. Piddock LJV, Griggs DJ, Hall MC, Jin YF. Ciprofloxacin resistance in clinical isolates of *Salmonella typhimurium* obtained from two patients. Antimicrob Agents Chemother 1993; 37: 662–6.
6. Bryan LE, Bedard J. Impermeability to quinolones in gram-positive and gram-negative bacteria. Eur J Clin Microbiol Infect Dis 1991; 10: 232–9.
7. Wolfson JS, Hooper DC. Introduction to DNA gyrase, quinolones and quinolone resistance. In: Fernandez PB, ed. Quinolones. Princeton: JR Prous Science Publishers, 1989: 219–33.
8. Moniot-Ville N, Guibert J, Moreau N, Acar JF, Collatz E, Gutmann L. Mechanisms of quinolone resistance in

a clinical isolate of *Escherichia coli* highly resistant to fluoroquinolones but susceptible to nalidixic acid. Antimicrob Agents Chemother 1991; 35: 519–23.

9. Cohen SP, McMurry LM, Hooper DC, Wolfson JS, Levy SB. Cross-resistance to fluoroquinolones in multiple-antibiotic-resistant (Mar) *Escherichia coli* selected by tetracycline or chloramphenicol: decreased drug accumulation associated with membrane changes in addition to OmpF reduction. Antimicrob Agents Chemother 1989; 33: 1318–25.

10. Chamberland S, Malouin F, Rabin HR, Schollaardt T, Parr TR Jr, Bryan LE. Persistence of *Pseudomonas aeruginosa* during ciprofloxacin therapy of a cystic fibrosis patient: transient resistance to quinolones and protein F-deficiency. J Antimicrob Chemother 1990; 25: 995–1010.

11. Celesk RA, Robillard NJ. Factors influencing the accumulation of ciprofloxacin in *Pseudomonas aeruginosa*. Antimicrob Agents Chemother 1989; 33: 1921–6.

12. Fukuda H, Hosaka M, Hirai K, Iyobe S. New norfloxacin resistance gene in *Pseudomonas aeruginosa* PAO. Antimicrob Agents Chemother 1990; 34: 1757–61.

13. Cohen SP, Hooper DC, Wolfson JS, Souza KS, McMurry LM, Levy SB. Endogenous active efflux of norfloxacin in susceptible *Escherichia coli*. Antimicrob Agents Chemother 1988; 32: 1187–91.

14. Hooper DC, Wolfson JS, Souza KS, Ng EY, McHugh GL, Swartz MN. Mechanisms of quinolone resistance in *Escherichia coli*: characterization of nfxB and cfxB, two mutant resistance loci decreasing norfloxacin accumulation. Antimicrobial Agents Chemother 1989; 33: 283–90.

15. Sreedharan S, Peterson LR, Fisher LM. Ciprofloxacin resistance in coagulase-positive and -negative staphylococci: role of mutations at serine 84 in the DNA gyrase A protein of *Staphylococcus aureus* and *Staphylococcus epidermidis*. Antimicrob Agents Chemother 1991; 35: 2151–4.

16. Cundy KV, Fasching CE, Willard KE, Peterson LR. Uptake of 3H-norfloxacin in methicillin-resistant *Staphylococcus aureus*. J Antimicrob Chemother 1991; 28: 491–7.

17. Neyfakh AA, Borsch CM, Kaatz GW. Fluoroquinolone resistance protein NorA of *Staphylococcus aureus* is a multidrug efflux transporter. Antimicrob Agents Chemother 1993; 37: 128–9.

18. Neyfakh AA. The multidrug efflux transporter of *Bacillus subtilis* is a structural and functional homolog of the *Staphylococcus* NorA protein. Antimicrob Agents Chemother 1992; 36: 484–5.

19. Ubukata K, Itoh-Yamashita N, Konno M. Cloning and expression of the *norA* gene for fluoroquinolone resistance in *Staphylococcus aureus*. Antimicrob Agents Chemother 1989; 33: 1535–9.

20. Munshi MH, Haider K, Rahaman MM, Sack DA, Ahmed ZU, Morshed MG. Plasmid-mediated resistance to nalidixic acid in *Shigella dysenteriae* type 1. Lancet 1987; 2: 419–21.

21. Smith JT. The mode of action of 4-quinolones and possible mechanisms of resistance. J Antimicrob Chemother 1986; 18 (Suppl D): 21–9.

22. Crump J, Cianciotto NP, Rogers J, Engleberg NC. Ciprofloxacin-resistant (Cfxr) mutants of *Legionella pneumophila* (Lpn). 29th Interscience Conference on Antimicrobial Agents and Chemotherapy, Houston, USA, 1989: Abstract 899.

23. Leigh DA, Emmanuel FXS, Petch VJ. Ciprofloxacin therapy in complicated urinary tract infections caused by *Pseudomonas aeruginosa* and other resistant bacteria. J Antimicrob Chemother 1986; 18: (Suppl D): 117–21.

24. Acar JF, Francoual S. The clinical problems of bacterial resistance to the new quinolones. J Antimicrob Chemother 1990; 26 (Suppl B): 207–13.

25. Diver JM, Schollaardt T, Rabin HR, Thorson C, Bryan LE. Persistence mechanisms in *Pseudomonas aeruginosa* from cystic fibrosis patients undergoing ciprofloxacin therapy. Antimicrob Agents Chemother 1991; 35: 1538–46.

26. Chapman ST, Speller DCE, Reeves DS. Resistance to ciprofloxacin. Lancet 1985; ii: 39.

27. Rozenberg-Arska M, Dekker AW, Verhoef J. Ciprofloxacin for selective decontamination of the alimentary tract in patients with acute leukaemia during remission induction treatment: the effect on faecal flora. J Infect Dis 1985; 152: 104–7.

28. Blumberg HM, Rimland D, Kiehlbauch JA, Terry PM, Wachsmuth IK. Epidemiological typing of *Staphylococcus aureus* by DNA restriction fragment length polymorphisms of rRNA genes: elucidation of the clonal nature of a group of bacteriophage-nontypeable, ciprofloxacin-resistant, methicillin-susceptible *S. aureus* isolates. J Clin Microbiol 1992; 30: 362–9.

29. Kaatz GW, Seo SM, Ruble CA. Mechanisms of fluoroquinolone resistance in *Staphylococcus aureus*. J Infect Dis 1991; 163: 1080–6.

30. Murphy PG, Ferguson WP. *Corynebacterium jeikeium* (Group JK) resistance to ciprofloxacin emerging during therapy. J Antimicrob Chemother 1987; 20: 922–3.

31. Jones RN, Hoban DJ and the North American Ofloxacin Study Group. North American (United States and Canada) comparative susceptibility of two fluoroquinolones: ofloxacin and ciprofloxacin: a 53-medical-center sample of spectra of activity. Diagn Microbiol Infect Dis 1994; 18: 49–56.

32. Smith BR. National cooperative study of ciprofloxacin susceptibility in the United States. Curr Ther Res 1990; 47: 962–70.

33. Dornbusch K and the European Study Group on Antibiotic Resistance. Resistance to β-lactam antibiotics and ciprofloxacin in gram-negative bacilli and staphylococci isolated from blood: a European

collaborative study. J Antimicrob Chemother 1990; 26: 269–78.

34. García-Rodríguez JA, Fresnadillo MJ, García García MI, García-Sánchez E, García-Sánchez JE, Trujillano I *et al.* Multicenter Spanish study of ciprofloxacin susceptibility in gram-negative bacteria. Eur J Clin Microbiol Infect Dis 1995; 14: 456–9.

35. Tillotson GS, Herbert JJF. National surveillance of susceptibility of various antimicrobial agents including a fluoroquinolone. 4th European Congress of Clinical Microbiology, Nice, France, 1989: 23 (Abstract 431).

36. King A, Phillips I. The comparative *in vitro* activity of eight newer quinolones and nalidixic acid. J Antimicrob Chemother 1986; 18 (Suppl D): 1–20.

37. Fernandes CJ, Ackerman VP. *In vitro* studies of ciprofloxacin and survey of resistance patterns in current isolates. Diagn Microbiol Infect Dis 1990; 13: 79–91.

38. Barry AL, Jones RN. Cross resistance among cinoxacin, ciprofloxacin, DJ-6783, enoxacin, nalidixic acid, norfloxacin and oxolinic acid after *in vitro* selection of resistant populations. Antimicrob Agents Chemother 1984; 25: 775–7.

39. Maple PAC, Hamilton-Miller JMT, Brumfitt W. World-wide antibiotic resistance in methicillin-resistant *Staphylococcus aureus*. Lancet 1989; i: 537–94.

40. Simberkoff MS, Rahal JJ. Bactericidal activity of ciprofloxacin against amikacin and cefotaxime resistant Gram-negative bacilli and methicillin-resistant staphylococci. Antimicrob Agents Chemother 1986; 29: 1098–100.

41. Venezio FR, Tatarowicz W, DiVencenzo CA, O'Keefe JP. Activity of ciprofloxacin against multiply resistant strains of *Pseudomonas aeruginosa*, *Staphylococcus epidermidis*, and Group JK Corynebacteria. Antimicrob Agents Chemother 1986; 30: 940–1.

42. Weightman NC, Brass AS. Ciprofloxacin-resistant methicillin-sensitive *Staphylococcus aureus*. J Antimicrob Chemother 1993; 31: 179–80.

43. Aubert G, Pozzetto B, Dorche G. Emergence of quinolone-imipenem cross-resistance in *Pseudomonas aeruginosa* after fluoroquinolone therapy. J Antimicrob Chemother 1992; 29: 307–12.

44. Nakanishi N, Yoshida S, Wakabe H, Inoue M, Mitsuhashi S. Mechanisms of clinical resistance to fluoroquinolones in *Enterococcus faecalis*. Antimicrob Agents Chemother 1991; 35: 1053–9.

45. Karjuki S, Gilks C, Brindle R, Batchelor B, Kimari J, Waiyaki P. Antimicrobial susceptibility and presence of extrachromosomal deoxyribonucleic acid in Salmonella and Shigella isolates from patients with AIDS. East Afr Med J 1994; 71: 292–6.

46. Gillespie SH, Fox R, Patel S, Ngowi FI, Tillotson GS. Antibiotic susceptibility of Enterobacteriaceae isolated from patients in northern Tanzania. J Antimicrob Chemother 1992; 29: 227–9.

47. Reina J, Borrell N, Serra A. Emergence of resistance to erythromycin and fluoroquinolones in thermotolerant Campylobacter strains isolated from feces 1987–1991. Eur J Clin Microbiol Infect Dis 1992; 11: 1163–6.

48. Bowler I, Day D. Emerging quinolone resistance in campylobacters. Lancet 1992; 340: 245.

49. Segreti J, Gootz TD, Goodman LJ, Parkhurst GW, Quinn JP, Martin BA *et al.* High-level quinolone resistance in clinical isolates of *Campylobacter jejuni*. J Infect Dis 1992; 165: 667–70.

50. Kresken M, Wiedemann B. Development of resistance to nalidixic acid and the fluoroquinolones after the introduction of norfloxacin and ofloxacin. Antimicrob Agents Chemother 1988; 32: 1285–8.

51. Grüneberg RN. Changes in urinary pathogens and their antibiotic sensitivities, 1971–1992. J Antimicrob Chemother 1994; 33 (Suppl A): 1–8.

52. Culshaw KD, Tillotson GS, O'Keeffe BJ. A five year survey of ciprofloxacin susceptibility amongst Gram-negative bacteria in the UK. 8th Mediterranean Congress of Chemotherapy, Athens, Greece, 1992: Abstract 44.

53. Grimm H. Resistance trend of ofloxacin and ciprofloxacin: monitoring of more than 300,000 strains in the last 5 years. 3rd International Symposium on New Quinolones, Vancouver, Canada, 1990: Abstract 94.

54. Kato N, Miyauchi M, Muto Y, Watanabe K, Ueno K. Emergence of fluoroquinolone resistance in *Bacteroides fragilis* accompanied by resistance to β-lactam antibiotics. Antimicrob Agents Chemother 1988; 32: 1437–8.

55. Bennish ML, Salam MA, Hossain MA, Myaux J, Khan EH, Chakraborty J *et al.* Antimicrobial resistance of Shigella isolates in Bangladesh, 1983–1990: increasing frequency of strains multiply resistant to ampicillin, trimethoprim–sulfamethoxazole, and nalidixic acid. Clin Infect Dis 1992; 14: 1055–60.

Chapter 4

Animal toxicity

Studies in animals, largely conducted by the manufacturer, have investigated the short- and long-term effects of ciprofloxacin in rats and monkeys, its effects on fertility and the embryo in rats, and on mutagenicity. Specific investigations of potential nephrotoxicity, cataracts and the well-publicised relationship with juvenile arthropathy have been performed. A long-term study of ciprofloxacin, up to 500 mg/kg/day for 24 months, showed no histological evidence of damage to the liver or kidneys.[1]

Kidneys

Renal changes have been commonly observed in toxicity studies. A 4-week study investigated the effects of intraperitoneal ciprofloxacin, 0–80 mg/kg/day, in 20 rats.[2] No animals died, but at 80 mg/kg/day growth was inhibited in male rats and blood urea nitrogen rose. Crystals were found in the urine and distal tubules with associated foreign-body reactions in the tubular epithelium. The crystals were shown to be a complex of ciprofloxacin (or its metabolites), magnesium and protein. Ciprofloxacin shows little solubility at neutral or alkaline pH, but this increases in acid conditions. Unlike humans, both rats and monkeys tend to maintain alkaline urine. In rats, lowering urinary pH to 5.2 reduced the rate of crystal formation.

In monkeys, ciprofloxacin, 20 mg/kg/day,

was administered as an injection or infusion over 1 hour for 10 days.[2] Renal tubular damage, as shown by a rise in plasma creatinine and a reduced rate of phenol red excretion, occurred only in the group receiving bolus injections. The dose producing crystalluria was always lower than that producing nephropathy (Figure 4.1). Nephropathy did not occur without crystalluria and was present only in a proportion of those showing obvious crystalluria. Nephropathy occurs as a result of a foreign-body reaction to the crystals and is rare in humans because the urine is usually acidic.

Joints

Juvenile and weight-bearing joints are affected by ciprofloxacin in rats and dogs.[2] In rats given 100–500 mg/kg orally, only 1 of 10 males given the highest dose showed weight-bearing joint lesions. In comparison, lesions were observed in 50% of male rats given nalidixic acid, 100 mg/kg, or ofloxacin, 100 mg/kg, and in 10% given the same dose of norfloxacin. In dogs, however, damage can occur at much lower doses and was found in 1 of 4 animals given 30 mg/kg/day orally.[2]

Beagle dogs aged 10–16 weeks were given oral ciprofloxacin, 0, 100, or 200 mg/kg/day (n = 4) or oral pipemidic acid, 100 or 500 mg/kg/day (n = 4).[2] After 2 weeks, one dog given ciprofloxacin, 100 mg/kg/day, had blisters in the knee joint cartilage and at 200 mg/kg/day all four animals had blisters or erosions in large joints. Damage was severe in

Wilson APR and Grüneberg RN.
Ciprofloxacin: 10 years of clinical experience
© 1997 Maxim Medical, Oxford.

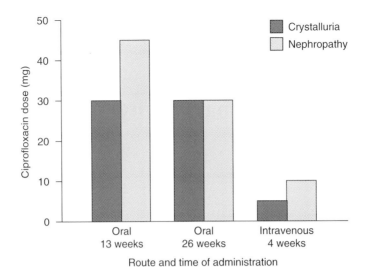

Figure 4.1. Crystalluria and nephropathy in studies of monkeys.[2]

all animals given pipemidic acid. Knee joint cartilage was affected in 15-week-old beagles given as little as 30–100 mg/kg/day ciprofloxacin for 3 weeks.[2] In these dogs, the arthropathy was irreversible and a safe dose was not established. Nalidixic acid, however, causes severe damage in dogs and yet is used therapeutically in children – with few adverse effects. Immobilisation of a limb reduces the severity of the lesions in that limb, but increases them in the other limb. Nuclear magnetic resonance imaging can show increased synovial fluid resulting from arthropathy at an early stage.[1]

Eyes

Another quinolone, pefloxacin, has been associated with subcapsular cataracts.[2] For this reason, lenses were examined in monkeys given ciprofloxacin for 6 months. No lens opacities were detected in animals given up to 20 mg/kg.[2] Furthermore, *in vitro* examination of the lens, including protein electrophoresis, did not show any changes. Concentrations of ciprofloxacin detected in the lens were similar to those in aqueous humour. Ciprofloxacin was not found to have any potential to form cataracts.

Mutagenicity

Standard tests of mutagenicity for ciprofloxacin were negative in mice and *in vitro* (micronucleus test, dominant lethal test and Salmonella/microsome tests).[2] Administration of 20 or 200 mg/kg/day to rats did not significantly affect chromosome numbers, but there was increased chromatid breakage at the higher dose.[3] Doses above 1.2 mg/kg are associated with increased sister chromatid exchange frequencies (i.e. DNA damage) in bone marrow cells in mice.[4]

An 'unscheduled DNA synthesis test' using rat hepatocytes *in vitro* has been used to determine effects on DNA. Mouse lymphoma and hamster cell line V79 tests have been used to show gene mutation. Ciprofloxacin, norfloxacin, ofloxacin and pefloxacin caused positive results only in the mouse lymphoma and hepatocyte tests. These findings may, however, be spurious because unscheduled DNA synthesis is not found in hepatocytes from rats given ciprofloxacin *in vivo*. Ciprofloxacin produced negative results in an *in vitro* cell transformation assay and no tumours were observed in 6-month chronic toxicity studies. Furthermore, mice and rats given ciprofloxacin, up to 500 mg/kg for 21–24 months, did not differ from controls in the number of tumours that developed.[1] No signs of genotoxicity were observed in cultured hepatocytes from rats given ciprofloxacin.[5]

Pregnancy

Norfloxacin administered in toxic doses to monkeys produces abortion. To assess the risk for ciprofloxacin, doses of 0–200 mg/kg orally or 0–25 mg/kg intravenously were given to groups of 6–10 monkeys at 20–50 days of pregnancy.[1] There was no effect on the rate of abortion or on foetal development.

Central nervous system

Central nervous system effects have been noted clinically when non-steroidal anti-inflammatory agents (NSAIDs) are administered with quinolones. In one study, various NSAIDs were administered orally at 20% of their lethal doses in combination with ciprofloxacin, 500 mg/kg.[1] Seizures developed in 5 of 5 rats given indomethacin, 3 of 5 given ketoprofen and 2 of 5 given ibuprofen.[1] EEG changes occurred only with an oral ciprofloxacin dose of 500 mg/kg following intravenous fenbufen, 15 mg/kg. Ciprofloxacin, up to 1000 mg/kg, had no effect on the general behaviour, co-ordination or movement of mice.[6] The same doses did not alter the sleeping time induced by hexobarbital nor prevent convulsions caused by strychnine or electric shock.

In rabbits, intravitreal injection of ciprofloxacin, 0.5 mg or more, resulted in patchy loss of the ganglion cell layer, but 0.25 mg was without effect.[7] Topical application of ciprofloxacin (0.75%) to guinea-pigs' ears for 1 week did not result in any ototoxic reaction or loss of hair cells.[8,9]

References

1. Schluter G. Ciprofloxacin: toxicologic evaluation of additional safety data. Am J Med 1989; 87 (Suppl 5A): 37–9.
2. Schluter G. Toxicology of ciprofloxacin. 1st International Ciprofloxacin Workshop, Leverkusen, Germany, 1985: 61–7.
3. Basaran A, Erol K, Basaran N, Günes HV, Açikalin E, Timuralp G *et al*. Effects of ciprofloxacin on chromosomes, and hepatic and renal functions in rats. Exp Chemother 1993; 39: 182–8.
4. Mukherjee A, Sen S, Agarwal K. Ciprofloxacin: mammalian DNA topoisomerase type II poison *in vivo*. Mutat Res 1993; 301: 87–92.
5. McQueen CA, Williams GM. Effects of quinolone antibiotics in tests for genotoxicity. Am J Med 1987; 82 (Suppl 4A): 94–6.
6. Kim EJ, Cha SW, Shin HS, Roh JK, Park MW, Kim WJ. The effects of KR-10876, a new quinolone antimicrobial agent, on the central nervous system. Arch Pharm Res 1993; 16: 6–12.
7. Slana VS, Marchese AL. Ocular toxicity of intravitreal ciprofloxacin injection in pigmented rabbit eyes. Invest Ophthalmol Vis Sci 1992; 33: 727.
8. Brownlee RL, Hulka GF, Prazma J, Pillsbury HC. Ciprofloxacin. Use as a topical otic preparation. Arch Otolaryngol Head Neck Surg 1992; 118: 392–6.
9. Lutz H, Lenarz T, Gotz R. Ototoxicity of gyrase antagonist ciprofloxacin? Adv Otorhinolaryngol 1990; 45: 175–80.

Chapter 5

Pharmacokinetics

Oral dose regimens

Ciprofloxacin is rapidly absorbed following oral doses and has a linear dose–response relationship (Figure 5.1).[1] Its elimination half-life is 3.0–4.5 hours, its oral systemic bioavailability is 85% and 35% is protein bound.[1] The concentrations found following a single oral dose are similar to those at the steady state (Tables 5.1 and 5.2).[1–31] For each 100 mg given by mouth, the peak serum level reached is about 0.5 mg/litre. Oral ciprofloxacin, 250 mg every 12 hours for 1 week, achieved a peak serum concentration of 1.4 mg/litre at 1 hour, falling to 0.16 mg/litre at 12 hours.[24] A dose regimen of 500 mg orally every 12 hours achieved peak levels of 2.5 mg/litre and trough levels of 0.3 mg/litre.[24] Oral ciprofloxacin, 750 mg every 12 hours, achieved peak and trough concentrations of 4.1 mg/litre (at 1.4 hours) and 0.5 mg/litre, respectively.[24] Administration of ciprofloxacin, 500 mg, as a single tablet, as two tablets of 250 mg or as an oral solution did not influence the serum concentration, but the distribution volume was greater with the two 250 mg tablets than with the solution.[7] An oral dose of 500 mg produced similar serum concentrations to an intravenous dose of 200 mg.[26] Ciprofloxacin, 750 mg, administered as a single oral dose achieved a maximum serum concentration of 3.2 mg/litre after 1.5 hours, but this was reduced to 1.3 mg/litre in the presence of papaveretum.[32] Multiple oral doses given for up to 8 days do not usually cause accumulation. The peak concentrations reached at the steady state are 1.4 mg/litre at 250 mg every 12 hours and 2.9 mg/litre at 500 mg every 12 hours (see Table 5.2).[24] A significant increase in serum concentrations during the course was found in one study of volunteers given oral ciprofloxacin, 500 mg every 12 hours.[28] After 1 and 7 days, peak serum levels were 1.9 and 2.8 mg/litre, respectively.

Intravenous dose regimens

Following an intravenous dose of ciprofloxacin, serum concentrations may be described by two- or three-compartment models.[1,23,33,34] The high distribution volume indicates penetration of the extravascular space.[35] The serum half-life of the drug is 3.5–4.8 hours, and serum concentrations fall four-fold within 30 minutes of injection, with little remaining at 12 hours. There is no accumulation. Intravenous ciprofloxacin, 200 mg every 12 hours for 1 week, achieved a peak concentration of 1.3 mg/litre at 1 hour and a trough of 0.1 mg/litre at 12 hours, with a terminal half-life of 4 hours (see Figure 5.2).[23] In volunteers given intravenous ciprofloxacin, 400 mg every 8 hours, the maximum serum concentration was 4.1 mg/litre at 1 hour, while in those given oral doses of 750 mg every 12 hours the peak was 3.6 mg/litre.[22,25] The area under the curve (AUC) over 24 hours for the two regimens was similar (33 mg/hour/litre and 32

Wilson APR and Grüneberg RN.
Ciprofloxacin: 10 years of clinical experience
© 1997 Maxim Medical, Oxford.

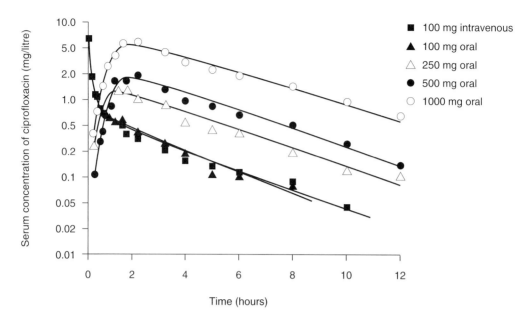

Figure 5.1. Mean serum concentrations of ciprofloxacin after single oral doses of 100, 250, 500 and 1000 mg and after a single intravenous dose of 100 mg. Reproduced with permission.[1]

mg/hour/litre, respectively). A single intravenous dose of 400 mg produces a similar AUC to 500 mg given orally.[4]

Recent work has suggested that higher dose regimens are required to treat some Gram-negative bacterial infections. Bauernfeind exposed organisms in broth culture to decreasing concentrations of ciprofloxacin, similar to those that would be observed clinically.[36] Three simulated intravenous doses of 400 mg killed 99.99% of the initial inoculum (106/ml) of *Klebsiella pneumoniae* (MIC 0.5 mg/litre) compared with a 99% kill using two simulated doses of 200 mg.[36] Similar results were obtained with *Pseudomonas aeruginosa*, *Staphylococcus aureus* and *Enterococcus faecalis*. Greater killing was achieved by giving 400 mg every 8 hours than by 600 mg every 12 hours for all test organisms.[36] Bauernfeind suggested that for a pathogen with an MIC of ≤ 0.4 mg/litre, 200 mg every 12 hours was an adequate dose, but for those with an MIC of 1 mg/litre, 400 mg every 12 hours was required, and 400 mg every 8 hours was needed for an

MIC of 2 mg/litre. Pathogens with MICs of ≥ 4 mg/litre should be classified as resistant.

Cystic fibrosis

The pharmacokinetic behaviour of ciprofloxacin in adult patients with cystic fibrosis appears to be similar to that in patients without the condition, and several authors recommend no changes to dose regimens.[20,30,37] LeBel *et al.* noted a significant fall in serum half-life after a single dose of ciprofloxacin, but clearance was unaffected.[38] Christensson *et al.* found higher total and renal clearance of ciprofloxacin and a larger distribution volume in patients with cystic fibrosis compared with healthy volunteers, factors which were offset by greater bioavailability.[19] In a crossover study, ofloxacin, 400 mg every 12 hours for 14 days, when compared to ciprofloxacin was found to have a longer half-life (6.4 versus 3.4 hours), greater penetration of sputum (79% versus 18%) and a higher mean serum concentration (5.9 versus 4.0 mg/litre).[31]

Table 5.1. Single-dose pharmacokinetics of ciprofloxacin.

Reference and patient group	No. of patients	Dose (mg)	C_{max} (mg/litre) and (time) (hours)	V_{ss} (litre/kg)	AUC (mg.hour/litre)	Clearance (ml/hour/kg)	Renal clearance (ml/hour/kg)	Terminal elimination half-life (hours)
2	10	100 i.v.	1.8 (0.5)	3.7	2.6	601*	351*	4.8
1	12	100 i.v.	–	2.4	2.6	600*	–	–
2	10	200 i.v.	3.9	2.5*	5.4	670	374	3.3
3	12	200 i.v.	3.4	2.4*	5.2	585*	–	3.6
3	12	300 i.v.	5.3	2.2*	8.7	595	–	3.7
4	12	300 i.v.	3.3	–	8.3	–	327*	5.7
3	12	400 i.v.	7.1	2.1*	11.1	608	–	3.5
4	12	400 i.v.	4.0	–	11.1	–	300*	4.7
1	12	100 p.o.	0.7 (0.9)	–	2.1	–	–	3.0
1	12	250 p.o.	1.7 (1.1)	–	5.9	–	–	3.2
1	12	500 p.o.	2.3 (1.5)	–	9.9	–	–	3.2
5	6	500 p.o.	2.3 (1.3)	–	9.9	–	–	3.9
6	7	500 p.o.	2.8 (1.4)	–	8.6	–	–	2.5
7	18	500 p.o.	3.0 (1.1)	4.3	12.2	600	300	4.9
4	12	500 p.o.	2.8	–	10.6	–	258*	4.6
4	12	750 p.o.	3.9	–	16.5	–	249*	4.6
1	12	1000 p.o.	5.9 (1.8)	–	29.4	–	–	3.4

Elderly
8

< 20 years	6	100 p.o.	0.5 (1.0)	–0.8 (0–8 hours)		– –	3.9	
30–40 years	4		0.6 (0.5)	– –	–	– –		
74 years	9		0.8 (1.0)	–1.9	–	–4.0		

9

20–30 years	10	250 p.o.	1.2 (1.3)	–5.6	–	2643.7	
60–73 years	10		1.3 (1.7)	–7.4	–	2044.3	

10

19–25 years	12	500 p.o.	2.3 (1.3)	2.610.0	616	3833.7	
71–86 years	12		3.2 (1.1)	1.620.9	254	1406.8	

Children
11

5–14 weeks	7	15 mg/kg p.o.	3.3 (1.2)	–16.1	–	–2.7
1–5 years	9		2.1 (1.0)	–5.3	–	–1.3

Renal failure
12

Normal	6	250 p.o.	1.5 (1.0)	–6.9	–	200*	4.4
Severe	6		1.7 (1.7)	–14.4	–	188.7	
Haemodialysis	5		2.1 (1.6)	–15.9	–	–5.8	

*Based on 70 kg body weight. C_{max} = peak serum drug concentration; V_{ss} = volume of distribution at steady state; AUC = area under the curve.

Table 5.1. (continued)

Reference and patient group	No. of patients	Dose (mg)	C_{max} (mg/litre) and (time) (hours)	V_{ss} (litre/kg)	AUC (mg.hour/litre)	Clearance (ml/hour/kg)	Renal clearance (ml/hour/kg)	Terminal elimination half-life (hours)
13								
Normal–	17	500 p.o.	2.2 (1.3)	–	9.8	791	193	4.3
mild		750 p.o.	2.8 (1.6)	–	15.6	926	215	3.5
Moderate–	15	500 p.o.	2.5 (1.8)	–	20.2	411	50	7.1
severe		750 p.o.	3.7 (2.3)	–	26.8	381	56	6.3
14								
Normal	8	200 i.v.	6.3 (0.1)	2.5	–	–	–	4.3
Mild	5		4.1 (0.5)	3.2	–	–	–	6.1
Moderate	11		5.4 (0.5)	2.4	–	–	–	7.7
Severe	8		5.4 (0.5)	2.7	–	–	–	8.6
15								
CAPD	8	750 p.o.	3.6 (1.6)	–	44.5	374*	–	16.8
Liver failure								
16								
Mild	8	500 p.o.	1.9 (1.0)	–	10.9	–	–	5.2
Moderate	5		2.0 (1.0)	–	12.4	–	–	5.5
Severe	6		2.6 (1.0)	–	17.7	–	–	7.0
Controls	7		1.8 (1.0)	–	10.1	–	–	5.2
17								
Cirrhosis	7	750 p.o.	3.7 (1.3)	2.8	18.4	655	183*	–
Controls	7		3.5 (1.0)	3.5	16.2	720*	171*	–
18								
Cirrhosis	5	250 p.o.	1.6 (1.6)	2.0	10.0	384	–	3.6
Controls	5		1.7 (1.9)	2.4	8.2	456	–	3.8
Cystic fibrosis								
19								
Normal	5	4 mg/kg i.v.	2 (0.5)	1.7	8.61	453*	213*	3.1
	5	15 mg/kg p.o.	4 (1.5)	–	18.6	–	271	3.2
Cystic	14	4 mg/kg i.v.	2 (0.5)	2.7	8.35	688	450	3.0
	13	15 mg/kg p.o.	3 (2.0)	–	17.2	–	307	2.9
20								
Normal	11	500 p.o.	2.1 (1.1)	–	8.8	–	265	4.7
		1000 p.o.	3.9 (1.1)	–	15.8	–	232	4.4
Cystic	12	500 p.o.	2.5 (2.5)	–	14.7	–	267	5.1
		1000 p.o.	5.6 (1.9)	–	31.7	–	385	5.1

*Based on 70 kg body weight. C_{max} = peak serum drug concentration; V_{ss} = volume of distribution at steady state; AUC = area under the curve; CAPD = continuous ambulatory peritoneal dialysis.

Table 5.2. Multiple-dose pharmacokinetics.

Reference and patient group	No. of patients	Dose (mg) and route	C_{max} (mg/litre) and (time) (hours)	V_{ss} (litre/kg)	AUC (mg.hour/ litre)	Clearance (ml/hour/kg)	Renal clearance (ml/hour/kg)	Terminal elimination half-life (hours)
21	12	200 i.v. b.d. × 6 days	–	2.6	10.0	332 (165–639)*	–	4.9
22	18	400 i.v. t.d.s. × 10 doses	4.1 (1)	–	11.0	556*	373*	–
		750 p.o. b.d. × 7 doses	3.6 (1)	–	15.8	768*	366*	–
1	12	500 p.o. b.d. × 5 days	2.5 (1.7)	–	11.3	–	–	3.1
23	9	100 i.v. b.d. × 7 days	0.6 (1)	1.95	3.4	430*	–	3.7
		150 i.v. b.d. × 7 days	0.8 (1)	1.97	5.1	426*	–	3.6
		200 i.v. b.d. × 7 days	1.3 (1)	1.97	7.7	384*	–	4.9
24	9	250 p.o. b.d. × 6 days	1.4 (1.0)	–	5.3	–	–	3.8
		500 p.o. b.d. × 6 days	2.9 (1.0)	–	13.9	–	–	4.7
		750 p.o. × 6 days	4.1 (1.4)	–	22.1	–	–	3.9
25	24	400 i.v. t.d.s.	4.1	–	11.1	–	372*	5.2
		750 p.o. t.d.s.	3.7	–	16.2	–	360*	5.7
26	6	500 p.o. b.d. × 5 days	2.0–3.4 (1.5)	–	14.4	540*	–	5.1
		200 i.v. b.d. × 5 days	1.7–3.7 (0.5)	–	7.0	439*	–	4.5
27	20	500 p.o. b.d. × 8 days	2.6 (1.1)	–	12.0	–	–	4.1
28	13	500 p.o. b.d. × 7 days	2.8 (1.9)	–	18.8	–	–	4
29 64–91 years	13	750 p.o. b.d. × 14 days	8.6 (1.4)	5.9	46	392	200	4.8
Liver failure 17								
Cirrhosis	7	750 p.o. b.d. × 5 days	4.1 (2.0)	2.8	21.0	567*	206*	–
Controls	7		3.7 (2.0)	2.8	19.2	568*	195*	–

*Based on 70 kg body weight. C_{max} = peak serum drug concentration; V_{ss} = volume of distribution at steady state; AUC = area under the curve.

Table 5.2. (continued)

Reference and patient group	No. of patients	Dose (mg) and route	C_{max} (mg/litre) and (time) (hours)	V_{ss} (litre/kg)	AUC (mg.hour/ litre)	Clearance (ml/hour/kg)	Renal clearance (ml/hour/kg)	Terminal elimination half-life (hours)
Cystic fibrosis								
19	11	6 mg/kg i.v. b.d. × 10–14 days	–	–	9.0	585*	328*	3.1
	13	15 mg/kg p.o. b.d. × 10–14 days	4.4 (1.8)	–	22.2	–	244*	3.4
30	29	750 p.o. b.d. × 14 days	4.0 (1.6)	–	21.1	690	–	5.3
		1000 p.o. b.d. × 14 days	5.0 (1.0)	–	27.2	800	–	4.8
31	18	750 mg b.d. × 14 days	1.6 (1.8)	–	19.3	744	144	3.4

*Based on 70 kg body weight. C_{max} = peak serum drug concentration; V_{ss} = volume of distribution at steady state; AUC = area under the curve.

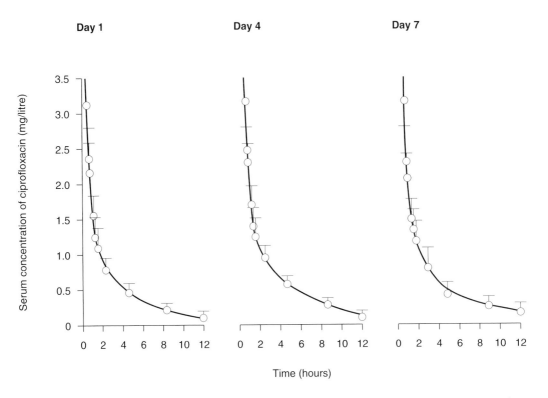

Figure 5.2. Mean serum concentration of ciprofloxacin following 200 mg intravenously every 12 hours for 1 week in nine volunteers. Reproduced with permission.[23]

Absorption

Although ciprofloxacin is well absorbed by the oral route, its absorption is reduced by antacids containing magnesium, aluminium or calcium ions, and this may affect clinical outcome.[39] The presence of food delays absorption of the drug and increases the time taken to reach peak concentration.[40] Absorption in patients with cystic fibrosis is not improved by the use of pancreatic enzyme supplements.[41]

Distribution

Ciprofloxacin is widely distributed throughout the body, as is suggested by its high distribution volume at the steady state (Tables 5.2 and 5.3).[1,5–7,17,19–31,42–76] The distribution phase half-life of oral ciprofloxacin is 0.5 hours for 250 mg and 1.0 hour for 750 mg.[1] The distribution phase half-life of intravenous ciprofloxacin is 0.18–0.29 hours for 100–200 mg.[23] The distribution volume at the steady state is 1.9–2.8 litre/kg. The volume of the central compartment is 0.16 litre/kg, which represents extracellular water.[33]

Tissue penetration

Ciprofloxacin is concentrated in the bile, kidney, gall bladder, liver, lung, pelvic organs and prostate (Table 5.3).[5–7,20,21,23,24,27,30,31,42–76] The levels found in human neutrophils are 3–6-fold greater than those in the extracellular space.[77] The concentrations in skin, fat, and cerebrospinal fluid tend to be lower than those in serum (Table 5.3).

In one study, oral ciprofloxacin, 500 mg, achieved saliva concentrations of 1.4–1.6 mg/litre, which is half that of serum.[24] Others report a saliva:serum ratio of 0.16–0.26.[7] In cystic fibrosis, salivary concentrations were initially lower than those in healthy volunteers, but achieved similar steady-state concentrations.[38] The concentration of ciprofloxacin in nasal secretions reached 1.9 mg/litre during continuous administration.[27]

A single intravenous dose of 200 mg is sufficient to maintain inhibitory concentrations in colonic mucosa for at least 2 hours.[72] In the gut, the proportion of ciprofloxacin existing in the form of metabolites is lower than that in serum (5% versus 20%).[73] The colon can accumulate ciprofloxacin, but it is lost quickly from the ileum.[73]

The ciprofloxacin concentrations in the lung generally exceed those found in blood, but there are wide variations between individuals.[54] At an intravenous dose of 200 mg every 12 hours, ciprofloxacin concentrations in the bronchial mucosa were 10–26-fold higher than those in the blood.[21] A single intravenous dose of 100 mg produced a peak lung concentration of 1.2 mg/kg, 2–7-fold higher than that of blood.[56] In one study, the mucosa:serum ratio exceeded that of oral amoxycillin (1.5 for oral or 2.3 for intravenous versus 0.75 for oral amoxycillin).[55] Sputum and pleural fluid concentrations, however, are much lower than those in bronchial mucosa.[30,58] Oral ciprofloxacin, 750 mg every 12 hours, achieved sputum concentrations (> 1.5 mg/litre) that usually exceeded the MIC of most strains of *Pseudomonas aeruginosa*, but not that of *Streptococcus pneumoniae*.[30] Even at a dose of 2 g/day, maximum sputum concentrations were found to vary between 0.8 and 5 mg/litre.[59] Intravenous ciprofloxacin, 1.5 mg/kg, achieved a concentration of 1.2 mg/litre in bronchial secretions.[57] In cystic fibrosis, sputum concentrations were half those found in the blood.[20,60]

The CSF:serum ciprofloxacin concentration ratios are 1:10–1:5 in the absence of meningeal inflammation, rising to 1:5–9:10 in patients with meningitis.[61,63] Oral ciprofloxacin, 500 mg, in patients with non-inflamed meninges, achieved a maximum CSF concentration of 0.14 mg/litre at 4 hours, falling to 0.08 mg/litre at 8 hours.[62] In patients with meningitis, concentrations in the CSF ranged from 0.1 to 0.6 mg/litre in the 1–2 hours after administration.[62–64] The concentrations were similar whether the drug was administered by the intra-

Table 5.3. Tissue distribution of ciprofloxacin.

Reference	No. of patients	Dose (mg) and route	Mean serum concentration (mg/litre) and (time) (hours)	Tissue/ fluid	Mean concentration (mg/kg or mg//litre)	Mean tissue: serum ratio
42	6	200 p.o. × 1 dose	0.9 (1)	Urine	485	540
			0.3 (3)		251	837
			0.15 (6)		57	380
			0.1 (10)		18	180
23	9	100 i.v. b.d. × 7 days	0.3–0.5 (2–4)	Urine	65	162
			0.1 (8–12)		7.1	71
		150 i.v. b.d. × 7 days	0.4–0.6 (2–4)		68	136
			0.1 (8–12)		12	12
		200 i.v. b.d. × 7 days	0.6–0.9 (2–4)		113	161
			0.2 (8–12)		19	95
7	18	500 p.o. × 1 dose	0.9 (2–4)	Urine	304	338
			0.2 (8–12)		111	555
24	9	250 p.o. b.d. × 7 days	0.5 (2–4)	Urine	147	294
			0.1 (8–12)		34	340
24	9	500 p.o. b.d. × 7 days	1.1 (2–4)	Urine	448	407
			0.3 (8–12)		82	273
24	9	750 p.o. b.d. × 7 days	1.6 (2–4)	Urine	704	440
			0.5 (8–12)		151	1408
24	9	750 p.o. b.d. × 7 days	1.6 (2–4)	Saliva	1.4–1.6	0.5
			0.5 (8–12)			
24	9	250 p.o. b.d. × 7 days	0.5 (2–4)	Saliva	0.4	0.5
			0.1 (8–12)			
24	9	500 p.o. b.d. × 7 days	1.1 (2–4)	Saliva	1.1–1.4	0.7
			0.3 (8–12)			
5	6	500 p.o. × 1 dose	1.7 (1)	Blister fluid	0.6	0.35
6	7	500 p.o. × 1 dose	1.2 (2.5)	Blister fluid	0.8	0.7
6	7	500 p.o. × 1 dose	0.4 (6)	Blister fluid	0.5	1.2
6	7	500 p.o. × 1 dose	1.2 (2.5)	Lymph	1.0	0.8
6	7	500 p.o. × 1 dose	0.4 (6)	Lymph	0.6	1.5
43	15	100 i.v. × 1 dose	0.9 (1)	Fat	0.35	0.3
44	23	100 i.v. × 1 dose	0.5 (1)	Fat	0.3	0.6
44	23	100 i.v. × 1 dose	0.13 (8)	Fat	0.04	0.4
45	18	500 p.o. × 1 dose	0.7 (2.5–3.2)	Fat	0.9	1.6
45	18	500 p.o. × 1 dose	0.5 (5–5.8)	Fat	0.5	1.1
46	11	750 p.o. b.d. × 4 doses	2.1 (1)	Fat	3.3	1.7
			0.6 (11)		1.9	1.7

Table 5.3. (continued)

Reference	No. of patients	Dose (mg) and route	Mean serum concentration (mg/litre) and (time) (hours)	Tissue/ fluid	Mean concentration (mg/kg or mg//litre)	Mean tissue: serum ratio
47	18	200 i.v. × 1 dose	2.2 (1)	Fat	1.0	0.5
43	15	100 i.v. × 1 dose	0.9 (1)	Muscle	0.9	1
43	15	500 p.o. × 1 dose	0.2 (12)	Muscle	0.2	–
44	23	100 i.v. × 1 dose	0.5 (1)	Muscle	1.2	2.4
44	23	100 i.v. × 1 dose	0.13 (8)	Muscle	0.2	1.6
45	18	500 p.o. × 1 dose	0.7 (2.5–3.2)	Muscle	1.0	2.0
45	18	500 p.o. × 1 dose	0.5 (5.0–5.8)	Muscle	1.9	3.4
48	7	500 p.o. × 1 dose	1.4 (3)	Muscle	1.1	0.8
48	7	750 p.o. × 1 dose	2.6 (3)	Muscle	1.3	0.5
48	7	1000 p.o. × 1 dose	2.9 (3)	Muscle	2.6	0.9
47	18	200 i.v. × 1 dose	2.2 (1)	Muscle	1.9	0.9
43	15	100 i.v. × 1 dose	0.9 (1)	Testicle	0.2	4.5
43	15	100 i.v. × 1 dose	0.9 (1)	Seminal vesicle	0.6 (2 hours)	–
45	18	500 p.o. × 1 dose	0.7 (2.5–3.2)	Skin	0.8	1.6
45	18	500 p.o. × 1 dose	0.5 (5.0–5.8)	Skin	1.0	2.2
44	23	100 i.v. × 1 dose	0.5 (1)	Skin	0.2	0.4
44	23	100 i.v. × 1 dose	0.13 (8)	Skin	0.1	1.0
44	23	100 i.v. × 1 dose	0.5 (1)	Kidney	4.7	9.4
44	23	100 i.v. × 1 dose	0.13 (8)	Kidney	0.9	7.1
48	7	500 p.o. × 1 dose	1.4 (3)	Bone	0.4	0.3
48	7	750 p.o. × 1 dose	2.6 (3)	Bone	0.7	0.3
48	7	1000 p.o. × 1 dose	2.9 (3)	Bone	1.6	0.6
48	7	500 p.o. × 1 dose	2.0 (3)	Bone (osteomyelitis)	0.7	0.4
48	7	750 p.o. × 1 dose	2.9 (3)	Bone (osteomyelitis)	1.4	0.5
49	20	200 i.v. × 1 dose	1.5 (1.1)	Cancellous bone	9.8	6.5
49	20	200 i.v. × 1 dose	1.5 (1.1)	Cortical bone	6.9	4.6
49	20	200 i.v. × 1 dose	1.5 (1.1)	Cartilage	4.9	2.1
27	20	500 p.o. b.d. × 8 days	2 (2)	Nasal secretion	1.9	0.9

Table 5.3. (continued)

Reference	No. of patients	Dose (mg) and route	Mean serum concentration (mg/litre) and (time) (hours)	Tissue/ fluid	Mean concentration (mg/kg or mg/litre)	Mean tissue: serum ratio
50	10	200 i.v. × 1 dose	0.3 (2)	Tonsil	0.3	1.1
			0.4 (3)		0.4	1.0
51	23	500 p.o. b.d. × 5 doses	2.5 (2)	Sinus mucosa	7.5	3
		500 p.o. b.d. × 18 doses	1.6 (2.9)	Middle ear mucosa	4.0	1.4
52	21	750 p.o. × 2 doses, then 400 i.v. × 2 doses	3.5 (2)	Intestinal mucosa Faeces	11.9 139	3.4 –
53	8	750 p.o. × 1 dose	3.5 (4.8)	Ascitic fluid	2.6	0.7
47	18	200 i.v. × 1 dose	2.2 (1)	Peritoneum	1.6	0.7
54	20	200 i.v. × 1 dose	0.6 (3–4)	Bronchial mucosa	2.5	4.0
21	12	200 i.v. b.d. × 6 days	1.0 (2)	Bronchial mucosa	22	16.9
55	29	500 p.o. b.d. × 8 doses	3.0 (4)	Bronchial mucosa	4.4	1.47
55	10	200 i.v. × 1 dose	1.6 (1)	Bronchial mucosa	3.9	2.3
54	20	200 i.v. × 1 dose	0.6 (3–4)	Lung	4.7	6.8
56	15	100 i.v. × 1 dose	0.4 (1)	Lung	1.1	2.8
54	20	200 i.v. × 1 dose	0.6 (3–4)	Pleura	1.7	3.0
57	5	0.75 mg/kg i.v. t.d.s. × 2 days	1.2 (1) 0.05 (8)	Bronchial secretion	0.38 0.09	0.32 1.8
57	5	1.5 mg/kg i.v. t.d.s. × 2 days	3.2 (1) 0.2 (8)	Bronchial secretion	1.2 0.29	0.38 1.2
57	5	1.5 mg/kg i.v. t.d.s. × 2 days	3.0 (1) 0.4 (8)	Pleural fluid	0.8 0.4	0.27 1.0
58	5	500–750 p.o. b.d.	1–4.5 C_{max}	Pleural fluid	1	0.4
30	29	750 p.o. b.d. × 14 days 1000 p.o. b.d. × 14 days	4.0 (1.6) 5.0 (1.7)	Sputum	1.5–3.4 2.5–3.7	1.15–1.25 0.87
59	20 40 20	500 p.o. b.d. × 10 days 750 p.o. b.d. × 10 days 1000 p.o. b.d. × 10 days	3.4 (2.4) 2.3–3.1 (1.7–2.2) 3.8 (2)	Sputum	1.3 1.6–1.9 2.3	0.5 0.77 0.79
60	8	500 p.o. b.d. × 10 days	2.5 (2)	Sputum (cystic fibrosis)	1.0	0.4
20	12	500 p.o. × 1 dose 1000 p.o. × 1 dose	2.5 (2.5) 5.6 (1.9)	Sputum (cystic fibrosis)	0.7 1.1	0.3 0.19
31	18	750 p.o. b.d. × 14 days	2.8	Sputum (cystic fibrosis)	0.5	0.18

Table 5.3. (continued)

Reference	No. of patients	Dose (mg) and route	Mean serum concentration (mg/litre) and (time) (hours)	Tissue/ fluid	Mean concentration (mg/kg or mg//litre)	Mean tissue: serum ratio
61	25	200 i.v. b.d. × 2 doses	0.5 (4)	CSF (non-inflamed)	0.08	0.12
			0.4 (5)		0.07	0.18
			0.5 (6)		0.11	0.24
62	48	500 p.o. × 1 dose	2.4 (2)	CSF (non-inflamed)	0.06	0.02
			0.5 (8)		0.08	0.2
63	23	200 i.v. b.d. × 3 doses	0.6 (1)	CSF (non-inflamed)	0.04	0.10
			1.1 (2)		0.3	0.22
			0.8 (4)		0.3	0.31
			0.2 (8)		0.15	0.78
61	9	200 i.v. b.d. × 2 doses	0.3 (3)	CSF (inflamed)	0.10	0.34
			0.4 (5)		0.14	0.34
62	4	500 p.o. × 1 dose	2.2 (2)	CSF (inflamed)	0.25	12
			1.0 (4)		0.15	15
64	20	200 i.v. × 1 dose	0.6 (1)	CSF (inflamed)	0.13	0.25
			0.7 (2)		0.09	0.15
			0.2 (4)		0.05	0.29
63	23	200 i.v. b.d. × 3 doses	0.9 (1)	CSF (inflamed)	0.2	0.12
			1.4 (2)		0.6	0.37
			1.0 (4)		0.5	0.57
			0.2 (8)		0.35	1.6
65	3	750 p.o. × 1 dose	2.7 (1.6)	Anterior chamber (eye)	0.15	0.6
	3	750 p.o. b.d. × 2 doses	3.4 (1.5)		0.53	0.16
	3	750 p.o. b.d. × 3 doses	3.8 (1.5)		0.69	0.18
	3	400 i.v. × 1 dose	2.5 (2)		0.40	0.16
	5	600 i.v. × 1 dose	2.5 (1.8)		0.42	0.17
	3	200 i.v. t.d.s. × 3 doses	1.1 (1.8)	Vitreous aspirate (eye)	0.24	0.22
66	16	200 i.v. × 1 dose	1.8 (1)	Aqueous humour	0.17	0.09
			0.9 (3)		0.13	0.15
			0.6 (6)		0.095	0.16
67	13	200 i.v. × 1 dose	0.5 (2.8)	Common bile duct	5.7	–
67	6	500 p.o. b.d. × 2 days, then 200 i.v. × 1 dose	1.0 (2.8)	Common bile duct	8.1	–
67	13	200 i.v. × 1 dose	0.5 (2.8)	Gall bladder (wall)	2.5	–
67	6	500 p.o. b.d. × 2 days, then 200 i.v. × 1 dose	1.0 (2.8)	Gall bladder (wall)	5.1	–
68	12	300 i.v. × 1 dose	(1)*	Gall bladder (wall)	5.4	–

*Peak not stated.

Table 5.3. (continued)

Reference	No. of patients	Dose (mg) and route	Mean serum concentration (mg/litre) and (time) (hours)	Tissue/ fluid	Mean concentration (mg/kg or mg/litre)	Mean tissue: serum ratio
68	12	300 i.v. × 1 dose	(1)*	Gall bladder (mucosa)	14.8	–
67	13	200 i.v.	0.5 (2.8)	Gall bladder (bile)	5.4	–
67	6	500 p.o. b.d. × 2 days, then 200 i.v. × 1 dose	1.0 (2.8)	Gall bladder (bile)	44.7	–
47	18	200 i.v. × 1 dose	2.2 (1)	Gall bladder (bile)	2.0	0.9
69	5	400 p.o. × 1 dose	0.8 (2)	Bile	1.3	1.6
			0.7 (4)		9.0	13
			0.5 (6)		5.6	11
70	12	500 p.o. × 1 dose	0.7 (1)	Bile	1.1	1.6
			0.95 (4)		5.4	5.7
			0.8 (8)		5.2	6.5
71	5	500 p.o. × 1 dose	0.7 (1)	Pancreatic juice	0.45	0.7
			2.2 (2)		1.3	0.7
			0.5 (8)		1.5	3.3
72	11	200 i.v. × 1 dose	(0.5)*	Colon mucosa	10	–
			–	Colon muscularis	6	–
73	7	200 i.v. × 1 dose	1.6 (1)	Colon muscularis	3.4	–
			–	Ileal mucosa	6.1	–
74	30	500 p.o. × 1 dose	3.1 (1)	Prostate	4.1	1.35
			2.3 (2)		4.4	1.92
			2.2 (4)		5.1	2.3
43	15	100 i.v. × 1 dose	0.9 (1)	Prostate	1.6–5.6	–
75	10	500 p.o. × 1 dose	1.5 (4)	Female pelvic organs	2–3	–
			0.5 (8)		1.8–4	–
76	18	500 p.o. × 1 dose	0.4 (1)	Female pelvic organs	0.21–0.44	–
	18	100 i.v. × 1 dose	0.6 (1)		0.58–1.2	–

*Peak not stated.

venous or oral route. Although these concentrations were low, they may be sufficient to exceed the MIC of *Neisseria meningitidis*. Intra-ocular penetration has been studied in patients undergoing elective surgery. Administration of multiple doses led to accumulation.[65] One pre-operative oral dose of 750 mg achieved a mean concentration of 0.15 mg/litre, whereas three such doses achieved a mean concentration of 0.69 mg/litre.[65] Single doses of intravenous ciprofloxacin, 400 and 600 mg, both achieved a concentration of 0.4 mg/litre. An intravenous infusion of ciprofloxacin, 200 mg, over 30 minutes achieved a concentration of 0.17 mg/litre in aqueous humour at 1 hour.[66]

In soft tissue and bone, ciprofloxacin reaches concentrations similar to, or greater than, those found in blood. Following an oral dose of 500 mg, blister fluid concentrations rose to a peak of 1.4 mg/litre compared with a peak of 2.3 mg/litre in serum.[5] In one study, ciprofloxacin, 750 mg every 12 hours, achieved high levels in fat of up to 3.3 mg/kg, approximately 1.7-fold higher than in serum.[46] Others have found concentrations in fat similar to those in serum, but lower than those in skin or muscle.[45] Oral doses of 500–1000 mg achieved muscle concentrations of 1.1–2.6 mg/kg, and similar concentrations were found following 200 mg administered intravenously.[47,48] High levels of ciprofloxacin (6.9–9.8 mg/litre) have been found in bone following intravenous doses of 200 mg.[49] In osteomyelitic bone, oral ciprofloxacin, 500–1000 mg, achieved concentrations between 0.7 and 1.4 mg/kg,

suggesting that most cases of Gram-negative bone infection could be treated orally.[48]

Oral ciprofloxacin, 500 mg, achieved concentrations in prostate up to 2.3-fold higher than those in serum.[43,74] In female pelvic organs, tissue concentrations were similar to those of serum.[76,78] Ciprofloxacin penetrates well into ascites, even following oral dosing.[53]

Elimination

Ciprofloxacin is eliminated by metabolism, renal glomerular filtration and active tubular secretion, and by the transintestinal route. Mild-to-moderate impairment of either liver or renal function does not affect ciprofloxacin clearance.[16,79] Only 10–20% of an administered dose is metabolised. Sulphociprofloxacin (M2) and oxociprofloxacin (M3) predominate, with

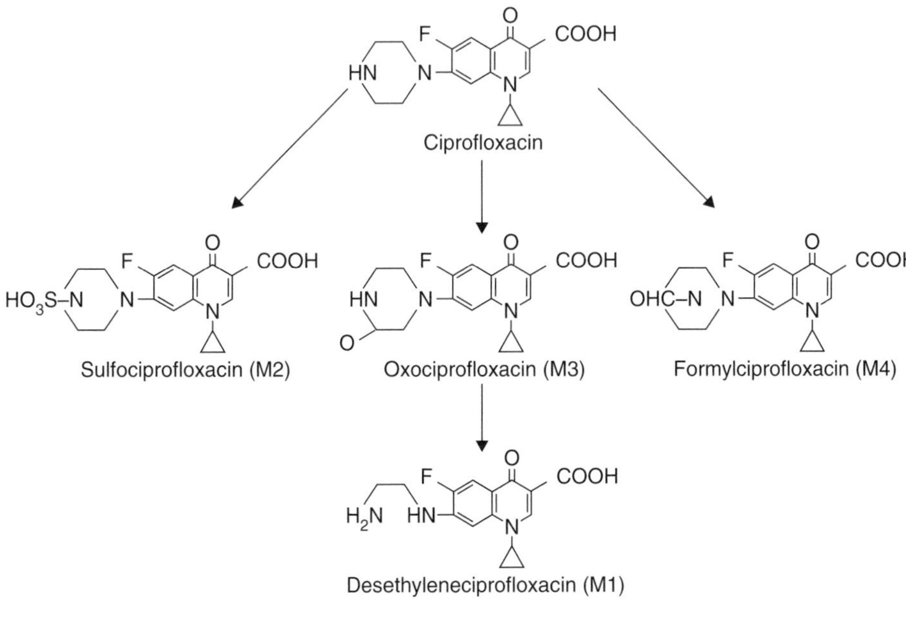

Figure 5.3. Metabolism of ciprofloxacin. Metabolites in urine and faeces after oral administration. Modified from Beermann *et al.*[39]

small amounts of desethyleneciprofloxacin (M1) (Figure 5.3).[39] The antibiotic activities of M3 and M1 are similar to that of norfloxacin, but M2 has little activity.[39] Following oral administration of ^{14}C-labelled ciprofloxacin to volunteers, 3.7% of the dose was excreted as M2 in the urine and 5.9% as M2 in the faeces.[39] M3 comprised 6.2% of the dose in urine and 1.1% of the dose in faeces. Only 1.4% and 0.5% of the dose was excreted in the urine and faeces, respectively, as M1. If formylciprofloxacin (M4) was detected at all, it was in very small amounts.[39] After intravenous administration, 12% of the ciprofloxacin dose is metabolised, appearing as M3 (5.6% in urine and 0.8% in faeces), M2 (2.6% in urine and 1.3% in faeces) and M1 (1.3% in urine and 0.5% in faeces). M2 forms during passage through the liver, and production of this metabolite is reduced with intravenous administration.

Elimination of ciprofloxacin and metabolites in the urine amounts to 60–70% of the dose and the remainder is secreted from the gut mucosa.[80] In the first 24 hours after administration of 500 mg of oral ciprofloxacin, 0.7% is excreted in the faeces, but the proportion is much higher in patients with renal failure.[70] The serum half-life varies from 3 to 5.7 hours after single or multiple doses (see Tables 5.1 and 5.2), and is independent of the size of the dose or its route of administration. The total serum clearance rate is also independent of dose, and is similar following single or repeated doses. Renal clearance of ciprofloxacin is responsible for two-thirds of the total clearance and exceeds the rate of creatinine clearance.[81] Active tubular secretion, which may be competitively inhibited by probenecid, takes place. Of an intravenous dose of 200 mg of ciprofloxacin, 65% is excreted unchanged in the urine in 1 week compared with 12% as metabolites.[80] Following oral administration of 200 mg, the mean urinary concentrations were found to be 250 mg/litre after 2–4 hours and 9 mg/litre at 12–24 hours.[42,44] At doses as low as 100 mg, renal levels reached 3.9 mg/kg and urinary concentrations of 7 mg/litre remained at 12 hours after administration.[23] The proportion

excreted in the urine does not differ significantly between doses of 250 mg and 750 mg given orally every 12 hours.[24]

Less than 1% of an intravenous ciprofloxacin dose is excreted in the bile, but levels in the gall bladder exceed serum concentrations by 10-fold.[67] Following a dose of 200 mg, ciprofloxacin concentrations in gall bladder bile were found to be between 2 and 11 mg/litre.[67] Unlike in serum, ciprofloxacin metabolites are concentrated in bile and with a single intravenous dose of 200 mg may reach 23 mg/litre in the gall bladder. With repeated dosing, gall bladder ciprofloxacin concentrations increase 10-fold, reaching 45 mg/litre. In the presence of gall bladder obstruction, bile concentrations of ciprofloxacin are lower (0.3–0.7 mg/litre), but are still sufficient to inhibit most pathogens. Oral ciprofloxacin, 500 mg, achieved a peak bile concentration of 7.5 mg/litre at 1–2 hours, eight-fold higher than in serum, falling to 4.7 mg/litre at 8–10 hours.[70]

Renal and hepatic failure

In patients with severe renal failure, the half-life of ciprofloxacin is double that of patients with normal renal function (8.7 versus 4.4 hours), and maximum serum concentrations after a single oral dose are increased.[12,13] Although the rate of non-renal clearance may be reduced because of other underlying conditions, it is high relative to renal clearance, and probably represents transintestinal elimination.[13] A single intravenous dose of 200 mg given to patients with severe renal failure was eliminated more slowly than in healthy volunteers (half-life 8.6 versus 4.3 hours), but serum clearance was still 15.4 litres/hour/1.73 m^2 compared with 26.8 litres/hour/1.73 m^2 in volunteers.[14]

Ciprofloxacin, 200 mg every 12 hours, did not accumulate when given to patients with moderate or severe renal failure.[79] The trough serum concentration was 0.6 mg/litre in moderate renal failure and 0.5 mg/litre in severe renal failure, compared with 0.3 mg/litre in patients with normal renal function. In severe renal failure, only 5% of the dose is excreted in the urine. Unlike Gasser et al.,[13] MacGowan et al. advised that dosing should not be reduced in patients with renal failure, and that if it was, subtherapeutic levels of drug would result.[79]

Dialysis

Haemodialysis reduces the serum half-life of ciprofloxacin from 5.8 to 3.2 hours.[12] The average extraction of ciprofloxacin by haemodialysis is 31%.[12] No additional dosing changes for haemodialysis are considered to be necessary.

Patients receiving continuous ambulatory peritoneal dialysis have higher serum concentrations of ciprofloxacin and slower elimination times than healthy volunteers.[82] Only 0.4–3.9% of the dose is eliminated in the dialysate. The serum and dialysate concentrations differ widely between individuals. No differences in pharmacokinetics were observed between patients with and without peritonitis, but oral ciprofloxacin, 1000 mg daily, was insufficient to maintain dialysate levels above the 2 mg/litre concentration required for treatment. The peak serum level recorded at that dose was 3.1 mg/litre, while the peak dialysate level was 0.7–6.2 mg/litre.[82] In another study, a single oral ciprofloxacin dose of 750 mg achieved a peak concentration of 3.6 mg/litre and a serum half-life of 10.7–25.2 hours.[15] The dialysate levels were 64% those of serum. Four 12-hourly doses of 750 mg achieved peak concentrations of 2.9–6.4 mg/litre in serum and 1.8–4.5 mg/litre in dialysate.[83] However, dialysate concentrations were reduced to 8–33% of these levels by ingestion of phosphate-binding aluminium antacids.[83] The ciprofloxacin concentrations in dialysate were found to increase with time, and reached 75% of serum concentrations after 8 hours. Intraperitoneal administration of ciprofloxacin, 50 mg/litre, in dialysate over 7 days, produced a mean serum concentration of 1.1 mg/litre and a wide range of dialysate concentrations from 0.2 to 33.4 mg/litre (mean 10 mg/litre).[84]

Liver cirrhosis

In severe liver cirrhosis, a higher maximum serum concentration (2.7 mg/litre) and longer half-life (7 hours) than controls have been observed following a single oral dose of 500 mg.[16] The values for patients with lesser degrees of liver failure did not differ significantly from controls. Other authors have found no significant differences in the serum concentrations of ciprofloxacin after the first dose in hepatic disease,[17,18] but metabolism was reduced.[17] The maximum serum concentrations of metabolites were 0.04 mg/litre for M1, 0.8 mg/litre for M2 and 0.14 mg/litre for M3. Only the maximum serum concentration for M3 was significantly lower than that of controls ($p < 0.05$).[17] During repeated dosing, the maximum serum concentration of M3 was half that found in control patients (0.18 versus 0.37 mg/litre).

Elderly patients

Elderly patients have an increased drug bioavailability, resulting in a higher AUC and peak concentrations. This is the result, in part, of reduced metabolism, changes in lean body mass and concomitant medication which alters oral absorption.[8,85] A fall in renal excretion with increasing age may also account for the correlation between age and serum concentrations.[86] The time-to-peak serum concentration, elimination half-life and urinary recovery have usually been found to be similar in elderly (60–73 years) and younger (20–30 years).[9] In elderly subjects, LeBel et al. noted a longer serum half-life of ciprofloxacin and a significantly higher mean peak serum concentration than in younger patients (3.2 mg/litre versus 2.6 mg/litre).[10] A multiple-dose study showed a trend to higher serum levels after a 14-day course, but the difference was not significant due to the large variation in results.[29] Dose reduction should be determined by organ dysfunction and not by age.

Children

There are few studies of ciprofloxacin pharmacokinetics in children and data from existing studies are highly variable. Following an oral dose of 15 mg/kg, the half-life was longer in infants aged 5–14 weeks than in children aged 1–5 years (2.7 versus 1.3 hours) with maximum serum concentrations of 3.3 mg/litre and 2.1 mg/litre respectively.[11] In children aged 2–16 years, oral ciprofloxacin, 40 mg/kg every 12 hours, resulted in peak concentrations of 1–5.7 mg/litre 2–3 hours after administration and trough concentrations of 0.06–0.8 mg/litre after 12 hours.[87] In children aged 8–16 years, oral ciprofloxacin, 500 mg achieved maximum serum concentrations of 2.1–5.8 mg/litre and minimum concentrations of 0.15–1.0 mg/litre.[88] In patients with cystic fibrosis aged 6–12 years, mean peak and trough serum concentrations were 5 mg/litre and 0.4 mg/litre, respectively, following intravenous ciprofloxacin, 10 mg/kg every 8 hours, and 3.2 mg/litre and 0.5 mg/litre, respectively, following intravenous ciprofloxacin, 20 mg/kg every 12 hours.[89] The serum half-life was 2.5 hours.[89] It has been suggested that oral dosing of 40 mg/kg/day or intravenous dosing of 30 mg/kg/day is necessary to maintain adequate therapeutic levels of ciprofloxacin in children.[11,89]

Measuring efficacy

In severe infections, it is important to achieve a high serum concentration:MIC ratio of ciprofloxacin to overcome sub-populations of bacteria with reduced susceptibilities. Ciprofloxacin is rapidly bactericidal, but levels above 4–8 mg/litre are needed to kill a strain with an MIC of 1 mg/litre. A regimen producing high peak concentrations would be less likely to select organisms with reduced susceptibilities. After an oral dose of 200 mg, the bactericidal titre against *Escherichia coli* is 1/90 at peak, 1/8 at 8 hours in serum, and 1/101 at 2 hours and 1/4 at 12 hours in urine.[42]

The period over which concentrations of drug exceed the MIC would also be expected to influence outcome. The AUC of serum concentration versus time and over the MIC (area under the inhibitory curve, AUIC) may be used to predict the regimen's efficacy (AUIC = [$AUC_{0-24\ hours}$]/MIC). The AUIC is predictive of bacterial eradication *in vivo*.[90] Doubling the administered dose doubles the peak serum concentration and AUC at therapeutic concentrations and causes the time over which the MIC is exceeded to be extended by a time that is equal to the half-life.[90]

Ciprofloxacin, 400–800 mg/day, provides serum levels above the MIC of highly susceptible organisms. For many Gram-negative bacteria, however, the MIC may not be exceeded for more than 80% of the dose interval. Early trials with intravenous ciprofloxacin used a dose of 100 mg every 12 hours, and reported failures with organisms of moderate susceptibility. The AUC for a 200 mg intravenous dose was still smaller than for an oral dose of 500 mg. Patients given oral ciprofloxacin after a course of intravenous antibiotic had a better outcome than those given the intravenous preparation alone.[91] A higher intravenous dose of 400 mg was then used against infections caused by less sensitive organisms, particularly *Pseudomonas* spp. Dosing every 12 hours was used for organisms with an MIC of less than 1 mg/litre and dosing every 8 hours for those with an MIC of 1–2 mg/litre. Dosing should be adjusted to the type of pathogen and the site of infection, but the AUIC is most predictive of success.[91]

Schentag *et al.* reported a pharmacodynamic analysis of 74 patients given intravenous ciprofloxacin at doses between 200 mg every 12 hours and 400 mg every 8 hours in the treatment of respiratory tract infections.[90,92] The pathogens, mostly *Pseudomonas* spp. and other Gram-negative aerobes, had ciprofloxacin MICs of between 0.008 and 4 mg/litre. If the AUIC was below 125 SIT^{-1}.hour (inverse serum inhibitory titre integrated over time), the microbiological and clinical cure rates were significantly lower than if it was above 125 SIT^{-1}.hour (26% versus 82% and 42% versus

82%; $p < 0.003$) (Figure 5.4).[90] An MIC of > 0.25 mg/litre or a peak:MIC ratio < 4 were associated with clinical and microbiological failure. By performing serial cultures, the delay from the start of treatment to consistent eradication of the pathogen was found to be greater than 32 days for an AUIC of less than 125 SIT⁻¹.hour, 6.6 days at AUIC 125–250 SIT⁻¹.hour and 1.9 days at AUICs above 250 SIT⁻¹.hour.[90,92] Doses of 400–800 mg/day should produce AUICs of greater than 250 SIT⁻¹.hour for *Haemophilus* spp. and the Enterobacteriaceae, but even a dose of 1200 mg/day was insufficient to achieve an AUIC above 125 SIT⁻¹.hour in some infections with *Staphylococcus aureus* and *Pseudomonas aeruginosa* (MIC = 0.5 mg/litre).[90] In such cases, addition of ureidopenicillins may provide sufficient synergistic interaction.

The 400 mg intravenous dose administered every 8 or 12 hours, has been approved in the USA, frequency of dosing depending on the severity of infection. In Europe, most countries have dosing every 12 hours approved, although there are some notable exceptions (e.g. Germany).

Effect on faecal flora

Ciprofloxacin has broad-spectrum activity against Gram-positive and Gram-negative aerobes, but little activity against anaerobes. Ciprofloxacin administration results in a rapid reduction in Enterobacteriaceae in faeces, but a less consistent fall in the numbers of staphylococci and enterococci. Anaerobes are either slightly reduced in number or remain unaffected by the drug. Overgrowth and the emergence of resistant bacteria are uncommon, but colonisation with coagulase-negative staphylococci and yeasts may occur.[81]

Two oral doses of 750 mg and two intravenous doses of 400 mg in 36 hours produced variable concentrations in faeces (≤ 0.1–858 mg/kg).[52] There was a marked decrease in the numbers of streptococci, enterococci and enterobacteria, all of which returned to normal levels in 2–4 weeks. Many species of anaerobes, cocci, bifidobacteria, eubacteria, lactobacilli, clostridia, fusobacteria and bacteroides were markedly reduced in number at 3 days, recovering by 2 weeks. Volunteers taking oral

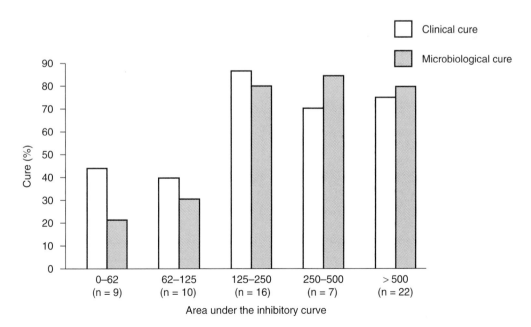

Figure 5.4. Area under the inhibitory curve compared with microbiological and clinical cure rates.[90]

ciprofloxacin, 500 mg every 12 hours for 1
week, were found to have between 185 and
2220 mg/kg of ciprofloxacin in their faeces at
the end of treatment.[28] Coliforms, of which
there were $\log_{10}$ 7.2 before treatment, were
eliminated at 1 week, but returned during the
subsequent week. There was a 2–3-log reduction in counts of streptococci, enterococci and
staphylococci at 7 days, but these had recovered by 14 days. No significant change was
found in the numbers of anaerobes or yeasts. At
14 days, coliforms, staphylococci and streptococci remained predominantly susceptible to
ciprofloxacin, but most anaerobes were then
resistant (9/36 versus 26/30). Holt *et al.* also
noted a 3-log fall in the numbers of
Enterobacteriaceae following a 5-day course of
oral ciprofloxacin, 500 mg every 12 hours, with
only a transient fall in anaerobe counts. No
ciprofloxacin-resistant Gram-negative bacteria
were isolated.[93]

References

1. Bergan T, Thorsteinsson SB, Solberg R, Bjornskau L, Kolstad IM, Johnson S. Pharmacokinetics of ciprofloxacin: intravenous and increasing oral doses. Am J Med 1987; 82 (Suppl 4A): 97–102.
2. Lode H, Höffken G, Olschewski P, Sievers B, Kirch A, Borner K *et al*. Comparative pharmaco-kinetics of intravenous ofloxacin and ciprofloxacin. J Antimicrob Chemother 1988; 22 (Suppl C): 73–9.
3. Nix DE, Spivey M, Norman A, Schentag JJ. Dose-ranging pharmacokinetic study of ciprofloxacin after 200-, 300-, and 400-mg intravenous doses. Ann Pharmacother 1992; 26: 8–10.
4. Lettieri JT, Rogge M, Echols R, Kaiser L, Heller AH. Pharmacokinetics of ciprofloxacin after single oral and intravenous doses. Drugs 1993; 45 (Suppl 3): 273–4.
5. Crump B, Wise R, Dent J. Pharmacokinetics and tissue penetration of ciprofloxacin. Antimicrob Agents Chemother 1983; 24: 784–6.
6. Bergan T, Engeset A, Olszewski W, Ostby N, Solberg R. Pharmacokinetics of ciprofloxacin in peripheral lymph and skin blisters. Eur J Clin Microbiol 1986; 5: 458–61.
7. Davis RL, Koup JR, Williams-Warren J, Weber A, Smith AL. Pharmacokinetics of three oral formulations of ciprofloxacin. Antimicrob Agents Chemother 1985; 28: 74–7.
8. Ball AP, Fox C, Ball ME, Brown IRF, Willis JV. Pharmacokinetics of oral ciprofloxacin, 100 mg single dose, in volunteers and elderly patients. J Antimicrob Chemother 1986; 17: 629–35.
9. Bayer A, Gajewska A, Stephens M, Marshal Stark J, Pathy J. Pharmacokinetics of ciprofloxacin in the elderly. Respiration 1987; 51: 292–5.
10. LeBel M, Barbeau G, Bergeron MG, Roy D, Vallee F. Pharmacokinetics of ciprofloxacin in elderly subjects. Pharmacotherapy 1986; 6: 87–91.
11. Peltola H, Väärälä M, Renkonen O-V, Neuvonen PJ. Pharmacokinetics of single dose oral ciprofloxacin in infants and small children. Antimicrob Agents Chemother 1992; 36: 1086–90.
12. Boelaert J, Valcke Y, Schurgers M, Daneels R, Rosseneu M, Rosseel MT *et al*. The pharmacokinetics of ciprofloxacin in patients with impaired renal function. J Antimicrob Chemother 1985; 16: 87–93.
13. Gasser TC, Ebert SC, Graversen PH, Madsen PO. Ciprofloxacin pharmacokinetics in patients with normal and impaired renal function. Antimicrob Agents Chemother 1987; 31: 709–12.
14. Drusano GL, Weir M, Forrest A, Plaisance K, Emm T, Standiford HC. Pharmacokinetics of intravenously administered ciprofloxacin in patients with various degrees of renal function. Antimicrob Agents Chemother 1987; 31: 860–4.
15. Shalit I, Greenwood RB, Marks MI, Pederson JA, Frederick DL. Pharmacokinetics of single dose oral ciprofloxacin in patients undergoing chronic ambulatory peritoneal dialysis. Antimicrob Agents Chemother 1986; 30: 152–6.
16. Esposito S, Miniero M, Barba D, Sagnelli E. Pharmacokinetics of ciprofloxacin in impaired liver function. Int J Clin Pharm Res 1989; 9: 37–41.
17. Frost RW, Lettieri JT, Krol G, Shamblen EC, Lasseter KC. The effect of cirrhosis on the steady-state pharmacokinetics of oral ciprofloxacin. Clin Pharmacol Ther 1989; 45: 608–16.
18. Miglioli PA, Palatini P, Orlando R, Sawadogo A. Evaluation of ciprofloxacin and ofloxacin pharmacokinetics in liver cirrhosis. Drugs 1993; 45 (Suppl 3): 270.
19. Christensson BA, Nilsson-Ehle I, Ljungberg B, Lindblad A, Malmborg A-S, Hjelte L *et al*. Increased oral bioavailability of ciprofloxacin in cystic fibrosis patients. Antimicrob Agents Chemother 1992; 36: 2512–17.
20. Bender SW, Dalhoff A, Shar PM, Strehl R, Posselt HG. Ciprofloxacin pharmacokinetics in patients with cystic fibrosis. Infection 1986; 14: 23–27.
21. Fabre D, Bressolle F, Gomeni R, Arich C, Lemesle F, Beziau H *et al*. Steady-state pharmacokinetics of ciprofloxacin in plasma from patients with nosocomial pneumonia: penetration of the bronchial mucosa. Antimicrob Agents Chemother 1991; 35: 2521–5.

22. Shah A, Lettieri J, Kaiser L, Echols R, Heller AH. Comparative pharmacokinetics and safety of ciprofloxacin 400 mg iv thrice daily versus 750 mg po twice daily. J Antimicrob Chemother 1994; 33: 795–801.

23. Gonzalez MA, Moranchel AH, Duran S, Pichardo A, Magana JL, Painter B et al. Multiple-dose pharmacokinetics of ciprofloxacin administered intravenously to normal volunteers. Antimicrob Agents Chemother 1985; 28: 235–9.

24. Gonzalez MA, Uribe F, Moisen SD, Fuster AP, Selen A, Welling PG et al. Multiple-dose pharmacokinetics and safety of ciprofloxacin in normal volunteers. Antimicrob Agents Chemother 1984; 26: 741–4.

25. Lettieri JT, Kaiser L, Krol G, Heller AH. Comparative pharmacokinetics of oral and intravenous ciprofloxacin. Drugs 1993; 45 (Suppl 3): 271–2.

26. Garraffo R, Lapalus P, Dellamonica P, Bernard E, Etesse H. Study on the bioequivalence of ciprofloxacin 500 mg orally versus 200 mg iv. Chemioterapia 1987; 6 (Suppl 2): 298–300.

27. Ullmann U, Giebel W, Dalhoff A, Koeppe P. Single and multiple dose pharmacokinetics of ciprofloxacin. Eur J Clin Microbiol 1986; 5: 193–6.

28. Brumfitt W, Franklin I, Grady D, Hamilton-Miller JMT, Iliffe A. Changes in the pharmacokinetics of ciprofloxacin and fecal flora during administration of a 7-day course to human volunteers. Antimicrob Agents Chemother 1984; 26: 757–61.

29. Guay DR, Awni WM, Peterson PK, Obaid S, Breitenbucher R, Matzke GR. Pharmacokinetics of ciprofloxacin in acutely ill and convalescent elderly patients. Am J Med 1987; 82 (Suppl 4A): 124–9.

30. Stutman HR, Shalit I, Marks MI, Greenwood R, Chartrand SA, Hilman BC. Pharmacokinetics of two dosage regimens of ciprofloxacin during a two-week therapeutic trial in patients with cystic fibrosis. Am J Med 1987; 82 (Suppl 4A): 142–5.

31. Pedersen SS, Jensen T, Hvidberg EF. Comparative pharmacokinetics of ciprofloxacin and ofloxacin in cystic fibrosis patients. J Antimicrob Chemother 1987; 20: 573–83.

32. Morran C, McArdle C, Pettitt L, Sleigh D, Gemmell C, Hichens M et al. Brief report: pharmacokinetics of orally administered ciprofloxacin in abdominal surgery. Am J Med 1989; 87 (Suppl 5A): 86–8.

33. Wingender W, Graefe KH, Gau W, Forster D, Beerman D, Schacht P. Pharmacokinetics of ciprofloxacin after oral and intravenous administration in healthy volunteers. Eur J Clin Microbiol 1984; 3: 355–9.

34. Drusano GL, Plaisance KI, Forrest A, Standiford HC. Dose ranging study and constant infusion evaluation of ciprofloxacin. Antimicrob Agents Chemother 1986; 30: 440–3.

35. Bergan T, Engeset A, Olszewski W. Does serum protein binding inhibit tissue penetration of antibiotics? Rev Infect Dis 1987; 9: 713–18.

36. Bauernfeind A. Questioning dosing regimens of ciprofloxacin. J Antimicrob Chemother 1993; 31: 789–98.

37. Davis RL, Koup JR, Williams-Warren J, Weber A, Smith AL. Pharmacokinetics of ciprofloxacin in cystic fibrosis. Antimicrob Agents Chemother 1987; 31: 915–19.

38. LeBel M, Bergeron MG, Vallee F, Fiset C, Chasse G, Bigonesse P et al. Pharmacokinetics and pharmacodynamics of ciprofloxacin in cystic fibrosis patients. Antimicrob Agents Chemother 1986; 30: 260–6.

39. Beermann D, Scholl H, Wingender W, Förster D, Beubler E, Kukovetz WR. Metabolism of ciprofloxacin in man. 1st International Ciprofloxacin Workshop, Leverkusen, Germany, 1985: 141–6.

40. Ledergerber B, Bettex JD, Joos B, Flepp M, Lüthy R. Effect of a standard breakfast on drug absorption and multiple dose pharmacokinetics of ciprofloxacin. Antimicrob Agents Chemother 1985; 27: 350–2.

41. Mack G, Cooper PJ, Buchanan N. Effects of enzyme supplementation on oral absorption of ciprofloxacin in patients with cystic fibrosis. Antimicrob Agents Chemother 1991; 35: 1484–5.

42. Zeiler H-J, Beermann D, Wingender W, Förster D, Schacht P. Bactericidal activity of ciprofloxacin, norfloxacin and ofloxacin in serum and urine after oral administration to healthy volunteers. Infection 1988; 16 (Suppl 1): S19–23.

43. Dalhoff A, Eickenberg H-U. Tissue distribution of ciprofloxacin following oral and intravenous administration. Infection 1985; 13: 78–81.

44. Daschner FD, Westenfelder M, Dalhoff A. Penetration of ciprofloxacin into kidney, fat, muscle and skin tissue. Eur J Clin Microbiol 1986; 5: 212–13.

45. Aigner KR, Dalhoff A. Penetration activities of ciprofloxacin into muscle, skin and fat following oral administration (letter). J Antimicrob Chemother 1986; 18: 644–5.

46. Licitra CM, Brooks RG, Sieger BE. Clinical efficacy and levels of ciprofloxacin in tissue in patients with soft tissue infection. Antimicrob Agents Chemother 1987; 31: 805–7.

47. Silverman SH, Johnson M, Burdon DW, Keighley MRB. Pharmacokinetics of single dose intravenous ciprofloxacin in patients undergoing gastrointestinal surgery. J Antimicrob Chemother 1986; 18: 107–12.

48. Fong IW, Ledbetter WH, Vandenbroucke AC, Simbul M, Rahm V. Ciprofloxacin concentrations in bone and muscle after oral dosing. Antimicrob Agents Chemother 1986; 29: 405–8.

49. Braun R, Dürig M, Harder F. Penetration of ciprofloxacin into bone tissues. 14th International Congress of Chemotherapy, Kyoto, Japan, 1985: Abstract 85.

50. Falser N, Dalhoff A, Weuta H. Ciprofloxacin concentrations in tonsils following a single intravenous infusion. Infection 1984; 12: 355–7.

51. Cohen B, Farinotti R, Gehanno P, Buffe P, Cudennec Y, Julien N et al. Penetration of ciprofloxacin into middle ear and sinus mucosa after repeated oral administration. 5th International Congress of Infectious Diseases, Nairobi, Kenya, 1992: Abstract 516.

52. Brismar B, Edlund C, Malmborg A-S, Nord CE. Ciprofloxacin concentrations and impact of the colon microflora in patients undergoing colorectal surgery. Antimicrob Agents Chemother 1990; 34: 481–3.

53. Dan M, Zuabi T, Quassem C, Rotmensch HH. Distribution of ciprofloxacin in ascitic fluid following administration of a single oral dose of 750 milligrams. Antimicrob Agents Chemother 1992; 36: 677–8.

54. Dan M, Torossian K, Weissberg D, Kitzes R. The penetration of ciprofloxacin into bronchial mucosa, lung parenchyma, and pleural tissue after intravenous administration. Eur J Clin Pharmacol 1993; 44: 101–2.

55. Honeybourne D, Lodwick R, Andrews JM, Ashby JP, Wise R. Assessment of the penetration of amoxycillin and ciprofloxacin into the bronchial mucosa. Thorax 1988; 43: 223P.

56. Schlenkoff D, Mayer M, Dalhoff A. Penetration of ciprofloxacin into human lung tissue following a single intravenous administration. 14th International Congress of Chemotherapy, Kyoto, Japan, 1985: 1620–1.

57. Thys JP, Klastersky J, Jacobs F, Berre J, Gangji D, Hanotte F et al. Penetration of ciprofloxacin into bronchial secretions and pleural fluid. 1st International Ciprofloxacin Workshop, Leverkusen, Germany, 1985: 153–6.

58. Bölcskei P, Burkhardt G, Klatte O, Dimpel M, Thoma B, Gill E. Penetration of ciprofloxacin in the pleural fluid. Chemioterapia 1987; 6 (Suppl 2): 290–2.

59. Davies BI, Maesen FPV, Baur C. Ciprofloxacin in the treatment of acute exacerbations of chronic bronchitis. Eur J Clin Microbiol 1986; 5: 226–31.

60. Smith MJ, White LO, Bowyer H, Willis J, Hodson ME, Batten JC. Pharmacokinetics and sputum penetration of ciprofloxacin in patients with cystic fibrosis. Antimicrob Agents Chemother 1986; 30: 614–16.

61. Gogos CA, Maraziotis TG, Papadakis N, Beermann D, Siamplis DK, Bassaris HP. Penetration of ciprofloxacin into human cerebrospinal fluid in patients with inflamed and non-inflamed meninges. Eur J Clin Microbiol Infect Dis 1991; 10: 511–14.

62. Kitzes-Cohen R, Miler A, Gilboa A, Harel D. Penetration of ciprofloxacin into the cerebrospinal fluid. Rev Infect Dis 1988; 10 (Suppl 1): S256–7.

63. Wolff M, Boutron L, Singlas E, Clair B, Decazes JM, Reginier B. Penetration of ciprofloxacin into cerebrospinal fluid of patients with bacterial meningitis. Antimicrob Agents Chemother 1987; 31: 899–902.

64. Trautmann M, Ruhnke M, Borner K. Penetration of ciprofloxacin into the spinal fluid in patients with viral and bacterial meningitis. Drug Res 1990; 40: 611–14.

65. Lüthy R, Joos B, Gassmann F. Penetration of ciprofloxacin into the human eye. 1st Ciprofloxacin Workshop, Leverkusen, Germany, 1985: 192–6.

66. Behrens-Baumann W, Martell J. Ciprofloxacin concentration in the rabbit aqueous humor and vitreous following intravenous and subconjunctival administration. Infection 1988; 16 (1): 54–7.

67. Parry MF, Smego DA , Digiovanni MA. Hepatobiliary kinetics and excretion of ciprofloxacin. Antimicrob Agents Chemother 1988; 32: 982–5.

68. Sayek I, Kaynaroglu V, Scholl H. Concentration of ciprofloxacin in non-functional gallbladder mucosa after single dose intravenous administration. Infection 1990; 18: 124–5.

69. Tanimura H, Tominaga S, Rai F, Matsumoto H. Transfer of ciprofloxacin to bile and determination of biliary metabolites in humans. Drug Res 1986; 36: 1417–20.

70. Brogard J-M, Jehl F, Monteil H, Adloff M, Blickle J-F, Levy P. Comparison of high-pressure liquid chromatography microbiological assay for the determination of biliary elimination of ciprofloxacin in humans. Antimicrob Agents Chemother 1985; 28: 311–14.

71. Pederzoli P, Massimo R, Bassi C, Vensentini S, Orcalli R, Seaglione F et al. Ciprofloxacin penetration in pancreatic juice. Pharmacology 1987; 33: 397–401.

72. Vestweber K-H, Viell B, Schaaf S, Scholl H. Perioperative prophylaxis in colorectal surgery: is a single-shot with 200 mg ciprofloxacin sufficient to maintain therapeutic levels in gut tissues? 6th Congress of Chemotherapy, Taormina, Italy, 1988: 179–81.

73. Viell B, Krause B, Vestweber K-H, Schaaf S, Scholl H. Transintestinal elimination of ciprofloxacin in humans – concomitant assessment of its metabolites in serum, ileum and colon. Infection 1992; 20: 22–5.

74. Waldron R, Arkell DG, Wise R, Andrews JM. The intraprostatic penetration of ciprofloxacin. J Antimicrob Chemother 1986; 17: 544–5.

75. Raspaud S, Konopka P, Taburet AM, Konopka CA, Singlas E. Diffusion of ciprofloxacin into female genital tract tissues. J Pharm Clin 1986; 5: 277–86.

76. Goormans E, Dalhoff A, Kazzazz B, Branolte JH. Penetration of ciprofloxacin to female genital tract tissues: possibilities of perioperative use as antibiotic prophylaxis. 1st International Ciprofloxacin Workshop, Leverkusen, Germany, 1985: 189–91.

77. Easmon CSF, Crane JP, Blowers A. Effect of ciprofloxacin on intracellular organisms: *in-vitro* and *in-vivo* studies. J Antimicrob Chemother 1986; 18 (Suppl D): 43–8.

78. Dalhoff A, Weuta H. Penetration of ciprofloxacin into gynecologic tissues. Am J Med 1987; 82 (Suppl 4A): 133–8.

79. MacGowan AP, White LO, Brown NM, Lovering AM, McMullin CM, Reeves DS. Serum ciprofloxacin concentrations in patients with severe sepsis being treated with ciprofloxacin 200 mg iv bd irrespective of renal function. J Antimicrob Chemother 1994; 33: 1051–4.

80. Rohwedder R, Bergan T, Thorsteinsson SB, Scholl H. Transintestinal elimination of ciprofloxacin. Chemotherapy 1990; 36: 77–84.

81. Campoli-Richards DM, Monk JP, Price A, Benfield P, Todd PA, Ward A. Ciprofloxacin. A review of its antibacterial activity, pharmacokinetic properties and therapeutic use. Drugs 1988; 35: 373–447.

82. Fleming LW, Moreland TA, Scott AC, Stewart WK, White LO. Ciprofloxacin in plasma and peritoneal dialysate after oral therapy in patients on continuous ambulatory peritoneal dialysis. J Antimicrob Chemother 1987; 19: 493–503.

83. Golper TA, Hartstein AI, Morthland VH, Christensen JM. Effects of antacids and dialysate dwell times on multiple dose pharmacokinetics of oral ciprofloxacin in patients on continuous ambulatory peritoneal dialysis. Antimicrob Agents Chemother 1987; 31: 1787–90.

84. Ludlam HA, Barton I, White L, McMullin C, King A, Phillips I. Intraperitoneal ciprofloxacin for the treatment of peritonitis in patients receiving continuous ambulatory peritoneal dialysis (CAPD). J Antimicrob Chemother 1990; 25: 843–51.

85. Robson RA. Quinolone pharmacokinetics. Int J Antimicrob Agents 1992; 2: 3–10.

86. Morita M, Hasuda A, Nakagawa H, Suzuki K. Accumulation of new quinolones in the blood of elderly patients. Drugs 1993; 45 (Suppl 3): 266.

87. Rubio TT. Clinical and laboratory experience with ciprofloxacin in children two to sixteen years of age.

88. Schaad UB, Salam MA, Aujard Y, Dagan R, Green SDR, Peltota H et al. Use of fluoroquinolones in pediatrics: consensus report of an International Society of Chemotherapy commission. Pediatr Infect Dis J 1995; 14: 1–9.

89. Rubio TT, Miles MV, Church DA, Echols RM, Pickering LK. Pharmacokinetic studies of ciprofloxacin in children with cystic fibrosis. Pediatr Res April 1994; Abstract 1153.

90. Schentag JJ. The relationship between ciprofloxacin blood concentrations, MIC values, bacterial eradication, and clinical outcome in patients with nosocomial pneumonia. In: Garrard C, ed. Ciprofloxacin iv. Defining its role in serious infection. Berlin: Springer Verlag, 1994: 49–57.

91. Echols RM. Antimicrobial practice: The selection of appropriate dosages for intravenous ciprofloxacin. J Antimicrob Chemother 1993; 31: 783–7.

92. Forrest A, Nix DE, Ballow CH, Goss TF, Birmingham MC, Schentag JJ. Pharmacodynamics of intravenous ciprofloxacin in seriously ill patients. Antimicrob Agents Chemother 1993; 37: 1073–81.

93. Holt HA, Lewis DA, White LO, Bastable SY, Reeves DS. The effects of oral ciprofloxacin on the faecal flora of healthy volunteers. 14th International Congress of Chemotherapy, Kyoto, Japan, 1985: 1573–4.

Ad Antimicrob Antineoplastic Chemother 1992; 11: S151–4.

Chapter 6

Therapeutic use

The broad antibacterial activity of ciprofloxacin makes it a good candidate for the empirical treatment of seriously ill patients. Both randomised and uncontrolled studies show it is effective, even in bacteraemia caused by Gram-negative bacterial endocarditis. Its activity might render the patient susceptible to superinfection but studies suggest that this is no more likely than during treatment with ceftazidime. Ciprofloxacin has little effect on the anaerobic flora of the gut, allowing preservation of some colonisation resistance.

Septicaemia

Any patients suspected of having bacteraemia, particularly those who are critically ill, must be treated empirically. If the patient has been in hospital for more than 3 days, the antibacterial spectrum should include potential nosocomial Gram-negative pathogens. Ciprofloxacin has several properties that make it an attractive choice for the treatment of bacteraemia. It has a broad spectrum of activity, rapid bactericidal action, good tissue penetration and few adverse effects, while resistance is rare among most Enterobacteriaceae.

Most early trials of the therapeutic use of ciprofloxacin covered a variety of infections. Either efficacy is not given by the site of infection or only small numbers of patients are

reported for each type of infection. Clinical response rates in a review of ten studies were between 76% and 96%, representing 434 of 487 (89%) patients.[1] Of the 341 with documented bacteraemia, 94% were cured. Gram-negative bacteria were the most common pathogens found, and it was concluded that the likelihood of resistance and clinical failure made ciprofloxacin unsuitable for treating Gram-positive bacteraemia. Results collected from several trials reported either a cure or improvement in 140 of 154 (91%) patients, with *Escherichia coli* and *Salmonella typhi* being the most common causes of bacteraemia.[2]

Uncontrolled trials

Uncontrolled trials have demonstrated high cure rates for ciprofloxacin. In one study, a total of 100 patients were treated with ciprofloxacin, 500 mg orally every 12 hours for 7–14 days.[3] In 41 of these cases, treatment was given for bacteraemia, mainly caused by *Salmonella typhi*. Fever resolved after a mean of 4 days in these cases, with only one patient, who had cholecystitis and *Escherichia coli* bacteraemia, failing to respond to treatment. In the remaining patients with other infections, all except two patients, who had both been treated for a staphylococcal respiratory tract infection, responded to treatment with disappearance of signs and symptoms of the disease.

In another multicentre trial with ciprofloxacin (200 mg given intravenously every 12 hours for 7–12 days, then 500–750 mg given orally every 12 hours), 105 of 113 (93%) serious infections were cured or improved,

Wilson APR and Grüneberg RN.
Ciprofloxacin: 10 years of clinical experience
© 1997 Maxim Medical, Oxford.

although 25 patients received other antibiotics (not stated).[4] Of these infections, 42 were septicaemia, with treatment failing in only 3 of these cases. In another trial, the success rate for improvement in similar infections was 87% (26/30 patients).[5] Multi-resistant infections, caused mainly by *Pseudomonas aeruginosa*, *Enterobacter* spp. and *Staphylococcus aureus*, responded to treatment in 52 of 62 (84%) cases.[6] In this study, the average course of treatment was 60 days, reflecting the 26 cases of osteomyelitis that required lengthy oral treatment. Eron *et al.* reported clinical success in 41 of 48 (85%) infections, mostly caused by *Pseudomonas aeruginosa*.[7] Kljucar *et al.* used a higher intravenous dosage, 400 mg every 12 hours, in 54 patients with severe nosocomial infections, predominantly pneumonias.[8] Cure or improvement was achieved in 44 patients (81%). There were only 2 treatment failures, in patients infected with *Pseudomonas* and *Serratia* spp., the remainder being indeterminate. Finally, in a study carried out by Gudiol *et al.*, ciprofloxacin was curative in 42 of 50 (84%) patients, 20 of whom were suffering from osteomyelitis, after a course averaging 14 days by the intravenous route followed by 57 days by the oral route.[9]

In patients with malignant disease, predominantly solid tumours, ciprofloxacin, 300 mg given intravenously every 12 hours, cured 24 of 27 (89%) cases of serious infection.[10] The condition of the other three patients was improved. In a further study, high oral doses, 750 mg given every 8 hours, were used to treat 46 febrile episodes in 43 patients with cancer, with a successful outcome, indicated by disappearance of clinical and laboratory evidence of infection, in 39 (85%) of the episodes.[11] The response rate in those with documented infections was higher (90%), with treatment failures occurring with pseudomonal osteomyelitis, staphylococcal empyema and polymicrobial pneumonia.

There has been a report that ciprofloxacin, 200 mg given intravenously every 12 hours or 750 mg given orally every 12 hours, cured 2 of 3 patients infected with multi-resistant

Flavobacterium meningosepticum.[12] Two HIV-infected patients with bacteraemia caused by *Campylobacter* spp. were also cured with ciprofloxacin, 500 mg given orally every 12 hours, after failing to respond to erythromycin.[13,14]

Randomised trials

Ciprofloxacin, 200 mg given intravenously every 12 hours followed by 750 mg orally every 12 hours, was compared with cefuroxime, 1.5 g given intravenously every 8 hours, plus tobramycin, given every 8 hours at a level to keep trough 1–2.5 mg/litre, in a randomised trial of 310 patients from eight centres.[15] All patients had serious infections, usually septicaemia or respiratory infection. Cure or improvement was observed in 120 of 160 (75%) patients given ciprofloxacin and 116 of 150 (77%) patients given cefuroxime plus tobramycin. More than half the failures in the ciprofloxacin group were of infections with *Streptococcus pneumoniae*, whereas less than 15% of treatment failures in the control group were caused by this pathogen.

Several randomised comparisons of ciprofloxacin and ceftazidime have been made in the treatment of serious infections. The trials were small and failed to show any significant differences in efficacy between the two antibiotics (total 188/206 versus 180/205).[16–22] In one trial, persistence of the pathogen was noted in 3 of 34 cases in the ciprofloxacin group (1 with *Staphylococcus epidermidis* and 2 with *Streptococcus* group B) compared with 7 of 32 cases in the ceftazidime group (4 with Gram-positive and 3 with Gram-negative pathogens).[17] Fass *et al.* used three treatment groups (intravenous and then oral ciprofloxacin, intravenous ciprofloxacin, and ceftazidime). Success rates were 81% (17/21), 85% (22/26) and 71% (22/31), respectively. Three patients with Gram-negative pneumonia and one with a mastoiditis were infected with pathogens that acquired ciprofloxacin resistance during treatment.[23]

The use of oral ciprofloxacin to complete the treatment of Gram-negative bacteraemia was tested in a randomised trial of 94 patients.[24] Another 171 patients were considered non-evaluable, usually because of a failure to isolate Gram-negative bacteria in the blood. Success rates in patients given only intravenous ciprofloxacin compared with those finishing treatment with oral ciprofloxacin were similar (35/36 versus 28/29). In a further study of 32 patients treated with ciprofloxacin (200 mg given intravenously every 12 hours for three days and then either continued with 200 mg given intravenously every 12 hours, or changed to 750 mg given orally every 12 hours) for serious infections, 14 (44%) were cured, 15 (47%) improved, treatment failed in 1 patient, 1 died and 1 was lost to follow-up.[25]

Endocarditis and endarteritis

Endocarditis is seldom caused by Gram-negative bacteria, and in these cases, ciprofloxacin has sometimes been used, with its advantages of good oral absorption, low toxicity and good tissue penetration. Ciprofloxacin reaches a mean concentration of 32 mg/kg in the myocardium and 5.8 mg/kg in the heart valve within 1 hour of an intravenous dose of 400 mg.[26] After four oral doses of 750 mg, myocardial and valvular concentrations have been found to be 22 mg/kg and 12 mg/kg, respectively.

Pseudomonas spp.

Daikos *et al.* reported two cases of pseudomonas endocarditis treated with oral ciprofloxacin.[27] In the first, a drug abuser in whom treatment with other agents had failed initially responded to a dose of 500 mg every 12 hours, but died at 16 weeks. The second patient responded quickly to ciprofloxacin, 500 mg every 8 hours, but relapsed when treatment was stopped after 1 year. Prolonged oral treatment, 750 mg given every 8 hours then 500 mg every 12 hours, was sufficient to suppress bac-

teraemia for over 18 months in a patient with prosthetic-valve endocarditis in whom re-operation was not feasible.[28] Intravenous ciprofloxacin, 200 mg every 8 hours, plus gentamicin, 80 mg given intravenously every 8 hours, was effective in another patient with pseudomonas prosthetic-valve endocarditis. However, the patient developed a paraprosthetic leak after gentamicin was stopped.[29] Although she responded to recommencement of gentamicin in combination with the ciprofloxacin, she later died as a result of haemodynamic problems. Treatment failure was reported following the emergence of resistance during treatment of pseudomonas endocarditis in a drug abuser.[6]

Salmonella spp.

Salmonella spp. are among the more common Gram-negative organisms to cause endocarditis. Ciprofloxacin has been used successfully to treat salmonella endocarditis on native and prosthetic valves.[30–32] However, ciprofloxacin treatment failed in one patient with salmonella infection of a ventricular aneurysm; ciprofloxacin (at its trough concentration) was shown not to inhibit the organism.[33] *Salmonella* spp. are a well-recognised cause of endarteritis of the aorta, which is usually complicated by the formation of aneurysms. Ciprofloxacin has been effective in salmonella aortitis.[34] A salmonella abscess that had developed around an iliac artery prosthetic graft was successfully treated by drainage and a 12-week course of oral ciprofloxacin, 750 mg given every 12 hours.[35]

Staphylococcus aureus

Staphylococcus aureus endocarditis in intravenous drug abusers has been treated in a randomised trial with a combination of oral ciprofloxacin, 750 mg every 12 hours, plus rifampicin, 300 mg every 12 hours, or intravenous oxacillin, 2 g every 4 hours, plus intravenous gentamicin, 2 mg/kg every 8 hours.[36] Treatment was continued for 28 days except for gentamicin which was given for only 5 days.

Of 574 patients, only 85 (15%) satisfied the criteria for recruitment, having right-side endocarditis. Of the 40 patients given oral treatment, 18 were cured, treatment failed in 1 and 21 were withdrawn. Of the 45 others given intravenous treatment, 22 were cured, treatment failed in 3 and 20 did not complete therapy. In another study, ciprofloxacin was given intravenously, 300 g every 12 hours for 1 week and then orally, 750 mg every 12 hours for 21 days.[37] Rifampicin was given orally, 300 mg every 12 hours for 28 days. All 10 evaluable patients, of the 14 recruited, were cured. These regimens are particularly useful if the patient wishes to be discharged from hospital. Compliance, however, may be poor and resistance to both agents can develop during treatment, leading to early treatment failure.[38] Neu et al. described two cases of endocarditis caused by Staphylococcus aureus that were treated with ciprofloxacin after failure with previous treatments.[6] One patient had persistent bacteraemia and the organism became resistant, but in the second patient, bacteraemia was cleared and the valve was sterile when removed.

Other Gram-negative species

Ciprofloxacin given over a period of 4–5 weeks, intravenously (then orally in one patient), cured two patients of endocarditis caused by Serratia marcescens, in one case following removal of the infected valve.[39] A combination of ciprofloxacin and rifampicin was effective in a case of endocarditis caused by Legionella pneumophila.[40] The patient responded to a 10-week course, but required a further 6 weeks of ciprofloxacin to treat residual inflammation discovered when the valve was removed. In individual cases, ciprofloxacin has been successfully used to treat cases caused by Haemophilus aphrophilus, 200 mg intravenously every 12 hours for 2 weeks, then 750 mg every 12 hours for 4 weeks;[41] Neisseria mucosa, 750 mg orally every 12 hours for 6 weeks;[42] and Erysipelothrix rhusiopathiae, 400 mg intravenously every 12 hours for 2 weeks then 750 mg every 12 hours

for 7 weeks.[43] Endocarditis caused by Coxiella burnetii was effectively suppressed by continued treatment with ciprofloxacin, 500 mg given orally every 12 hours, in a patient who refused surgery.[44]

Superinfection

Despite its broad spectrum of activity, treatment with ciprofloxacin does not commonly result in superinfection, though rates vary widely between clinical trials. Only 5% of 1046 patients in early clinical trials developed superinfection,[45] but 6 of 19 (32%) patients treated for soft tissue infection became infected with Stenotrophomonas maltophilia or enterococci.[46] In 3822 patients, there were superinfections with enterococci in 17 patients, pneumococci in 6 patients, Staphylococcus aureus in 13 patients and Pseudomonas aeruginosa in 16 patients.[47]

Pseudomembranous colitis associated with growth of Clostridium difficile in the gut during treatment with ciprofloxacin has been reported and is discussed in Chapter 16.

Neutropenic patients are most susceptible to superinfection.[48] Of 36 neutropenic patients given ciprofloxacin and penicillin for fever, one developed Staphylococcus epidermidis bacteraemia and four proven or suspected fungal infections. In comparison, of 46 patients given netilmicin and piperacillin, two developed bacterial superinfections, but none had fungal infections. In another trial, 3 of 38 febrile neutropenic patients became infected with Aspergillus spp., cytomegalovirus (CMV) and Staphylococcus epidermidis, respectively, during treatment with ciprofloxacin and teicoplanin.[49] Somolinos et al. reported an increase in bacteraemia caused by ciprofloxacin-resistant Escherichia coli, associated with use of the antibiotic.[50] Infections were mostly limited to patients given long courses of ciprofloxacin and were thought to have been selected from endogenous flora.

The risk of superinfection arising from the use of ciprofloxacin is similar to that for ceftazidime. In a comparative trial of treatment of serious infections, 5 of 19 patients given ciprofloxacin and 7 of 20 given ceftazidime were affected.[20] Five patients in each group developed fungal urinary infections. Of a further 26 patients treated with intravenous ciprofloxacin, 3 developed infection with *Acinetobacter* spp., one strain being ciprofloxacin resistant.[19] Of the 26 patients given ceftazidime, 2 developed superinfections. In another trial, 1 of 33 patients given ciprofloxacin and 2 of 26 patients given ceftazidime developed candidal urinary infection.[18] Another two patients in the ceftazidime group developed fatal enterococcal septicaemias.

In an uncontrolled trial carried out by Ramirez *et al.*, superinfection was observed in 3 of 100 patients treated for 7–14 days with oral ciprofloxacin for various infections.[3] Two of the superinfections were bladder infections of chronically catheterised patients. Of 50 patients given prolonged courses of treatment for severe infections, 3 developed superinfection with ciprofloxacin-resistant *Pseudomonas aeruginosa* and 2 became colonised with *Candida* spp. in the urinary tract.[9] In a further trial of 27 patients with carcinoma, one developed septicaemia caused by *Listeria monocytogenes* and another by *Candida* spp.[10] Three of 10 patients treated for osteomyelitis developed superinfection with resistant organisms (*Achromobacter xylosoxidans*, *Pseudomonas aeruginosa* and *Staphylococcus epidermidis*).[51]

In most trials of treatments for respiratory tract infection, few superinfections are reported. Of 66 elderly patients treated with ciprofloxacin, 3 developed superinfections: 1 *Pseudomonas aeruginosa* pneumonia and 1 enterococcal bacteraemia, both resulting in death, and 1 pneumococcal pneumonia.[52] Of another 56 patients treated with ceftazidime, 6 acquired a superinfection and 1 died. In a trial using oral ciprofloxacin, 250–750 mg given every 12 hours, and a course of treatment averaging 9 days, superinfection with *Candida albicans* was recorded in 3 of 419 patients.[53] In a

further study, 1 of 26 patients developed pneumococcal infection during a course of oral ciprofloxacin, 500 mg given every 12 hours.[54]

Colonisation resistance and effects on commensal flora

The normal bacterial population found in humans is disturbed by the use of broad-spectrum antibiotics, resulting in the proliferation of resistant species within the flora and the acquisition of resistant strains from the patient's environment. Severe infections can develop if these patients are debilitated or if their immune system is suppressed by their underlying disease, treatment or age. The normal resistance of the bacterial flora to colonisation by exogenous organisms is impaired.[55] The antimicrobial spectrum and the concentration of antibiotic in the gut or tissues govern the extent to which there is disruption of the normal flora.

Ciprofloxacin has little effect on the anaerobic flora and may allow some preservation of the normal response to colonisation. In the prevention of urinary infection or selective decontamination, however, suppression of one part of the normal flora may be useful. In volunteers, oral ciprofloxacin principally reduces the numbers of Gram-negative aerobes in the gut and has a limited effect on the anaerobes (see Chapter 5).[56–58] Brumfitt *et al.* noted that anaerobes were little reduced in numbers by ciprofloxacin but acquired resistance.[59] Elderly patients being treated with oral ciprofloxacin, 250–1000 mg/day for urinary infection similarly showed a suppression of Enterobacteriaceae in the stool.[60] Although *Candida* spp. were later isolated in 2 of 14 patients, no staphylococci or resistant Gram-negative species emerged. In another study, the enterobacteria were eliminated from the faecal flora in patients with cirrhosis treated with ciprofloxacin for urinary or respiratory infections for 5–10 days, while the levels of Gram-positive and anaerobic flora were little changed.[61]

Salivary and faecal flora were studied in 12 volunteers receiving oral ciprofloxacin, 500 mg given every 12 hours for 5 days.[62] In the saliva, the numbers of streptococci, staphylococci and anaerobes were unchanged and only levels of *Neisseria* spp. decreased. There were significant reductions in the aerobic faecal flora, however, and smaller falls in the anaerobic flora, although both had recovered by 14 days after treatment had ceased. There was no colonisation by resistant strains at either site. Others found no effect on oral flora but the faecal flora were found to be colonised with yeasts in all volunteers.[63]

The effect of ciprofloxacin, 250 mg every 12 hours for 3 days, on the faecal flora in comparison with placebo has been studied in 42 patients who travelled to Mexico from Texas, USA.[64] *Escherichia coli*, with one of various virulence genes, were found in 67 of 592 isolates from 14 travellers after 4 days in Mexico before treatment for diarrhoea. However, similar numbers were found in both the ciprofloxacin and the placebo groups. During the stay in Mexico, the numbers of enterococci increased significantly in all travellers with no diarrhoea at that time and there were smaller rises in the numbers of *Escherichia coli*, *Clostridium* spp., lactobacilli and *Candida albicans*. In those treated with ciprofloxacin, the numbers of *Klebsiella* spp. and *Escherichia coli* were significantly reduced, with small rises in anaerobic cocci and bifidobacteria compared with those found in the travellers given placebo. From four travellers, 23 isolates of ciprofloxacin-resistant *Escherichia coli* were found that were also resistant to chloramphenicol, ampicillin and doxycycline. Those given placebo similarly acquired strains resistant to several antibiotics, but not to ciprofloxacin.

Ciprofloxacin has been assessed for use in selective decontamination of the gut of leukaemic patients. During prolonged administration of ciprofloxacin, 500 mg every 12 hours for more than 40 days, plus oral amphotericin, 200 mg every 6 hours, to a total of 15 patients, the levels of enterobacteria were greatly reduced, with enterococci levels being reduced or unchanged.[65] There was no change in the levels of anaerobic Gram-negative bacilli and *Clostridium* spp., and only small reductions in the numbers of anaerobic cocci. Only 6 ciprofloxacin-resistant *Pseudomonas* spp. were isolated from 186 faecal samples and none were established colonisers. A total of 7 patients were colonised with resistant *Staphylococcus epidermidis* and 4 were colonised with *Candida* spp. Fifteen patients developed a total of 10 infections during the study, of which 2 were caused by *Staphylococcus epidermidis*, 2 by *Streptococcus sanguis* and 1 by *Bacteroides* spp., all with reduced sensitivity to ciprofloxacin. The same authors found that prophylactic use of ciprofloxacin was associated with significantly fewer infections than with co-trimoxazole (5/28 versus 14/28) ($p < 0.025$).[65] Colonisation with resistant Gram-negative bacteria was similarly less likely.[66] In another study, more infections occurred in patients given ciprofloxacin than in those given co-trimoxazole (82/117 versus 69/113), but there were no episodes of Gram-negative bacteraemia with ciprofloxacin compared with 5 with co-trimoxazole.[67] Both agents cleared *Escherichia coli* and most *Staphylococcus aureus* from the stools, and during prophylaxis, most patients remained clear of Enterobacteriaceae and *Staphylococcus aureus* in the mouth (92% versus 93%) and stools (95% versus 92%). Oral candidiasis was noted in 32% of those given ciprofloxacin and in 43% of those given co-trimoxazole.

In a randomised study of prophylaxis in 255 neutropenic episodes, in a total of 189 patients, ciprofloxacin was more effective than pefloxacin in preventing bacteraemia.[68] As in other trials, there was a marked reduction in Enterobacteriaceae with little effect on anaerobic flora. Ciprofloxacin was less likely to be associated with isolation of resistant *Pseudomonas aeruginosa* or *Staphylococcus aureus* than pefloxacin (2/78 versus 14/77, 5/78 versus 14/77). The number of patients in the ciprofloxacin group colonised with resistant Enterobacteriaceae rose from 6 to 11 by the end of prophylaxis (10–59 days).

Thus, in summary, ciprofloxacin is excreted at high concentrations in the faeces and strongly suppresses the Gram-negative aerobic flora but leaves the anaerobic flora intact, despite the minimum inhibitory concentrations of these organisms being exceeded. The potential for the development of resistance does not seem to be high, but the widespread therapeutic use of ciprofloxacin suggests that when applied prophylactically, it should be carefully controlled.

Conclusions

Ciprofloxacin is a common choice in the empirical treatment of bacteraemia because of the low prevalence of resistance, broad-spectrum activity and intravenous or oral administration. Initial intravenous treatment is at a dose of 200 mg every 12 hours for 3–12 days followed if necessary by oral doses of 750 mg 8–12 hourly for up to 1 week. Bacterial spectrum can be further increased by the addition of a glycopeptide or metronidazole. Gram-negative bacterial endocarditis has been treated by intravenous (200 mg every 8 hours) or oral (500 mg every 8 hours) ciprofloxacin for at least 12 weeks, sometimes combined with gentamicin initially. Ciprofloxacin (750 mg administered orally every 12 hours) plus rifampicin (300 mg administered orally every 12 hours) for 28 days has been used to allow out-patient treatment of intravenous drug abusers with staphylococcal endocarditis of the tricuspid valve. Superinfections are uncommon and similar to those with ceftazidime. Ciprofloxacin spares the anaerobic flora of the gut and can be used for selective decontamination.

References

1. Piper JL, Chang GL. Quinolone use in critical care. Probl Crit Care 1992; 6: 64–83.
2. Neumann C, Echols R, Arcieri G, Becker N. Intravenous ciprofloxacin (CIP) alone (iv only) or with sequential oral (iv/po) CIP in the treatment of bacteraemia. 3rd International Symposium on New Quinolones, Vancouver, Canada, 1990: 482.
3. Ramirez CA, Bran JL, Mejia CR, Garcia JF. Open, prospective study of the clinical efficacy of ciprofloxacin. Antimicrob Agents Chemother 1985; 28: 128–32.
4. Modai J, French Multicenter Study Group. Treatment of serious infections with intravenous ciprofloxacin. Am J Med 1989; 87 (Suppl 5A): 243–7.
5. Scully BE, Neu HC. Treatment of serious infections with intravenous ciprofloxacin. Am J Med 1987; 82 (Suppl 4A): 369–75.
6. Neu HC, Davidson S, Briones F. Intravenous/oral ciprofloxacin therapy of infections caused by multi-resistant bacteria. Am J Med 1989; 87 (Suppl 5A): 209–12.
7. Eron LJ, Harvey L, Hixon DL, Poretz DM. Ciprofloxacin therapy of infections caused by *Pseudomonas aeruginosa* and other resistant bacteria. Antimicrob Agents Chemother 1985; 27: 308–10.
8. Kljucar S, Heimesaat M, von Pritzbuer E, Timm J, Scholl H, Beerman D. Efficacy and safety of higher dose intravenous ciprofloxacin in severe hospital-acquired infections. Am J Med 1989; 87 (Suppl 5A): 52–6.
9. Gudiol F, Cabellos C, Pallares R, Linares J, Ariza J. Intravenous ciprofloxacin therapy in severe infections. Am J Med 1989; 87 (Suppl 5A): 221–4.
10. Brown AE, Smith G. Treatment of sepsis in patients with neoplastic diseases with intravenous ciprofloxacin. Am J Med 1989; 87 (Suppl 5A): 266–8.
11. Haron E, Rolston KVI, Cunningham C, Holmes F, Umsawasadi T, Bodey GP. Oral ciprofloxacin therapy for infections in cancer patients. J Antimicrob Chemother 1989; 24: 955–62.
12. Bolash NK, Liu HH. Oral and/or intravenous ciprofloxacin for treatment of multiply-resistant *Flavobacterium meningosepticum* septicaemia. Drugs 1993; 45 (Suppl 3): 430–1.
13. Sacks LV, Labriola AM, Gill VJ, Gordin FM. Use of ciprofloxacin for successful eradication of bacteremia due to *Campylobacter cinaedi* in a human immuno-deficiency virus-infected person. Rev Infect Dis 1991; 13: 1066–8.
14. Decker CF, Martin GJ, Barham WB, Paparello SF. Bacteremia due to *Campylobacter cinaedi* in a patient infected with the human immunodeficiency virus. Clin Infect Dis 1992; 15: 178–9.
15. Kalager T, Andersen BM, Bergan T, Brubakk O, Bruun JN, Døskeland B *et al*. Ciprofloxacin versus a tobramycin/cefuroxime combination in the treatment of serious systemic infections: a prospective randomized and controlled study of efficacy and safety. Scand J Infect Dis 1992; 24: 637–46.
16. Quintero-Perez NP, Andrade-Villanueva JF, Leon-Garnica G, Bertin-Montano M, Rodriguez-Chagollan JJ, Rodriguez-Noriega E. Efficacy and safety of intravenous ciprofloxacin in the treatment of serious infections. Am J Med 1989; 87 (Suppl 5A): 198–201.

17. Ramirez-Ronda C, Saavedra S, Rivera-Vazquez CR. Brief report: comparative, double-blind study of intravenous ciprofloxacin and intravenous ceftazidime in serious infection. Am J Med 1989; 87 (Suppl 5A): 195–7.

18. Sifuentes-Osornio J, Macias A, Amieva RI, Ramos A, Ruiz-Palacios GM. Intravenous ciprofloxacin and ceftazidime in serious infections. Am J Med 1989; 87 (Suppl 5A): 202–5.

19. Villavicencio J, de Fernandez MEA, Ramirez CA. Intravenous ciprofloxacin or ceftazidime in selected infections. A prospective, randomized, controlled study. Am J Med 1989; 87 (Suppl 5A): 191–4.

20. Peacock JE, Pegram PS, Weber ST, Leone PA. Prospective, randomized comparison of sequential intravenous followed by oral ciprofloxacin with intravenous ceftazidime in the treatment of serious infections. Am J Med 1989; 87 (Suppl 5A): 185–90.

21. Levine DP, McNeil P, Lerner SA. Randomized, double-blind comparative study of intravenous ciprofloxacin in the treatment of serious infections. Am J Med 1989; 87 (Suppl 5A): 160–3.

22. Gallis HA, Brennan RO, Goodwin SD, Swinney V, Rumbaugh MM, Drew RH. Comparison of the safety and efficacy of intravenous ceftazidime in the treatment of selected infections. Am J Med 1989; 87 (Suppl 5A): 176–80.

23. Fass RJ, Plouffe JR, Russell JA. Intravenous/oral ciprofloxacin versus ceftazidime in the treatment of serious infections. Am J Med 1989; 87 (Suppl 5A): 164–8.

24. Gangji D, Jacobs F, de Jonckheer J, Coppens L, Serruys E, Hanotte F et al. Brief report: randomized study of intravenous versus sequential intravenous/oral regimen of ciprofloxacin in the treatment of Gram-negative septicaemia. Am J Med 1989; 87 (Suppl 5A): 206–8.

25. Daly JS, Worthington MG, Razvi SA, Robillard R. Brief report: intravenous and sequential intravenous and oral ciprofloxacin in the treatment of severe infections. Am J Med 1989; 87 (Suppl 5A): 232–4.

26. Mertes PM, Voiriot P, Dopff C, Scholl H, Clavey M, Villemot JP et al. Penetration of ciprofloxacin into heart valves, myocardium, mediastinal fat and sternal bone marrow in humans. Antimicrob Agents Chemother 1990; 34: 398–401.

27. Daikos GL, Kathpalia SB, Lolans VT, Jackson GG, Fosslien E. Long term oral ciprofloxacin: experience in the treatment of incurable infective endocarditis. Am J Med 1988; 84: 786–90.

28. Uzun Ö, Akalin HE, Ünal S, Demircin M, Yorgancioğlu AC, Uğurlu B. Long term oral ciprofloxacin in the treatment of prosthetic valve endocarditis due to Pseudomonas aeruginosa. Scand J Infect Dis 1992; 24: 797–800.

29. Breuer J, Bragman SGL, Sahathevan MD, Philpott-Howard JN, Casewell MW. The possible role of ciprofloxacin in the treatment of endocarditis caused by Pseudomonas aeruginosa. J Infect 1988; 16: 106–7.

30. Hufnagel B, Saul F, Rosin H, Polonius MJ, Losse B. Mitralklappenendokarditis durch Salmonella enteritidis. Z Kardiol 1993; 82: 654–7.

31. Choo PW, Gantz NM, Anderson C, Maguire JH. Salmonella prosthetic valve endocarditis. Diagn Microbiol Infect Dis 1992; 15: 273–6.

32. Bíró L, Lengyel M, Koltai M és Hodics. Salmonella enteritidis endocarditis. Orv Hetil 1995; 136: 777–9.

33. O'Neill D, Landis SJ, Carey LS. Salmonella infection of a ventricular aneurysm. Clin Infect Dis 1992; 14: 175–7.

34. Oskoui R, Davis WA, Gomes MN. Salmonella aortitis. Arch Intern Med 1993; 153: 517–25.

35. Parry CM, Cheesbrough JS, Corcoran GD. Salmonella dublin infection of a prosthetic vascular graft successfully treated with ciprofloxacin. J Infect 1991; 22: 175–7.

36. Heldman AW, Hartert TV, Ray SC, Daourd EG, Kowalski TE, Pompili VJ et al. Oral antibiotic treatment of right-sided staphylococcal endocarditis in injection drug users: prospective randomized comparison with parenteral therapy. Am J Med 1996; 10: 68–76.

37. Dworkin RJ, Sande MA, Lee BL, Chambers HF. Treatment of right sided Staphylococcus aureus endocarditis in intravenous drug users with ciprofloxacin and rifampicin. Lancet 1989; ii: 1071–3.

38. Tebas P, Martinez-Ruiz R, Roman F, Mendaza P, Rodriguez-Diaz JC, Daza R et al. Early resistance to rifampicin and ciprofloxacin in the treatment of right-sided Staphylococcus aureus endocarditis. J Infect Dis 1991; 163: 204–5.

39. Ena J, Amador C, Parras F, Bouza E. Ciprofloxacin as an effective antibacterial agent in Serratia endocarditis. J Infect 1991; 22: 103–5.

40. Tucker RM, Baldwin JC, Pohlod DJ, Saravolatz LD, Remington JS. Ciprofloxacin for the treatment of endocarditis due to Legionella pneumophila. Rev Infect Dis 1989; 11 (Suppl 5): S1203–4.

41. Dawson SJ, White LA. Treatment of Haemophilus aphrophilus endocarditis with ciprofloxacin. J Infect 1992; 24: 317–20.

42. Anderson MD, Miller LK. Endocarditis due to Neisseria mucosa. Clin Infect Dis 1993; 16: 184.

43. MacGowan AP, Reeves DS, Wright C, Glover SC. Tricuspid valve infective endocarditis and pulmonary sepsis due to Erysipelothrix rhusiopathiae successfully treated with high doses of ciprofloxacin but complicated by gynaecomastia. J Infect 1991; 22: 100–1.

44. Yebra M, Ortigosa J, Albarran F, Crespo MG. Ciprofloxacin in a case of Q fever endocarditis. N Engl J Med 1990; 323: 614.

45. Arcieri G, August R, Becker N, Doyle C, Griffith E, Gruenwald G et al. Clinical experience with ciprofloxacin. Eur J Clin Microbiol 1986; 5: 220–5.

46. Pien FD, Yamane KK. Ciprofloxacin treatment of soft tissue and respiratory infections in community outpatient practice. Am J Med 1987; 82 (Suppl 4A): 236–8.

47. Campoli-Richards DM, Monk JP, Price A, Benfield P, Todd PA, Ward A. Ciprofloxacin. A review of its antibacterial activity, pharmacokinetic properties and therapeutic use. Drugs 1988; 35: 373–447.

48. Kelsey SM, Wood ME, Shaw E, Jenkins GC, Newland AC. A comparative study of intravenous ciprofloxacin and benzylpenicillin versus netilmicin and piperacillin for the empirical treatment of fever in neutropenic patients. J Antimicrob Chemother 1990; 25: 149–57.

49. Kelsey SM, Collins PW, Delord C, Weinhard B, Newland AC. A randomized study of teicoplanin plus ciprofloxacin versus gentamicin plus piperacillin for the empirical treatment of fever in neutropenic patients. Br J Haematol 1990; 76 (Suppl 2): 10–13.

50. Somolinos N, Arranz R, Del Rey MC, Jimenez ML. Superinfections by *Escherichia coli* resistant to fluoro-quinolones in immunocompromised patients. J Antimicrob Chemother 1992; 30: 730–1.

51. Snydman DR, Barza M, McGowan K, Kaplan K, Cuchural GC. Randomised comparative trial of ciprofloxacin for treatment of patients with osteomyelitis. Rev Infect Dis 1989; 11(Suppl 5): S1271–2.

52. Khan FA. Sequential intravenous–oral administration of ciprofloxacin vs ceftazidime in serious bacterial res-piratory tract infections. Chest 1989; 96: 528–37.

53. Maggiolo F, Bianchi W, Ohnmeiss H. Clinical and microbiological evaluation of ciprofloxacin in respira-tory tract infections. 4th European Congress of Clinical Microbiology, Nice, France, 1989: Abstract 127/PP3.

54. Gleadhill IC, Ferguson WP, Lowry RC. Efficacy and safety of ciprofloxacin in patients with respiratory infections in comparison with amoxycillin. J Antimicrob Chemother 1986; 18 (Suppl D): 133–8.

55. Van der Waaij D. Colonization pattern of the digestive tract by potentially pathogenic microorganisms: colo-nization-controlling mechanisms and consequences for antibiotic treatment. Infection 1983; 11 (Suppl 2): 90–2.

56. Pecquet S, Ravoire S, Andremont A. Faecal excretion of ciprofloxacin after a single dose and its effect on faecal bacteria in healthy volunteers. J Antimicrob Chemother 1990; 26: 125–9.

57. Holt HA, Lewis DA, White LO, Bastable SY, Reeves DS. Effect of oral ciprofloxacin on the faecal flora of healthy volunteers. Eur J Clin Microbiol 1986; 5: 201–5.

58. Nord CE. Effect of new quinolones on the human gastrointestinal microflora. Rev Infect Dis 1988; 10 (Suppl 1): S193–6.

59. Brumfitt W, Franklin I, Grady D, Hamilton-Miller JMT, Iliffe A. Changes in the pharmacokinetics of ciprofloxacin and fecal flora during administration of a 7-day course to human volunteers. Antimicrob Agents Chemother 1984; 26: 757–61.

60. Hoffler U, Grunig F, Brehmer B. Effect of oral ciprofloxacin on fecal bacteria in elderly patients. 6th Medical Congress on Chemotherapy, Taormina, Italy, 1988: 161–3.

61. Esposito S, Barba D, Galante D, Gaeta GB, Laghezza O. Intestinal microflora changes induced by ciprofloxacin and treatment of portal-systemic encephalopathy. Drugs Exp Clin Res 1987; 10: 641–6.

62. Bergan T, Delin C, Johansen S, Kolstad IM, Nord CE, Thorsteinsson SB. Pharmacokinetics of ciprofloxacin and effect of repeated dosage on salivary and fecal microflora. Antimicrob Agents Chemother 1986; 29: 298–302.

63. De Vries-Hospers HG, Welling GW, van der Waaij D. Influence of quinolones on throat and faecal flora of healthy volunteers. Pharm Weekbl (Sci) 1987; 9: 41–4.

64. Wistrom J, Gentry LO, Palmgren AC, Price M, Nord CE, Ljungh A *et al*. Ecological effects of short term ciprofloxacin treatment of traveller's diarrhoea. J Antimicrob Chemother 1992; 30: 693–706.

65. Rozenberg-Arska M, Dekker AW, Verhoef J. Ciprofloxacin for selective decontamination of the alimentary tract in patients with acute leukemia during remission induction treatment: the effect on faecal flora. J Infect Dis 1985; 152: 104–7.

66. Dekker A, Rozenberg-Arska M, Verhoef J. Infection prophylaxis in acute leukaemia: a comparison of ciprofloxacin with trimethoprim–sulfamethoxazole and colisitin. Ann Intern Med 1987; 106: 7–12.

67. Donnelly JP, Maschmeyer G, Daenen S. Selective oral antimicrobial prophylaxis for the prevention of infection in acute leukaemia – ciprofloxacin versus co-trimoxazole plus colistin. Eur J Cancer 1992; 28A: 873–8.

68. D'Antonio D, Piccolomini R, Iacone A, Fiortoni G, Parruti G, Betti S *et al*. Comparison of ciprofloxacin, ofloxacin and pefloxacin for the prevention of bacterial infection in neutropenic patients with haematological malignancies. J Antimicrob Chemother 1994; 33: 837–44.

Chapter 7

Urinary tract infection

Early studies using ciprofloxacin for urinary tract infection indicated high cure rates of 98% (502/514), 95% (574/602) and 87% (803/924).[1] Predictably, cure rates were higher in uncomplicated infections (98%, 282/287) than in complicated upper or lower urinary tract infections (79%, 70/89; 74%, 241/325, respectively).[2] The activity of ciprofloxacin against most Gram-negative species, including *Pseudomonas* spp., and its oral administration have resulted in an increasing popularity for its use as treatment of complicated urinary tract infections.

Uncomplicated infections

The increase in resistance of bacterial pathogens to common agents such as amoxycillin or trimethoprim has encouraged the assessment and use of ciprofloxacin in general practice. If the need for retreatment is reduced, cost savings will be made (see Chapter 17). However, the widespread use of ciprofloxacin in the community may ultimately reduce its usefulness in hospital-acquired infections by exerting a selective pressure for bacterial resistance. As observed with other agents, susceptibility of community-acquired urinary pathogens to ciprofloxacin has declined slowly in the UK since 1984 (94% in 1984, 90% in 1992).[3]

Ciprofloxacin is at least as effective as comparative antibiotics in randomised trials. In a comparison of ciprofloxacin (250 mg, given every 12 hours for 5 days) with co-amoxiclav (375 mg, given every 8 hours for 5 days), treatment failed in only 2 of 102 patients given ciprofloxacin compared with 10 of 87 given co-amoxiclav ($p < 0.01$).[4] No isolates developed resistance to ciprofloxacin. In elderly patients, cure was reported in all 16 given ciprofloxacin and in 15 of 16 given trimethoprim.[5] All 46 patients given ciprofloxacin for 10 days in another study were cured or improved compared with 43 of 45 given co-trimoxazole.[6] Persistent infection was noted in 2% of those given ciprofloxacin versus 13% of the control group. All 28 patients given ciprofloxacin (500 mg every 12 hours) to treat infections resistant to co-trimoxazole were cured. Another double-blind trial reported no treatment failures in 31 patients given ciprofloxacin and 2 failures in 34 given co-trimoxazole.[7] A non-randomised trial also reported similar cure rates to co-trimoxazole (54/59 versus 14/16).[8]

The duration of treatment has been investigated in three double-blind trials described by Iravani *et al* .[9] A single oral dose of 500 mg in the first trial, and 100 mg or 250 mg, every 12 hours for 3 days in the second trial, were compared with 250 mg every 12 hours for 7 days. In the third trial, 500 mg given orally once daily for 3 or 5 days was compared with norfloxacin, 400 mg every 12 hours for 7 days. In the three trials, 425 of the 1389 patients were not evaluable, usually because of failure to isolate a pathogen. A significantly higher bacterial

Wilson APR and Grüneberg RN.
Ciprofloxacin: 10 years of clinical experience
© 1997 Maxim Medical, Oxford.

eradication rate was found in patients given a 7-day course compared with those given a single dose (101/103 versus 95/107, $p = 0.01$). However, the bacteriological efficacy was similar in the two 3-day courses to that in the 7-day course (98/105, 95/105, 98/106, respectively). Similar success was achieved whether once-daily ciprofloxacin was given for 3 or 5 days, or norfloxacin was given for 7 days (137/149, 134/149, 133/141, respectively).

Single-dose regimens using 100 mg and 250 mg of ciprofloxacin produced similar results (16/19 versus 17/19).[10] Patients with liver disease responded equally well to treatment whether a single dose of 500 mg, 250 mg every 12 hours, or 500 mg every 12 hours were given (20/20, 19/20, 20/22, respectively).[11] Although single-dose treatments ensure compliance, are cheap and reduce the risk of adverse effects, they should be used only in uncomplicated infections in non-pregnant women. Three-day regimens are preferred in most cases. Men need investigation of any urinary infection except in old age and pregnant women should be treated with a β-lactam following investigation.

The incidence of adverse effects associated with ciprofloxacin was not significantly different from those of comparative antibiotics, but in one trial there was a trend to a higher proportion of patients affected during treatment with co-trimoxazole (3/13 versus 10/34).[7] Headaches and nausea were the most common effects. In one trial, 2 of 102 (2%) patients given ciprofloxacin reported adverse effects while 4 of 87 (5%) given co-amoxiclav were affected.[4]

Complicated infections

Complicated urinary tract infections are a common indication for the use of ciprofloxacin because they are often caused by *Pseudomonas* spp. and other Enterobacteriaceae resistant to trimethoprim and amoxycillin. Paraplegic patients often have permanent urethral or suprapubic catheters, or intermittently self-catheterise, and are particularly prone to repeated infection. In nursing homes, urinary tract infections are the principal cause of bacteraemia but resistance to agents other than ciprofloxacin is common.

Controlled trials

Most trials have used small numbers of patients so their usefulness in distinguishing the efficacy of different treatments is limited. In addition, many require pathogens to be susceptible to all trial antibiotics. One trial thereby excluded half the patients because of bacterial resistance to the comparator agent, cephalexin, risking a selective bias. Nevertheless, the efficacy of ciprofloxacin was the same in those excluded as those in-cluded (ciprofloxacin 30/30, cephalexin 24/30, cephalexin-resistant organisms treated with ciprofloxacin 56/59).[12]

Ciprofloxacin, 500 mg every 12 hours for 7–10 days, was compared with the aminoglycoside, gentamicin, 1 mg/kg every 8 hours for 7 days, in the treatment of predominantly symptomatic catheter-related infections.[13] A total of 30 of the 37 patients given ciprofloxacin and 18 of the 28 patients given gentamicin were paraplegic. The cure rate was similar in the two groups (30/37 and 23/28, respectively). Bacteriological success was greater with ciprofloxacin at 5–9 days after the end of treatment. The same comparison was made in another 76 patients, again with no significant difference between the two (20/34 versus 21/27).[14] However, there were significantly fewer relapses in patients given ciprofloxacin (500 mg, orally every 12 hours) than in those given tobramycin, with or without ampicillin, followed by oral co-trimoxazole (0/40 versus 6/39, $p = 0.02$).[15] Re-infection was observed in 8 and 6 patients, respectively.

Ciprofloxacin was significantly more effective in complicated infection than norfloxacin (104/131 versus 81/121, $p < 0.05$) including those patients with catheters or in whom treatment had previously failed.[16] Bacteriological eradication was significantly more likely following ciprofloxacin (170/190 versus 138/173, $p < 0.025$). Smaller trials found no significant difference between the two antibiotics (29/30 versus 29/30, 28/35 versus 27/37).[17,18] Efficacy of ciprofloxacin was found to be similar to that of ofloxacin in a double-blind comparison (19/22 versus 15/18),[19] and parenteral courses of both ciprofloxacin and ofloxacin may be successfully completed by oral treatment (20/20 versus 20/20).[20] Ciprofloxacin (500 mg every 12 hours for 7–14 days) was as effective as lomefloxacin (400 mg once daily for 7–14 days) (67/70 versus 70/72).[21] A low intravenous dose of ciprofloxacin (200 mg/day) produces a similar outcome to mezlocillin (2 g every 12 hours) (18/20 versus 17/20).[22]

Similar results have been obtained in complicated infections whether the daily oral dose of ciprofloxacin is 0.5 g, 1 g or 1.5 g for 7 days (42/43 versus 36/37 versus 41/43, respectively).[23]

Uncontrolled trials

Ciprofloxacin produces a high early cure rate even in difficult infections but relapses or re-infections are not uncommon. Of 28 patients, 23 were free of infection 1 week after treatment with ciprofloxacin (250 mg every 12 hours for 10 days) but only 18 remained free after 1 month.[24] An initial cure of pseudomonal urinary infection was achieved in 25 of 28 paraplegic or disabled patients after a 5-day course of treatment, but infection had recurred in nine patients by 1 month.[25] Bacteriological cure was achieved in 23 of 28 patients with pseudomonal infections after treating for 7–14 days. Two patients had recurring infections within a month.[26] All 83 patients with serious urinary tract infections in another study responded to ciprofloxacin, 0.5–0.75 g given orally once daily.[27] A total of 5 infections recurred and 6 patients developed urinary tract colonization with yeasts. Re-infection but not relapse was found to be responsible for a return of bacteriuria in 11 of 33 patients previously treated with ciprofloxacin.[28] In another 36 paraplegic or tetraplegic patients with multi-resistant infections, 35 responded during treatment with ciprofloxacin, 250 mg every 12 hours.[29] By day 35, 92% of patients had

bacteriuria again. High rates of superinfection (8/32) and re-infection (3/32) have been reported in a trial using a dose of 1 g per day to treat multi-resistant infections.[30]

Very long courses of oral treatment were used in one study of pseudomonal infections (28 days for cystitis, 83 days for pyelonephritis and 84 days for prostatitis).[31] All cystitis infections were cleared compared with 10 of 17 chronic pyelonephritis and 10 of 15 prostatitis. Resistant pathogens emerged during treatment in 5 patients and in 7 patients the infection recurred during follow-up.

A total of 10 of 11 elderly patients with asymptomatic bacteriuria were cured by a single 500 mg dose of ciprofloxacin, as were 13 of 15 patients with previous urological infections who were given 250 mg every 12 hours for 7 days.[32] It is not clear if such treatment is clinically beneficial because asymptomatic bacteriuria is common in elderly patients and rarely justifies treatment.

Pyelonephritis

Ciprofloxacin is effective in the treatment of acute pyelonephritis. A double-blind, randomised comparison of ciprofloxacin (500 mg administered orally every 12 hours for 10 days) and rufloxacin (400 mg then 200 mg administered orally once daily for 10 days) recruited 110 patients with suspected pyelonephritis.[33] Of these, 47 were excluded, usually because urinary culture was negative. Bacteriological eradication was achieved in 29 of 35 (83%) evaluable patients given ciprofloxacin, and 18 of 28 (64%) patients given rufloxacin. However, clinical cure or improvement was observed in 34 of 37 (92%) ciprofloxacin patients and in all 29 (100%) rufloxacin patients.

The cure rate in another randomised study was identical at a dose of 100 mg given intravenously every 12 hours for 5 days to that of netilmicin (15/17 versus 15/17).[34] However, the use of oral administration of ciprofloxacin to complete the course resulted in a significantly shorter in-patient stay (3.7 days versus 5.3 days).

Prostatitis and epididymo-orchitis

Prostatitis is the commonest cause of relapsing urinary infection in men. Back or perineal pain and dysuria are common symptoms. Ciprofloxacin is one of the few antibiotics to produce high prostatic fluid concentrations and fewer bacteria are resistant to it than to tetracycline or trimethoprim. Of 32 patients given 500 mg every 12 hours for 4 weeks, cure or improvement was achieved in 29.[35] Six other patients were cured by a 3–6-month course.[36] A 2-week course of ciprofloxacin, at a dose of 1 g/day, cured 10 patients with prostatitis caused by *Escherichia coli*, but only 1 of 3 patients infected with *Enterococcus* spp. and neither of the patients who were infected with *Pseudomonas aeruginosa*.[37]

Epididymo-orchitis was treated successfully with ciprofloxacin (14/14) or ampicillin plus gentamicin (15/16) in a randomised trial.[38] Use of the oral route during ciprofloxacin treatment allowed the patient to be treated outside hospital (see Chapter 17).

Conclusions

Ciprofloxacin is highly effective in both uncomplicated and complicated urinary infections and the prevalence of bacterial resistance remains low. A 3-day regimen (100–250 mg administered orally every 12 hours) is sufficient in uncomplicated community-acquired infection, but effective, cheaper alternatives are available for first episodes. In view of its broad antibacterial spectrum, ciprofloxacin is better reserved for complicated, hospital-acquired or recurrent infections and is particularly useful as an oral treatment of urinary infections in paraplegic patients or those needing repeated catheterisation. A higher dose is required than for uncomplicated infection (500 mg administered orally every 12 hours for 7 days). Ciprofloxacin, 500–750 mg administered orally every 12 hours for 4–6 weeks, is used for the treatment of bacterial prostatitis.

References

1. Campoli-Richards DM, Monk JP, Price A, Benfield P, Todd PA, Ward A. Ciprofloxacin. A review of its antibacterial activity, pharmacokinetic properties and therapeutic use. Drugs 1988; 35; 373–447.
2. Kumazawa J. Clinical evaluation of BAY 09867 in the urological infections in Japan. 14th International Congress of Chemotherapy, Kyoto, Japan, 1985: Abstract WS-6-9.
3. Grüneberg RN. Changes in urinary pathogens and their antibiotic sensitivities, 1971–1992. J Antimicrob Chemother 1994; 33 (Suppl A): 1–8.
4. Abbas AMA, Chandra V, Dongaonkar PP, Goel PK, Kacker P, Patel NA *et al*. Ciprofloxacin versus amoxycillin/clavulanic acid in the treatment of urinary tract infections in general practice. J Antimicrob Chemother 1989; 24: 235–9.
5. Newsom SWB, Murphy P, Matthews J. A comparative study of ciprofloxacin and trimethoprim in the treatment of urinary tract infections in geriatric patients. J Antimicrob Chemother 1986; 18 (Suppl D): 111–15.
6. Childs SJ. Ciprofloxacin in the outpatient treatment of urinary tract infections. In: Ishijami J, ed. Recent advances in chemotherapy. Proceedings of the 14th International Congress of Chemotherapy. Tokyo: University of Tokyo Press, 1985: 1632–3.
7. Henry NK, Schultz HJ, Grubbs NC, Muller SM, Ilstrup DM, Wilson WR. Comparison of ciprofloxacin and co-trimoxazole in the treatment of uncomplicated urinary tract infections in women. J Antimicrob Chemother 1986; 18 (Suppl D): 103–6.
8. Williams AH, Grüneberg RN. Ciprofloxacin and co-trimoxazole in urinary tract infection. J Antimicrob Chemother 1986; 18 (Suppl D): 107–10.
9. Iravani A, Tice AD, McCarty J, Sikes DH, Nolen T, Galis HA *et al*. Short course ciprofloxacin treatment of acute uncomplicated urinary tract infection in women. Arch Intern Med 1995; 155: 485–94.
10. Garlando F, Rietiker S, Tauber MG, Flepp M, Meier B, Luthy R. Single dose ciprofloxacin at 100 versus 250 mg for treatment of uncomplicated urinary tract infections in women. Antimicrob Agents Chemother 1987; 31: 354–6.
11. Esposito S, Galante D, Barba D, Bianchi W, Gagliardi R, Giusti R. Efficacy and safety of ciprofloxacin in the treatment of UTIs and RTIs in patients affected by liver diseases. Infection 1988; 16 (Suppl 1): S57–61.
12. Polubiec A, Weuta H, Stepka K, Ktos K, Stazynska R, Jorasz J. Bacterial infections of the lower urinary tract treated with ciprofloxacin or cefalexin – a comparative study. Infection 1988; 16 (Suppl 1): S62–4.
13. Fang G, Brennen C, Wagener M, Swanson D, Hilf M, Zadecky L *et al*. Use of ciprofloxacin versus use of aminoglycosides for therapy of complicated urinary tract infection: prospective, randomized clinical and pharmacokinetic study. Antimicrob Agents Chemother 1991; 35: 1849–55.

14. Mehtar S, Drabu Y, Sanderson P, Perinpanayagam M, Chapman S. Ciprofloxacin versus gentamicin in complicated urinary tract infections. 17th International Congress of Chemotherapy, Berlin, Germany, 1991: Abstract 1752.

15. Harding G, Nicolle L, Wenman W, Richards G, Louie T, Martel A *et al*. Randomised comparison of oral ciprofloxacin vs standard parenteral therapy in the treatment of complicated urinary tract infections. Drugs 1993; 45 (Suppl 3): 333–4.

16. Kumazawa J, Matsumoto T, Tsuchida S, Niijima T, Machida T, Ohkoshi M *et al*. Comparative clinical study of ciprofloxacin and norfloxacin in the treatment of complicated urinary tract infections. Nishinihon J Urol 1987; 49: 1620–2.

17. Naber KG, Bartosik-Wich B. Ciprofloxacin versus norfloxacin in the treatment of complicated urinary tract infections: in vitro activity, serum and urine concentrations, safety and therapeutic efficacy. 1st International Ciprofloxacin Workshop, Leverkusen, Germany, 1985: 314–17.

18. Schaeffer AJ, Anderson RU. Efficacy and tolerability of norfloxacin vs. ciprofloxacin in complicated urinary tract infection. Urology 1992; 40: 446–9.

19. Kromann-Andersen B, Sommer P, Pers C, Larsen V, Rasmussen F. Ofloxacin compared with ciprofloxacin in the treatment of complicated lower urinary tract infections. J Antimicrob Chemother 1988; 22 (Suppl C): 143–7.

20. Peters HJ. Sequential therapy with ofloxacin in complicated urinary tract infections: a randomized comparative study with ciprofloxacin. Infection 1992; 20: 172–3.

21. Cox CE. A comparison of the safety and efficacy of lomefloxacin and ciprofloxacin in the treatment of complicated or recurrent urinary tract infections. Am J Med 1992; 92 (Suppl 4A): 82–6.

22. Peters HJ. Comparison of intravenous ciprofloxacin and mezlocillin in treatment of complicated urinary tract infection. Eur J Clin Microbiol 1986; 5: 253–5.

23. Gasser TC, Graversen PH, Madsen PO. Treatment of complicated urinary tract infections with ciprofloxacin. Am J Med 1987; 82 (Suppl 4A): 278–9.

24. Boerema J, Boll B, Muytjens H, Branolte J. Efficacy and safety of ciprofloxacin (BAY 09867) in the treatment of patients with complicated urinary tract infections. J Antimicrob Chemother 1985; 16: 211–17.

25. Leigh DA, Emmanuel FXS, Petch VJ. Ciprofloxacin therapy in complicated urinary tract infections caused by *Pseudomonas aeruginosa* and other resistant bacteria. J Antimicrob Chemother 1986; 18 (Suppl D): 117–21.

26. Saavedra S, Ramirez-Ronda CH, Nevarez M. Ciprofloxacin in the treatment of urinary tract infections caused by *Pseudomonas aeruginosa* and multiresistant bacteria. Eur J Clin Microbiol 1986; 5: 255–7.

27. Fass RJ. Efficacy and safety of oral ciprofloxacin for treatment of serious urinary tract infections. Antimicrob Agents Chemother 1987; 31: 148–50.

28. Cox C. Brief report. Ciprofloxacin in the treatment of urinary tract infections caused by *Pseudomonas* species and organisms resistant to trimethoprim/sulphamethoxazole. Am J Med 1987; 82 (Suppl 4A): 288–9.

29. Stannard AJ, Sharples SJ, Norman PM, Tillotson GS. Ciprofloxacin therapy of urinary tract infections in paraplegic and tetraplegic patients: a bacteriological assessment. J Antimicrob Chemother 1990; 26 (Suppl F): 13–18.

30. Ryan JL, Berenson CS, Greco TP, Mangi RJ, Sims M, Thornton GF *et al*. Oral ciprofloxacin in resistant urinary infections. Am J Med 1987; 82 (Suppl 4A): 303–6.

31. Guibert JM, Destrée DM, Acar JF. Ciprofloxacin (BAY 09867): clinical evaluation in urinary tract infections due to *Pseudomonas aeruginosa*. Chemioterapia 1987; 6 (Suppl 2): 524–5.

32. Del Rio G, Mestre J, Dalet F. Prevalence and treatment of asymptomatic bacteriuria in the elderly. Drugs 1993; 45 (Suppl 3): 349–50.

33. Bach D, van den Berg-Segers A, Hubner A, van Breukelen G, Cesana M, Pletan Y. Rufloxacin once daily versus ciprofloxacin twice daily in the treatment of patients with acute uncomplicated pyelonephritis. J Urol 1995; 154: 19–24.

34. Bailey RR, Lynn KL, Robson RA, Peddie BA, Smith A. Comparison of ciprofloxacin with netilmicin for the treatment of acute pyelonephritis. N Z Med J 1992; 105: 102–3.

35. Langmeyer TNM, Ferwerda WHH, Hoogkamp-Korstanje J AA, de Leur EJA, van Oort H, Schipper JJ *et al*. Treatment of chronic bacterial prostatitis with ciprofloxacin. Pharm Weekbl (Sci) 1987; 9 (Suppl): S78–81.

36. Pfau A. The treatment of chronic bacterial prostatitis. Infection 1991; 19 (Suppl 3): S160–4.

37. Weidner W, Schiefer HG, Dalhoff A. Treatment of chronic bacterial prostatitis with ciprofloxacin: results of a one year follow up study. Am J Med 1987; 82 (Suppl 4A): 280–3.

38. Reif W, Bornman MS, Mutamirwa S. A comparative study with ciprofloxacin in patients with acute epididymo-orchitis. Drugs 1993; 45 (Suppl 3): 351.

Chapter 8

Respiratory tract infection

The increasing resistance of many respiratory pathogens to the antibiotics used against them and the identification of 'new' infectious agents, such as *Chlamydia pneumoniae*, suggest that there is a place for the use of quinolones in respiratory infection. While ciprofloxacin is highly active against *Haemophilus influenzae* and *Moraxella catarrhalis*, it is less active against *Streptococcus pneumoniae*. Nevertheless, in recent reviews a high cure rate has been reported for ciprofloxacin, plus equivalence with most comparators and superiority over some of the cephalosporins.[1] In acute-on-chronic bronchitis, trials using clinical endpoints have suggested that ciprofloxacin is effective, whereas those using bacteriological endpoints report lower response rates because of the persistence of pneumococci.[1] The minimum inhibitory concentration (MIC) of ciprofloxacin against *Streptococcus pneumoniae* is 1–2 mg/litre, while the concentrations in sputum and bronchial secretions are 1–4 mg/litre. Consequently, efficacy against pneumococcal infection has been the subject of many investigations (Table 8.1).[2–46]

Upper respiratory tract infections

Most upper respiratory tract infections are caused by viruses and should be treated

symptomatically without further investigation. If, by its clinical appearance, the infection is suspected to be bacterial, the penicillins are both effective and cheap and should be used in preference to the quinolones. Ciprofloxacin is an effective alternative, however, and may be needed for specific infections (e.g. malignant otitis externa or chronic bacterial sinusitis).

In a trial carried out by García-Rodríguez *et al.*, ciprofloxacin, 250 mg orally every 12 hours, was effective in 126 of 133 (95%) patients with upper respiratory tract infections.[47] Pain was relieved in 102 of 118 (86%) patients. Otitis media was cured or improved in 37 of 42 (88%) patients, sinusitis in 34 of 35 (97%) patients, pharyngotonsillitis in 33 of 34 (97%) patients, and mixed infections in 22 of 22 (100%) patients. In another open trial, 154 patients were treated for sinusitis with ciprofloxacin, 0.5–1 g/day for 1 week. Cure was achieved in 124 (81%), 28 (18%) improved, and treatment failed in only 2 patients (1%).[48] In further trials, radio-opacity disappeared in 90 of 91 (99%) patients with sinusitis given ciprofloxacin, 1 g/day for 10 days,[49] and sinusitis and otitis media were also cured or improved in 37 of 39 (95%) patients given ciprofloxacin, 300–600 mg/day.[50]

Treatment of acute sinusitis was assessed in a large, double-blind, randomised trial comparing ciprofloxacin, 500 mg given orally every 12 hours for 10 days, and clarithromycin, 500 mg given orally every 12 hours for 14 days.[51] The clinical response was significantly greater in the clarithromycin group 1–7 days after the completion of therapy (202/221 [91%] versus

Wilson APR and Grüneberg RN.
Ciprofloxacin: 10 years of clinical experience
© 1997 Maxim Medical, Oxford.

Table 8.1. Randomised, controlled trials of the use of ciprofloxacin in lower respiratory tract infections.

Disease	Year	Blind	Agent	Dose (mg/day)	Duration (days)	No. patients	No. men	Age (years)	No. withdrawn	No. cured	No. improved	No. failed (+ indeterminates*)	Quality	Reference
Chronic bronchitis	1990	NB	Ciprofloxacin Amoxycillin	1000–1500 p.o. 750–1500 p.o.	7 7	75 67	41 52	62 63	2 0	16 7	51 42	2 (+6) 11 (+7)	0.18	2
Pneumonia, bronchiectasis, lung abscess, acute bronchitis	1986	NB	Ciprofloxacin Amoxycillin	1000 p.o. 750 p.o.	5–10 4–10	26 22	14 11	69 74	0 0	12 7	9 11	4 (+1) 2 (+2)	0.38	3
Acute exacerbation of chronic bronchitis	1990	DB	Ciprofloxacin Ampicillin	500 p.o. 2000 p.o.	10 10	29 28	28 27	63 66	0 0	16 20	13 8	0 0	0.42	4
Acute-on-chronic bronchitis	1989	DB	Ciprofloxacin Ampicillin	1500 p.o. 2000 p.o.	14 14	22 22	17 17	35–69 35–69	0 0	22 22	0 0	0 0	0.43	5
Bronchitis	1987	DB	Ciprofloxacin Ampicillin	1500 p.o. 2000 p.o.	9 9	42 45	– –	– –	0 0	41 40	0 0	1 5	0.49	6
Bronchitis/ pneumonia	1987	NB	Ciprofloxacin Ampicillin	500 p.o. 1500 p.o.	10 10	40 40	21 22	51 56	0 0	38 34	2 6	0 0	0.14	7
LRTI	1988	NB	Ciprofloxacin Ampicillin	1000 p.o. 3000 p.o.	10 10	15 15	8 9	41–67 21–61	0 0	14 5	1 5	0 5	0.15	8
LRTI	1985	NB	Ciprofloxacin Cephalexin	1000 p.o. 2000 p.o.	7–13 7–13	30 30	29 29	35–83 34–81	2 7	27 22	0 0	1 1	0.15	9
COAD, bronchiectasis	1989	NB	Ciprofloxacin Ceftazidime	400 i.v./p.o. 3000 i.v./p.o.	4.8–7.4 9–9.6	37 34	13 15	67 63	0 0	36 33	0 0	1 1	0.27	10

*Indeterminates = number of patients neither withdrawn, cured, improved nor failed.
LRTI, lower respiratory tract infection; COAD, chronic obstructive airways disease; DB, double blind; NB, not blinded.

Table 8.1. (continued)

Disease	Year	Blind	Agent	Dose (mg/day)	Duration (days)	No. patients	No. men	Age (years)	No. withdrawn	No. cured	No. improved	No. failed (+ indeterminates*)	Quality	Reference
LRTI	1990	NB	Ciprofloxacin	400–600 i.v. then 1000–1500 p.o.	13	180	–	–	73	100	0	7	0.08	11
			Ceftazidime	4000 i.v./p.o.	10	173	–	–	77	91	0	5		
Community or nosocomial LRTI	1989	NB	Ciprofloxacin	400 i.v. then 1000 p.o.	5	66	–	–	8	60	0	6	0.21	12
			Ceftazidime	2000–6000 i.v.	5	56	–	–	10	50	0	6		
Pneumonia	1989	NB	Ciprofloxacin	400 i.v. then 1500 p.o.	–	17	10	21–70	0	13	4	0	0.14	13
			Ceftazidime	3000 i.v.	–	20	12	24–76	0	13	6	1		
Nosocomial pneumonia	1991	DB	Ciprofloxacin	600 i.v.	5–17	17	14	19–81	Not stated	15	0	2	0.44	14
			Ceftazidime	6000 i.v.	7–14	15	10	22–84	Not stated	13	0	2		
Pneumonia in elderly patients	1989	NB	Ciprofloxacin	200–1000 i.v./p.o.	2–10	24	10	56–102	1	23	0	0	0.26	15
			Ceftazidime	6000 i.v.	1–15	23	11	35–91	2	15	0	6		
Pneumonia in neutropenic patients	1993	NB	Ciprofloxacin + vancomycin	400 i.v.	–	26	–	–	0	23	0	3	0.13	16
			Ceftazidime + gentamicin	6000 i.v.	–	32	–	–	0	23	0	9		
Pneumonia in AIDS	1993	NB	Ciprofloxacin	1500 p.o.	–	17	–	–	0	10	2	5	0.18	17
			Cefotaxime	6000 i.v.	–	17	–	–	0	11	2	4		
Pneumonia	1996	DB	Ciprofloxacin	800 i.v./p.o.	9	107	–	19–90	57	44	0	5 (+1)	0.57	18
			Ceftriaxone	1000 i.v./p.o.	8	110	–	25–97	64	38	0	7 (+1)		
LRTI in elderly patients	1991	NB	Ciprofloxacin	400–1500 i.v./p.o.	2–6	24	13	65–101	2	12	0	10 (+2)	0.26	19
			Ceftriaxone	1–2 g i.v./i.m.	2–11	26	18	64–97	2	14	0	10 (+2)		

*Indeterminates = number of patients neither withdrawn, cured, improved nor failed.
LRTI, lower respiratory tract infection; DB, double blind; NB, not blinded.

Table 8.1. (continued)

Disease	Year	Blind	Agent	Dose (mg/day)	Duration (days)	No. patients	No. men	Age (years)	No. withdrawn	No. cured	No. improved	No. failed (+ indeterminates*)	Quality	Reference
LRTI	1992	NB	Ciprofloxacin	400–1500 i.v./p.o.	12	39	–	20–93	Not stated	37	0	2	0.37	20
			Tobramycin/ cefuroxime	By assay/ 4500	9.5	40	–	18–93	Not stated	34	0	6		
Bronchitis	1990	NB	Ciprofloxacin	1000 p.o.	13	28	5	48	0	20	6	2	0.18	21
			Cefaclor	750 p.o.	13	27	11	42	0	18	9	0		
Acute-on-chronic bronchitis, diffuse panbronchiolitis	1986	DB	Ciprofloxacin	600 p.o.	14	111	–	–	8	3	84	16	0.49	22
			Cefaclor	750 p.o.	14	119	–	–	17	0	60	37 (+5)		
Pneumonia, acute bronchitis	1988	NB	Ciprofloxacin	1500 p.o.	14	30	13	64–95	0	23	0	7	0.28	23
			Cefamandole	4000 p.o.	14	30	16	55–96	0	21	0	9		
LRTI	1991	NB	Ciprofloxacin	1000 p.o.	–	100	–	–	15	56	24	2 (+3)	0.21	24
			Co-amoxiclav	1875 p.o.	–	96	–	–	18	61	14	3		
Exacerbations of chronic bronchitis	1994	NB	Ciprofloxacin	1000 p.o.	10	70	–	–	0	60	0	10	0.06	25
			Co-amoxiclav	900 p.o.	10	78	–	–	0	71	0	7		
			Cefixime	400 p.o.	10	68	–	–	0	54	0	14		
Pneumonia, acute-on-chronic bronchitis	1989	NB	Ciprofloxacin	500 p.o.	–	34	–	–	1	26	0	7	0.11	26
			Co-amoxiclav	1875 p.o.	–	30	–	–	0	23	0	7		
Pneumonia, community acquired	1991	NB	Ciprofloxacin	1500 p.o.	5	41	25	61	11	22	0	8	0.23	27
			Co-amoxiclav	2000 p.o.	5	28	12	60	3	20	0	5		
			Erythromycin	3000 p.o.	5	16	14	65	8	7	0	1		
Chronic bronchitis	1992	DB	Ciprofloxacin	1000 p.o.	7–14	234	–	–	6	199	0	15 (+14)	0.48	28
			Roxithromycin	300 p.o.	7–14	235	–	–	4	176	0	29 (+26)		

*Indeterminates = number of patients neither withdrawn, cured, improved nor failed.
LRTI, lower respiratory tract infection; DB, double blind; NB, not blinded.

Table 8.1. (continued)

Disease	Year	Blind	Agent	Dose (mg/day)	Duration (days)	No. patients	No. men	Age (years)	No. withdrawn	No. cured	No. improved	No. failed (+ indeterminates*)	Quality	Reference
Acute-on-chronic bronchitis	1996	DB	Ciprofloxacin	1000 p.o.	14	185	–	–	18	147	0	20	0.41	29
			Clarithromycin	1000 p.o.	14	185	–	–	23	139	0	26		
Bronchitis	1989	NB	Ciprofloxacin	1000 p.o.	9	69	–	–	0	49	17	3	0.18	30
			Josamycin	2000 p.o.	9	62	–	–	0	31	17	14		
Bronchitis	1988	NB	Ciprofloxacin	500 p.o.	9	70	–	–	0	50	17	3	0.17	31
			Josamycin	2000 p.o.	9	62	–	–	0	31	17	14		
Acute-on-chronic bronchitis, pneumonia	1991	DB	Ciprofloxacin	1000 p.o.	7–14	188	38	20–95	121	58	5	4	0.49	32
			Temafloxacin	1200 p.o.	7–14	188	40	19–79	124	51	7	6		
Acute-on-chronic bronchitis, bronchiectasis	1992	DB	Ciprofloxacin	1500 p.o.	7–14	283	98	18–85	95	161	14	13	0.52	33, 34
			Temafloxacin	1200 p.o.	7–14	281	119	19–99	89	165	15	12		
LRTI in community	1991	DB	Ciprofloxacin	1000 p.o.	7–14	138	–	21–88	17	117	0	4	0.42	35
			Temafloxacin	600 p.o.	7–14	140	–	27–89	24	114	0	2		
Acute-on-chronic bronchitis, pneumonia	1993	NB	Ciprofloxacin	1000 p.o.	7–14	31	–	–	0	16	15	0	0.12	36
			Lomefloxacin	800 p.o.	7–14	28	–	–	0	12	16	0		
Acute-on-chronic bronchitis	1995	NB	Ciprofloxacin	1000 p.o.	7	89	–	–	0	81	0	8	0.08	37
			Rufloxacin	400 p.o.	5	90	–	–	0	80	0	10		
Acute-on-chronic bronchitis, pneumonia	1994	NB	Ciprofloxacin	500 p.o.	10–12	50	28	26–90	1	48	1	0	0.16	38
			Ofloxacin	400 p.o.	10–12	50	22	18–94	0	43	3	2 (+2)		

*Indeterminates = number of patients neither withdrawn, cured, improved nor failed.
LRTI, lower respiratory tract infection; DB, double blind; NB, not blinded.

Table 8.1. (continued)

Disease	Year	Blind	Agent	Dose (mg/day)	Duration (days)	No. patients	No. men	Age (years)	No. withdrawn	No. cured	No. improved	No. failed (+ indeterminates*)	Quality	Reference
Pneumonia, LRTI	1990	NB	Ciprofloxacin	200–600 i.v. or 1500 p.o.	13	98	–	–	16 (total) (individual group withdrawals unknown)	36	46	10	0.15	39
			Ofloxacin	400–600 i.v./p.o.	14	70	–	–		26	29	7		
			β-lactams	various	–	102	–	–		37	48	13		
Acute-on-chronic bronchitis	1995	NB	Ciprofloxacin	1000 p.o.	–	30	–	–	0	28	0	2	0.19	40
			Pefloxacin	800 i.v./p.o.	–	30/30	–	–	0	27/29	0	3/1		
Bronchitis	1989	NB	Ciprofloxacin	500 p.o.	5	28	14	42	1	23	4	0	0.17	41
			Co-trimoxazole	960 p.o.	5	28	10	41	0	8	16	4		
Acute-on-chronic bronchitis, bronchiectasis	1994	PB	Ciprofloxacin	1000 p.o.	–	104	71	25–85	66	19	16	2 (+1)	0.30	42
			Co-trimoxazole	1920 p.o.	–	113	70	27–82	86	14	10	3		
LRTI	1985	NB	Ciprofloxacin	1000 p.o.	9	15	–	56	0	11	4	0	0.17	43
			Co-trimoxazole	1920 p.o.	9	15	–	54	1	8	4	2		
Acute bronchitis, chronic bronchitis	1988	NB	Ciprofloxacin	500 p.o.	11	20	10	46	0	20	0	0	0.15	44
			Doxycycline	200 p.o.	11	20	11	49	0	20	0	0		
Bronchitis, pneumonia	1987	NB	Ciprofloxacin	500 p.o.	4–12	56	21	19–89	1	45	8	1 (+1)	0.22	45
			Doxycycline	100 p.o.	5–12	54	33	22–83	1	42	11	0		
Community and nosocomial pneumonia	1994	DB	Ciprofloxacin	1200 i.v.	10.5	205	140	59.9	107	68	0	30	0.64	46
			Imipenem	3000 i.v.	10.1	200	142	59.6	93	58	0	46 (+3)		

*Indeterminates = number of patients neither withdrawn, cured, improved nor failed.

LRTI, lower respiratory tract infection; DB, double blind; NB, not blinded; PB, patient blind.

199/236 [84%], $p < 0.05$) but by 28 days, resolution in the two groups was similar (168/175 [96%] for ciprofloxacin versus 169/187 [90%] for clarithromycin).

Chronic sinusitis is associated with infection by *Haemophilus influenzae*, Enterobacteriaceae, *Pseudomonas* spp., *Staphylococcus aureus* and streptococci. In a randomised, double-blind trial, ciprofloxacin, 1 g/day given orally, was compared with co-amoxiclav, 1.5 g/day, both over a 9-day course.[52] Cure or improvement was observed in 101 of the 118 (86%) patients given ciprofloxacin and 100 of the 123 (81%) patients given co-amoxiclav (p = ns). Bacteriological eradication was 80% in both groups. Ciprofloxacin (250 mg given orally every 12 hours) showed similar efficacy to cefuroxime axetil (250 mg given orally every 12 hours), given for 10–14 days in the treatment of patients with acute sinusitis or exacerbations of chronic bacterial sinusitis.[53] An open study using the same dose of ciprofloxacin reported a response rate of 85% (46/54).[54]

Ciprofloxacin has also been used as an oral treatment for chronic suppurative otitis media, a condition commonly caused by infection with *Pseudomonas aeruginosa*.[55] In a randomised trial with co-amoxiclav, 24 of the 40 (60%) patients given ciprofloxacin, 1 g/day, were cured compared with 13 of the 35 (37%) given co-amoxiclav, 500 mg orally every 8 hours.[55] Bacteriological eradication was also significantly more likely to occur in the ciprofloxacin group (23/33 versus 6/22, p = 0.01). In an open trial, exacerbation of chronic otitis was cured or improved in 49 of 69 (71%) patients.[56]

Malignant external otitis, caused by infection with *Pseudomonas aeruginosa*, is an invasive infection of the aural canal culminating in osteomyelitis of the petrous bone and meningitis. It occurs in individuals with diabetes and those with a suppressed immune system, and can involve the cranial nerves. Other organisms, such as *Staphylococcus aureus*, Enterobacteriaceae and anaerobes, are involved in 5% of cases. Ciprofloxacin has been given as an oral treatment in 13 trials, usually at a dose of 750 mg every 12 hours for 3 months.[57] All

of the 47 strains of *Pseudomonas aeruginosa* isolated from the patients in these trials were susceptible to ciprofloxacin. A clinical cure was achieved in 81 of the 84 (96%) cases and the organism eradicated in all except 1 case. In another review, 101 patients from several trials were treated with ciprofloxacin and 96 (95%) were cured 1 year later.[58]

Ciprofloxacin (0.2% and 0.5%) was used topically in the treatment of otitis media and externa. Of 50 patients, there were 8 treatment failures associated with chronic otitis media or following surgery.[59] The risk of resistance emerging during treatment was not discussed.

Lower respiratory tract infections

Nosocomial and ventilator-associated pneumonia

Gram-negative bacteria account for 60% of nosocomial pneumonias, *Staphylococcus aureus* causing 10–28% and *Streptococcus pneumoniae* 2–10%.[60] In the intensive care unit, *Pseudomonas aeruginosa* and *Staphylococcus aureus* are the most common pathogens. The work of Schentag (see Chapter 5) has shown that the MIC of *Pseudomonas aeruginosa* is not reliably exceeded at ciprofloxacin doses of 400 mg/day, and to achieve a satisfactory area under the inhibitory curve (AUIC) in the treatment of pseudomonal pneumonia, a dose of 400 mg every 8 hours is recommended.[61] In some cases, a combination of agents might be preferable until microbiological results are available.

In a large, multicentre, double-blind, randomised trial, the efficacy of ciprofloxacin was tested against that of imipenem in patients with severe pneumonia. The infections had been predominantly acquired in hospital and the patients required mechanical ventilation (Table 8.1).[46] Ciprofloxacin was administered intravenously at a dose of 400 mg every 8 hours and imipenem was administered intravenously at 1 g every 8 hours. As patients without a recognised causative organism were withdrawn, only 205 patients were evaluable (98 ciprofloxacin, 107 imipenem) of the 405 who enrolled. Vancomycin or metronidazole was given concomitantly in 43–47% of patients. Clinical response was significantly higher following treatment with ciprofloxacin (69% versus 56%, $p = 0.02$). Bacteriological eradication was also greater but the difference was not significant (69% versus 59%). Ciprofloxacin achieved eradication in 41 of the 44 (93%) patients infected with Enterobacteriaceae compared with 45 of the 68 (66%) patients treated with imipenem, persistence after imipenem being observed with *Enterobacter* spp., *Klebsiella* spp. and *Escherichia coli*. Failure was common in both groups when *Pseudomonas aeruginosa* was isolated before treatment (11/33 versus 11/27). Seizures were observed in only 3 of 202 (1%) patients given ciprofloxacin compared with 11 of 200 (6%) patients given imipenem ($p = 0.028$), but overall, the difference in adverse events was not significant (132/202 versus 148/200, $p = 0.06$).

A similar trial reported high rates of clinical success in patients given ciprofloxacin, ofloxacin or a β-lactam (imipenem, ticarcillin/clavulanic acid or cefpirome) for severe respiratory infections (82/92 versus 55/62 versus 85/98).[39] Most patients had underlying cardiac or respiratory diseases and a high proportion of the treatment failures were critically ill patients infected with *Staphylococcus aureus* or *Pseudomonas aeruginosa*.

In another randomised trial, Khan and Basir found ciprofloxacin, 200 mg intravenously every 12 hours, followed by 500 mg orally every 12 hours, and ceftazidime, 1–2 g intravenously every 8–12 hours to be similarly effective against severe nosocomial or community-acquired pneumonia (Table 8.1).[12] *Pseudomonas aeruginosa* was isolated in 25 patients and *Streptococcus pneumoniae* in 12 patients in the ciprofloxacin group. Of those given ciprofloxacin, 42 of 46 (91%) proven infections and 18 of 20 (90%) presumed infections were cured. In the ceftazidime group, 38 of 42 (90%) proven infections and 12 of

14 (86%) presumed infections were cured. All of the pneumococcal and all but one of the pseudomonal infections were cured by ciprofloxacin. Ciprofloxacin and ceftriaxone were also found to be of comparable efficacy in the treatment of lower respiratory tract infections in a study of elderly patients in nursing homes (12/24 versus 14/26).[19]

An uncontrolled trial of the treatment of Gram-negative pneumonia showed ciprofloxacin, 200 mg every 12 hours, to be effective in eradicating Enterobacteriaceae and *Haemophilus* spp.[62] However, in 10 of 13 patients with infections caused by *Pseudomonas* spp., the organism developed resistance to ciprofloxacin during treatment and persisted. In patients with serum concentrations exceeding the MIC of the organism for 95% of the dose interval, the organisms were eradicated but in treatment failures, the plasma concentration exceeded the MIC for only 75% of the interval. Similar findings have been reported from other studies.[63,64]

Cystic fibrosis

Patients with cystic fibrosis are subject to damaging colonisation and infective exacerbations arising from mucus-producing strains of *Pseudomonas aeruginosa*. Ciprofloxacin provides an oral alternative to in-patient parenteral treatment with penicillins and aminoglycosides or cephalosporins. Clinical trials have examined the use of ciprofloxacin as an oral treatment for chronic respiratory infection with *Pseudomonas aeruginosa* in adults rather than children with cystic fibrosis. In a small, double-blind crossover study of 21 patients, the clinical response was similar when either ciprofloxacin, 1.5 g/day orally, or ofloxacin, 800 mg/day orally, was used for 2 weeks.[65] A four-fold increase in MIC was seen in 7 patients given ciprofloxacin and 3 patients given ofloxacin, but clinically significant resistance was observed in only 1 patient (in the ofloxacin group). As is the case with other antibiotics, the improvement was not maintained 3 months later. Another trial of 40 patients compared oral ciprofloxacin, 1.5 g/day, with intravenous azlocillin, 5 g every 8 hours, plus gentamicin, 80 mg intravenously every 8 hours, in the treatment of pseudomonal respiratory infection.[66] Both groups showed a significant improvement in lung function but the ciprofloxacin group had a greater improvement in peak expiratory flow ($p < 0.001$). In other respects, improvements were similar in the two groups, but two patients in the ciprofloxacin group were found to have ciprofloxacin-resistant strains by the end of treatment. Two further small trials with 19 and 20 patients, respectively, suggested that oral ciprofloxacin had similar efficacy in acute pulmonary exacerbations to intravenous azlocillin plus tobramycin.[67,68]

Open trials have confirmed the improvements in various clinical scores and respiratory parameters following treatment of adults with oral ciprofloxacin.[69,70] *Pseudomonas* spp. are not eradicated, but purulence and bacterial load are reduced. Resistance emerged during treatment and, although susceptibility returned after a 3-month interval, the response to repeated courses gradually diminished.[71] When given as a 14-day course in 29 patients, there was no significant difference in the efficacy of doses of 1.5 g/day versus 2 g/day, both groups improving significantly.[72] However, the number of patients with ciprofloxacin-resistant strains increased from just 2 of 24 patients before treatment to 14 of 23 patients by day 14.

Regular courses of ciprofloxacin given for 10 days every 3 months resulted in an improvement in peak expiratory flow during treatment but did not reduce hospital admissions or the requirement for antibiotics.[73] The MIC of bacterial isolates rose from 0.5 mg/litre to 0.8 mg/litre. Treatment should, therefore, be limited to acute exacerbations only.

Ciprofloxacin is of major benefit to patients because oral use is both cheaper and more pleasant than parenteral administration for the patient, but courses must be kept short (≤ 10 days) and rotated with other agents to maintain the efficacy of this drug. A permanent cure is not expected with any agent. If the MIC of the infecting organism is greater than 1 mg/litre, an additional antibiotic should be used.

Community-acquired infections

Pneumonia, acute exacerbation of chronic bronchitis and bronchiectasis were the common infections investigated in the comparative trials because they form a large proportion of the workload in general practice (Table 8.1). Cure or improvement was achieved in 175 of 188 (93%) patients given a high dose of ciprofloxacin, 750 mg every 12 hours for 7–14 days, in a double-blind trial of treatment versus temafloxacin (no longer available).[33,34] However, bacteriological eradication was inferior to that achieved with temafloxacin because only 32 of 41 (78%) isolates of *Streptococcus pneumoniae* were eradicated compared with all 27 in the temafloxacin group. Another double-blind trial at a lower dose of ciprofloxacin, 500 mg orally every 12 hours, again showed a very high rate of cure (117/121, 97%) not significantly different from that of temafloxacin (114/116, 98%).[35] *Streptococcus pneumoniae* was eradicated by ciprofloxacin in 31 of 34 (91%) patients. A further large, investigator-blind trial that included both upper and lower respiratory tract infections suggested that ciprofloxacin was similar in efficacy to erythromycin in general practice (245/308 versus 252/311).[74]

In a small, randomised trial, ciprofloxacin, 200 mg given intravenously every 12 hours or 750 mg given orally every 12 hours, was compared with ceftazidime in predominantly pneumococcal pneumonia.[13] Treatment failed in only one patient who had been given ceftazidime (17/17 versus 19/20). A similar trial reported cures in 36 of 37 (97%) patients given ciprofloxacin and 33 of 34 (97%) given ceftazidime, the only treatment failures occurring in patients with pneumonia (1 in each group).[10]

In a randomised trial of 163 patients with lower respiratory tract infections, ciprofloxacin, 500 mg every 12 hours, appeared to be as effective as co-amoxiclav (80/85 versus 75/78).[24] Ciprofloxacin eradicated all of the 45 pathogens isolated, whereas co-amoxiclav resulted in persistence (mostly Gram-negative species) at 6 of 48 sites. Ciprofloxacin, 1 g/day, also showed a similar efficacy to amoxycillin, 750 mg/day, in a 10-day course of treatment (21/26 versus 18/22).[3] The same dose was as effective as cephalexin in one study (27/28 versus 22/23) and as cefamandole in another (23/30 versus 21/30), but many patients were excluded from the trial, principally because of failure to take oral medication or lack of consent.[9,23] In a comparison with lomefloxacin, all patients in both arms of the trial were cured or improved (31/31 versus 28/28).[36]

At a lower dose of 250 mg every 12 hours, ciprofloxacin was as effective as co-amoxiclav, 1875 mg/day (26/33 versus 23/30) and ofloxacin, 400 mg/day (48/49 versus 43/50).[26,38] One trial comparing ciprofloxacin and doxycycline reported cure in all patients (20/20 versus 20/20) and another showed no significant difference in response (45/55 versus 42/53).[44,45]

Pneumonia and acute bronchitis
Streptococcus pneumoniae is the most common cause of community-acquired pneumonia and the majority of trials suggest that ciprofloxacin is effective in its treatment (Table 8.1). Some authors find persistence of the organism, however, sometimes with a rise in MIC during treatment.[1,33,75] Three reports describe single cases of treatment that failed, with or without a subsequent response to penicillin.[76–78] A meta-analysis of 45 trials in 1991 found 34 to be evaluable and included 2836 patients.[79] The odds ratio of failure compared with other antibiotics was 0.6 (95% confidence interval, CI 0.5–0.8), and was only 0.3 with respect to bronchitis. The outcome for pneumonia was similar. The differences between individual classes of antibiotic and ciprofloxacin were not significant. Eradication of *Streptococcus pneumoniae* (n = 100) was similar to that of comparators but eradication of *Haemophilus influenzae* by ciprofloxacin was superior. Nevertheless, a high oral dose, 750 mg every 12 hours, was advised for lower respiratory tract infections. Similar results have been obtained in a new meta-analysis (see later).

Patients with severe community-acquired pneumonia were treated with ciprofloxacin, 400 mg every 12 hours, or ceftriaxone in a double-blind trial. By intent-to-treat, the cure rates were 90% (96/107) and 84% (92/110). More than half of the patients were not strictly evaluable but cure rates in the remaining patients were similar (44/49 versus 38/45).[18] In another randomised trial, ciprofloxacin, 1.5 g/day orally, was as effective as co-amoxiclav for community-acquired pneumonia, although the 8 failures in the 30 patients treated were related to *Streptococcus pneumoniae*.[27] The cure rate for pneumococcal infections was lower for ciprofloxacin than for the other antibiotics (6/14 versus 14/15, p = 0.05).

For acute bronchitis, ciprofloxacin, 500 mg/day, was more likely to result in cure (as opposed to just improvement) than co-trimoxazole as a 5-day course (cure plus improvement, 23 + 4/28 versus 8 + 16/28).[41] Others found efficacy to be similar but resistance to co-trimoxazole developed more readily among causative pathogens.[42] In a double-blind trial, ciprofloxacin, 1.5 g/day, was successful in all but 1 of 42 (98%) patients with bacterial bronchitis compared with success in 40 of 45 (89%) given ampicillin.[6] It eradicated the likely pathogen in a significantly higher proportion of patients than ampicillin (40/42 versus 30/40, p = 0.02, Fisher's test). Ampicillin-resistant pathogens were isolated in 10 patients given ampicillin, of whom 7 recovered. Drug toxicity was the reason for failure in 2, and in only 1 patient was antibiotic resistance the cause of failure.

Acute-on-chronic bronchitis
Chronic bronchitis is the presence of a chronic cough productive on most days and present for 3 consecutive months of the year for at least 2 years. When the patient develops increased breathlessness, sputum production and/or sputum purulence, an acute exacerbation is present. *Haemophilus influenzae* is the most common pathogen, present in 40% of cases, with *Streptococcus pneumoniae* being present in 14% and *Moraxella catarrhalis* in 19%.[80] Ciprofloxacin is usually given at a dose of

500–750 mg orally every 12 hours for 5 days, the higher dose being reserved for more severe or potential pneumococcal infections.[80] Treatment in most cases will be empirical and have to be effective against all three pathogens.

Clinical success in acute exacerbations was observed in 60 of 70 (86%) patients given ciprofloxacin, 1 g/day orally, 71 of 78 (91%) given co-amoxiclav and 54 of 68 (79%) given cefixime (p = ns).[25] Ciprofloxacin and co-amoxiclav had identical success rates in another comparative trial (both 14/20).[81] Similarly, 58 of 67 (87%) patients given the same dose of ciprofloxacin were cured or improved, compared with 51 of 64 (80%) patients given temafloxacin in a double-blind study.[32] Of 18 isolates of *Streptococcus pneumoniae*, only 11 were susceptible to ciprofloxacin, but all those treated were eradicated. The same authors found no significant difference in clinical efficacy between ciprofloxacin, 500 mg given orally every 12 hours, and cefuroxime axetil in 271 patients.[82] The numbers in each group were not stated (cure rates 90% versus 89%). All 64 infections with *Moraxella catarrhalis* or *Haemophilus influenzae* and 11 of 12 infections with *Streptococcus pneumoniae* were eradicated by ciprofloxacin. Overall, the bacterial eradication rate was greater with ciprofloxacin than with cefuroxime (89/93 [96%] versus 80/97 [82%], p = 0.006). A higher bacterial eradication rate (92/101[91%] versus 71/94 [76%]) was again found in a comparison with clarithromycin with similar clinical cure rates (147/167 [88%] versus 139/165 [84%]).[29] A dose of only 0.5 g/day resulted in cure or improvement of all 29 patients treated, compared with all 28 given ampicillin in a further double-blind trial.[4]

Chodosh *et al.* used a higher dose, 750 mg every 12 hours, in a double-blind crossover study in patients suffering repeated acute exacerbations of chronic bronchitis.[5] All of the 22 patients given ciprofloxacin and the 22 given ampicillin were cured. A total of 6 of 38 pathogens persisted at the end of treatment with ciprofloxacin compared with 21 of 33 isolates after treatment with ampicillin. Only 3

and 5, respectively, were associated with relapse. A similar dose of ciprofloxacin, 1–1.5 g/day, was significantly more effective than amoxycillin in another trial (67/73 versus 49/67); bacteriological eradication was similar in the two groups, including that for infections caused by *Streptococcus pneumoniae* (7/10 versus 3/5).[2] Ciprofloxacin, at the dose used in Japan (200 mg orally every 8 hours) was more effective clinically and bacteriologically than cefaclor, 750 mg/day, in a further large, blinded trial (87/103 [85%] versus 60/97 [62%]).[22] In particular, there was a higher rate of eradication of *Haemophilus influenzae* by ciprofloxacin but this was not statistically significant (14/17 versus 13/24, p > 0.05). A smaller comparative trial failed to show any difference (26/28 versus 27/27).[21] Another community-based trial demonstrated a significantly higher cure rate of bronchitis by ciprofloxacin, 1 g/day orally, than josamycin (p = 0.004).[30] A total of 13 of 14 pneumococcal infections were cured despite only 64% of strains being susceptible to ciprofloxacin. Ciprofloxacin, 1 g/day orally, was also significantly more effective than roxithromycin in a double-blind study in general practice but no microbiological results were available (199/214 versus 176/205, p < 0.05).[28]

A potential advantage to the use of ciprofloxacin is that it can be administered orally to complete a course of treatment. Patients treated with intravenous ciprofloxacin, 200–300 mg every 12 hours for 1 week and then given another week of oral ciprofloxacin, 500–750 mg every 12 hours, demonstrated similar cure rates to 10 days of ceftazidime treatment.[11] Elderly patients in nursing homes similarly had a significantly better response rate to intravenous and then oral ciprofloxacin than to intravenous ceftazidime (p = 0.02).[15]

Meta-analysis

The disagreement between clinical trials with regard to the efficacy of ciprofloxacin in the treatment of lower respiratory tract infections, particularly pneumococcal pneumonia, requires a systematic review. Most clinical trials fail to include sufficient numbers of patients to avoid a type II error (i.e. claiming no significant difference exists between two treatments when just too few patients have been recruited to demonstrate a clinically important difference). Meta-analysis is a means of critical review and statistical pooling of the results of previous research to increase statistical power and to form a conclusion from conflicting reports.[83] It is important that all available randomised controlled studies on the subject are included and that defined protocol is used. A test of heterogeneity is needed to show with what caution to view the results of combining the results of different populations in different trials. The quality of the methods used in each trial are an indicator of the reliability of the results. Less weight should be placed on trials reported in abstract form only. For example, the means of randomisation, compliance, blinding, analysis and withdrawal of patients should be considered and this can be done most easily by using an index of quality in the pooling method.

We performed a meta-analysis of all randomised, comparative studies of the efficacy of ciprofloxacin versus other antibiotic regimens in the treatment of lower respiratory tract infections using the method of L'Abbé et al.[84] Trials in which a number of infections were treated within the same randomisation were excluded. Relevant studies were identified on Medline® from 1983 to 1995 and from references in other reviews. Assessment of quality was made using the method of Chalmers et al. [85] Differences in efficacy were indicated by the odds ratio and results pooled using the method of Mantel-Haenszel.[84,86] Heterogeneity was tested with the method of Woolf with an adjustment for small subsets.[86] The quality index was used as described by Klein et al.[87]

Of the 44 trials, 12 were double blind and one was patient blind. Type II error was considered to have occurred in the planning of only four trials.[20,33,42,46] The pooled results included 2497 patients treated with ciprofloxacin and 2404 treated with a comparator, with median rates of failure of 6% and 11%, respectively (Table 8.2). The pooled odds ratio was 0.57

(95% CI 0.47–0.68), and was in favour of ciprofloxacin, even when the quality of the trials was considered (Table 8.2, Figure 8.1). Six trials showed a significant difference in efficacy between ciprofloxacin and the comparator, all in favour of ciprofloxacin (versus amoxycillin, cefaclor, roxithromycin and josamycin) (Table 8.1). Ciprofloxacin was significantly more effective than amoxycillin/ampicillin when the results of seven trials were pooled, but the difference was lost if trial quality was considered. There was no significant difference compared with ceftazidime or co-amoxiclav. Six trials included more than ten patients given ciprofloxacin for infections with *Streptococcus pneumoniae*. Treatment failed in 26 of 136 (19%) patients given ciprofloxacin compared with 9 of 104 (9%) given comparators, indicating that ciprofloxacin was significantly less effective (odds ratio 2.4, 95% CI 1.06–5.3). However, if the quality of the trials was considered the difference was not statistically significant. In the ten trials reporting more than ten patients treated for *Haemophilus influenzae* infections, ciprofloxacin was not significantly different in efficacy from comparators (odds ratio 0.75, 95% CI 0.3–2.1). The findings were similar in the two trials reporting *Moraxella catarrhalis* infections (Table 8.2).

Ciprofloxacin is, therefore, as effective as, or more effective than, its comparators in Gram-negative respiratory infections. Against *Streptococcus pneumoniae*, however, other agents may be more effective. Nevertheless, Ball and Tillotson reviewed many of the trials reporting failure of ciprofloxacin in the treatment of pneumococcal infection and concluded that many of the cases failed because of inadequate or inappropriate treatment.[88] By examining controlled and uncontrolled studies (3500 patients in 37 studies), they found that the eradication of *Streptococcus pneumoniae* was achieved in more than 86% of patients and the overall clinical cure rate was 94%.

Uncontrolled trials

The collected experience of early USA trials suggested a 96% cure or improvement rate

Table 8.2. Pooled results of randomised comparative trials of ciprofloxacin in the treatment of lower respiratory tract infections.

Trial category	No. trials	Ciprofloxacin			Comparator			Pooled odds ratio 95% CI (Mantel–Haenszel)	Heterogeneity Chi square (Woolf)	Using quality index	
		No. patients	No. failed	Median % (range)	No. patients	No. failed	Median % (range)			Pooled odds ratio (Woolf)	Heterogeneity (Chi square)
All	44	2497	212	6 (0–45)	2404	339	11 (0–49)	0.57 (0.47–0.68)	45 NS	0.55 (0.40–0.77)	11 NS
Ciprofloxacin versus ampicillin/amoxycillin	7	242	7	0 (0–16)	230	23	10 (0–33)	0.31 (0.14–0.69)	7 NS	0.44 (0.09–2.29)	2 NS
Ciprofloxacin versus ceftazidime	7	299	19	7 (0–12)	280	30	10 (3–29)	0.61 (0.32–1.2)	5 NS	0.66 (0.15–2.94)	1 NS
Ciprofloxacin versus co-amoxiclav	4	215	27	18 (2–27)	211	22	14 (4–23)	1.21 (0.53–2.77)	1 NS	1.14 (0.21–6.3)	0.2 NS
Streptococcus pneumoniae	6	136	26	15 (7–57)	104	9	5 (2–44)	2.37 (1.06–5.32)	13 NS	3.19 (0.52–19.5)	2.8 NS
Haemophilus influenzae	10	298	11	1 (0–23)	286	15	9 (0–39)	0.75 (0.27–2.13)	5.5 NS	0.62 (0.15–2.55)	1.2 NS
Moraxella catarrhalis	2	51	0	0	47	3	(0–7)	0.18 (0.005–7.4)	0.3 NS	0.10 (0–9)	0.10 NS

CI, confidence interval; NS, not significant.

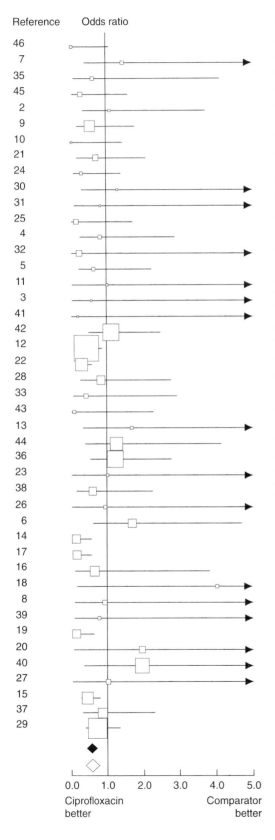

Reference   Odds ratio

46
7
35
45
2
9
10
21
24
30
31
25
4
32
5
11
3
41
42
12
22
28
33
43
13
44
36
23
38
26
6
14
17
16
18
8
39
19
20
40
27
15
37
29

0.0   1.0   2.0   3.0   4.0   5.0
Ciprofloxacin   Comparator
better   better

(201/209), with 8% of bacterial pathogens persisting.[89] In Japan, clinical success was achieved using a wide range of doses in 81 of 100 (81%) patients with pneumonia, 149 of 214 (70%) patients with acute-on-chronic bronchitis, and 94 of 121 (78%) patients with infected bronchiectasis.[90] A large general practice study observed cure or improvement in 965 of 1016 (95%) patients. Bacterial eradication was achieved in all 57 pneumococcal infections, 14 of 15 *Staphylococcus aureus* infections, 26 of 28 pseudomonal infections and all other Gram-negative infections.[91] Poorer cure rates were observed in infections caused by *Pseudomonas aeruginosa* (31/74, 42%), with only 21 of 94 strains being eradicated. Although there was a clinical cure rate of 92% for pneumococcal infection, only 29 of 42 isolates were killed. Yamaguchi and Hara reported clinical success in 529 of 717 (74%) patients with respiratory infections, the lowest rate of cure being in acute bronchitis (72%).[92] Another study reported cures in 46 of 70 (66%) patients with bronchiectasis or chronic bronchitis, using a dose of 600 mg/day.[93]

An open trial reported 290 of 299 (97%) patients with acute bronchitis cured or improved as were 81 of 82 (99%) with acute-on-chronic bronchitis and 20 of 21 (95%) with primary atypical pneumonia, using doses of 0.5–1 g/day.[48] Cure or improvement was recorded in 342 of 361 (94%) patients given 0.5–1.5 g/day for various respiratory infections.[94] A total of 42 patients with bronchitis or pneumonia were all cured or improved after treatment with 500–750 mg/day for 2 weeks in another trial.[63] The pathogen persisted in 7 patients, usually with a rise in MIC.

Figure 8.1. Odds ratio with 95% confidence intervals for 44 trials comparing ciprofloxacin versus control regimens in lower respiratory tract infections. Values between 0.0 and 1.0 represent an advantage with ciprofloxacin. Open squares represent odds ratio. Occluded diamond represents pooled odds ratio. Open diamond represents pooled odds ratio with quality index. The size of the symbols is proportional to the number of patients.

All 50 patients with acute pneumonia were cured with ciprofloxacin, 0.5–1.5 g/day for 5–15 days, in two trials.[95,96] Ciprofloxacin, 200 mg intravenously every 12 hours, then 500 mg orally every 12 hours, had cured 73 of 78 (94%) patients treated for pneumonia in an earlier trial by the same authors.[97] Of the cases, 8 were nosocomial and 12 caused by pneumococci. In AIDS patients, one small trial suggested similar cure rates for pneumonia using ciprofloxacin, 1 g/day orally, or parenteral cefotaxime.[17]

In acute-on-chronic bronchitis, ciprofloxacin was found to be clinically effective but could fail to eradicate *Streptococcus pneumoniae*. However, many of the patients recruited had severe disease and may not be typical of the patient population in general practice. Of 129 patients given 1.5 g/day, 96% were cured and the pathogen was eradicated in 95% with a proven infection. *Streptococcus pneumoniae* was responsible for only 1 of the 5 failures.[98] In a smaller trial, clinical success was recorded in 18 of 20 (90%) patients given 2 g/day and 14 of 20 (70%) given 1 g/day, but *Streptococcus pneumoniae* was isolated in 7 patients after treatment compared with 11 before treatment.[99] The mean MIC of post-treatment strains was 0.9 mg/litre compared with a maximum sputum concentration of 2.3 mg/litre (range 0.8–5 mg/litre) at the highest dose (2 g/day). Poor cure rates were reported for patients with acute-on-chronic bronchitis treated with ciprofloxacin, 1, 1.5 and 2 g/day (10/19, 21/38, 11/18).[100] Analysing their studies, Davies and Maesen found *Streptococcus pneumoniae* was re-isolated after treatment in 20 of 75 (27%) patients.[101] Only 4 of 9 pseudomonal infections were eradicated. In another study using 1 g/day, only 1 failure was recorded in 34 patients with acute-on-chronic bronchitis, but clearance of pneumococci was slower than that of *Haemophilus influenzae*.[102]

Prolonged courses of treatment with ciprofloxacin have been given to patients with chronic lung disease. Diffuse panbronchiolitis is a type of obstructive lung disease with a poor prognosis.[103] Of 37 patients treated with ciprofloxacin, 600 mg/day for 3 months, 21 (57%) improved. Although the bacterial eradication rate was high for most pathogens, only 18% of *Pseudomonas aeruginosa* were eliminated. Ciprofloxacin (range 8–27 mg/kg/day administered orally for 90–860 days) has been used to reduce bacterial colonisation in ten patients with severe bronchiectasis.[104] *Pseudomonas aeruginosa* was eradicated in 3 of 5 patients colonised with the organism. Of the 10 patients, 7 improved on treatment but 3 had infective exacerbations, 2 due to ciprofloxacin-resistant *Pseudomonas aeruginosa*. Only 1 patient reported any adverse effect (nausea) despite the length of the courses.

Legionnaire's disease

Ciprofloxacin can be used to treat Legionnaire's disease, preferably in combination with other agents, but as with all treatments in this disease, the evidence is from uncontrolled trials. *Legionella pneumophila* is commonly an intracellular pathogen and ciprofloxacin reaches a concentration within the alveolar macrophage 14–18 times that found in serum.[105] Low extracellular concentrations of ciprofloxacin can still be associated with inhibition of intracellular growth. Legionnaire's disease has been reported to respond to ciprofloxacin after failure of treatment with erythromycin.[106] Of 15 treated cases in the literature, 6 failed but only 3 were treated with ciprofloxacin alone.[107] Ciprofloxacin was effective in 8 of another 10 cases treated with monotherapy (400 mg/day).[108] One patient in whom treatment failed had previously been unresponsive to erythromycin and rifampicin and one responded to erythromycin after ciprofloxacin had been stopped. Another relapsed 12 days after a 2-week course and then responded to a second course having failed with erythromycin. Two patients who developed legionellosis after cardiac transplantation responded well to 200 mg given intravenously every 12 hours.[109] Finally, 6 of

10 patients with severe disease requiring ventilation survived when given ciprofloxacin in addition to erythromycin.[110]

Atypical pneumonia

Clinical experience is very limited but ciprofloxacin may have a role, at least in combination with a macrolide or tetracycline in the treatment of atypical pneumonia. At a dose of 500 mg every 12 hours, it was effective in 17 cases caused by *Chlamydia psittaci* and another 33 caused by *Mycoplasma pneumoniae*.[111] Fever resolved within a mean of 2 days and there were no failures. A Japanese study reported cure in 8 of 10 patients treated for mycoplasmal pneumonia.[92]

Mycobacterial infections

Ciprofloxacin is used in the treatment of mycobacterial disease because of its activity, good oral absorption and intracellular penetration. As part of a multi-drug regimen, acquired development of resistance has not been seen. Sputum clearance was observed in 7 of 9 patients treated with ciprofloxacin, isoniazid and other agents for multi-resistant tuberculosis.[112] Another 15 patients in whom first-line agents failed or who had resistant pathogens, were treated with ciprofloxacin, usually combined with rifampicin. Seven of 10 evaluable patients improved. A randomised trial reported sputum clearance at 6 months in 17 of 18 patients given a four-drug regimen, including ciprofloxacin, compared with all 18 given a standard regimen.[113]

Two hundred patients were treated in Tanzania with either rifampicin, 600 mg/day for 6 months, isoniazid, 300 mg/day for 6 months, and ciprofloxacin, 750 mg/day for 4 months, or rifampicin, isoniazid, ethambutol and pyrazinamide.[114] All patients were smear-negative at 6 months, but patients who were HIV positive had a slower response to the ciprofloxacin regimen. Relapses occurred in 7 of 75 patients given ciprofloxacin compared with none of 81 given standard treatment ($p = 0.005$). Possibly, ciprofloxacin did not significantly increase the bactericidal activity of rifampicin–isoniazid.

The *Mycobacterium avium–intracellulare* complex (MAC) infects at least one-third of patients with AIDS and is a significant contributor to their death. A combination of oral ciprofloxacin, 1.5 g/day, oral clarithromycin, 1 g every 12 hours, and intravenous amikacin, 7.5 mg/kg every 12 hours, was used in 12 patients with MAC bacteraemia over periods of 10–44 weeks.[115] Blood cultures became negative between 2 and 8 weeks after starting treatment and none of the four patients who died showed signs of active disease.

Conclusions

Ciprofloxacin is effective in complicated and severe respiratory infections caused by organisms resistant to β-lactam and other antibiotics and has the advantage of oral as well as intravenous administration. Ciprofloxacin, often in prolonged courses, is used to treat chronic sinusitis (250–500 mg administered orally every 12 hours for 10 days) and malignant external otitis (750 mg administered orally every 12 hours for 3 months). Ciprofloxacin is an alternative to extended-spectrum cephalosporins and other agents in the treatment of nosocomial or ventilator-associated pneumonia. A dose of 400 mg every 8–12 hours is recommended for the treatment of pseudomonal pneumonia and has been shown to be more effective than imipenem. Ciprofloxacin is a valuable oral treatment of infective exacerbations of cystic fibrosis at a dose of 1.5 g/day for 10 days, but if courses are repeated, response gradually diminishes as the result of reduced susceptibility of *Pseudomonas* spp.

Ciprofloxacin has been found to be as effective as co-amoxiclav, erythromycin and cephalosporins in community-acquired pneumonia. A dose of 250–750 mg administered orally every 12 hours or 200–400 mg administered intravenously every 12 hours for 5–10 days is usually effective, the higher dose being required in pneumococcal pneumonia. Meta-analyses suggest that ciprofloxacin is similar to or better than its comparators in eradication of

Haemophilus influenzae but should not be a first choice for treatment of severe pneumococcal infections. However, at a dose of 400 mg every 12 hours, outcome of severe community-acquired pneumonia is similar to that with ceftriaxone. In acute-on-chronic bronchitis, an oral dose of 500–750 mg every 12 hours has been shown to be as clinically effective as co-amoxiclav, amoxycillin or cefixime, although *Streptococcus pneumoniae* may not be eradicated in every case.

Ciprofloxacin has good intracellular penetration and activity. It is an alternative agent to erythromycin in legionellosis (200 mg administered intravenously every 12 hours for 2 weeks), and to first-line antibiotics in mycobacterial disease (750 mg/day administered orally for 4 months with rifampicin and isoniazid for 6 months).

References

1. Ball AP. Clinical evidence for the efficacy of ciprofloxacin in lower respiratory tract infections. Rev Contemp Pharmacother 1992; 3: 133–42.
2. Basran GS, Joseph J, Abbas AMA, Hughes C, Tillotson G. Treatment of acute exacerbations of chronic obstructive airways disease – a comparison of amoxycillin and ciprofloxacin. J Antimicrob Chemother 1990; 26 (Suppl F): 19–24.
3. Gleadhill IC, Ferguson WP, Lowry RC. Efficacy and safety of ciprofloxacin in patients with respiratory infections in comparison with amoxycillin. J Antimicrob Chemother 1986; 18 (Suppl D): 133–8.
4. Chmel H, Emmanuel G, Lie T, Anderson L, Ireland J. A prospective double blind randomized study comparing the efficacy and safety of low dose ciprofloxacin with ampicillin in the treatment of bronchitis. Diagn Microbiol Infect Dis 1990; 13: 149–51.
5. Chodosh S, Tuck J, Stottmeier KD, Pizzuto D. Comparison of ciprofloxacin with ampicillin in acute infectious exacerbations of chronic bronchitis. Am J Med 1989; 87 (Suppl 5A): 107–12.
6. Wollschlager CM, Raoof S, Khan FA, Guarneri JJ, LaBombardi V, Afzal Q. Controlled comparative study of ciprofloxacin versus ampicillin in treatment of bacterial respiratory tract infections. Am J Med 1987; 82 (Suppl 4A): 164–8.
7. Gellerman HJ. Therapie von unteren Atemwegsinfektionen mit Ciprofloxacin. Med Welt 1987; 38: 69–72.
8. Felgner U. Ciprofloxacin and ampicillin in acute bacterial exacerbations of lower respiratory tract infections. International Symposium on Ciprofloxacin, Dresden, Germany, 1988: 88–92.
9. Feist H, Vetter N, Drlicek M, Otupal I, Weutta H. Comparative study of ciprofloxacin and cefalexin in the treatment of patients with lower respiratory tract infection. 1st International Ciprofloxacin Workshop, Leverkusen, Germany, 1985: 265–7.
10. Haddow A, Greene S, Heinz E, Wantuck D. Ciprofloxacin (intravenous/oral) versus ceftazidime in lower respiratory tract infections. Am J Med 1989; 87 (Suppl 5A): 113–15.
11. Echols R, Arcieri G, Neumann C, Seligman M. Sequential intravenous/oral (iv/po) ciprofloxacin (cip) versus ceftazidime (CFZ) in the treatment of lower respiratory tract infection. International Congress of Infectious Diseases, Montreal, Canada, 1990: Abstract 466.
12. Khan FA, Basir R. Sequential intravenous–oral administration of ciprofloxacin vs ceftazidime in serious bacterial respiratory tract infections. Chest 1989; 96: 528–37.
13. Menon L, Ernst JA, Ernesto RS, Flores D, Pacia A, Lorian V. Brief report: sequential intravenous/oral ciprofloxacin compared with intravenous ceftazidime in the treatment of serious lower respiratory tract infections. Am J Med 1989; 87 (Suppl 5A): 119–20.
14. Rapp RP, Billeter M, Hatton J, Young AB, Tibbs PA, Dempsey RJ. Intravenous ciprofloxacin vs ceftazidime for treatment of nosocomial pneumonia and urinary tract infections. Clin Pharm 1991; 10: 49–55.
15. Trenholme GM, Schmitt BA, Spear J, Gvazdinskas LC, Levin S. Randomized study of intravenous/oral ciprofloxacin versus ceftazidime in the treatment of hospital and nursing home patients with lower respiratory tract infections. Am J Med 1989; 87 (Suppl 5A): 116–18.
16. Krcméry V, Fuchsberger P, Trupl J, Sufliarsky J, Spánik S, Koza I *et al.* Ciprofloxacin plus vancomycin vs ceftazidime plus gentamicin in the treatment of pneumonia in granulocytopenic patients. Drugs 1993; 45 (Suppl 3): 311.
17. Franzetti F, Cernuschi M, Ridolofo A, Antinori S, Coppin P, Negri C *et al.* Oral ciprofloxacin vs intravenous cefotaxime in the treatment of pneumonias in AIDS patients. Drugs 1993; 45 (Suppl 3): 425–6.
18. Johnson RH, Levine S, Traub SL, Echols RM, Haverstock D, Arnold E *et al.* Sequential intravenous/oral ciprofloxacin compared to parenteral ceftriaxone in the treatment of hospitalised patients with community-acquired pneumonia. Infect Dis Clin Pract 1996; 5(4): 265–72.
19. Hirata-Dulas CAI, Stein DJ, Guay DRP, Gruninger RP, Peterson PK. A randomized study of ciprofloxacin versus ceftriaxone in the treatment of nursing home-

acquired lower respiratory tract infections. J Am Geriatr Soc 1991; 39: 979–85.

20. Kalager R, Anderson BM, Bergan T, Brubakk O, Bruun JN, Døskeland B *et al*. Ciprofloxacin versus a tobramycin/cefuroxime combination in the treatment of serious systemic infections: a prospective, randomised and controlled study of efficacy and safety. Scand J Infect Dis 1992; 24: 637–46.

21. Quenzer RW, Davis RL, Neidhart MM. Prospective randomized study comparing the efficacy and safety of ciprofloxacin with cefaclor in the treatment of patients with purulent bronchitis. Diagn Microbiol Infect Dis 1990; 13: 143–8.

22. Kobayashi H, Takamura H, Takeda H, Kono K, Saito A, Tomizawa M *et al*. Comparative clinical study of ciprofloxacin and cefaclor in the treatment of respiratory tract infections. Chemotherapy (Tokyo) 1986; 34: 1011–37.

23. Peterson PK, Stein D, Guay DRP, Logan G, Obaid S, Gruninger R *et al*. Prospective study of lower respiratory tract infections in an extended care nursing home program: potential role of oral ciprofloxacin. Am J Med 1988; 85: 164–71.

24. Barash M, Khan F, Clark R, Heyd A, Seligman M. Efficacy and safety of oral ciprofloxacin versus amoxicillin/clavulanate in the treatment of lower respiratory tract infections in adults. Eur J Clin Microbiol Infect Dis 1991; Special issue: 395–7.

25. Cazzola M, Legnani D, Beghi G, Giura R, Madonini V, Florentini F *et al*. Exacerbation of chronic bronchitis. Clinical and microbiological efficacy of amoxicillin + clavulanic acid vs cefixime or ciprofloxacin. 6th International Congress on Infectious Diseases, Prague, Czech Republic, 1994: 383.

26. Schwigon CD, Barckow D, Gotz D, Hopfenmüller G. Comparative clinical study of augmentin and ciprofloxacin in the treatment of respiratory infection in hospitalized patients. 16th International Congress of Chemotherapy, Jerusalem, Israel, 1989: Abstract 105.

27. Mouton Y, Beuscart C, Leroy O, Ajana F, Charrel J, Groupe Multicentrique. Evaluation de la ciprofloxacine versus amoxicilline plus acide clavulanique ou erythromycine pour le traitement empirique des pneumonies communautaires. Pathol Biol Paris 1991; 39: 34–7.

28. Leophonte P. Ciprofloxacin vs roxithromycin in lower respiratory tract infections: a double-blind comparison. In: Shah PM, ed. Ciprofloxacin in pulmonology II. Munich: Zuckschwerdt Verlag, 1992: 1–13.

29. Chodosh S, Schreurs AJM, Shan M, Moesker HL, Kowalsky S, the Bronchitis Study Group. The efficacy of oral ciprofloxacin vs clarithromycin for the treatment of acute bacterial exacerbations of chronic bronchitis. Clin Infect Dis 1996; 23: 913 (Abstract).

30. Canton P, Hoen B, Richet H, Ravoire S, Acar JF. Brief report: comparative efficacy of ciprofloxacin versus josamycin in the treatment of acute, recurrent, or exacer-

bated bronchitis. Am J Med 1989; 87 (Suppl 5A): 121–2.

31. Acar JF, Richet H, Ravoire S, Vray M. A randomised comparative study of ciprofloxacin versus josamycin in respiratory tract infections of adults. International Congress on Infectious Diseases, Rio de Janeiro, Brazil, 1988: Abstract 606.

32. Chodosh S. Temafloxacin compared with ciprofloxacin in mild to moderate lower respiratory tract infections in ambulatory patients. Chest 1991; 100: 1497–502.

33. Lindsay G, Scorer HJN, Carnegie CMD. Safety and efficacy of temafloxacin versus ciprofloxacin in lower respiratory tract infections: a randomized, double-blind trial. J Antimicrob Chemother 1992; 30: 89–100.

34. Dewhurst J, Carpentier P, Cerasoli J, Pernet A. Temafloxacin vs ciprofloxacin in the treatment of lower respiratory tract infections. 3rd International Symposium on New Quinolones, Vancouver, Canada 1990: 393.

35. Kosmidis J. A double blind study of once daily temafloxacin in the treatment of bacterial lower respiratory tract infections. J Antimicrob Chemother 1991; 28 (Suppl C): 73–9.

36. Nonikov VE, Makarova OV, Zubkov MN, Gugutzidze EN. Lomefloxacin vs. ciprofloxacin in lower respiratory infection. Drugs 1993; 45 (Suppl 3): 413.

37. Catena E, Cesana M, Rufloxacin in Acute Exacerbations of Chronic Bronchitis Study Group. 5 day rufloxacin treatment versus 7 day ciprofloxacin treatment in patients with acute exacerbations of chronic bronchitis. Clin Drug Invest 1995; 9: 334–43.

38. Polubiec A, Jorasz I, Pietrzak J, Soszka A, Stepka K, Zaryn A. A randomized study comparing low dose ciprofloxacin and ofloxacin in the treatment of lower respiratory tract infections. Infection 1994; 22: 62–4.

39. Lode H, Wiley E, Olschewski, Sievers H, Wintermantel M, Baetz R *et al*. Prospective randomized clinical trials of new quinolones versus β-lactam antibiotics in lower respiratory tract infections. Scand J Infect Dis 1990; 68: 50–5.

40. Scaglione F, Scamazzo F, Arcidiacono MM, Cogo R, Monzani GP, Fraschini F. Comparative activities of pefloxacin and ciprofloxacin in the treatment of chronic respiratory tract infections. J Chemother 1995; 7: 140–5.

41. Gritz HA, Gross M, Marten W. Lower respiratory tract infections. Efficacy and tolerability of ciprofloxacin in comparison with trimethoprim/sulphamethoxazole. Med Welt 1989; 40: 398–402.

42. Grossman RF, Beaupre A, LaForge J, Lampron N, Hanna K. A prospective randomised parallel single blind comparison of oral ciprofloxacin with oral co-trimoxazole in the treatment of respiratory tract infections in patients with chronic obstructive lung disease. Drug Invest 1994; 8: 110–17.

43. Magnani C, Fregni S, Valli G, Cosentina R, Bisetti A. Comparative clinical study of ciprofloxacin and co-

trimoxazole in respiratory tract infections. 1st International Ciprofloxacin Workshop, Leverkusen, Germany, 1985: 260–4.

44. Möller M. A study on the efficiency of antibiotics in acute airway infections. Ciprofloxacin versus doxycycline. 6th Medical Congress on Chemotherapy, Taormina, Italy, 1988; 143–6.

45. Bantz P-M, Grote J, Peters-Haertel W. Low-dose ciprofloxacin in respiratory tract infections. A randomized comparison with doxycycline in general practice. Am J Med 1987; 82 (Suppl 4A): 208–10.

46. Fink MP, Snydman DR, Niederman MS, Leeper KV, Johnson RH, Heard SO et al. Treatment of severe pneumonia in hospitalized patients: results of a multicenter, randomized, double-blind trial comparing intravenous ciprofloxacin with imipenem-cilastatin. Antimicrob Agents Chemother 1994; 38: 547–57.

47. García-Rodríguez JA, del Cañizo A, Pérez Samitier E, Cánovas EC, González Pérez J, Fabra JM et al. Efficacy and safety of ciprofloxacin in ENT infections (sinusitis, otitis media, pharyngotonsillitis). Rev Esp Quimoterap 1990; 3(3): 235–40.

48. Braun H, Radzyner M. Ciprofloxacin in respiratory tract infections: a phase IV surveillance study. Curr Ther Res 1994; 55: 729–35.

49. del Cañizo A, Alvarez A, Lavilla Martín de Valmaseda MJ. Efficacy of ciprofloxacin in the treatment of acute sinusitis. Rev Esp Quimoterap 1991; IV (Suppl 3): 5–7.

50. Miyamoto N, Kobayashi T, Baba S. Ciprofloxacin in the treatment of suppurative otitis media and sinusitis. Drugs 1993; 45 (Suppl 3): 325–6.

51. Data on file (Project file D93–007), Bayer plc.

52. Legent F, Bordure P, Beauvillain C, Berche P. A double blind comparison of ciprofloxacin and amoxycillin/clavulanic acid in the treatment of chronic sinusitis. Chemotherapy 1994; 40 (Suppl 1): 8–15.

53. Klein GL, Heyd A, Echols R. Oral ciprofloxacin vs cefuroxime axetil in acute bacterial sinusitis. Drugs 1993; 45 (Suppl 3): 324.

54. Fombeur JP, Barrault S, Koubbi G, Laurier JN, Ebbo D, Lecomte F et al. Study of the efficacy and safety of ciprofloxacin in the treatment of chronic sinusitis. Chemotherapy 1994; 40 (Suppl 1): 24–8.

55. Legent F, Bordure P, Beauvillain C, Berche P. Controlled prospective study of oral ciprofloxacin versus amoxycillin/clavulanic acid in chronic suppurative otitis media in adults. Chemotherapy 1994; 40 (Suppl 1): 16–23.

56. Fombeur JP, Barrault S, Koubbi G, Laurier JN, Ebbo D, Lecomte F et al. Study of the efficacy and safety of ciprofloxacin in the treatment of chronic otitis. Chemotherapy 1994; 40 (Suppl 1): 29–34.

57. Gehanno P. Ciprofloxacin in the treatment of malignant external otitis. Chemotherapy 1994; 40 (Suppl 1): 35–40.

58. Giamarellou H. Malignant otitis externa: the therapeutic evolution of a lethal infection. J Antimicrob Chemother 1992; 30: 745–51.

59. García-Rodríguez JA, del Cañizo A, García Sanchez JE, Garcia Garcia MI, de Miguel Martinez I, Munoz Bellido JL et al. Efficacy of 2 regimens of local ciprofloxacin in the treatment of ear infections. Drugs 1993; 45 (Suppl 3): 327–8.

60. Aoun M, Klastersky M. Drug treatment of pneumonia in hospital. Drugs 1991; 11: 586–99.

61. Schentag JJ. The relationship between ciprofloxacin blood concentrations, MIC values, bacterial eradication, and clinical outcome in patients with nosocomial pneumonia. In: Garrard C, ed. Ciprofloxacin i.v. Defining its role in serious infection. Berlin: Springer-Verlag, 1994: 49–57.

62. Peloquin CA, Cumbo TJ, Nix DE, Sands MF, Schentag JJ. Evaluation of intravenous ciprofloxacin in patients with nosocomial lower respiratory tract infections. Arch Intern Med 1989; 149: 2269–73.

63. Fass RJ. Efficacy and safety of oral ciprofloxacin in the treatment of serious respiratory infections. Am J Med 1987; 82 (Suppl 4A): 202–7.

64. Haverkorn MJ. Ciprofloxacin therapy of respiratory tract infection with *Pseudomonas aeruginosa*. Eur J Clin Microbiol Infect Dis 1988; 7: 661–4.

65. Jensen T, Pedersen SS, Nielsen CH, Hoiby N, Koch C. The efficacy and safety of ciprofloxacin and ofloxacin in chronic *Pseudomonas aeruginosa* infections in cystic fibrosis. J Antimicrob Chemother 1987; 20: 585–94.

66. Hodson ME, Roberts CM, Butland RJA, Smith MJ, Batten JC. Oral ciprofloxacin compared with conventional intravenous treatment for *Pseudomonas aeruginosa* infection in adults with cystic fibrosis. Lancet 1987; I(8527): 235–7.

67. Bosso JA, Black PG, Matsen JM. Ciprofloxacin versus tobramycin plus azlocillin in pulmonary exacerbations in adult patients with cystic fibrosis. Am J Med 1987; 82 (Suppl 4A): 180–4.

68. Rubio TT, Shapiro C. Ciprofloxacin in the treatment of pseudomonas infection in cystic fibrosis patients. J Antimicrob Chemother 1986; 18 (Suppl D): 147–52.

69. Bosso JA, Black PG. Efficacy of ciprofloxacin in patients with cystic fibrosis. Drug Intell Clin Pharm 1988; 22: 551–3.

70. Steen HJ, Scott EM, Stevenson MI, Black AE, Redmond AOB, Collier PS. Clinical and pharmacokinetic aspects of ciprofloxacin in the treatment of acute exacerbations of pseudomonas infection in cystic fibrosis patients. J Antimicrob Chemother 1989; 24: 787–95.

71. Scully BE, Nakatomi M, Ores C, Davidson S, Neu HC. Ciprofloxacin therapy in cystic fibrosis. Am J Med 1987; 82 (Suppl 4A): 196–201.

72. Shalit I, Stutman HR, Marks MI, Chartrand SA, Hilman BC. Randomized study of two dosage regimens of ciprofloxacin for treating chronic

broncho-pulmonary infection in patients with cystic fibrosis. Am J Med 1987; 82 (Suppl 4A): 189–95.

73. Sheldon CD, Assoufi BK, Hodson ME. Regular three monthly oral ciprofloxacin in adult cystic fibrosis patients infected with *Pseudomonas aeruginosa*. Respir Med 1993; 87: 587–93.

74. Feld MS, Carnegie C, Macklin J, Coles S. Comparison of oral erythromycin ethylsuccinate and ciprofloxacin in the treatment of acute respiratory tract infection. Br J Clin Pract 1990; 44: 404–8.

75. Mehtar S, Drabu Y, Blakemore PH, Walsh B. Clinical evaluation of oral ciprofloxacin in serious infection: an open study. Eur J Intern Med 1990; 1: 383–90.

76. Cooper B, Lawlor M. Pneumococcal bacteraemia during ciprofloxacin therapy for pneumococcal pneumonia. Am J Med 1989; 87 (Suppl 5A): 225–7.

77. Gordon JJ, Kauffman CA. Superinfection with *Streptococcus pneumoniae* during therapy with ciprofloxacin. Am J Med 1990; 89: 383–4.

78. Levine DP, McNeil P, Lerner SA. Randomised double blind comparative study of intravenous ciprofloxacin versus ceftazidime in the treatment of serious infections. Am J Med 1989; 87 (Suppl 5A): 160–3.

79. Byl B, Kaufman L, Jacobs F, Derde MP, Thys JP. Ciprofloxacin vs comparative antibiotics in LRTI. A meta-analysis. Drugs 1993; 45 (Suppl 3): 428–9.

80. Evans DM. Ciprofloxacin in the treatment of bronchitis in general practice. Rev Contemp Pharmacother 1992; 3: 143–52.

81. Schmidt EW, Zimmermann I, Ritzerfeld W, Voss E, Ulmer WT. Controlled prospective study of oral amoxycillin/clavulanate vs ciprofloxacin in acute exacerbations of chronic bronchitis. J Antimicrob Chemother 1989; 24 (Suppl B): 185–93.

82. Chodosh S, Echols R, Kowalsky S, Painter B, Valalik E. A prospective, randomized, double-blind, comparative study of ciprofloxacin and cefuroxime axetil for the treatment of acute bacterial exacerbations of chronic bronchitis. Annual Meeting of the Infectious Disease Society of America, Washington, USA, 1995: 58 (Abstract 166).

83. Sacks HS, Berrier J, Reitman D, Ancona-Berk VA, Chalmers TC. Meta-analyses of randomized controlled trials. N Engl J Med 1987; 316: 450–5.

84. L'Abbé K, Detsky AS, O'Rourke K. Meta-analysis in clinical research. Ann Intern Med 1987; 107: 224–33.

85. Chalmers TC, Smith H, Blackburn B, Silverman B, Schroeder B, Reitman D *et al*. A method for assessing quality of a randomized control trial. Control Clin Trials 1981; 2: 31–49.

86. Armitage P, Berry G. Statistical methods in epidemiology. In: Statistical methods in medical research. Chapter 16, 2nd ed. Oxford: Blackwell Scientific Publications, 1987: 459–64.

87. Klein S, Simes J, Blackburn GL. Total parenteral nutrition and cancer clinical trials. Cancer 1986; 58: 1378–86.

88. Ball AP, Tillotson GS. Lower respiratory tract infection therapy – the role of ciprofloxacin. J Int Med Res 1995; 23: 315–27.

89. Arcieri G, August R, Becker N, Doyle C, Griffith E, Gruenwaldt G *et al*. Clinical experience with ciprofloxacin. Eur J Clin Microbiol 1986; 5: 220–5.

90. Kobayashi H. Clinical efficacy of ciprofloxacin in the treatment of patients with respiratory tract infections in Japan. Am J Med 1987; 82: 169–73.

91. Pankey GA, Kalish GH, Wallach M, Garbus SB, Cohen G. Ciprofloxacin in lower respiratory tract and skin/skin structure infections: a phase IV surveillance study. Infect Med 1990; Sept: 1–6.

92. Yamaguchi K, Hara K. Clinical evaluation of ciprofloxacin in the field of internal medicine in Japan. 14th International Congress on Chemotherapy, Kyoto, Japan, 1985: 41–5.

93. Odagiri S, Takigami T, Fukaya K. Ciprofloxacin in the treatment of exacerbations of chronic respiratory tract infections. Drugs 1993; 45 (Suppl 3): 403–4.

94. Maggiolo F, Bianchi W, Ohnmeiss H. Clinical and microbiological evaluation of ciprofloxacin in respiratory tract infections. 4th European Congress of Clinical Microbiology, Nice, France, 1989: Abstract 127/PP3.

95. Chrysanthopoulos CJ, Bassaris HP. Use of oral ciprofloxacin in community acquired pneumonia. J Chemother 1989; 1: 103–6.

96. Ernst JA, Sy ER, Colon-Lucca H, Sandhu N, Rallos T, Lorian V. Ciprofloxacin in the treatment of pneumonia. Antimicrob Agents Chemother 1986; 29: 1088–9.

97. Chrysanthopoulos CJ, Skoutelis AT, Starakis JC, Anastassiou ED, Bassaris HP. Use of intravenous ciprofloxacin in respiratory tract infections and biliary sepsis. Am J Med 1987; 82 (Suppl 4A): 357–9.

98. Raoof S, Wollschlager C, Khan F. Treatment of respiratory tract infection with ciprofloxacin. J Antimicrob Chemother 1986; 18 (Suppl D): 139–45.

99. Davies BI, Maesen FPV, Baur C. Ciprofloxacin in the treatment of acute exacerbations of chronic bronchitis. Eur J Clin Microbiol 1986; 5: 226–31.

100. Maesen FPV, Davies BI, Geraedts WH, Baur C. The use of quinolones in respiratory tract infections. Drugs 1987; 34 (Suppl 1): 74–9.

101. Davies BI, Maesen FPV. Respiratory infections: clinical experiences with the new quinolones. Pharm Weekbl (Sci) 1987; 9 (Suppl): 53–7.

102. Hoogkamp-Korstanje JAA, Klein SJ. Ciprofloxacin in acute exacerbations of chronic bronchitis. J Antimicrob Chemother 1986; 18: 407–13.

103. Tanimoto H, Kobayashi H, Takizawa T, Kabe J, Nakata K, Kira S *et al*. Clinical study of long term ciprofloxacin therapy in diffuse panbronchiolitis. Drugs 1993; 45 (Suppl 3): 398.

104. Rayner CFJ, Tillotson G, Cole PJ, Wilson R. Efficacy and safety of long-term ciprofloxacin in the manage-

ment of severe bronchiectasis. J Antimicrob Chemother 1994; 34: 149–56.

105. Spiteri MA, Di Benedetto G. Mucociliary clearance and alveolar macrophages in pulmonary infection: the modulatory role of ciprofloxacin. Rev Contemp Pharmacother 1992; 3: 125–31.

106. Clara F. Severe *Legionella pneumophila* infection resistant to parenteral erythromycin that responded to ciprofloxacin. 7th Mediterranean Congress of Chemotherapy, Barcelona, Spain, 1990: Abstract 411.

107. Ruckdeschel G, Ehret W, Lenhart FP, Unertl K. Ciprofloxacin in legionellosis. In: Fass RJ, ed. Ciprofloxacin in pulmonology. Munich: Zuckschwerdt Verlag, 1990: 84–91.

108. Unertl KE, Lenhart FP, Forst H, Vogler G, Wilm V, Ehret W *et al*. Brief report: ciprofloxacin in the treatment of legionellosis in critically ill patients including those cases unresponsive to erythromycin. Am J Med 1989; 87 (Suppl 5A): 128–31.

109. Hooper TL, Gould FK, Swinburn CR, Featherstone G, Odom NJ, Corris PA *et al*. Ciprofloxacin: a preferred treatment for legionella infections in patients receiving cyclosporin A. J Antimicrob Chemother 1988; 22: 952–3.

110. Winter JH, McCartney C, Bingham J, Telfer M, White LO, Fallon RJ. Ciprofloxacin in the treatment of severe Legionnaire's disease. Rev Infect Dis 1988; 10 (Suppl 1): 218–19.

111. Schönwald S, Petricevic CV, Soldo I, Skerk V. Ciprofloxacin applied in treatment of interstitial pneumonias of infectious etiology. 15th International Congress of Chemotherapy, Istanbul, Turkey, 1987: 1148–50.

112. Tillotson GS. Tuberculosis – new aspects of chemotherapy. J Med Microbiol 1996; 44: 16–20.

113. Mohanty KC, Dhamgaye TK. Controlled trial of ciprofloxacin in short-term chemotherapy for pulmonary tuberculosis. Chest 1993; 104: 1194–8.

114. Kennedy N, Berger L, Curram J, Fox R, Gutmann J, Kisyombe GM *et al*. Randomised controlled trial of a drug regimen which includes ciprofloxacin in the treatment of pulmonary tuberculosis: outcome in HIV-negative and HIV-positive patients. Clin Infect Dis 1996; 22; 827–33.

115. De Lalla F, Maserati R, Scarpellini P, Marone P, Nicolin R, Caccamo F *et al*. Clarithromycin–ciprofloxacin–amikacin for therapy of *Mycobacterium avium-Mycobacterium intracellulare* bacteremia in patients with AIDS. Antimicrob Agents Chemother 1992; 36: 1567–9.

Chapter 9

Febrile neutropenia

Infection is the major cause of death in neutropenic cancer patients, particularly when caused by *Escherichia coli*, *Klebsiella* spp., *Pseudomonas aeruginosa*, *Staphylococcus aureus* or *Aspergillus* spp. Ciprofloxacin is used both to prevent Gram-negative bacteraemia and for empirical treatment of febrile episodes in neutropenic patients. Therapeutic ciprofloxacin following oral prophylaxis with ciprofloxacin might be avoided on theoretical grounds, but little direct clinical evidence of loss of efficacy exists.[1] If ciprofloxacin is used after a period of prophylaxis, however, early combination with a glycopeptide might be advisable.

Empirical treatment of febrile episodes in neutropenic patients requires a broad-spectrum agent with activity against most Gram-negative species including *Pseudomonas* spp. Treatment should start promptly, regardless of the availability of microbiological results identifying the species responsible. Ciprofloxacin as part of combination therapy has been adopted because of low levels of bacterial resistance, oral and intravenous routes of administration, avoidance of the need for monitoring of serum concentration and a low risk of adverse effects. However, increasing resistance of *Pseudomonas* spp. and *Acinetobacter* spp. and poor activity against streptococci and methicillin-resistant *Staphylococcus aureus* limit its usefulness.[2] Gram-positive pathogens are usually covered by the addition of a glycopeptide

if there has been no response to the primary agent after 48 hours.

Therapeutic use

Comparison of cure rates between trials using ciprofloxacin is difficult because some investigators categorise treatments that have been modified as successes, while others regard these treatments as failures. The proportion of patients with bone marrow transplantation, acute leukaemia, lymphoma and solid tumours varies between trials. There are further differences in the depth and duration of neutropenia and the type of chemotherapy compromising mucosal integrity.[2] Antibiotic prophylaxis is used in some patients and not others. Nevertheless, ciprofloxacin seems to be as effective as standard regimens, when used in combination. As with other antibiotics, when used as monotherapy, cure is less certain and failure is often caused by the resistant coagulase-negative staphylococci and streptococci.

Uncontrolled studies suggest that ciprofloxacin is effective. Febrile episodes in 147 cancer patients were treated with ciprofloxacin at a dose of 200 mg every 8 hours for at least 7 days.[3] Of these, 30 patients were neutropenic at the onset of infection. Response was observed in 114 (78%) of the patients including 73% of the neutropenic patients. Failure occurred in 1 patient with pseudomonal pneumonia, 3 with staphylococcal bacteraemia and 1 with pneumococcal bacteraemia. For 64 episodes in 42 patients, ciprofloxacin (300 mg every 12 hours) effected

Wilson APR and Grüneberg RN.
Ciprofloxacin: 10 years of clinical experience
© 1997 Maxim Medical, Oxford.

cure or improvement in 38 (59%), therapy being modified in 11 of these episodes.[4] One patient died of septicaemia caused by a *Pseudomonas* sp. resistant to ciprofloxacin. A third of the patients were receiving ciprofloxacin by mouth by the end of their course.

Ciprofloxacin (400 mg administered intravenously every 12 hours for 24 hours, then 200 mg every 12 hours) plus vancomycin was successful in treating 27 of 35 (77%) episodes in neutropenic patients with a temporary improvement in a further 3 patients.[5] Two documented infections failed to improve, both caused by *Pseudomonas* spp. Ciprofloxacin plus piperacillin cured 24 of 47 (51%) episodes by 72 hours, greater success being achieved in those cases that were microbiologically proven bacteraemias (15/24, 63%).[6]

Randomised comparisons with standard regimens have confirmed that ciprofloxacin is as effective as other agents and is equivalent to an aminoglycoside in the treatment of Gram-negative causes of febrile episodes. Gram-positive bacteraemia usually requires the addition of a glycopeptide to the treatment regimen. The use of ciprofloxacin alone was found to be effective in two trials, but as might be expected for monotherapy, a third trial was stopped when a significantly higher failure rate was observed compared with a standard combination.[7–9] Monotherapy with intravenous ciprofloxacin (200 mg every 12 hours) or intravenous ceftazidime (2 g every 8 hours) resulted in improvement at 72 hours in 10 of 21 (48%) patients and 13 of 25 (52%) patients, respectively.[7] At the end of treatment, success was achieved in 71% of patients with ciprofloxacin and 64% with ceftazidime by the addition of vancomycin, but only in 14% and 21%, respectively, without modification. Comparison of ciprofloxacin (300 mg every 12 hours administered intravenously then 750 mg every 12 hours administered orally) with a combination of azlocillin and netilmicin showed response without addition of antibiotics was similar (25/73, 34% versus 28/70, 40%).[8] Treatment failed in 34% of patients receiving monotherapy compared with 30% of patients receiving the combination therapy. However, an EORTC trial in patients with solid tumours and lymphoma was stopped prematurely when the efficacy of ciprofloxacin alone (200 mg every 12 hours) fell significantly below that of piperacillin plus amikacin (31/48 versus 48/53, $p = 0.002$) (Figure 9.1).[9] The difference in failure rates was due to

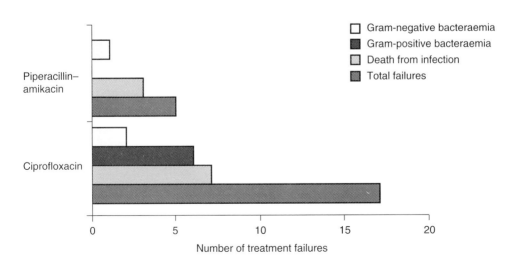

Figure 9.1. Reason for treatment failure in a trial comparing ciprofloxacin alone (n = 48) with piperacillin plus amikacin (n = 53).[9] Gram-positive bacteraemia was cured in 2 patients in the ciprofloxacin group and 4 in the control group.

the poor response to ciprofloxacin in patients with Gram-positive bacteraemia and might have been overcome by the use of a higher dose (400 mg every 8 hours) or combination with a β-lactam or aminoglycoside. Results of further clinical trials are awaited.[2] As with other antibiotics, monotherapy may predispose to the development of resistance to ciprofloxacin. An outbreak of bacteraemia caused by resistant *Escherichia coli* has been reported in neutropenic patients during treatment.[10]

In a trial comparing intravenous ciprofloxacin (200 mg every 12 hours) plus netilmicin, with piperacillin plus netilmicin, patients were stratified according to the presence of an haematological or solid tumour.[11] Treatment was continued until neutropenia resolved. Of 115 patients given the ciprofloxacin regimen, 68 (59%) recovered compared with 61 of 99 (62%) given the piperacillin regimen. Gram-positive bacteria, usually coagulase-negative staphylococci, caused 67% of the 76 cases of bacteraemia and only 41% of patients on the ciprofloxacin regimen and 40% on the piperacillin regimen responded without addition of a glycopeptide.

To improve activity against streptococci, ciprofloxacin (200 mg every 12 hours) was given with benzylpenicillin and compared in a randomised trial with piperacillin plus netilmicin.[12] In the ciprofloxacin group, response was observed in 33 of 51 (65%) patients similar to the rate in the piperacillin group (30/46, 65%). The success rate with documented infections was higher in the ciprofloxacin group (24/36, 67% versus 19/34, 56%). A third of the failures in both groups was related to bacteraemia with coagulase-negative staphylococci. The number of adverse events in each group was not significantly different (32% for the ciprofloxacin group and 28% for the piperacillin group), but more patients in the netilmicin group tended to have renal impairment. Another trial compared ciprofloxacin (200 mg every 12 hours) with gentamicin; both groups also received azlocillin. Response was observed in 58 of 80 (73%) patients in the ciprofloxacin group and in 42 of

67 (63%) patients in the gentamicin group (not significant).[13] One patient experienced convulsions thought to be related to ciprofloxacin. Comparison with netilmicin instead of gentamicin produced similar results (20/37, 54% for ciprofloxacin plus azlocillin and 13/36, 36% for netilmicin plus azlocillin without modification).[14]

To avoid failures due to coagulase-negative staphylococci, teicoplanin has been used with ciprofloxacin (200 mg every 12 hours) from the onset of a febrile episode.[15] No antagonism between the two antibiotics was detected *in vitro*.[16] A total of 28 of 36 (78%) patients were cured or improved after the ciprofloxacin regimen compared with 17 of 35 (49%) given piperacillin and gentamicin ($p < 0.05$). Ten of 12 cases of infection with *Staphylococcus epidermidis* responded to teicoplanin and ciprofloxacin in contrast to 2 of 8 cases treated with piperacillin and gentamicin ($p = 0.03$). Another randomised trial compared ciprofloxacin with ceftazidime, but added teicoplanin whenever there was a suspicion of a catheter-related infection. Cure rates were not significantly different either with monotherapy (23/28, 82% for cipro-floxacin versus 18/31, 58% for ceftazidime) or in combination with teicoplanin (11/15, 73% and 8/12, 67%, respectively).[17] In patients receiving ciprofloxacin alone, eight cases of bacteraemia caused by resistant organisms, mostly Gram-positive bacteria, were detected during treatment.

Flaherty *et al.* compared ciprofloxacin, 300 mg administered intravenously every 12 hours, plus azlocillin with ceftazidime plus amikacin, both groups converting to oral ciprofloxacin, 550 mg every 12 hours, after 72 hours.[18] A third group was given ceftazidime plus amikacin only. Clinical success was reported in 8 of 25 in the first group, 12 of 24 in the second and 15 of 30 in the third. Another 15, 10 and 12 patients, respectively, improved after changing the antibiotic regimen. Oral ciprofloxacin was used successfully in 13 patients in the first group and in 19 in the second group.

Ciprofloxacin can be used to treat febrile neutropenic episodes in out-patients by the oral route. Oral ciprofloxacin has been given to complete treatment courses that were started in hospital[11] but can also be used to avoid admission.[19] Reduction of the number of hospital admissions has important benefits in terms of costs, reduced exposure to hospital pathogens and improved quality of life, particularly in children. Ciprofloxacin at a dose of 750 mg every 8 hours administered orally, cured 85% of 46 febrile episodes treated as out-patients.[20]

A combination of oral ciprofloxacin (750 mg every 12 hours) plus intravenous teicoplanin (400 mg once daily) was successful in 26 of 35 (74%) febrile out-patient episodes.[19] Ciprofloxacin plus co-amoxiclav, both administered orally, seemed to be as effective as intravenous aztreonam plus clindamycin (25/27 and 22/25, respectively).[21] Patients treated with ceftazidime or piperacillin–tobramycin have been changed successfully onto oral ciprofloxacin after 4 days and their hospital stay shortened.[22] Only 1 of 43 patients required readmission. Oral ciprofloxacin (1.5 g/day) plus penicillin V and amikacin plus carbenicillin–ceftazidime both resulted in a 94% cure rate in a trial of 108 patients.[23]

Prophylactic use

Antibiotics are commonly used prophylactically to prevent infection during neutropenia in cancer patients, particularly those with profound neutropenia for more than 1 week, (administered 2–3 days before the onset of neutropenia until recovery). Faecal concentrations of ciprofloxacin are high after oral administration and sufficient to inhibit even less susceptible species, for example, *Stenotrophomonas* spp.[24] Concentrations in the saliva, however, may be inadequate, inhibiting only 75% of *Pseudomonas* spp. Most Gram-positive organisms causing bacteraemia in neutropenic patients are resistant to quinolones.

Co-trimoxazole is effective in preventing Gram-negative bacteraemia, but lacks antipseudomonal activity and may prolong granulo-cytopenia. Ciprofloxacin (1 g/day) appeared to be more effective in preventing bacteraemia than co-trimoxazole–colistin in one trial.[25] Five infections were diagnosed in 28 patients given ciprofloxacin compared with 14 in 28 patients given the standard regimen. There were no Gram-negative infections in the ciprofloxacin group, but seven in the control group. Ciprofloxacin was less effective, however, in another trial (though still more effective than controls) with 35 of 113 patients versus 21 of 117 remaining free of any infection ($p = 0.02$).[26] The delay from the start of neutropenia to infection was longer with co-trimoxazole, and patients given ciprofloxacin required more antibiotics for treatment. Nevertheless, there were no bacteraemic episodes due to Gram-negative bacteria or staphylococci in the ciprofloxacin group compared with five in the co-trimoxazole group. The difference in findings may have related to the longer period of uninterrupted neutropenia in the second trial. Oral ciprofloxacin (500 mg every 12 hours) compares favourably with the more complicated standard prophylactic regimen of neomycin (250 mg every 6 hours), polymyxin B (100 mg every 6 hours) and nalidixic acid (1 g every 12 hours).[27] Signs of infection developed in 31 of 63 (49%) patients given ciprofloxacin and 22 of 33 (67%) of patients given the standard regimen during neutropenia.

Ciprofloxacin appears to be superior to other quinolones for the prevention of febrile episodes, but there is a risk of the emergence of bacterial resistance. A large randomised trial showed a significant reduction in febrile episodes and Gram-negative infection when ciprofloxacin was used compared with norfloxacin (Figure 9.2).[28] Patients had a longer period from the start of neutropenia to the first febrile episode and less antibiotic treatment was needed. D'Antonio *et al.* found that the development of fever was not affected by the choice of quinolone (500 mg oral ciprofloxacin every 12 hours: 44/78, 56%; 300 mg oral ofloxacin every 12 hours: 48/80, 60%; and 400 mg oral pefloxacin every 12 hours: 50/77, 65%, respectively, not significant).[29] However, there

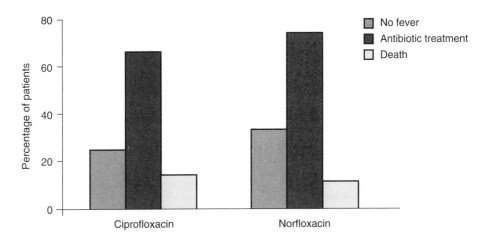

Figure 9.2. Comparison of ciprofloxacin (n = 319) and norfloxacin (n = 300) in the prevention of febrile neutropenic episodes.[28]

were no episodes of Gram-negative bacteraemia in the ciprofloxacin group compared with 3 and 7 in the other groups (p = 0.01). The isolated pathogens were resistant to quinolones. The numbers colonised with resistant Enterobacteriaceae increased from 6 to 11 during a course of ciprofloxacin, from 6 to 16 during ofloxacin and from 7 to 18 during pefloxacin prophylaxis. A third group found no significant difference in the number of infections in leukaemic patients given ciprofloxacin, ofloxacin or co-trimoxazole–colistin (7/30 versus 7/31 versus 10/27, respectively).[30]

In patients undergoing bone marrow transplantation, ciprofloxacin (500 mg administered every 12 hours) was effective in preventing Gram-negative bacteraemia but Gram-positive bacteraemia occurred in 42 patients, usually with streptococci.[31] Erythromycin has been used to try to improve the activity of the regimen,[24] but in a consecutive non-randomised study of 53 patients having bone marrow transplantation, there was no significant difference in the proportion of days of fever whether ciprofloxacin was given with or without erythromycin.[32] Ciprofloxacin (500 mg/day) plus ketoconazole was also effective as prophylaxis in 50 patients with advanced lymphoma, 42 remaining free of infection after 17 months.[33]

Conclusions

Ciprofloxacin is an established agent in the treatment of febrile neutropenic episodes and has the advantage of intravenous or oral dosage (200 mg administered intravenously every 12 hours or 750 mg given orally every 12 hours). Patients can be treated at home or on a day-case basis if sufficiently well. There is some evidence that the use of combinations, with aminoglycosides or ureidopenicillins, for example, are preferable to monotherapy. Combination with teicoplanin reduces the number of early failures caused by coagulase-negative staphylococci, but may not alter the final outcome. Ciprofloxacin can be given to prevent febrile episodes particularly those caused by Gram-negative bacteria. However, pathogens resistant to ciprofloxacin may emerge.

References

1. Maschmeyer G. Therapeutic use of quinolones in oncology. In: Garrard C, ed. Ciprofloxacin i.v. Berlin: Springer-Verlag, 1994: 97–108.
2. Giamarellou H. Ciprofloxacin in neutropenic host infection. In: Garrard C, ed. Ciprofloxacin i.v. Berlin: Springer-Verlag, 1994: 109–19.

3. Rolston KVI, Haron E, Cunningham C, Bodey GP. Intravenous ciprofloxacin for infections in cancer patients. Am J Med 1989; 87 (Suppl 5A): 261–5.
4. Johnson PRE, Liu Yin JA, Tooth JA. High dose intravenous ciprofloxacin in febrile neutropenic patients. J Antimicrob Chemother 1990; 26 (Suppl F): 101–7.
5. Smith GM, Leyland MJ, Farrell ID, Geddes AM. A clinical, microbiological and pharmacokinetic study of ciprofloxacin plus vancomycin as initial therapy of febrile episodes in neutropenic patients. J Antimicrob Chemother 1988; 21: 647–55.
6. Samuelsson J, Nilsson P, Wahlin A, Lerner R, Winqvist I, Palmblad J. A pilot study of piperacillin and ciprofloxacin as initial therapy for fever in severely neutropenic leukaemia patients. Scand J Infect Dis 1992; 24: 467–75.
7. Bayston KF, Want S, Cohen J. A prospective, randomized comparison of ceftazidime and ciprofloxacin as initial empiric therapy in neutropenic patients with fever. Am J Med 1989; 87 (Suppl 5A): 269–73.
8. Johnson PRE, Liu Yin JA, Tooth JA. A randomized trial of high-dose ciprofloxacin versus azlocillin and netilmicin in the empirical therapy of febrile neutropenic patients. J Antimicrob Chemother 1992; 30: 203–14.
9. Meunier F, Zinner SH, Gaya H, Calandra T, Viscoli C, Klastersky J et al. Prospective randomized evaluation of ciprofloxacin versus piperacillin plus amikacin for empiric therapy of febrile granulocytopenic cancer patients with lymphomas and solid tumors. Antimicrob Agents Chemother 1991; 35: 873–8.
10. Somolinos N, Arranz R, Del Rey MC, Jiménez ML. Superinfections by Escherichia coli resistant to fluoroquinolones in immunocompromised patients. J Antimicrob Chemother 1992; 30: 730–1.
11. Chan CC, Oppenheim BA, Anderson H, Swindell R, Scarffe JH. Randomized trial comparing ciprofloxacin plus netilmicin versus piperacillin plus netilmicin for empiric treatment of fever in neutropenic patients. Antimicrob Agents Chemother 1989; 33: 87–91.
12. Kelsey SM, Wood ME, Shaw E, Jenkins GC, Newland AC. A comparative study of intravenous ciprofloxacin and benzylpenicillin versus netilmicin and piperacillin for the empirical treatment of fever in neutropenic patients. J Antimicrob Chemother 1990; 25: 149–57.
13. Philpott-Howard JN, Barker KF, Wade JJ, Kaczmarski RS, Smedley JC, Mufti GJ. Randomized multicentre study of ciprofloxacin and azlocillin versus gentamicin and azlocillin in the treatment of febrile neutropenic patients. J Antimicrob Chemother 1990; 26 (Suppl F): 89–99.
14. Hyatt DS, Rogers TRF, McCarthy DM, Samson DS. A randomized trial of ciprofloxacin plus azlocillin versus netilmicin plus azlocillin for the empirical treatment of fever in neutropenic patients. J Antimicrob Chemother 1991; 28: 324–6.
15. Kelsey SM, Weinhardt B, Collins PW, Newland AC. Teicoplanin plus ciprofloxacin versus gentamicin plus piperacillin in the treatment of febrile neutropenic patients. Eur J Clin Microbiol Infect Dis 1992; 11: 509–14.
16. Lewin CS, Kelsey SM, Paton R, Newland AC, Amyes SGB. Assessment of the interaction between ciprofloxacin and teicoplanin in vitro and in neutropenic patients. J Antimicrob Chemother 1990; 26: 549–59.
17. Lim SH, Smith MP, Goldstone AH, Machin SJ. A randomized prospective study of ceftazidime and ciprofloxacin with or without teicoplanin as an empiric antibiotic regimen for febrile neutropenic patients. Br J Haematol 1990; 76 (Suppl 2): 41–4.
18. Flaherty JP, Waitley D, Edlin B, George D, Arnow P, O'Keefe P et al. Multicenter, randomized trial of ciprofloxacin plus azlocillin versus ceftazidime plus amikacin for empiric treatment of febrile neutropenic patients. Am J Med 1989; 87 (Suppl 5A): 278–82.
19. Ketley NJ, Kelsey SM, Newland AC. Teicoplanin and oral ciprofloxacin as outpatient treatment of infective episodes in patients with indwelling central venous catheters and haematological malignancy. Clin Lab Haematol 1995; 17: 71–4.
20. Haron E, Rolston KVI, Cunningham C, Holmes F, Umsawasdi T, Bodey GP. Oral ciprofloxacin therapy for infections in cancer patients. J Antimicrob Chemother 1989; 24: 955–62.
21. Rolston K, Rubenstein E, Frisbee-Hume S, Escalante C, Manzullo E, Wheeler A et al. Outpatient treatment of febrile episodes in low-risk neutropenic cancer patients. 29th American Society for Clinical Oncology, Orlando, USA 1993; 12: 436 (Abstract 1505).
22. Tomiak A, Yau J, Huan S, Cripps C, Young Y, Goel R et al. Duration of intravenous antibiotic and hospital stay for patients with febrile neutropenia after chemotherapy: Experience of Ottawa Regional Cancer Centre. 29th American Society for Clinical Oncology, Orlando, USA 1993; 12: 435 (Abstract 1500).
23. Velasco E, Costa MA, Rabinowits M, Martins CA, Arnaud DG. Randomized trial comparing oral ciprofloxacin plus penicillin V with amikacin plus carbenicillin or ceftazidime in cancer patients with neutropenic fever. 29th American Society for Clinical Oncology, Orlando, USA 1993; 12: 445 (Abstract 1541).
24. Warren RE, Wimperis JZ, Baglin TP, Constantine CE, Marcus R. Prevention of infection by ciprofloxacin in neutropenia. J Antimicrob Chemother 1990; 26 (Suppl F): 109–23.
25. Dekker A, Rozenberg-Arska M, Verhoef J. Infection prophylaxis in acute leukaemia: a comparison of ciprofloxacin with trimethoprim–sulfamethoxazole and colistin. Ann Intern Med 1987; 106: 7–12.
26. Donnelly JP, Maschmeyer G, Daenen S. EORTC-Gnotobiotic Project Group. Selective oral antimicrobial prophylaxis for the prevention of infection in acute leukaemia – ciprofloxacin versus co-trimoxazole plus colistin. Eur J Cancer 1992; 28A: 873–8.

27. Jansen J, Cromer M, Akard L, Black JR, Wheat LJ, Allen SD. Infection prevention in severely myelosuppressed patients: a comparison between ciprofloxacin and a regimen of selective antibiotic modulation of the intestinal flora. Am J Med 1994; 96: 335–41.

28. Del Favero A, Menchetti F, Martino P, Mandelli F. Prevention of bacterial infection in neutropenic patients with hematologic malignancies: a randomized, multicenter trial comparing norfloxacin with ciprofloxacin. Ann Intern Med 1991; 115: 7–12.

29. D'Antonio D, Piccolomini R, Iacone A, Fioritoni G, Parruti G, Betti S et al. Comparison of ciprofloxacin, ofloxacin and pefloxacin for the prevention of bacterial infection in neutropenic patients with haematological malignancies. J Antimicrob Chemother 1994; 33: 837–44.

30. Arning M, Wolf HH, Aul C, Heyll A, Scharf RE, Scheider W. Infection prophylaxis in neutropenic patients with acute leukaemia: a randomized, comparative study with ofloxacin, ciprofloxacin and co-trimoxazole/colistin. J Antimicrob Chemother 1990; 26 (Suppl D): 137–42.

31. De Pauw BE, Donnelly JP, De Witte T, Novakova IR, Schattenberg A. Options and limitations of long term oral ciprofloxacin as antibacterial prophylaxis in allogeneic bone marrow transplant recipients. Bone Marrow Transplant 1990; 5: 179–82.

32. Wimperis JZ, Baglin TP, Marcus RE, Warren RE. An assessment of the efficacy of antimicrobial prophylaxis in bone marrow autografts. Bone Marrow Transplant 1991; 8: 363–7.

33. Landys KE, Berg GEB, Michanek AMK. Prophylactic use of oral ciprofloxacin and ketoconazole in patients with advanced lymphoma. In: Gemmell CG, ed. Ciprofloxacin in hematology and oncology. New York: Raven Press, 1993: 57–63.

Chapter 10

Sexually transmitted diseases

Ciprofloxacin is highly effective against gonorrhoea and chancroid, including the increasing proportion of strains resistant to penicillins and tetracyclines, and can be effective as a single dose. An effective single-dose treatment is extremely useful in the management of patients with sexually transmitted diseases. Unfortunately, despite the success against gonorrhoea, single-dose ciprofloxacin is not effective against chlamydial urethritis or in the treatment of syphilis.

Gonorrhoea

In many countries the treatment of gonorrhoea is complicated by the prevalence of multiple antibiotic resistance and frequent failure of single-dose treatment of rectal or pharyngeal gonorrhoea using older agents. Parenteral administration of antibiotics may not be acceptable to the patient, may be too expensive or, in some countries, may carry the risk of transmission of HIV. Consequently, there is a need for a widely effective single-dose agent. Ciprofloxacin, administered as a single 500 mg oral dose, is recommended by the Centers for Disease Control, Atlanta, USA, as an alternative to ceftriaxone for the treatment of gonorrhoea, including pharyngeal infections.[1]

A single oral dose of ciprofloxacin (250 mg) is effective against penicillinase-producing

strains and strains with chromosomal resistance to penicillin and tetracycline. In one study, there was no significant difference in efficacy between single doses of 250 mg or 500 mg (85/85 versus 79/79) but post-gonococcal urethritis developed in one-third of patients whatever the dose.[2] All 73 patients treated with a single dose in a Nigerian study were cured of gonorrhoea, with a prevalence of penicillinase-producing strains of 73%.[3] A review of 18 trials using the individual case record forms included 2026 patients treated with single oral doses ranging from 100 mg to 2000 mg.[4] The review included comparative studies in which cure rates were between 97% and 100%. Cure was achieved in 19 of 20 (95%) patients with pharyngeal infection and 38 of 39 (97%) patients with rectal gonorrhoea. Control regimens eradicated 472 of 498 (95%) infections. In the uncontrolled studies, gonorrhoea was cured in 671 of 673 (99.7%) patients by a single dose of ciprofloxacin. All 75 patients with rectal disease and 37 of 38 with pharyngeal disease were also cured.

In a study in Zambia, a double-blind trial showed that a single oral dose of ciprofloxacin (250 mg) cured all 83 men treated and ceftriaxone (250 mg, single intramuscular dose) cured 81 of 82 who were treated, despite a third of isolates being penicillinase producers and a fifth being multi-resistant[5] (Table 10.1).[5–15] A total of 30 patients (15 in each group) did not return for follow-up and 5 had negative cultures for gonorrhoea. Oral ciprofloxacin (250 mg) was again found to be as effective as an intramuscular dose of ceftriaxone in separate double-blind trials of treatment of uncomplicated

Wilson APR and Grüneberg RN.
Ciprofloxacin: 10 years of clinical experience
© 1997 Maxim Medical, Oxford.

Table 10.1. Randomised comparative trials of treatment of sexually transmitted diseases with ciprofloxacin.

Disease	Agent	Dose and route	Duration (days)	No. patients	No. withdrawn	No. cured	No. improved	No. failed	Reference
Gonococcal urethritis (men)	Ciprofloxacin	250 mg p.o. × 1 dose	1	100	17	83	0	0	5
	Ceftriaxone	250 mg i.m. × 1 dose	1	100	18	81	0	1	
Gonococcal urethritis (men)	Ciprofloxacin	250 mg p.o. × 1 dose	1	37	2	35	0	0	6
	Ceftriaxone	250 mg i.m. × 1 dose	1	37	6	28	0	3	
Gonococcal urethritis (men)	Ciprofloxacin	250 mg p.o. × 1 dose	1	53	4	48	0	1	7
	Ampicillin + probenecid	3.5 g p.o. × 1 dose 1 g p.o. × 1 dose	1	53	2	47	0	4	
Gonorrhoea (men)	Ciprofloxacin	250 mg p.o. × 1 dose	1	39		38	0	1	8
	Ampicillin + probenecid	2 g p.o. × 1 dose 1 g p.o. × 1 dose	1	45	2	43	0	2	
Gonorrhoea (women)	Ciprofloxacin	250 mg p.o. × 1 dose	1	130	36	94	0	0	9
	Ceftriaxone	250 mg i.m. × 1 dose	1	128	41	86	0	1	
Pelvic inflammatory disease	Ciprofloxacin	200 mg b.d. i.v. × 2 days then 750 mg b.d. p.o. × 12 days	14	20	4	15	0	1	10
	Doxycycline + metronidazole	100 mg b.d. i.v. × 2 days then 150 mg once daily p.o. × 12 days + 500 mg t.d.s. i.v. × 2 days then 400 mg t.d.s. p.o. × 12 days	14	20	0	14	0	6	

Table 10.1. (continued)

Disease	Agent	Dose and route	Duration (days)	No. patients	No. withdrawn	No. cured	No. improved	No. failed	Reference
Endometritis/ acute salpingitis	Ciprofloxacin	300 mg b.d. i.v. × 3 days then	10–14	48	0	41	0	7	11
		750 mg b.d. p.o. × 9 days		10	0	10	0	0	
	Clindamycin + gentamicin	900 mg t.d.s. i.v. + 1.5	10–14	46	0	34	0	12	
	Clindamycin	mg/kg t.d.s. i.v. × 3 days then 450 mg q.d.s. p.o. × 9 days		15	0	13	0	2	
Non-gonococcal urethritis (men)	Ciprofloxacin	500 mg b.d. p.o.	7	36		27	0	9	12
	Ofloxacin	200 mg b.d. p.o.	7	43	16	32	0	11	
Non-gonococcal urethritis (men)	Ciprofloxacin	750 mg b.d. p.o.	7	121	50	37	0	34	13
	Doxycycline	100 mg b.d. p.o.	7	104	30	45	0	29	
Chlamydial cervicitis/salpingitis	Ciprofloxacin	500 mg b.d. p.o.	10	18	0	15	0	3	14
	Doxycycline	200 mg b.d. p.o.	10	19	0	17	0	2	
Chancroid (men)	Ciprofloxacin	500 mg p.o. × 1 dose	1	46	2	28	13	3	15
	Ciprofloxacin	500 mg b.d. p.o.	3	47	4	27	13	3	
	Co-trimoxazole	960 mg b.d. p.o.	3	46	1	28	12	5	

gonorrhoea (35/35 versus 28/31, 94/94 versus 86/87).[6,9] In another double-blind trial, ciprofloxacin (250 mg, single oral dose) and ampicillin–probenecid (3.5 g/1.0 g administered orally) showed similar efficacy against urethral gonorrhoea in 106 men.[7]

Rectal and pharyngeal gonorrhoea have been treated successfully by a single oral dose of 250 mg of ciprofloxacin.[16] All 26 rectal infections and 15 of 16 pharyngeal infections were cured. A larger open study included 16 men and 23 women with rectal gonorrhoea, 10 men and 3 women with pharyngeal disease and 6 men and 6 women with both.[17] A single dose of ciprofloxacin cured all but one man who responded to a second dose. Urethral gonorrhoea was cured in 147 of 151 (97%) men and 52 of 53 (98%) women.

Chancroid

Chancroid is a common sexually transmitted disease in developing countries, caused by *Haemophilus ducreyi*. These organisms are often multi-resistant but retain susceptibility to ciprofloxacin. In a double-blind trial, a single oral dose of ciprofloxacin (500 mg) was similar in efficacy to 3-day courses of ciprofloxacin (500 mg, given orally every 12 hours for 3 days) or co-trimoxazole (960 mg, given orally every 12 hours for 3 days).[15] There were no clinical failures in the 40 patients given a 3-day course of ciprofloxacin but 2 patients given a single dose and 3 patients given co-trimoxazole did not respond. In another trial, a single dose of 500 mg of ciprofloxacin cured 15 of 18 patients with chancroid within 6 days and the remaining 3 patients within 3 weeks.[18]

Chlamydia

A single dose of ciprofloxacin is not effective in chlamydial infections. Patients have been treated for gonococcal infection but then developed post-gonococcal urethritis due to concomitant chlamydial or ureaplasma infections.[19,20] A review of 18 trials showed that chlamydia was not eradicated in 65 of 82 patients.[4] In one trial, single-dose ciprofloxacin failed to cure 10 of 11 patients compared with 10 of 14 failures after ampicillin–probenecid.[7] A course of 500 mg ciprofloxacin every 12 hours for 1 week was effective in only 3 of 14 patients with chlamydial urethritis in one trial and, of 29 of the 32 patients initially cured in another study, one quarter relapsed.[21,22] A comparative trial reported 27 of 36 (75%) patients with non-gonococcal urethritis were cured with ciprofloxacin compared with 32 of 43 (74%) patients given ofloxacin. If *Chlamydia trachomatis* was isolated, ofloxacin seemed to be more likely to eradicate the organism than ciprofloxacin (11/11 versus 8/13, $p = 0.03$) (Table 10.1).[12] At a higher dose (1.5 g/day), a double-blind comparison with doxycycline showed overall cure rates were similar (52%, 37/71 versus 61%, 45/74) but ciprofloxacin was inferior in chlamydial infections (10/22 versus 15/20, $p = 0.04$).[13] Ciprofloxacin tended to be more effective against *Ureaplasma urealyticum* (9/13 versus 9/20).

Pelvic inflammatory disease (PID) is the result of organisms from the vagina invading the endometrium and fallopian tubes. *Chlamydia trachomatis*, *Neisseria gonorrhoeae*, anaerobes, Gram-negative bacteria and mycoplasmas are implicated. Of 36 patients with PID, *Chlamydia trachomatis* was isolated from 15 patients and both chlamydiae and gonococci were isolated from six.[10] Ciprofloxacin (750 mg every 12 hours) given as a 2-week course was effective in 15 of 16 patients compared with 14 of 20 patients given doxycycline plus metronidazole.[10] The single failure with ciprofloxacin was an infection with *Escherichia coli* and *Bacteroides fragilis*. In another study, 14 of 48 patients with endometritis given ciprofloxacin and 8 of 46 others given clindamycin plus gentamicin had chlamydial infection.[11] *Chlamydia trachomatis* persisted in only one patient from each group. Treatment failed overall in 7 of 48 and 12 of 46 patients, respectively, with three of the ciprofloxacin failures being caused by microaerophilic streptococci. All 10 patients treated for acute salpingitis with ciprofloxacin and 13 of 15 treated with clindamycin/gentamicin were cured.[11]

Bacterial vaginosis

Ciprofloxacin has been assessed in the treatment of bacterial vaginosis in one uncontrolled trial.[23] Resolution of signs and symptoms was observed in 17 of 22 patients and improvement in another 4 following ciprofloxacin, 500 mg given orally every 12 hours for 1 week. However, follow-up continued for only 1 week and clue cells persisted in 11 cases.

Conclusions

Ciprofloxacin is a recommended single dose for gonorrhoea treatment (250 mg administered orally), even at rectal and pharyngeal sites. Chancroid also responds to a single 500 mg oral dose. Ciprofloxacin is less effective than standard treatments in chlamydial infection, although a prolonged course can cure pelvic inflammatory disease.

References

1. Centers for Disease Control and Prevention. 1993 Sexually transmitted diseases treatment guidelines. Morbid Mortal Weekly Rep 1993; 42: RR-14, 57.

2. Tegelberg-Stassen MJAM, van der Hoek JCS, Mooi L, Wagenvoort JHT, van Joost T, Michel MF et al. Treatment of uncomplicated gonococcal urethritis in men with two dosages of ciprofloxacin. Eur J Clin Microbiol 1986; 5: 244–6.

3. Otubu JAM, Imade GE, Sagay AS, Towobola OA. Resistance of recent Neisseria gonorrhoeae isolates in Nigeria and outcome of single-dose treatment with ciprofloxacin. Infection 1992; 20: 339–41.

4. Echols RM, Heyd A, O'Keefe BJ, Schacht P. Single dose ciprofloxacin for the treatment of uncomplicated gonorrhoea: a worldwide summary. Sex Transm Dis 1994; 21: 345–52.

5. Bryan JP, Hira SK, Brady W, Luo N, Mwale C, Mpoko G et al. Oral ciprofloxacin versus ceftriaxone for the treatment of urethritis from resistant Neisseria gonorrhoeae in Zambia. Antimicrob Agents Chemother 1990; 34: 819–22.

6. Fleites E, Rivera C, Ramirez-Ronda CH, Rivera-Castaño R, Saavedra S, Padilla B et al. Ciprofloxacin (CIP) versus ceftriaxone (CEF) in gonorrhea in males: a double blind study. 3rd International Symposium on New Quinolones. Vancouver, Canada, 1990: Abstract 304.

7. Roddy RE, Handsfield HH, Hook EW. Comparative trial of single-dose ciprofloxacin and ampicillin plus probenecid for treatment of gonococcal urethritis in men. Antimicrob Agents Chemother 1986; 30: 267–9.

8. Scott GR, McMillan A, Young H. Ciprofloxacin versus ampicillin and probenecid in the treatment of uncomplicated gonorrhoea. J Antimicrob Chemother 1987; 20: 117–21.

9. Hook EW, Jones RB, Martin DH, Bolan GA, Mroczkowski TF, Neumann TM et al. Comparison of ciprofloxacin and ceftriaxone as single dose therapy for uncomplicated gonorrhea in women. Antimicrob Agents Chemother 1993; 37: 1670–3.

10. Heinonen PK, Teisala K, Miettinen A, Aine R, Punnonen R, Grönroos P. A comparison of ciprofloxacin with doxycycline plus metronidazole in the treatment of acute pelvic inflammatory disease. Scand J Infect Dis 1989; 60 (Suppl): 66–73.

11. Apuzzio JJ, Stankiewicz R, Ganesh V, Jain S, Kaminski Z, Louria D. Comparison of parenteral ciprofloxacin with clindamycin–gentamicin in the treatment of pelvic infection. Am J Med 1989; 87 (Suppl 5A): 148–51.

12. Perea EJ, Aznar J, Herrera A, Mazuecos J, Rodriguez-Pichardo A. Clinical efficacy of new quinolones for therapy of nongonoccal urethritis. Sex Transm Dis 1989; 16: 7–10.

13. Fong IW, Linton W, Simbul M, Thorup R, McLaughlin B, Rahm V et al. Treatment of nongonococcal urethritis with ciprofloxacin. Am J Med 1987; 82 (Suppl 4A): 311–16.

14. Petersen EE. Chlamydia trachomatis infections in women. Therapy of ciprofloxacin against doxycycline. 6th Mediterranean Congress on Chemotherapy. Taormina, Italy, 1988: 129–31.

15. Naamara W, Plummer FA, Greenblatt SM, d'Costa LJ, Ndinya-Achola JO, Ronald AR. Treatment of chancroid with ciprofloxacin. Am J Med 1987; 82 (Suppl 4A): 317–20.

16. Coker DM, Ahmed-Jushuf I, Arya OP, Chessbrough JS, Pratt BC. Evaluation of single dose ciprofloxacin in the treatment of rectal and pharyngeal gonorrhoea. J Antimicrob Chemother 1989; 24: 271–2.

17. Balachandran T, Roberts AP, Evans BA, Azadian BS. Single dose therapy of anogenital and pharyngeal gonorrhoea with ciprofloxacin. Int J STD AIDS 1992; 3: 49–51.

18. Traisupa A, Wongba C, Tesavibul P. Efficacy and safety of a single dose therapy of a 500 mg ciprofloxacin tablet in chancroid patients. Infection 1988; 16 (Suppl 1): S44–5.

19. Loo PS, Ridgway GL, Oriel JD. Single dose ciprofloxacin for treating gonococcal infections in men. Genitourin Med 1985; 61: 302–5.

20. Aznar J, Prados R, Rodriguez-Pichardo A, Hernandez I, De Miguel C, Perea EJ *et al.* Comparative clinical efficacy of two different single dose ciprofloxacin treatments for uncomplicated gonorrhoea. Sex Transm Dis 1986; 13: 169–71.

21. Arya OP, Hobson D, Hart CA, Bartzokas C, Pratt BC. Evaluation of ciprofloxacin 500 mg twice daily for one week in treating uncomplicated gonococcal, chlamydial and non-specific urethritis in men. Genitourin Med 1986; 62: 170–4.

22. Stolz E, Wagenvoort JHT, Van der Willigen AH. Quinolones in the treatment of gonorrhoea and *Chlamydia trachomatis* infection. Pharm Weekbl (Sci) 1987; 9 (Suppl): 82–5.

23. Carmona O, Hernández-González S, Kobelt R. Ciprofloxacin in the treatment of nonspecific vaginitis. Am J Med 1987; 82 (Suppl 4A): 321–3.

Chapter 11

Osteomyelitis and septic arthritis

Osteomyelitis caused by Gram-negative bacteria is usually a result of severe trauma, penetrating injuries or surgery. *Pseudomonas aeruginosa* is a frequent isolate, either alone or in a mixed infection. Common sources of infection are a compound fracture, surgical intervention for fracture of a long bone, a nail puncturing the skin, or peripheral neuropathy resulting in pressure necrosis. Ischaemic ulcers can penetrate adjacent bone. Treatment requires surgical debridement and prolonged antibiotic administration, which prior to the advent of ciprofloxacin, was usually parenteral. It is difficult to assess the success of treatment because of the various factors that need to be taken into account, such as the type of bone, severity of infection, presence of sequestrum or foreign material, compliance and length of follow-up. Oral administration and good tolerance are particularly important because treatment is prolonged. With parenteral agents, such as ceftazidime, the cure/improvement rates for osteomyelitis caused by Gram-negative bacteria are high (96/101; 95%),[1] but prolonged hospitalisation is often necessary.

A number of studies have demonstrated the efficacy of a 6–12-week course of oral ciprofloxacin (750 mg, given every 12 hours) together with debridement for predominantly Gram-negative osteomyelitis (Table 11.1).[2–18] In one study, 13 of 20 patients were cured at 1-year follow-up, although 15 had undergone

surgery.[7] In a series of patients with chronic pseudomonal osteomyelitis, initial cures were observed in 27 of 32 patients but follow-up was only for 2 months.[9] Of 6 persistent pseudomonal infections, the pathogen was sensitive to ciprofloxacin in 3 cases. In another trial, 20 of 22 infections were cured by an oral course of ciprofloxacin, 750 mg, given every 12 hours for 37–122 days.[11] Sixteen patients had surgery and 8 received other antibiotics. Follow-up was between 1 and 17 months. Renal failure resulted in discontinuation of ciprofloxacin in one patient and vertigo (probably caused by aminoglycoside) resulted in the withdrawal of another patient from the trial. Other adverse effects were minor.

Ciprofloxacin is less reliably effective against osteomyelitis caused by staphylococci than that caused by Gram-negative bacteria. In one study, only 11 of 21 patients were treated successfully with ciprofloxacin alone for staphylococcal osteomyelitis, with oral administration being used after the first 3 days.[14] Treatment failed in 3 of 5 patients in another study.[19] Another investigation, however, reported cure in 8 of 10 cases caused by *Staphylococcus aureus*.[3] The organism may become resistant during treatment.[2] Osteomyelitis associated with prosthetic joints was cured without loss of the prosthesis in 20 of 27 patients treated with oral ciprofloxacin but, of the 3 failures, 2 infections were due to *Staphylococcus aureus*.[3] Long-term cure of staphylococcal infection is more likely when there is a high ratio of peak serum ciprofloxacin concentration to minimum inhibitory concentration (MIC).[4] In a series of 14 patients,

Wilson APR and Grüneberg RN.
Ciprofloxacin: 10 years of clinical experience
© 1997 Maxim Medical, Oxford.

Table 11.1. Open clinical trials of the use of ciprofloxacin in the treatment of osteomyelitis and septic arthritis.

Disease and pathogens	Sex (M:F) Age (years)	Dose	Duration	Single agent	Follow-up	Cured/ improved	Failed/ recurred	Odds ratio (95% CI)	Reference
Osteomyelitis									
Staphylococcus aureus, Enterobacteriaceae	12:5 40–94	750 mg p.o. b.d.	28–254 days	All	1 year	13	4	24 (7–50)	2
Enterobacteriaceae, *Pseudomonas aeruginosa*, *Staphylococcus aureus*	6:21 18–90	500–750 mg p.o. b.d.	17–189 days	All	6 months	24	3	11 (2–29)	3
Staphylococcus aureus, *Pseudomonas aeruginosa*	10:1 29–74	750 mg p.o. b.d.	53 days (mean)	All	1 year	6	8	57 (29–82)	4
Mixed, predominantly Gram-negative	12:6 21–73	750 mg p.o. b.d.	2–52 weeks	14/18	4–35 months	15	3	17 (4–41)	5
Enterobacteriaceae	24:6 24–85	750 mg p.o. b.d.	39–163 days	All	6 months	22	8	27 (12–46)	6
Pseudomonas aeruginosa, Enterobacteriaceae	14:6 20–75	750 mg p.o. b.d.	6–12 weeks	All	1 year	13	7	35 (15–59)	7
Pseudomonas aeruginosa	12:8 14–84	750 mg p.o. b.d.	1–4 months	All	6 months	19	1	5 (1–25)	8
Pseudomonas aeruginosa, coagulase-negative staphylococci	24:11 18–86	500–1500 mg p.o. b.d.	15–476 days	All	2 months	27	7	26 (11–46)	9
Pseudomonas aeruginosa, coagulase-negative staphylococci	16:7	750 mg p.o. b.d. 23–77	41–191 days	18/23	6 months	14	0	0 (0–23)	10
Pseudomonas aeruginosa, Enterobacteriaceae	16:7 23–88	750 mg p.o. b.d.	37–122 days	All	1–17 months	20	2	9 (11–29)	11

Table 11.1. (continued)

Disease and pathogens	Sex (M:F) Age (years)	Dose	Duration	Single agent	Follow-up	Cured/ improved	Failed/ recurred	Odds ratio (95% CI)	Reference
Pseudomonas aeruginosa, Enterobacteriaceae	10:5	750 mg p.o. b.d.	28–100 days	Not known	9 months	12	3	20 (4–48)	12
Pseudomonas aeruginosa	14:5 16–89	750 mg p.o. b.d.	3 weeks– 4 months	All	1 year	18	1	6 (1–27)	13
Staphylococcus aureus, Pseudomonas aeruginosa	14:7 22–66	200 mg i.v. b.d. × 3 days, then 750 mg p.o. b.d.	25–139 days	20/21	3–13 days	20	1	5 (1–25)	14
Pseudomonas aeruginosa, Staphylococcus aureus	24:5 15–85	500–750 mg p.o. b.d.	17–181 days	34/41	1 year	14	8	28 (13–47)	15
Staphylococcus aureus, Staphylococcus epidermidis, Enterobacteriaceae (diabetic patients)	29 64 (mean)	750–1000 mg p.o. b.d.	3 months	All	1 year	19	10	35 (18–54)	16
Pseudomonas spp., Staphylococcus aureus, Enterobacter spp., Serratia spp.	– 55–64 (mean)	500–750 mg p.o. b.d.	11–127 days	30/37	–	30	7	19 (8–35)	17
Pseudomonas aeruginosa	21:8 17–79	500–750 mg p.o. b.d.	2–36 weeks	All	9 months	16	4	20 (6–44)	18
Septic arthritis									
Escherichia coli, Staphylococcus aureus, Pseudomonas aeruginosa	–	500–750 mg p.o. b.d.	14–28 days	All	1 year	1	2	–	15
Pseudomonas aeruginosa	21:8 17–79	500–750 mg p.o. b.d.	2–36 weeks	All	9 months	6	3	33 (8–70)	18

treatment failed or resulted in relapse in 8, but the peak serum ciprofloxacin concentration: MIC ratio was 12.8 in patients who were cured compared with 5.9 in patients in whom treatment failed.

Treatment of osteomyelitis caused by methicillin-resistant *Staphylococcus aureus* (MRSA) has resulted in poor cure rates. Of 22 patients with osteomyelitis of various causes, 14 were cured, 2 failed to respond and 6 relapsed.[15] However, 4 of the 6 patients with infections caused by MRSA were among those with recurrent disease. Two of 4 treatment failures in another series of 17 patients also occurred with MRSA infections.[2]

Oral administration of ciprofloxacin is a considerable advantage in the prolonged treatment required in osteomyelitis and avoids the need for prolonged in-patient stay. Costs are greatly reduced and the quality of life improved (see Chapter 17). Out-patient treatment of 30 patients with acute or chronic osteomyelitis caused by Gram-negative or mixed bacteria resulted in cure of 22 at 6 months after an average course of 78 days.[6] The common causative organisms were *Escherichia coli*, *Serratia marcescens* and *Enterobacter aerogenes*.

Oral ciprofloxacin, 100 mg/day for 9 weeks, was used successfully to treat osteomyelitis in a child caused by a multi-resistant *Salmonella* sp.[20] following the failure of treatment with high-dose chloramphenicol, 100 mg/kg/day. A course of 200–400 mg, given every 12 hours intravenously for 8 weeks, cured osteomyelitis around a prosthetic hip joint caused by *Campylobacter jejuni*.[21] Osteomyelitis caused by *Mycobacterium haemophilum* in AIDS patients was treated successfully by regimens incorporating ciprofloxacin.[22]

Randomised trials

Randomised trials are unusual in the treatment of bone and joint infection because few patients can be recruited. Those trials that are available are small or of poor design. One randomised trial compared oral ciprofloxacin with a parenteral regimen of ceftazidime or nafcillin plus amikacin[23] (Table 11.2).[23–27] All patients had undergone debridement before treatment and infections due to MRSA were excluded. There was no significant difference in efficacy, with 24 of 31 (77%) patients cured with ciprofloxacin versus 22 of 28 (79%). Three of 4 polymicrobial infections were not cured by ciprofloxacin, nor were 2 similar infections treated under the control regimen. However, all 9 infections caused by *Pseudomonas aeruginosa* alone were cured. Superinfections occurred in 4 patients given ciprofloxacin and in 2 given the control regimen, but none of the organisms were resistant to ciprofloxacin.

Another randomised trial of oral ciprofloxacin against standard regimens suggested the rate of cure was similar but numbers were small (7/14 [50%] versus 11/16 [69%]).[24] Although ciprofloxacin alone was well tolerated (2 mild adverse events), neutropenia, diarrhoea or allergies developed in 5 of 16 patients given combination regimens. Two other trials included cases caused by *Staphylococcus aureus* and showed similar cure rates to standard regimens in small numbers of patients (7/10 versus 7/11; 11/14 versus 10/12).[25,26] A larger trial comparing ciprofloxacin and ceftriaxone found no treatment failures in any of the 70 patients, but fewer developed adverse effects following a course of ciprofloxacin.[27]

Combining the results of four trials, Lew and Waldvogel showed that out of a total of 94 patients treated with ciprofloxacin, 81% were cured, 2% improved and treatment failed in 18%.[28] Standard parenteral therapy resulted in cure in 85% and improvement in 15% of patients in comparator groups.

Septic arthritis

Experience of the treatment of septic arthritis with ciprofloxacin is limited and prosthetic joint infection usually requires surgical intervention. Three of 4 cases reported by Kaufmann *et al.*[18] were cured of knee infections due to Gram-negative bacteria. In

Table 11.2. Comparative clinical trials of treatment of osteomyelitis.

Pathogens	Sex (M:F) Age (years)	Regimen	Duration (days)	Single agent	Follow-up	Cured/ improved	Failed/ recurred	Odds ratio (95% CI)	Reference
Pseudomonas aeruginosa, Staphylococcus aureus, Enterobacteriaceae	26:5 36 (mean)	Ciprofloxacin 750 mg p.o. b.d. versus	28–96	All	1 year	24	7	0.9 (0.3–3)	23
	25:3 38 (mean)	Ceftazidime/nafcillin + amikacin	8–77	–	–	22	6	–	
Enterobacteriaceae, *Pseudomonas aeruginosa, Staphylococcus aureus,*	20:10 52 (mean)	Ciprofloxacin, 750 mg p.o. b.d. versus various	44–73	All	0–13 months	7	7	3.2 (0.8–1.4)	24
			19–150		0–13 months	11	5		
Staphylococcus aureus, mixed infections	–	Ciprofloxacin, 750 mg p.o. b.d. versus various	72 (mean)	All	–	7	3	1.3 (0.2–8)	25
			44 (mean)			7	4		
Staphylococcus aureus, coagulase-negative staphylococci, Enterobacteriaceae	12:2 34 (mean) 7:5 33 (mean)	Ciprofloxacin, 750 mg p.o. b.d. versus various	28–64	All	25–39 months	11	3	1.3 (0.2–9.9)	26
			29–60		24–36 months	10	2		
Enterobacteriaceae, *Staphyloccus aureus*	31:4	Ciprofloxacin, 200 mg i.v. b.d. for 2 weeks, then 500 mg p.o. b.d. versus	90	All	1 year	35	0	–	27
	32:3	Ceftriaxone + amikacin				35	0		

another study, infections in 2 of 3 patients treated with oral ciprofloxacin (500–750 mg, given every 12 hours for 2–4 weeks) failed to respond to the treatment.[15] Both failures were mixed infections (*Staphylococcus aureus* with Gram-negative bacteria), and in one of these patients ciprofloxacin-resistant *Pseudomonas aeruginosa* was isolated during treatment.

The successful treatment of septic arthritis caused by *Salmonella* spp. has been described in several case reports, including some associated with prosthetic joints.[29–33] One infection had failed to respond to treatment with ceftazidime and amikacin and the organism was resistant to chloramphenicol and ampicillin.[29] The patient recovered, however, with intravenous then oral ciprofloxacin.

Conclusions

Ciprofloxacin is an effective and widely used treatment (250 mg given intravenously every 12 hours, then 750 mg given orally every 12 hours) for osteomyelitis caused by Gram-negative organisms, particularly when combined with debridement. It has the advantage over other agents that, once the patient is improving, it can be given orally (750 mg every 12 hours) for the 6–12-week course. Staphylococcal osteomyelitis is better treated with alternative antibiotics. Septic arthritis has been treated occasionally with ciprofloxacin but treatment should be limited to Gram-negative infections.

References

1. Gentry LO. Treatment of skin, skin structure, bone and joint infections with ceftazidime. Am J Med 1985; 79 (Suppl 2A): 67–74.
2. Yamaguti A, Trevisanello C, Lobo IMF, Carvalho MCS, Bortoletto ML, Silva MLR *et al.* Oral ciprofloxacin for treatment of chronic osteomyelitis. Int J Clin Pharm Res 1993; XIII: 75–9.
3. Hoogkamp-Korstanje JAA, van Bottenburg HA, van Bruggen J, Detmar SJ, de Graaf W, Rijinks J *et al.* Treatment of chronic osteomyelitis with ciprofloxacin. J Antimicrob Chemother 1989; 23: 427–32.
4. Lentino JR, Preheim LC, Mellencamp MA, Dworzack DL. Oral ciprofloxacin versus parenteral ceftriaxone in the therapy of acute and chronic osteomyelitis due to *Staphylococcus aureus* and other pathogens. Eur J Clin Microbiol Infect Dis Special Issue 1991: 411–12.
5. MacGregor RR, Graziani AL, Esterhai JL. Oral ciprofloxacin for osteomyelitis. Orthopedics 1990; 13: 55–60.
6. Slama TG, Misinski J, Sklar S. Oral ciprofloxacin therapy for osteomyelitis caused by aerobic Gram-negative bacilli. Am J Med 1987; 82 (Suppl 4A): 259–61.
7. Gilbert DN, Tice AD, Marsh PK, Craven PC, Preheim LC. Oral ciprofloxacin therapy for chronic contiguous osteomyelitis caused by aerobic Gram-negative bacilli. Am J Med l987; 82 (Suppl 4A): 254–8.
8. Dan M, Siegman-Igra Y, Pitlik S, Raz R. Oral ciprofloxacin treatment of *Pseudomonas aeruginosa* osteomyelitis. Antimicrob Agents Chemother 1990; 34: 849–52.
9. Swedish Study Group. Therapy of acute and chronic Gram-negative osteomyelitis with ciprofloxacin. J Antimicrob Chemother 1988; 22: 221–8.
10. Lesse AJ, Freer C, Salata RA, Francis JB, Scheld WM. Oral ciprofloxacin therapy for Gram-negative bacillary osteomyelitis. Am J Med 1987; 82 (Suppl 4A): 247–53.
11. Trexler Hessen M, Ingerman MJ, Kaufman DH, Weiner P, Santoro J, Korzeniowski OM *et al.* Clinicial efficacy of ciprofloxacin therapy for gram-negative bacillary osteomyelitis. Am J Med 1987; 82 (Suppl 4A): 262–5.
12. Tice AD, Marsh PK, Craven PC. Ciprofloxacin administered orally as therapy for osteomyelitis. Rev Infect Dis 1988; 10 (Suppl 1): 187.
13. Giamarellou H, Galanakis N, Charalampopoulous D, Stephanou J, Daphinis E, Daikos GK. Ciprofloxacin in the treatment of bone infections. Rev Infect Dis 1988; 10 (Suppl 1): S190–1.
14. Stuyck J, Verbist L, Mulier JC. Treatment of chronic osteomyelitis with ciprofloxacin. Pharm Weekbl (Sci) 1987; 9 (Suppl): 93–6.
15. Greenberg RN, Kennedy DJ, Reilly PM. Treatment of bone, joint and soft-tissue infections with oral ciprofloxacin. Antimicrob Agents Chemother 1987; 31: 151–5.
16. Peterson LR, Lissack LM, Canter K, Fasching CE, Clabots C, Gerding DN. Therapy of lower extremity infections with ciprofloxacin in patients with diabetes mellitus, peripheral vascular disease or both. Am J Med 1989; 86: 801–8.
17. Nix DE. Oral ciprofloxacin in the treatment of serious soft tissue and bone infections. Am J Med 1987; 82 (Suppl 4A): 146–53.
18. Kaufmann G, Bindschedler M, Frei R, Follath F. Ciprofloxacin as therapy for infections of bones and joints due to Gram-negative organisms. Rev Infect Dis 1989; 11 (Suppl 5): 1266–7.

19. Dellamonica P, Bernard E, Etesse H, Garaffo R, Drugeon HB. Evaluation of pefloxacin, ofloxacin and ciprofloxacin in the treatment of thirty-nine cases of chronic osteomyelitis. Eur J Clin Microbiol Infect Dis 1989; 8: 1024–30.

20. Kiess W, Haas R, Marget W. Chloramphenicol-resistant *Salmonella tennessee* osteomyelitis. Infection 1984; 12: 359.

21. Peterson MC, Farr RW, Castiglia M. Prosthetic hip infection and bacteremia due to *Campylobacter jejuni* in a patient with AIDS. Clin Infect Dis 1993; 16: 439–40.

22. Yarrish RL, Shay W, LaBombardi VJ, Meyerson M, Miller DK, Larone D. Osteomyelitis caused by *Mycobacterium haemophilum*: successful therapy in two patients with AIDS. AIDS 1992; 6: 557–61.

23. Gentry LO, Rodriguez GG. Oral ciprofloxacin compared with parenteral antibiotics in the treatment of osteomyelitis. Antimicrob Agents Chemother 1990; 34: 40–3.

24. Greenberg RN, Tice AD, Marsh PK, Craven PC, Reilly PM, Bollinger M *et al.* Randomized trial of ciprofloxacin compared with other antimicrobial therapy in the treatment of osteomyelitis. Am J Med 1987; 82 (Suppl 4A): 266–9.

25. Snydman DR, Barza M, McGowan K, Kaplan K, Cuchural GC, Gill M *et al.* Randomized comparative trial of ciprofloxacin for treatment of patients with osteomyelitis. Rev Infect Dis 1989; 11 (Suppl 5): 1271–2.

26. Mader JT, Cantrell JS, Calhoun J. Oral ciprofloxacin compared with standard parenteral antibiotic therapy for chronic osteomyelitis in adults. J Bone Joint Surg 1990; 72A: 104–10.

27. Zavala IG, Valladares G, Nava A. Ciprofloxacin in the treatment of chronic osteomyelitis in adults. Drugs 1993; 45 (Suppl 3): 454–5.

28. Lew DP, Waldvogel FA. Quinolones and osteomyelitis: state of the art. Drugs 1995; 49 (Suppl 2): 100–11.

29. Díaz-Tejeiro R, Díez J, Maduell F, Esparza N, Errasti P, Purroy A. Successful treatment with ciprofloxacin of multiresistant salmonella arthritis in a renal transplant recipient. Nephrol Dial Transplant 1989; 4: 390–2.

30. Widmer AF, Colombo VE, Gacher A, Thiel G, Zimmerli W. Salmonella infection in total hip replacement: tests to predict the outcome of antimicrobial therapy. Scand J Infect Dis 1990; 22: 611–18.

31. Praet J-P, Peretz A, Goossens H, Van Laethem Y, Fameay J-P. Salmonella septic arthritis: additional 2 cases with quinolone treatment (letter). J Rheumatol 1989; 16: 1610–11.

32. Allard S, O'Driscoll J, Laurie A. Salmonella osteomyelitis in aplastic anaemia after antilymphocyte globulin and steroid treatment. J Clin Pathol 1992; 45: 174–5.

33. John R, Mathai D, Daniel AJ, Lalitha MK. Bilateral septic arthritis due to *Salmonella enteritidis*. Diagn Microbiol Infect Dis 1993; 17: 167–9.

Chapter 12

Skin and soft tissue infection

Cellulitis and abscesses in the skin and soft tissues are often caused by *Staphylococcus aureus* and *Streptococcus pyogenes* and can usually be treated with oral antibiotics and local drainage. Traumatic wounds and foot ulcers in diabetic patients and postoperative wound infections are more likely to be caused by Gram-negative bacteria, particularly *Pseudomonas aeruginosa*, *Klebsiella* spp., *Escherichia coli*, and *Enterobacter* spp. Ciprofloxacin allows treatment of these infections to be given by mouth to out-patients rather than parenterally in hospital, as is necessary for most cephalosporins. Most studies suggest that ciprofloxacin is clinically effective but persistence of *Staphylococcus aureus* is not uncommon.

Uncontrolled studies

Clinical histories collected by the manufacturer of ciprofloxacin in the USA, Miles Pharmaceuticals, Connecticut, indicated resolution in 151 (71%) and improvement in 44 (21%) of 212 patients.[1] Bacteriological eradication was achieved in 176 of 216 (82%) patients. Other early series suggested response rates of 96% (247/257), 89% (131/148) and 87% (264/305).[2]

In a general practice surveillance study, clinical success was achieved in 1250 of 1302 (96%) patients with soft tissue infections.[3] Of 498 patients with an initial positive culture, 481

(97%) were judged to have had their pathogen eradicated when ciprofloxacin was used to treat soft tissue infection.[3] *Staphylococcus aureus* was eradic-ated in 235 of 245 cases (96%), *Enterobacter* spp. in all 53 cases (100%) and *Pseudomonas aeruginosa* in 26 of 28 (93%) patients. Improvement in the appearance of 12 of 13 leg ulcers was achieved by treatment with ciprofloxacin, 500 mg given every 12 hours for 5–13 days, while the remaining ulcer was cured on the same regimen.[4] Of another 21 patients, all were cured or showed improvement, but resistant *Pseudomonas* spp. emerged during treatment in 2 of the patients.[5]

Other studies have found ciprofloxacin to be less effective in the eradication of Gram-positive infections. Five of 17 (29%) patients with severe staphylococcal infection failed to improve clinically or bacteriologically after treatment with ciprofloxacin.[6] In the treatment of cellulitis in 21 patients, ciprofloxacin failed to eradicate 7 bacterial isolates, 6 of which were Gram-positive organisms.[7] Of a total of 33 patients in another trial, 28 (85%) were cured or improved after treatment with ciprofloxacin.[8] Of these patients, 17 were infected with *Staphylococcus aureus* and in 3 cases the organism persisted.

Ciprofloxacin was assessed for the treatment of postoperative surgical infections in 24 patients.[9] It was effective in treating wound infections in 6 patients after cardiac surgery, 6 after general surgery and 11 of 12 after surgery at other sites, despite a wide variety of Gram-positive and Gram-negative pathogens. In another 25 patients with serious surgical wound

Wilson APR and Grüneberg RN.
Ciprofloxacin: 10 years of clinical experience
© 1997 Maxim Medical, Oxford.

infections or infected ulcers, improvement was observed in 23 (92%) cases.[10] A total of 6 pathogens persisted, 3 of which became resistant to ciprofloxacin (2 *Staphylococcus aureus* and 1 *Pseudomonas aeruginosa*).

Randomised trials

Comparisons with penicillins or erythromycin have not been reported but ciprofloxacin has been assessed against parenteral cephalosporins for predominantly Gram-negative infections.

There was no significant difference in cure or eradication rates between ciprofloxacin and ceftazidime in two comparative trials[11,12] (Table 12.1).[11-17] In the first trial, infections in 8 of the 32 patients given ciprofloxacin failed to improve.[11] In 3 patients, the pathogen became resistant to ciprofloxacin during treatment compared with 7 of 8 treatment failures in the ceftazidime group. In the second trial, resistance to the treatment emerged in only two cases in the ceftazidime group.[12] Bacteriological eradication was similar with either antibiotic, with 32 of 36 (89%) being cured with ciprofloxacin versus 22 of 32 (69%) with ceftazidime.

Several trials have been devoted to comparisons of ciprofloxacin and cefotaxime, each with similar results (Table 12.1). A large double-blind study showed clinical success in 97% of patients given ciprofloxacin and 93% of patients given cefotaxime.[14] There was a significant difference in favour of ciprofloxacin with respect to bacteriological eradication or reduction to clinically insignificant numbers (371/387 [96%] versus 383/424 [91%]; χ^2 test, $p < 0.005$). The persistence of pathogens in mixed infections of ulcers was more common in the cefotaxime-treated group.[14] The incidence of adverse reactions was similar in each group. An earlier study by the same authors also claimed a higher cure rate for ciprofloxacin than cefotaxime but this failed to reach statistical significance (Table 12.1).[15] Another double-blind trial suggested similar cure rates for ciprofloxacin and cefotaxime, but

again noted a trend in favour of ciprofloxacin.[13] In this trial, most of the patients were elderly women with decubitus ulcers. *Staphylococcus aureus* persisted in 2 of 13 patients after treatment with ciprofloxacin, and 2 of 12 patients following cefotaxime treatment. By using an algorithm that included the clinical and bacteriological responses in determining the overall response, ciprofloxacin appeared to be significantly more effective than cefotaxime (21/24 [88%] versus 17/32 [53%], respectively, $p = 0.02$). In severe soft-tissue infections, cure rates were high for both antibiotics in two blinded trials,[16,17] though in one study, *Staphylococcus aureus* persisted in 1 of 8 patients in the ciprofloxacin group and 2 of 16 patients in the cefotaxime group.[16]

Unusual infections

Rhinoscleroma, a granulomatous infection of the soft tissue of the nose caused by *Klebsiella rhinoscleromatis*, can be cured by a course of oral ciprofloxacin. In a non-randomised comparison, 28 patients were given ciprofloxacin, 250 mg given every 12 hours for 4 weeks, and 22 patients were given oral rifampicin, 300 mg every 12 hours, and oral co-trimoxazole, every 12 hours, for 6 months.[18] At 6 months' follow-up, symptoms and signs were markedly improved in the ciprofloxacin-treated group compared with the comparator group. The organism was cultured from a biopsy at 2 months in only 3 (11%) specimens after ciprofloxacin treatment compared with 20 (91%) specimens after treatment with the comparator agents. A 17-year-old woman responded to a 3-month course of oral ciprofloxacin, 750 mg given every 12 hours, having failed to respond to treatment with oral tetracycline, 0.5 mg given every 6 hours for 3 months, and streptomycin, given intramuscularly for 3 months.[19]

A severe wound infection caused by *Bacillus cereus* was cured by a 3-month course of ciprofloxacin (750 mg, every 12 hours).[20]

Table 12.1. Comparative clinical trials of treatment of skin and soft tissue infection. NB, not blinded; SB, single blind; DB, double blind.

Studies	Sex (M:F) Age (years)	Dose regimen	Duration (days)	No. of patients	No. cured/ improved	No. failed/ recurred	Odds ratio (95% CI)	Reference
Gentry and Koshdel, 1989 NB	– 21–76	Ciprofloxacin, 200 mg i.v. b.d., then 750 mg p.o. b.d.	2–50	32	24	8	0.5 (0.1–1.5)	11
	– 36–77	Ceftazidime, 2 g i.v. t.d.s.	3–42	19	11	8		
Rivera-Vasquez et al., 1989 SB	34:0 60 (mean)	Ciprofloxacin, 200 mg i.v. b.d.	11 (mean)	34	30	4	0.6 (0.1–2.3)	12
	32:0 61 (mean)	Ceftazidime, 1–2 g i.v. t.d.s.	10 (mean)	32	26	6		
Parish and Asper, 1987 DB	8:16 75 (mean)	Ciprofloxacin, 750 mg p.o. b.d.	5–21	25	24	1	0.7 (0.06–8)	13
	8:23 79 (mean)	Cefotaxime, 2 g i.v. t.d.s.	–	36	34	2		
Gentry et al., 1989 DB	152:72 47 (mean)	Ciprofloxacin, 750 mg p.o. b.d.	4–34	230	224	6	0.4 (0.2–1.2)	14
	153:84 50 (mean)	Cefotaxime, 2 g i.v. t.d.s.	4–27	246	228	14		

Table 12.1. (continued)

Studies	Sex (M:F) Age (years)	Dose regimen	Duration (days)	No. of patients	No. cured/ improved	No. failed recurred	Odds ratio (95% CI)	Reference
Ramirez-Ronda et al., 1987 DB	30:0 29–79	Ciprofloxacin, 750 mg p.o. b.d.	9.6 (mean)	30	27	1	0.14 (0.02–1.2)	15
	30:0 24–69	Cefotaxime, 2 g i.v. t.d.s.	9.3 (mean)	30	22	6		
Perez-Ruvalcaba et al., 1987 DB	14:17 52.6 (mean)	Ciprofloxacin, 750 mg p.o. b.d.	–	31	31	0	–	16
	19:9 52.3 (mean)	Cefotaxime, 2 g i.v. t.d.s.	–	29	28	1		
Self et al., 1987 DB	28:10 34.3 (mean)	Ciprofloxacin, 750 mg p.o. b.d.	–	38	37	1	–	17
	27:8 30.2 (mean)	Cefotaxime, 2 g i.v. t.d.s.	–	35	35	0		

Conclusions

Ciprofloxacin (500–750 mg administered orally every 12 hours, or 200 mg administered intravenously every 12 hours for 1–2 weeks) has been found to be effective in large uncontrolled trials, but persistence of *Staphylococcus aureus* has been reported in some studies. Combination with metronidazole might be appropriate for wound infections after abdominal surgery, although monotherapy may be effective. Rhinoscleroma can be cured by ciprofloxacin, 250 mg administered orally every 12 hours for 2 weeks.

References

1. Arcieri G, August R, Becker N, Doyle C, Griffith E, Gruenwald G *et al.* Clinical experience with ciprofloxacin. Eur J Clin Microbiol 1986; 5: 220–5.
2. Campoli-Richards DM, Monk JP, Price A, Benfield P, Todd PA, Ward A. Ciprofloxacin. A review of its antibacterial activity, pharmacokinetic properties and therapeutic use. Drugs 1988; 35; 373–447.
3. Pankey GA, Kalish GH, Wallach M, Garbus SB, Cohen G. Ciprofloxacin in lower respiratory tract and skin/skin structure infections: a phase IV surveillance study. Infections Med September 1990: 1–6.
4. Gorkiewicz-Petkow A, Weuta H, Jablonska S, Petkow L, Bielunska S, Gawkonska M. Bacterial infections of the skin treated with ciprofloxacin. Infection 1988; 16 (Suppl 1): 55–6.
5. Licitra CM, Brooks RG, Sieger BE. Clinical efficacy and levels of ciprofloxacin in tissue in patients with soft tissue infection. Antimicrob Agents Chemother 1987; 31: 805–7.
6. Righter J. Ciprofloxacin in the treatment of *Staphylococcus aureus* infections. J Antimicrob Chemother 1987; 20: 595–7.
7. Wood MJ, Logan MN. Ciprofloxacin for soft tissue infections. J Antimicrob Chemother 1986; 18 (Suppl D): 159–64.
8. Valainis GT, Pankey GA, Katner HP, Cortez LM, Dalovisio JR. Ciprofloxacin in the treatment of bacterial skin infections. Am J Med 1987; 82 (Suppl 4A): 230–2.
9. Ehrenkranz NJ. IV/PO ciprofloxacin in treatment of surgical infections. 6th Mediterranean Congress of Chemotherapy, Taormina, Italy, 1988: 109–14.
10. Fass RJ. Treatment of skin and soft tissue infections with oral ciprofloxacin. J Antimicrob Chemother 1986; 18 (Suppl D): 153–7.
11. Gentry LO, Koshdel A. Intravenous/oral ciprofloxacin versus intravenous ceftazidime in the treatment of serious Gram-negative infections of the skin and skin structure. Am J Med 1989; 87 (Suppl 5A): 132–5.
12. Rivera-Vasquez C, Saavedra S, Ramirez-Ronda CH. IV ciprofloxacin vs IV ceftazidime in severe soft tissue infections: a randomized blinded comparison. 16th International Congress of Chemotherapy, Jerusalem, Israel, 1989: 240.1–2.
13. Parish LC, Asper R. Systemic treatment of cutaneous infections. Am J Med 1987; 82 (Suppl 4A): 227–9.
14. Gentry LO, Ramirez-Ronda CH, Rodriguez-Noriega E, Thadepalli H, Leal del Rosal P, Ramirez C. Oral ciprofloxacin versus parenteral cefotaxime in the treatment of difficult skin and soft tissue structure infections. A multicenter trial. Arch Intern Med 1989; 149: 2579–83.
15. Ramirez-Ronda CH, Saavedra S, Rivera-Vazquez CR. Comparative double blind study of oral ciprofloxacin and intravenous cefotaxime in skin and skin structure infections. Am J Med 1987; 82 (Suppl 4A): 220–3.
16. Perez-Ruvalcaba JA, Quintero-Perez NP, Morales-Reyes JJ, Huitron-Ramirez JA, Rodriguez-Chagollan JJ, Rodriguez-Noriega E. Double-blind comparison of ciprofloxacin with cefotaxime in the treatment of skin and skin structure infections. Am J Med 1987; 82 (Suppl 4A): 242–6.
17. Self PL, Zeluff BA, Sollo D, Gentry LO. Use of ciprofloxacin in the treatment of serious skin and skin structure infections. Am J Med 1987; 82 (Suppl 4A): 239–41.
18. Borgstein J, Sada E, Cortes R. Ciprofloxacin for rhinoscleroma and ozena. Lancet 1993; 342: 122.
19. Trautmann M, Held Th, Ruhnke M, Schnoy N. A case of rhinoscleroma cured with ciprofloxacin. Infection 1993; 21: 403–6.
20. Kemmerly SA, Pankey GA. Oral ciprofloxacin therapy for *Bacillus cereus* wound infection and bacteremia. Clin Infect Dis 1993; 16: 189.

Chapter 13

Gastrointestinal and intra-abdominal infections

Most cases of gastroenteritis are self-limited and do not require antibiotic treatment. Antibiotics disturb the faecal flora and promote the emergence of resistance, but will shorten the duration of diarrhoea and can reduce the risk of cross-infection in an institutional environment. Goodman *et al.*[1] compared the use of ciprofloxacin or co-trimoxazole with placebo in the treatment of acute diarrhoea (Table 13.1).[1–17] Ciprofloxacin was significantly more effective than co-trimoxazole in eradicating bacterial pathogens (mostly *Salmonella* spp., *Campylobacter* spp. and *Shigella* spp.) from the stool, and the clinical response to ciprofloxacin was significantly better than placebo on 4 of 5 treatment days, while the difference in response between co-trimoxazole and placebo was significant only on day 3. In another trial, all stool cultures became negative within 48 hours of treatment with ciprofloxacin. With placebo, however, stool cultures became negative in only 4 of 43 patients.[14] A study carried out by Pichler *et al.* also compared ciprofloxacin with placebo in acute diarrhoea. Within 72 hours, significantly more patients treated with ciprofloxacin had become afebrile than with placebo and their diarrhoea had stopped (37/38 versus 25/38, $p < 0.005$).[13] In a further, uncontrolled study, diarrhoea stopped in 25 of 30 patients within 1 day of the start of treatment with oral ciprofloxacin, 500 mg every 12 hours.[18]

Traveller's diarrhoea

Traveller's diarrhoea is a self-limited condition that occurs in one-third of visitors to developing countries.[19] Enterotoxigenic *Escherichia coli* is the most common cause, and the diarrhoea, though it lasts only 3–4 days, can disrupt travel considerably. Although antibiotics shorten the course of the diarrhoea, their use has been restricted by the risk of adverse effects and the emergence of bacterial resistance in this benign disease.

In a study carried out by Wistrom *et al.*, 8 patients were treated with ciprofloxacin, with 4 subsequently harbouring *Escherichia coli* with a reduced susceptibility to ciprofloxacin (9 strains with a minimum inhibitory concentration (MIC) ≥ 0.12 mg/litre) and resistant *Bacteroides* spp. (MIC ≥ 64 mg/litre).[15] Of these 8 patients, 7 were analysed for efficacy and all 8 were assessed for the emergence of resistance. In all patients who later developed diarrhoea, there was a significant increase in resistance to ampicillin, doxycycline and co-trimoxazole in faecal isolates of *Escherichia coli*. A further study found that *Escherichia coli* and other Gram-negative bacteria increased in numbers in the faecal flora of patients given placebo but were absent in those treated with ciprofloxacin.[20]

In a double-blind trial carried out by Ericsson *et al.*, patients were treated with oral ciprofloxacin for 5 days. The duration of diarrhoea was 27 hours compared with 30 hours in those given co-trimoxazole and 81 hours in those receiving placebo.[11] Persistence of the

Wilson APR and Grüneberg RN.
Ciprofloxacin: 10 years of clinical experience
© 1997 Maxim Medical, Oxford.

Table 13.1. Comparative clinical trials of treatments for gastrointestinal and intra-abdominal infections.

Reference/ disease	Sex (M:F) Age (years)	Agent	Dose regimen	Duration (days)	No. patients	No. cured/ improved	No. failed/ recurred	Odds ratio (95% CI)
2								
Acute cholecystitis	–	Ciprofloxacin	200 mg i.v. b.d.	–	32	30	2	1.0 (0.06–1.6)
		Ceftazidime	1 g i.v. b.d.		30	29	1	
3								
Acute cholangitis	20:26	Ciprofloxacin	200 mg i.v. b.d.	–	46	39	7	0.6 (0.2–1.8)
	22:22	Ceftazidime + ampicillin + metronidazole	1 g i.v. b.d. 500 mg p.o. q.d.s. 500 mg i.v. t.d.s.		44	34	10	
4								
Intra-abdominal infection	17:23 45*	Ciprofloxacin + metronidazole	200 mg i.v. b.d. + 500 mg i.v. b.d.	5	40	37	1	0.2 (0.025–2.2)
	24:16 52*	Co-amoxiclav + metronidazole	200 mg i.v. t.d.s. + 500 mg i.v. b.d.	5	40	36	4	
5‡								
Intra-abdominal infection	95:127 52.1*	Ciprofloxacin + metronidazole	400 mg i.v. b.d. + 500 mg i.v. q.d.s.	10	222	182	40	
	81:138 52.3*	Ciprofloxacin + metronidazole	400 mg i.v. b.d., then 500 mg p.o. b.d. + 500 mg i.v. q.d.s., then p.o.	8	219	183	36	1.1 (0.7–1.8)
	102:128 54.5*	Imipenem	500 mg i.v. q.d.s.	10	230	189	41	1.0 (0.6–1.7)

*Mean; ‡double-blind trial.

Table 13.1. (continued)

Reference/ disease	Sex (M:F) Age (years)	Agent	Dose regimen	Duration (days)	No. patients	No. cured/ improved	No. failed/ recurred	Odds ratio (95% CI)
6[†]								
Intra-abdominal infection	19:21 20–95	Ciprofloxacin + metronidazole	300 mg i.v. b.d 500 mg i.v. t.d.s.	13	40	31	9	0.3 (0.1–1.0)
	22:17 21–94	Cefotaxime + gentamicin + metronidazole	1 g .i.v. q.d.s. 120 mg i.v. b.d. 500 mg i.v. t.d.s.	12	39	22	17	
7[‡]								
Shigellosis	– 18–60	Ciprofloxacin	500 mg p.o. b.d.	5	60	57	0	–
	– 18–55	Ampicillin	500 mg p.o. q.d.s.	5	61	amp-S 23 amp-R 15	2 17	
8[‡]								
Shigellosis	40:0 31*	Ciprofloxacin	1 g p.o.	1	40	36	4	–
	43:0 26*	Ciprofloxacin	1 g p.o.	2	43	38	2	
	35:0 32*	Ciprofloxacin	500 mg b.d.	5	35	33	0	
9								
Enteric fever	13:7 18–70	Ciprofloxacin	500 mg p.o. b.d.	10	20	20	0	–
	11:9 18–77	Co-trimoxazole	960 mg p.o. b.d.	14	20	18	2	

*Mean; [‡]double-blind trial; [†]not randomised, allocation by alternate patients; amp-S, ampicillin-sensitive; amp-R, ampicillin-resistant.

Table 13.1. (continued)

Reference/ disease	Sex (M:F) Age (years)	Agent	Dose regimen	Duration (days)	No. patients	No. cured/ improved	No. failed/ recurred	Odds ratio (95% CI)
10 Enteric fever	– 26.8*	Ciprofloxacin	500 mg p.o. b.d.	7	20	20	0	–
	– 28.2*	Ceftriaxone	3 g i.v. b.d.	7	22	16	6	
1‡ Acute diarrhoea	–	Ciprofloxacin	500 mg p.o. b.d.	5	59	56	2	0.4 (0.09–1.5)
		Co-trimoxazole	960 mg p.o. b.d.	5	56	49	7	0.2 (0.05–0.7)
		Placebo	p.o. b.d.	5	58	45	13	
11‡ Acute diarrhoea	–	Ciprofloxacin	500 mg p.o. b.d.	5	60	56	4	1.3 (0.3–6.2)
		Co-trimoxazole	960 mg p.o. b.d.	5	59	56	3	0.2 (0.07–0.7)
		Placebo	p.o. b.d.	5	62	42	20	
12‡ Acute diarrhoea	– –	Ciprofloxacin	500 mg p.o.	1	45	44	1	0.1 (0.01–1.1)
		Placebo		1	38	32	6	
13‡ Acute diarrhoea	26:18 20–89 21:20 19–76	Ciprofloxacin	500 mg p.o. b.d.	5	38	37	1	0.04 (0.05–0.3)
		Placebo	p.o. b.d.	5	38	25	13	
14‡ Acute diarrhoea	– –	Ciprofloxacin	500 mg p.o. b.d.	5	40	40	0	–
		Placebo	p.o. b.d.	5	43	4	39	

*Mean; ‡double-blind trial.

Table 13.1. (continued)

Reference/ disease	Sex (M:F) Age (years)	Agent	Dose regimen	Duration (days)	No. patients	No. cured/ improved	No. failed/ recurred	Odds ratio (95% CI)
15‡ Acute diarrhoea	4:3 25–46	Ciprofloxacin	250 mg p.o. b.d.	3	7	7	0	–
	5:3 20–46	Placebo	p.o. b.d.	3	8	6	2	
16‡ Salmonellosis	6:2 29*	Ciprofloxacin	750 mg p.o. b.d.	14	8	4	4	0.4 (0.05–3.4)
	2:5 30*	Placebo		14	7	2	5	
17‡ Salmonellosis	11:12 37.5*	Ciprofloxacin	500 mg p.o. b.d.	5	23	18	5	0.5 (0.1–1.8)
	14:12 38.3*	Co-trimoxazole	960 mg p.o. b.d.	5	25	16	9	0.3 (0.07–1.2)
	5:11 31.7*	Placebo		5	14	7	7	

*Mean; ‡double-blind trial.

diarrhoea beyond 5 days was significantly more likely following placebo than with either antibiotic, and there was no significant difference in the efficacies of ciprofloxacin and co-trimoxazole. In a study of 88 marines posted to Belize (83 of whom were evaluable), a single 500 mg dose of ciprofloxacin produced a significant reduction in the severity and duration of diarrhoea compared with placebo.[12] At 48 hours, 39 of 45 marines given ciprofloxacin no longer had diarrhoea compared with 19 of 38 given placebo. Selection of resistance would be less likely to occur with a short course of treatment. The addition of loperamide to ciprofloxacin did not appear to have any benefit at 48 hours, but tended to reduce symptoms at 24 hours (41/50 patients given ciprofloxacin plus loperamide versus 36/54 given ciprofloxacin plus placebo were cured at 24 hours, p = ns).[21]

'Critical' travel

It has become popular to use ciprofloxacin in the prevention of traveller's diarrhoea in those going on 'critical' trips, despite the potential risk of emergence of resistance. A total of 344 adults travelling to South America were randomly prescribed oral ciprofloxacin (500 mg every 24 hours), oral co-trimoxazole (960 mg every 24 hours) or placebo.[22] Diarrhoea developed in 5 of 99 (5%) travellers in the ciprofloxacin group, 14 of 87 (16%) in the co-trimoxazole group and 30 of 92 (33%) in the placebo group. Ciprofloxacin was significantly more effective than co-trimoxazole or placebo (p < 0.05). Ten patients experienced some degree of adverse effects, of which only 2 discontinued with ciprofloxacin. In another double-blind, volunteer study, a course of ciprofloxacin (500 mg/day) prevented almost all cases of diarrhoea compared with placebo (1/25 versus 18/28, p < 0.001).[20] Only one patient suffered what was possibly an adverse effect (severe sunburn).

Salmonellosis

Antibiotics are usually not advised for the treatment of acute salmonella gastroenteritis because of the risk of emergence of resistant organisms. Despite this, ciprofloxacin has been used to control hospital and institutional outbreaks.

In psychiatric hospitals, patients may have poor personal hygiene, and source isolation is difficult to enforce on disturbed patients. Of 36 psychiatric patients treated with ciprofloxacin during an outbreak of salmonella gastroenteritis, only 2 continued to excrete the organisms once treatment with ciprofloxacin (200 mg administered intravenously every 12 hours, or 500 mg administered orally every 12 hours) had been started.[23] In another psychiatric hospital, salmonella gastroenteritis was controlled by treating all infected cases and carriers with oral ciprofloxacin, 500 mg every 12 hours for 7 days. Of 59 cases, all had negative stool cultures by the seventh day of treatment and no relapses occurred in the next 6 months.[24] A hospital for mentally handicapped adults was affected by a salmonella outbreak in 101 patients and 8 staff. All 292 hospital patients and infected staff were treated with oral ciprofloxacin, 500 mg every 12 hours for 1 week, resulting in an immediate cessation of the outbreak without recurrence.[25] Treatment of all infected patients and carriers also terminated a further two hospital outbreaks, caused by *Salmonella virchow* and *Salmonella enteritidis*, allowing patients to return to their wards within 10 days.[26]

Two double-blind trials have reported poor results when using ciprofloxacin to treat salmonella gastroenteritis. In one trial, 4 of 8 patients infected with *Salmonella java* began excreting the organism again within 14–21 days of a 2-week course of ciprofloxacin, with excretion persisting for longer than in the patients given placebo.[16] However, the relapses were asymptomatic and the organism's susceptibility was unchanged. *Salmonella typhi* with reduced susceptibility to ciprofloxacin (MIC 0.3 mg/litre) was isolated from a child infected in India.[27]

This organism was also resistant to chloramphenicol, ampicillin, trimethoprim and nalidixic acid. In the second double-blind trial of 65 patients, no significant differences were found between those given ciprofloxacin, co-trimoxazole or placebo in the loss of symptoms or fever, or in the clearance of the organism from stools.[17] In contrast, an open trial found that all 60 patients given a 5-day course of ciprofloxacin were cured, although the duration of follow-up was not stated.[28]

Enteric fever

Enteric fever is currently a major indication for the use of ciprofloxacin. Resistance to the previous drug of choice, chloramphenicol, is widespread. Ciprofloxacin remains active and it has good oral absorption and a high concentration in bile.

Rowe *et al.*[29] have recommended that ciprofloxacin should be given to patients with typhoid fever who have travelled from India, and, as a result, it has been vigorously promoted in the Indian subcontinent.[30] A clinical response to oral ciprofloxacin, 500 mg every 12 hours, occurred within 1 week in 32 of 38 patients with typhoid fever.[31] In a further 30 patients, all became afebrile after a mean of 4 days when treated with the same dose over 10–14 days.[32] In the latter study, half the patients received ciprofloxacin intravenously for the first 2–10 days. Another open study reported loss of fever after 3–6 days of treatment and the resolution of other symptoms within 2 days in 38 patients given ciprofloxacin.[33]

A further randomised trial compared ciprofloxacin with co-trimoxazole in the treatment of typhoid and paratyphoid fever. The courses lasted 10 and 14 days, respectively. Of 40 patients treated, only 2 failed to respond. Both were in the co-trimoxazole group and were infected with *Salmonella paratyphi* A.[9] In the remainder, blood cultures were negative within 48 hours and symptoms improved within 5 days. Ciprofloxacin was significantly more effective ($p = 0.01$) against multi-resistant *Salmonella typhi* than ceftriaxone in another

randomised trial, with fever resolved within a mean of 4 days instead of 5.2 days.[10] A further, comparative, but inadequately randomised, study found that twice-daily doses of 500 mg of ciprofloxacin were as effective as twice-daily doses of 750 mg (28/28 versus 34/34).[34]

Long-term carriage

Long-term carriage occurs in 1–2% of patients and is a major factor in the transmission of typhoid and other salmonelloses. Ciprofloxacin is an effective treatment and results in few adverse effects. A total of 12 chronic carriers of *Salmonella typhi* were treated with oral ciprofloxacin, 750 mg every 12 hours for 28 days.[35] Carriage was eliminated in 11 patients, the single relapse being caused by a strain still susceptible to ciprofloxacin.

Of 4 carriers of *Salmonella heidelberg* identified during an outbreak, 3 were cured by a course of oral ciprofloxacin, 500 mg every 12 hours for 2 weeks.[36] The fourth patient relapsed after being given second and third courses of ciprofloxacin treatment; the MIC of ciprofloxacin was 2 mg/litre and the organism was resistant to nalidixic acid. In another trial, salmonella carriage persisted in 3 of 14 patients treated with ciprofloxacin, 500 mg every 12 hours for 28 days, but none of these cases were due to resistance.[14]

Shigellosis

Shigellosis has a mortality rate of 11% in developing countries, particularly following infections with *Shigella dysenteriae* type 1 and *Shigella flexneri*.[37] These species in Asia, as well as *Shigella sonnei* in the USA, may be resistant to co-trimoxazole and ampicillin.[7] In Bangladesh, almost all isolates of *Shigella dysenteriae* are resistant to these antibiotics. At present, ciprofloxacin remains active against almost all *Shigella* spp. and is widely used. In the Third World, as courses of treatment are often not completed, duration should be minimised and must be affordable. A single dose of ciprofloxacin has been found to be effective for shigellosis other than that caused by *Shigella dysenteriae* type 1.[7]

In a randomised comparison of ciprofloxacin with ampicillin, 35 of 61 infections in the ampicillin-treated group were found to be caused by strains already resistant to ampicillin.[7] Predictably, the cure rate among these patients was poor (43%). Ciprofloxacin was active against all isolates in the entire study group. All 60 patients treated with ciprofloxacin were bacteriologically cured compared with 23 (88%) of the patients treated with ampicillin for an ampicillin-sensitive infecting organism. Overall, ciprofloxacin was significantly more effective than ampicillin. Stool frequency was reduced significantly after the first day of therapy in the ciprofloxacin group compared with the ampicillin group. Of 16 patients who did not respond to treatment with ampicillin, all but 1 were later cured with ciprofloxacin. In a separate study, ciprofloxacin eradicated *Shigella* spp. from all 7 patients treated with 750 mg/day for 5 days.[38]

Treatments using one or two doses of ciprofloxacin have been compared in a randomised, double-blind trial with a standard 5-day course of ciprofloxacin.[8] Treatment failed in 4 of 40 patients given a single dose of ciprofloxacin and in 2 of 43 given two doses. There were no treatment failures in the group given a 5-day course. However, organisms were more rapidly eradicated from the stool by the 1–2-dose courses. All those who did not respond to treatment and 5 other patients who showed little improvement were infected with *Shigella dysenteriae* type 1. Another 27 patients who were given a single 1 g dose of ciprofloxacin all responded quickly, even though 12 were infected with *Shigella dysenteriae* type 1.[39]

Campylobacter infections

Ciprofloxacin has been found to be effective in treating campylobacter infections. Diarrhoea of moderate-to-severe intensity caused by campylobacter was cured, with eradication of the organism, in 5 patients given ciprofloxacin, 750 mg/day for 5 days, and all 19 patients infected with *Campylobacter* spp. in another study became culture-negative within 48 hours of treatment with ciprofloxacin.[14, 38] In a further randomised trial of 32 patients infected with *Campylobacter* spp., 8 of 10 patients given ciprofloxacin were cured compared with all 7 given co-trimoxazole and 2 of 6 given placebo,[1] and as part of another double-blind trial, the duration of diarrhoea in 19 patients with campylobacter infection was 1.1 days, significantly shorter than the 2.2 days in 11 patients given placebo.[13]

Other pathogens

Yersinia spp. was eradicated from 6 patients with diarrhoea by a 5-day course of ciprofloxacin, 750 mg/day.[38] Administration of ciprofloxacin to 3 patients with severe diarrhoea associated with *Aeromonas hydrophila* was followed by resolution of symptoms within 48 hours.[40] However, it was not possible to demonstrate that ciprofloxacin was the sole cause of improvement.

Intra-abdominal infections

Infections following gastrointestinal surgery and perforation of the gut are polymicrobial and the primary treatment is surgical lavage and correction. Antibiotic treatment must be broad-spectrum to cover Enterobacteriaceae and anaerobes, and a cephalosporin or a β-lactam–aminoglycoside combination with metronidazole is commonly used. Ciprofloxacin is an effective and well-tolerated alternative and penetrates well into the peritoneum, where it reaches 60% of the serum concentration.[41]

A large, multicentre, double-blind trial compared ciprofloxacin plus metronidazole, given either intravenously or orally, with imipenem for intra-abdominal sepsis.[5] The two antibiotic regimens appeared equivalent and cure rates were similar whether the course of treatment was completed using oral or parenteral ciprofloxacin. There were only 2 treatment failures in the 46 patients given oral treatment. Bacterial eradication occurred in 98 of 111 (88%) patients in the parenteral ciprofloxacin plus metronidazole group and in 100 of 113 (88%) patients given imipenem. Treatment failure occurred in 20 of 71 (28%) patients from whom enterococci were isolated compared with 35 of 259 (14%) patients in whom enterococci were not isolated. In a non-randomised study, ciprofloxacin, 300 mg administered intravenously every 12 hours, plus metronidazole was compared with cefotaxime plus gentamicin plus metronidazole. Significantly more patients were cured following the ciprofloxacin regimen than after the control regimen (31/40 versus 22/39, $p < 0.05$).[6] Superinfection was also more common in those given cefotaxime.

Of 40 patients with peritonitis or an intra-abdominal abscess treated with ciprofloxacin (0.6–1 g/day) plus metronidazole, 20 were cured without further surgery and 13 with surgery.[42] Three bacterial strains developed resistance to ciprofloxacin during treatment. A randomised trial suggested a similar outcome if infection was treated with ciprofloxacin plus metronidazole or co-amoxiclav plus metronidazole, but only 40 patients were included in each group.[4]

The activity against Enterobacteriaceae, significant biliary excretion and high tissue penetration suggest that ciprofloxacin would be effective in biliary sepsis. In a randomised trial of treatment of acute cholangitis, ciprofloxacin (200 mg administered intravenously every 12 hours) was compared with a combination of ceftazidime, ampicillin and metronidazole (Table 13.1).[3] Metronidazole was given to two patients in the ciprofloxacin group after anaerobes were isolated from blood cultures. Endoscopic drainage was performed in all patients. Bile samples yielded a mixture of organisms in 82% of patients and commonly included *Escherichia coli* or enterococci. There was no significant difference in clinical response between the antibiotic groups (39/46 [85%] versus 34/44 [77%]). A smaller randomised trial has also suggested that ciprofloxacin has a similar efficacy to ceftazidime in the treatment of acute cholecystitis.[2] All patients had cholecystectomy and/or common bile duct exploration. In an open trial, acute cholecystitis or acute cholangitis was cured in 25 of 30 (83%) patients given intravenous ciprofloxacin, 400 mg/day for 3–8 days, followed by an oral antibiotic, 1.5 g/day for another 3–8 days.[43] A similar investigation reported cure in 28 of 32 patients following treatment with ciprofloxacin.[44]

Ciprofloxacin is effective in intra-abdominal infections and a policy of waiting for culture results before adding additional antibiotics to cover enterococci and anaerobes has not caused problems in clinical practice.

Conclusions

Ciprofloxacin (500 mg administered orally every 12 hours for 5 days) is effective in the treatment and prevention of traveller's diarrhoea. Administration to patients and carriers (500 mg administered orally every 12 hours for 1 week) halts an outbreak of salmonellosis. Ciprofloxacin is currently the first choice for treatment of typhoid (500 mg administered orally every 12 hours for 10–14 days). However, there are concerns that resistance will eventually emerge as has been observed with earlier antibiotic choices. Ciprofloxacin is still effective in the management of shigellosis (500 mg administered orally every 12 hours for 5 days). In combination with metronidazole it is an alternative to cephalosporins for eradication of intra-abdominal sepsis. The recommended dose is 400 mg administered intravenously every 12 hours followed by 500 mg administered orally every 12 hours for 10 days.

References

1. Goodman W, Trenholme GM, Kaplan RL, Segreti J, Hines D, Petrak R *et al*. Empiric antimicrobial therapy of domestically acquired acute diarrhea in urban adults. Arch Intern Med 1990; 150: 541–6.

2. Berne TV, Yellin AE, Heseltine PNR, Appleman MD. Ceftazidime versus ciprofloxacin as an adjunct to surgery in acute cholecystitis. 16th International Congress of Chemotherapy, Jerusalem, Israel, 1989: 287.

3. Sung JJY, Lyon DJ, Suen R, Chung SCS, Co AL, Cheng AFB *et al*. Intravenous ciprofloxacin as treatment for patients with acute suppurative cholangitis: a randomized, controlled clinical trial. J Antimicrob Chemother 1995; 35: 855–64.

4. Yoshioka K, Youngs DJ, Keighley MRB. A randomised prospective controlled study of ciprofloxacin with metronidazole versus amoxycillin/clavulanic acid with metronidazole in the treatment of intra-abdominal infection. Infection 1991; 19: 25–9, 29–33.

5. Solomkin JS, Reinhart HH, Dellinger EP, Bohnen JM, Rotstein OD, Vogel SB *et al*. (Intra-abdominal Infection Study Group). Results of a randomized trial comparing sequential intravenous oral treatment with ciprofloxacin plus metronidazole to imipenem/cilastatin for intra-abdominal infections. Ann Surg 1996; 223: 303–15.

6. Hoogkamp-Korstanje JAA. Ciprofloxacin vs cefotaxime regimens for the treatment of intra-abdominal infections. Infection 1995; 23: 278–82.

7. Bennish ML, Salam MA, Haider R, Barza M. Therapy for shigellosis. II. Randomized, double-blind comparison of ciprofloxacin and ampicillin. J Infect Dis 1990; 162: 711–16.

8. Bennish, ML, Salam MA, Khan WA, Khan AM. Treatment of Shigellosis: III. Comparison of one- or two-dose ciprofloxacin with standard 5-day therapy. Ann Intern Med 1992; 117: 727–34.

9. Limson BM, Littaua RT. Comparative study of ciprofloxacin versus co-trimoxazole in the treatment of *Salmonella* enteric fever. Infection 1989; 17: 105–6.

10. Wallace MR, Yousif AA, Mahroos GA, Mapes T, Threlfall EJ, Rowe B *et al*. Ciprofloxacin versus ceftriaxone in the treatment of multiresistant typhoid fever. Eur J Clin Microbiol Infect Dis 1993; 12: 907–10.

11. Ericsson CD, Johnson PC, DuPont HL, Morgan DR, Bitsura JM, de la Cabada FJ. Ciprofloxacin or trimethoprim-sulfamethoxazole as initial therapy for traveller's diarrhea. Ann Intern Med 1987; 106: 216–20.

12. Salam I, Katelaris P, Leigh-Smith S, Farthing MJG. Randomised trial of single-dose ciprofloxacin for traveller's diarrhoea. Lancet 1994; 344: 1357–9.

13. Pichler HET, Diridl G, Stickler K, Wolf D. Clinical efficacy of ciprofloxacin compared with placebo in bacterial diarrhea. Am J Med 1987; 82 (Suppl 4A): 329–32.

14. Diridl G, Pichler H, Stickler K, Wolf D. Ciprofloxacin in the treatment of acute bacterial gastroenteritis and *Salmonella* carriage. International Symposium on Ciprofloxacin, Dresden, Germany, 1988: 122–3.

15. Wistrom J, Gentry LO, Palmgren AC, Price M, Nord CE, Ljungh A *et al*. Ecological effects of short term ciprofloxacin treatment of traveller's diarrhoea. J Antimicrob Chemother 1992; 30: 693–706.

16. Neill MA, Opal SM, Heelan J, Giusti R, Cassidy JE, White R *et al*. Failure of ciprofloxacin to eradicate convalescent faecal excretion after salmonellosis: experience during an outbreak in health care workers. Ann Intern Med 1991; 114: 195–9.

17. Sanchez C, Garcia-Restoy E, Garau J, Bella F, Freixas N, Simó M *et al*. Ciprofloxacin and trimethoprim–sulfamethoxazole versus placebo in acute uncomplicated *Salmonella* enteritis: a double-blind trial. J Infect Dis 1993; 168: 1304–7.

18. Nelwan RHH, Soemarsono H, Zulkarnain HI, Pohan HT, Hendarwanto, Kosasih AS *et al*. An open study on the use of ciprofloxacin for acute diarrhea in hospitalized adult patients. Mikrob Klinik Indonesia 1989; 4: 89–93.

19. Black R. Epidemiology of traveller's diarrhoea and relative importance of various pathogens. Rev Infect Dis 1990; 12 (Suppl 1): S73–9.

20. Rademaker CMA, Hoepelman IM, Wolfhagen MJHM, Beumer H, Rozenberg-Arska M, Verhoef J. Results of a double-blind placebo-controlled study using ciprofloxacin for prevention of travelers' diarrhoea. Eur J Clin Microbiol Infect Dis 1989; 8: 690–4.

21. Taylor DN, Sanchez JL, Candler W, Thornton S, McQueen C, Echeverria P. Treatment of traveler's diarrhea: ciprofloxacin plus loperamide compared with ciprofloxacin alone. Ann Intern Med 1991; 114: 731–4.

22. Heck JE, Staneck JL, Cohen MB, Weckbach LS, Giannella RA, Hawkins J *et al*. Prevention of traveller's diarrhoea: ciprofloxacin versus trimethoprim/sulfamethoxazole in adult volunteers working in Latin America and the Caribbean. J Travel Med 1994; 1: 136–42.

23. Willocks LJ, Thompson C, Emmanuel FXS, Bligh J, Jones ME, Scott AC *et al*. Hospital outbreak of *Salmonella enteritidis* infection treated with ciprofloxacin. Lancet 1990; 335: 1404–5.

24. Ahmad F, Bray G, Prescott RWG, Aquilla S, Lightfoot NF. Use of ciprofloxacin to control a *Salmonella* outbreak in a long-stay psychiatric hospital. J Hosp Infect 1991; 17: 171–8.

25. Dyson C, Ribeiro CD, Westmoreland D. Large-scale use of ciprofloxacin in the control of a *Salmonella* outbreak in a hospital for the mentally handicapped. J Hosp Infect 1995; 29: 287–99.

26. Lightfoot NF, Ahmad F, Cowden J. Management of institutional outbreaks of *Salmonella* gastroenteritis. J Antimicrob Chemother 1990; 26 (Suppl F): 37–46.

27. Rowe B, Ward LR, Threlfall EJ. Ciprofloxacin and typhoid fever. Lancet 1992; 339: 740.

28. Tkacz B, Busch W, Stepka K. Ciprofloxacin in the treatment of acute infectious diarrhea. 6th Mediterranean Congress on Chemotherapy, Taormina, Italy, 1988: Abstract 400.

29. Rowe B, Ward LR, Threlfall EJ. Treatment of multi-resistant typhoid fever. Lancet 1991; 337: 1422.

30. Kumar PD. Ciprofloxacin for typhoid fever. Lancet 1991; 338: 1143.

31. Choe K-W, Kim EJ, Chang WH. Evaluation of ciprofloxacin in the treatment of enteric fever. 15th International Congress of Chemotherapy, Istanbul, Turkey, 1987: 35.

32. Stanley PJ, Flegg PJ, Mandal BK, Geddes AM. Open study of ciprofloxacin in enteric fever. J Antimicrob Chemother 1989; 23: 789–91.

33. Ramirez CA, Bran JL, Mejia CR, Garcia JF. Clinical efficacy of ciprofloxacin in typhoid fever. 1st International Ciprofloxacin Workshop, Leverkusen, Germany, 1985: 365–9.

34. Uwadydah AK, Al Soub H, Matar I. Randomized prospective study comparing two dosage regimens of ciprofloxacin for the treatment of typhoid fever. J Antimicrob Chemother 1992; 30: 707–11.

35. Ferreccio C, Morris JG, Valdivieso C, Prenzel I, Sotomayor V, Drusano GL et al. Efficacy of ciprofloxacin in the treatment of chronic typhoid carriers. J Infect Dis 1988; 157: 1235–9.

36. Cherubin CE, Eng RHK. Quinolones for the treatment of infections due to *Salmonella*. Rev Infect Dis 1991; 13: 343–4.

37. Bennish ML, Wojtyniak BJ. Mortality due to shigellosis: community and hospital data. Rev Infect Dis 1991; 13 (Suppl 4): S245–51.

38. Schönwald S, Breitenfeld V, Car V, Gmajnicki B. Treatment of acute diarrhoeal syndrome with ciprofloxacin: pilot study. 1st International Ciprofloxacin Workshop, Leverkusen, Germany, 1985: 353–6.

39. Bhattacharya SK, Bhattacharya MK, Dutta D, Dutta P, Paul H, Sen D et al. Single dose ciprofloxacin for shigellosis in adults. J Infect 1992; 25: 117–19.

40. Nathwani D, Laing RBS, Harvey G, Smith CC. Treatment of symptomatic enteric *Aeromonas hydrophila* infection with ciprofloxacin. Scand J Infect Dis 1991; 23: 653–4.

41. Lockley MR, Waldron R, Wise R, Donovan IA. Intraperitoneal penetration of ciprofloxacin. Eur J Clin Microbiol 1986; 5: 209–10.

42. Hoogkamp-Korstanje JAA. Treatment of intra-abdominal infections with ciprofloxacin. 16th International Congress of Chemotherapy, Jerusalem, Israel, 1989: 243.1–2.

43. Chrysanthopoulos CJ, Skoutelis AT, Starakis JC, Arvaniti A, Bassaris HP. Use of ciprofloxacin in biliary sepsis. Infection 1988; 16: 249.

44. Karachalios GN, Zografos G, Patrikakos V, Nassopoulou D, Kehagioglou K. Biliary tract infections treated with ciprofloxacin. Infection 1993; 21: 262–4.

Chapter 14

Other infections

Ciprofloxacin is effective in certain infections when administered by routes other than parenteral or oral, for example, in the peritoneal dialysate treatment of peritonitis or topically for eye infections. Despite its potential efficacy, little clinical information is available in other infections, such as meningitis or malaria.

CAPD peritonitis

Chronic ambulatory peritoneal dialysis (CAPD) is a popular means of support for patients with chronic renal failure. Compared with haemodialysis it is inexpensive, but peritonitis and exit-site infections are common complications that can result in the removal of the catheter. The most common pathogens are the coagulase-negative staphylococci and *Staphylococcus aureus*, followed by the Enterobacteriaceae. Antibiotics are usually administered in the peritoneal dialysate to achieve high concentrations at the infection site, but an oral regimen would improve compliance. Ciprofloxacin has been assessed using the oral or the intraperitoneal routes. It is stable in dialysate fluid: in a solution of 4.25% dextrose, 89% of ciprofloxacin remains after 14 days of storage at 4°C.[1]

The oral administration of ciprofloxacin is associated with low concentrations of the drug in the peritoneal fluid and most authorities recommend peritoneal administration. Some have observed, however, a completely successful outcome with oral ciprofloxacin (21/21),[2] and others an acceptable failure rate secondary to bacterial resistance (28/33).[3] Oral ciprofloxacin, 750 mg every 12 hours, has been compared with intraperitoneal ciprofloxacin, 25 mg/litre of dialysate, in a randomised trial.[4] Cure rates were poor in both arms of the study, and there was no significant difference between groups; 10 of 24 (42%) of patients given oral ciprofloxacin were cured compared with 16 of 24 (67%) given the antibiotic intraperitoneally. Gram-positive bacteria accounted for most of the failures; 42% of the Gram-positive bacteria showed resistance or reduced susceptibility to ciprofloxacin. Oral ciprofloxacin, 500–750 mg every 6 hours, has also been compared with intraperitoneal vancomycin and netilmicin in 50 episodes of peritonitis.[5] Cure rates were similar (19/25 [76%] versus 18/25 [72%]). However, in a comparative trial of oral ciprofloxacin versus intraperitoneal vancomycin (25 mg/litre of dialysate) and gentamicin (4–8 mg/litre of dialysate) there was a trend towards more failures in the ciprofloxacin group (10/22 [45%] versus 17/26 [65%], p = ns).[6] A total of 3 of 4 infections caused by coagulase-negative staphylococci failed to respond to ciprofloxacin, whereas all 6 treated with vancomycin were cured.[6]

Intraperitoneal ciprofloxacin has been found to be effective in other studies. Ciprofloxacin, 20 mg/litre of dialysate for 10 days, was effective in 19 of 20 (95%) patients compared with 16 of 20 (80%) patients given intraperitoneal vancomycin, 12.5 mg/litre of

Wilson APR and Grüneberg RN.
Ciprofloxacin: 10 years of clinical experience
© 1997 Maxim Medical, Oxford.

dialysate in each dialysate bag, and gentamicin, 4 mg/litre in alternate bags.[7] For 115 episodes of peritonitis reported in an uncontrolled trial, ciprofloxacin, 50 mg/litre of dialysate, was administered by the intraperitoneal route for 5 days, followed by a 10-day oral course of 500 mg every 8 hours.[8] Cure was observed in 99 cases (86.5%), failure in 5 (4%), relapse in 8 (7%) and superinfection in 3 (2.5%). Susceptibility of the staphylococci to ciprofloxacin decreased during the study. In a similar study, 117 episodes of peritonitis were treated for 5 days with intraperitoneal ciprofloxacin, 25 mg/litre of dialysate.[9] The outcome was successful in 79 of 100 (79%) of evaluable cases, but resistant coagulase-negative staphylococci were isolated in 9 of 117 (8%) of the episodes. Ludlam et al. used a higher dose of ciprofloxacin, 50 mg/litre of dialysate, for 7 days and reported cure in 73 of 75 (97%) of episodes.[10] The two treatment failures were caused by resistant organisms, and 11 patients relapsed.[10]

Ocular infections

Following oral ciprofloxacin, 750 mg given orally every 12 hours, modest concentrations (0.15–0.7 mg/litre) were found within the eye (see Chapter 5).[11] The concentration of ciprofloxacin was studied in the aqueous humour of 101 patients having routine cataract operations.[12] After an oral dose of 0.5 g, concentrations in the aqueous were 0.04–0.52 mg/litre and after an oral dose of 1.5 g, they were 0.18–0.62 mg/litre, representing 3–12% of serum levels. However, the ophthalmic solution of ciprofloxacin, 0.3%, is widely used for topical treatment of corneal ulcers and superficial bacterial infections, and appears to be effective and well tolerated. After topical ciprofloxacin application of four drops of 0.3% ophthalmic solution over 60 minutes, intracorneal concentrations of ciprofloxacin were 0.6 mg/kg.[13] To achieve maximum corneal levels, drops must be applied every 15 minutes for the first 4 hours.[14]

Ophthalmic ciprofloxacin has been found to be significantly more effective than placebo in the eradication of bacterial pathogens from patients with proven bacterial conjunctivitis (132/140 [94%] versus 22/37 [59%], $p < 0.001$).[15] In this study, in which staphylococci were isolated from the eyes of 69% and Gram-negative bacteria from the eyes of 34% of 288 patients, the efficacy of ophthalmic ciprofloxacin was similar to that of tobramycin (102/111 [92%]).[15] In another study, topical ciprofloxacin and tobramycin were compared in a double-blind manner in patients with blepharitis and blepharoconjunctivitis.[16] A total of 230 patients were treated with an ophthalmic solution of 0.3% ciprofloxacin, 1–2 drops applied topically every 2 hours for 1 day and then every 4 hours for 6 days, and 234 with an ophthalmic solution of 0.3% tobramycin, 1–2 drops applied topically every 2 hours for 1 day and then every 4 hours for 6 days. There were no statistically significant differences observed between the treatment groups, but more than 80% of patients were cured or improved after 7 days (104/127 [82%] with ciprofloxacin versus 98/117 [84%] with tobramycin). Side-effects caused treatment to be discontinued in only one patient given ciprofloxacin, compared with eight given tobramycin ($p = 0.03$, Fisher's test).[16]

Ophthalmic ciprofloxacin, 0.3%, has also been compared with an ophthalmic solution of rifamycin, 1%, in a double-blind trial of bacterial conjunctivitis and blepharitis treatment.[17] More than 90% of patients in both groups had some improvement, but cure was achieved in 10 of 19 (53%) of patients treated with ciprofloxacin compared with 5 of 22 (23%) given rifamycin ($p = $ ns). The rate of bacteriological eradication was similar in the two groups.[17] In a comparison with an ophthalmic solution of chloramphenicol, 0.5%, in the treatment of conjunctivitis and blepharitis, an ophthalmic solution of ciprofloxacin, 0.3% for 1 week, resulted in a clinical success rate of 94% (29/31), compared with 85% (22/26) for chloramphenicol.[18] The differences in cure rates and adverse effects were not significant,[18] but ciprofloxacin is not associated with aplastic anaemia, which is encountered occasionally after topical treatment with chloramphenicol.[19]

Meningitis

Ciprofloxacin concentrations in the cerebrospinal fluid (CSF) are only 10–20% of serum levels in patients with non-inflamed meninges, but reach 20–90% of serum levels in patients with meningitis.[20,21] In one neonate treated for meningitis, CSF levels exceeded serum concentrations during the first 4 days of treatment.[22] Concentrations in the CSF after oral doses of the drug are similar to those after intravenous doses, and may be sufficient to kill Gram-negative bacteria, including *Neisseria meningitidis*, but probably not *Streptococcus pneumoniae*.

Experience of ciprofloxacin in the treatment of meningitis is limited. Of 3822 patients given ciprofloxacin, only 3 cases of meningitis were reported, all of which were cured.[23] In 20 patients treated for meningitis caused by Gram-negative bacteria, the causative organisms included *Escherichia coli*, *Pseudomonas aeruginosa* and *Klebsiella* spp.[24] Ciprofloxacin, 200 mg every 12 hours for 12 days, cured 18 patients, though 2 were also given other agents. Improvement usually occurred within 3–6 days of starting treatment. Two patients responded only after modifying the treatment.[24]

Gram-negative meningitis in neonates carries a high risk of mortality, but ciprofloxacin can be used to treat patients infected by multi-resistant Gram-negative bacilli. Green *et al.* described two neonates, infected with *Escherichia coli* and *Flavobacterium meningosepticum*, respectively, who were successfully treated with ciprofloxacin, 50 mg daily in two divided doses for 2–3 weeks.[22] Another infant was cured of pseudomonal ventriculitis by a 28-day course of ciprofloxacin, 4–6 mg/kg every 12 hours, after failure with intraventricular netilmicin.[25] Other infants have been cured of meningitis caused by multi-resistant *Salmonella paratyphi* A (10 mg/kg ciprofloxacin given intravenously every 12 hours for

3 weeks) or *Salmonella typhimurium* (25 mg given intravenously every 12 hours for 13 days in an infant weighing 3.2 kg), after failure with cefotaxime or chloramphenicol treatment.[26,27]

Ciprofloxacin failed to sterilise the CSF of a leukaemic patient with meningitis caused by *Pseudomonas aeruginosa*, because CSF penetration was inadequate.[28] However, a woman who developed meningitis caused by *Stenotrophomonas maltophilia* was cured by a 3-week course of oral ciprofloxacin, 500 mg every 12 hours.[29] In another study, cefotaxime and gentamicin failed in a patient infected with multi-resistant pseudomonas.[30] However, a 2-week course of ciprofloxacin, 200 mg given intravenously every 12 hours, in combination with tobramycin, 120 mg given intravenously every 8 hours, cured the patient.[30]

Malaria

The problem of resistance to chloroquine and pyrimethamine in *Plasmodium falciparum* has led to the clinical assessment of a wide variety of agents with some antimalarial activity. Of the quinolones, ciprofloxacin is the most active against chloroquine-resistant *Plasmodium falciparum*, and is effective at a concentration of 5.2 mg/litre.[31]

In a randomised trial in Thailand, patients were treated with oral ciprofloxacin, 750 mg every 12 hours, or quinine sulphate (650 mg given orally every 8 hours) plus tetracycline (250 mg given orally every 6 hours).[32] Although it was planned to recruit 50 patients to the study, the study was stopped prematurely as none of the first four patients randomised to ciprofloxacin could complete the study. Within 36 hours of treatment with ciprofloxacin, parasitaemia had increased on average three-fold. Treatment was changed to quinine and tetracycline, and subsequent recovery was rapid. Failure was not the result of poor oral absorption as peak serum concentrations were 3.7–6.8 mg/litre peak, nor was it the result of failure to penetrate the erythrocytes, as erythrocyte concentrations were 3.8–6.0 mg/litre. The concentration needed to inhibit growth of the parasites *in vitro* at the median infective dose (ID_{50}), however, was 6.6 mg/litre, which was higher than the peak serum levels achieved.[32] A similar lack of efficacy has been reported in another patient with falciparum malaria.[33] There is some evidence, however, that ciprofloxacin can act synergistically with standard antimalarial agents against infections which are slow to respond to conventional treatment.[34] Four children with malaria caused by *Plasmodium falciparum* showed no clinical improvement during treatment with quinine and chloroquine with or without Fasidar® (pyrimethamine). In each case, the fever settled and the blood film became negative within 4 days of adding ciprofloxacin to existing treatment.

Conclusions

Due to its breadth of activity and mode of action, ciprofloxacin is being used in an increasing number of infections and by various routes of administration. For the treatment of peritonitis during CAPD, oral administration has proved unreliable, but intraperitoneal dosing (20 mg/litre added to the dialysate for 10 days) is effective. Combination with a glycopeptide would prevent failure due to coagulase-negative staphylococci. Topical application is a major form of treatment of ocular infections (0.3% ophthalmic solution administered every 2 hours for 1 day then every 4 hours for 6 days). An oral liquid form, ear drops and liposomal ciprofloxacin are likely to become available in the future (G Tillotson, personal communication). Ciprofloxacin (50–75 mg/day administered intravenously) can be considered for the treatment of neonatal meningitis caused by Gram-negative bacteria. The use of ciprofloxacin in the treatment of non-resistant malaria, however, no longer seems appropriate, although resistant/recalcitrant disease may warrant concomitant use of ciprofloxacin in addition to standard therapy.

References

1. Kane MP, Bailie GR, Moon DG, Siu I. Stability of ciprofloxacin injection in peritoneal dialysis solutions. Am J Hosp Pharm 1994; 51: 373–7.
2. Hancock K, Hulme B. Treatment of CAPD peritonitis with oral ciprofloxacin. Nephrol Dial Transplant 1989; 4: 759.
3. Fleming LW, Phillips G, Stewart WK, Scott AC. Oral ciprofloxacin in the treatment of peritonitis in patients on continuous ambulatory peritoneal dialysis. J Antimicrob Chemother 1990; 25: 441–8.
4. Cheng IK, Chan CY, Wong WT, Cheng SW, Ritchie CW, Cheung WC et al. A randomized prospective comparison of oral versus intraperitoneal ciprofloxacin as the primary treatment of peritonitis complicating continuous ambulatory peritoneal dialysis. Perit Dial Int 1993; 13 (Suppl 2): S351–4.
5. Tapson JS, Orr KE, George JC, Stansfield E, Bint AJ, Ward MK. A comparison between oral ciprofloxacin and intraperitoneal vancomycin and netilmicin in CAPD peritonitis. J Antimicrob Chemother 1990; 26 (Suppl F): 63–71.
6. Bennett-Jones DN, Russell GI, Barrett A. A comparison between oral ciprofloxacin and intra-peritoneal vancomycin and gentamicin in the treatment of CAPD peritonitis. J Antimicrob Chemother 1990; 26 (Suppl F): 73–6.
7. Friedland JS, Iveson TJ, Fraise AP, Winearls CG, Selkon JB, Oliver DO. A comparison between intraperitoneal vancomycin and gentamicin in the treatment of peritonitis associated with continuous ambulatory peritoneal dialysis. J Antimicrob Chemother 1990; 26 (Suppl F): 77–81.
8. Peréz Fontan M, Rosales M, Rodríguez-Carmona A, García Falcón T, Adeva M, Fernández Rivera C et al. Treatment of peritonitis in CAPD with ciprofloxacin: long-term experience. Adv Perit Dial 1993; 9: 211–14.
9. Dryden MS, Wing AJ, Phillips I. Low dose intraperitoneal ciprofloxacin for the treatment of peritonitis in patients receiving continuous ambulatory peritoneal dialysis (CAPD). J Antimicrob Chemother 1991; 28: 131–9.
10. Ludlam HA, Barton I, White L, McMullin C, King A, Phillips I. Intraperitoneal ciprofloxacin for the treatment of peritonitis in patients receiving continuous ambulatory peritoneal dialysis (CAPD). J Antimicrob Chemother 1990; 25: 843–51.
11. Lüthy R, Joos B, Gassmann F. Penetration of ciprofloxacin into the human eye. 1st Ciprofloxacin Workshop, Leverkusen, Germany, 1985: 192–6.
12. Sweeney G, Fern AI, Lindsay G, Doig MW. Penetration of ciprofloxacin into the aqueous humour of the uninflamed human eye after oral administration. J Antimicrob Chemother 1990; 26: 99–105.
13. Diamond JP, White L, Leeming JP, Bing-Hoh H, Easty DL. Topical 0.3% ciprofloxacin, norfloxacin, and

ofloxacin in treatment of bacterial keratitis: a new method for comparative evaluation of ocular drug penetration. Br J Ophthalmol 1995; 79: 606–9.

14. Price FW Jr, Whitson WE, Collins KS, Gonzales JS. Corneal tissue levels of topically applied ciprofloxacin. Cornea 1995; 14: 152–6.

15. Leibowitz HM. Antibacterial effectiveness of ciprofloxacin 0.3% ophthalmic solution in the treatment of bacterial conjunctivitis. Am J Ophthalmol 1991; 112 (Suppl 4): S29–33.

16. Bloom PA, Leeming JP, Power W, Laidlaw DA, Collum LM, Easty DL. Topical ciprofloxacin in the treatment of blepharitis and blepharoconjunctivitis. Eur J Ophthalmol 1994; 4: 6–12.

17. Adenis JP, Colin J, Verin P, Saint-Blancat P, Malet F. Ciprofloxacin ophthalmic solution versus rifamycin ophthalmic solution for the treatment of conjunctivitis and blepharitis. Eur J Ophthalmol 1995; 5: 82–7.

18. Power WJ, Collum LM, Easty DL, Bloom PA, Laidlaw DA, Libert J et al. Evaluation of efficacy and safety of ciprofloxacin ophthalmic solution versus chloramphenicol. Eur J Ophthalmol 1993; 3: 77–82.

19. Abrams SM, Degnan TJ, Vinciguerra V. Marrow aplasia following topical application of chloramphenicol ointment. Arch Intern Med 1980; 140: 576–7.

20. Gogos CA, Maraziotis TG, Papadakis N, Beermann D, Siamplis DK, Bassaris HP. Penetration of ciprofloxacin into human cerebrospinal fluid in patients with inflamed and non-inflamed meninges. Eur J Clin Microbiol Infect Dis 1991; 10: 511–14.

21. Wolff M, Boutron L, Singlas E, Clair B, Decazes JM, Regnier B. Penetration of ciprofloxacin into cerebrospinal fluid of patients with bacterial meningitis. Antimicrob Agents Chemother 1987; 31: 899–902.

22. Green SDR, Ilunga F, Cheesbrough JS, Tillotson GS, Hichens M, Felmingham D. The treatment of neonatal meningitis due to Gram-negative bacilli with ciprofloxacin: evidence of satisfactory penetration into the cerebrospinal fluid. J Infect 1993; 26: 253–6.

23. Schacht P, Arcieri G, Branolte J, Bruck H, Chysky V, Griffith E et al. Worldwide clinical data on efficacy and safety of ciprofloxacin. Infection 1988; 16 (Suppl 1): 29–43.

24. Schonwald S, Beus I, Lisic M, Car V, Gmajnicki B. Ciprofloxacin in the treatment of Gram-negative bacillary meningitis. Am J Med 1989; 87 (Suppl 5A): 248–9.

25. Isaacs D, Slack MPE, Wilkinson AR, Westwood AW. Successful treatment of pseudomonas ventriculitis with ciprofloxacin. J Antimicrob Chemother 1986; 17: 535–8.

26. Bhutta ZA, Farooqui BJ, Sturm AW. Eradication of a multiple drug resistant Salmonella paratyphi A causing meningitis with ciprofloxacin. J Infect 1992; 25: 215–19.

27. Ragunathan PL, Potkins DV, Watson JG, Kearns AM, Carroll A. Neonatal meningitis due to Salmonella typhimurium treated with ciprofloxacin. J Antimicrob Chemother 1990; 26: 727–8.

28. Saha V, Stansfield R, Masterton R, Eden T. The treatment of Pseudomonas aeruginosa meningitis – old regime or newer drugs? Scand J Infect Dis 1993; 25: 81–3.

29. Girijaratnakumari T, Raja A, Ramani R, Antony B, Shivananda PG. Meningitis due to Xanthomonas maltophilia. J Postgrad Med 1993; 39: 153–5.

30. Millar MR, Bransby-Zachary MA, Tompkins DS, Hawkey PM, Gibson RM. Ciprofloxacin for Pseudomonas aeruginosa meningitis. Lancet 1986; i: 1325.

31. Midgley JM, Keter DW, Phillipson JD, Grant S, Warhurst DC. Quinolones and multiresistant Plasmodium falciparum. Lancet 1988; ii: 281.

32. Watt G, Shanks GD, Edstein MD, Pavanand K, Webster HK, Wechgritaya S. Ciprofloxacin treatment of drug-resistant falciparum malaria. J Infect Dis 1991; 164: 602–4.

33. Stromberg A, Bjorkman A. Ciprofloxacin does not achieve radical cure of Plasmodium falciparum infection in Sierra Leone. Trans R Soc Trop Med Hyg 1992; 86: 373.

34. Smithson JC, Harbottle JA, Hunter PR. Ciprofloxacin is effective in the treatment of drug-resistant malaria when combined with other anti-malaria drugs. Travel Med Int 1995; 13: 136–7.

Chapter 15

Prophylaxis

Surgery

Perioperative antibiotics are used routinely in many procedures to reduce the incidence of postoperative wound infections.[1] Prospective, randomised trials have demonstrated the effectiveness of prophylaxis, provided the antibiotics are given before skin incision to ensure therapeutic tissue concentrations are present at the time of possible contamination. The antibiotics chosen must be active against the majority of contaminating organisms. Prophylaxis should not be continued beyond 3 hours after the end of surgery because no additional benefit accrues and the risk of antibiotic resistance emerging should be kept to a minimum.[2] Although prophylactic antibiotics can reduce the costs attributable to infection and prolonged hospital stay, indiscriminate use can result in greater costs arising from adverse effects (e.g. pseudomembranous colitis) and the selection and dissemination of resistant organisms.[1]

The antibacterial spectrum and pharmacokinetic behaviour of ciprofloxacin suggest that it would be effective as an agent for surgical prophylaxis.[3] Ciprofloxacin is highly active against the Enterobacteriaceae that commonly infect wounds after abdominal surgery, but it is less effective against the staphylococci, particularly methicillin-resistant *Staphylococcus aureus* (MRSA), which can cause infection in wounds after clean surgery. However, the penetration of ciprofloxacin into body fat is good, reaching 3.3 mg/kg with a dose of 750 mg every 12 hours.[4] A single intravenous dose of 200 mg maintains inhibitory concentrations in the colonic mucosa for at least 2 hours[5] and, although only 1% of an intravenous dose of ciprofloxacin is excreted in the bile, levels in the gall bladder are ten times higher than serum concentrations. Concentrations of metabolites of ciprofloxacin reach 21 mg/litre in the common bile duct, but their antibiotic activity is only 5% of the parent compound.[6]

Orally administered prophylaxis is possible with ciprofloxacin, as 30–60 ml of fluid can be administered before surgery without complications.[7] The oral route reduces costs and improves the ease of drug administration, but depends on surgery being performed within an hour of giving the dose. Unfortunately, surgery often has to be delayed beyond the expected time, and tissue concentrations of the antibiotic may, therefore, fall to low levels by the time it actually takes place. In addition, the oral dose cannot be given within 60 minutes of opiate administration because absorption is reduced.[8] Temazepam and other benzodiazepines do not have any effect on absorption.

Vascular surgery

In vascular surgery, the predominant pathogens causing wound infections are *Staphylococcus aureus* and the coagulase-negative staphylococci, particularly in late infections, but the contribution of antibiotics to the prevention of infections more than 6 months after surgery is

Wilson APR and Grüneberg RN.
Ciprofloxacin: 10 years of clinical experience
© 1997 Maxim Medical, Oxford.

unclear. Ciprofloxacin appears to be as effective as the cephalosporins[9,10] (Table 15.1).[9–32] A double-blind, randomised trial compared oral ciprofloxacin, two doses of 750 mg, with intravenous cefuroxime, 1.5 g every 8 hours for 3 days, in 580 patients undergoing arterial surgery.[10] Purulent wound infections, caused by *Staphylococcus aureus* in most cases, developed in 27 (9%) of the patients in the ciprofloxacin group and in 26 (9%) of the patients in the cefuroxime group. Another smaller trial (n = 33) compared three oral doses of ciprofloxacin, 500 mg, 1 hour before, and 8 and 24 hours after surgery, with intravenous cephazolin, 1 g every 8 hours for 3 days.[9] Two patients in each group developed cellulitis.

Gastroduodenal surgery

Antibiotic prophylaxis is used in gastric surgery because of the frequent bacterial colonisation of the mucosa in patients with achlorhydria, cancer or bleeding, or in those receiving H_2-receptor antagonists. In a randomised trial of 149 patients using intravenous or oral ciprofloxacin (oral given 1 hour before the operation) or intravenous cefuroxime (Table 15.1), McArdle *et al.* found no significant differences between the groups.[11] Intravenous and not oral doses of ciprofloxacin, however, are recommended for patients with gastric outlet obstruction.

Biliary surgery and endoscopy

Bile is usually sterile and the treatment of acute cholecystitis generally supportive, with antibiotics being used only if there is ascending infection, demonstrated by rigors, fever or signs of septicaemia. Septic complications are more common in patients older than 75 years, or in those with positive bile cultures, acute cholecystitis or obstructive jaundice.[33] Acute cholangitis requires early endoscopic drainage (ERCP) and antibiotics, and sphincterotomy if stones are present. Of 347 patients undergoing surgery for biliary stent insertion, 34 developed bacteraemia (14 of these patients were receiving antibiotics at the time),[34] the quality of drainage being the most important risk factor.

The bacteria in infected bile reflect those of the small intestine and colon: *Escherichia coli*, *Klebsiella* spp., *Proteus* spp., *Enterobacter* spp., enterococci, streptococci and staphylococci. Anaerobes (*Bacteroides* spp., *Clostridium* spp.) are less common.[35] With the exception of the anaerobes, ciprofloxacin would be effective against these organisms at the expected tissue or fluid levels. Following ERCP, *Pseudomonas aeruginosa* is a common pathogen, particularly if the endoscope is not adequately disinfected. In the 34 episodes of bacteraemia reported by Motte *et al.*, *Pseudomonas aeruginosa* was found in 17, compared with 12 due to *Escherichia coli*.[34]

Ciprofloxacin given orally is an effective and convenient form of prophylaxis of bacteraemia following ERCP. Alveyn *et al.* reported the results of two randomised trials.[15] The first study was double blind, enrolling patients without biliary obstruction to receive either one dose of oral ciprofloxacin, 750 mg, or placebo. No cases of bacteraemia occurred. In the second study, patients with biliary obstruction were treated with three doses of ciprofloxacin, 750 mg orally, or one dose of intravenous cephazolin, 1 g, and only two cases of bacteraemia occurred, both in the cephazolin group.[15] Another study reported only single cases of cholangitis in 103 patients given oral ciprofloxacin and in 106 patients given intravenous cefuroxime.[16] Pancreatitis occurred in 2 and 5 patients, respectively.

Kujath treated 200 patients intravenously with either ciprofloxacin, 200 mg, or ceftriaxone, 2 g, before biliary surgery (Table 15.1).[12] All patients had at least one risk factor for cholangitis (e.g. emergency surgery, obesity or age over 70 years). There were two wound infections in the ciprofloxacin group (2%) and one in the ceftriaxone group (1%), although 12 and 15 patients, respectively, required prolonged antibiotic administration. Another trial compared oral and intravenous ciprofloxacin with intravenous cefuroxime in 208 patients.[13] Wound infections occurred in 8%, 9% and 10%

Table 15.1. Randomised, controlled trials of the use of ciprofloxacin in the prevention of surgical wound infection.

Reference/specialty	Men:women	Age (mean or range) (years)	Agent	Dose regimen (loading) × number of doses	No. patients (no. evaluable)	Success (%)	Failure (%)	Odds ratio (95% CI)
9								
Vascular	–	–	Ciprofloxacin	500 mg p.o. at –1, 8 & 24 hours	18	16 (89)	1 (6)	0.8 (0.1–6.6)
			Cephazolin	1 g i.v. t.d.s. × 9	15	13 (87)	1 (7)	
10								
Vascular	–	72.5	Ciprofloxacin	750 mg p.o. b.d. × 2	293	266 (91)	27 (9)	1.0 (0.6–1.3)
		71.5	Cefuroxime	1.5 g i.v. t.d.s. × 3	287	261 (90)	26 (10)	
11								
Gastroduodenal	36:13	55	Ciprofloxacin	200 mg i.v. × 1	49	43 (88)	6 (12)	0.9 (0.3–2.8)
	35:15	53	Ciprofloxacin	750 mg p.o. × 1	50	46 (92)	4 (8)	0.5 (0.2–2.0)
	28:22	55	Cefuroxime	1.5 g i.v.	50	43 (86)	7 (14)	
12								
Biliary	27:73	59	Ciprofloxacin	200 mg i.v. × 1	100	98 (98)	2 (2)	0.5 (0.04–5.6)
	32:68	57	Ceftriaxone	2 g i.v. × 1	100	99 (99)	1 (1)	
13								
Biliary	17:50	–	Ciprofloxacin	200 mg i.v. × 1	67	61 (91)	6 (9)	1.1 (0.3–3.5)
	21:51		Ciprofloxacin	750 mg p.o. × 1	72	66 (92)	6 (8)	1.1 (0.4–3.6)
	19:50		Cefuroxime	1.5 g i.v. × 1	69	62 (90)	7 (10)	
14								
Biliary	–	–	Ciprofloxacin	500 mg p.o. × 1	95	91 (96)	4 (4)	0.7 (0.2–2.4)
			Ciprofloxacin	500 mg p.o. × 3	97	97 (100)	0	
			Cefuroxime	1.5 g i.v. × 1	96	90 (94)	6 (6)	

Table 15.1. (continued)

Reference/ specialty	Men:women	Age (mean or range) (years)	Agent	Dose regimen (loading) × number of doses	No. patients (no. evaluable)	Success (%)	Failure (%)	Odds ratio (95% CI)
15 ERCP*	14:10	–	Ciprofloxacin	750 mg p.o. × 1	24	24 (100)	0	–
	9:14		Placebo	–	23	23 (100)	0	–
	25:16		Ciprofloxacin	750 mg b.d. × 6	41	41 (100)	0	
	19:24		Cephazolin	1 g b.d. × 6	43	41 (95)	2 (5)	
16 ERCP*	50:53	32–78	Ciprofloxacin	750 mg p.o. × 2 14 hours apart	103	102	1	1.0 (0.06–17)
	47:59	35–83	Cefuroxime	1.5 g i.v. single dose then 750 mg i.v. single dose 12 hours later	106	105	1	
17 Colorectal	–	Not stated	Ciprofloxacin + metronidazole	200 mg + 500 mg i.v. × 1	54	50 (93)	4 (7)	4.4 (0.5–41)
			Latamoxef + metronidazole	2 g + 500 mg i.v. × 1	57	56 (98)	1 (2)	
18 Colorectal	79:80	21–89	Ciprofloxacin + piperacillin	500 mg p.o. b.d. × 2 + 4 i.v. × 1	159	136 (86)	23 (14)	0.35 (0.2–0.6)
	79:89	19–88	No oral agent + piperacillin	4 g i.v. × 1	168	113 (67)	55 (33)	
19 Colorectal	18:23	64	Ciprofloxacin + metronidazole	1000 mg p.o. × 1 + 500 mg i.v. t.d.s. × 3	41 (40)	36 (88)	4 (10)	0.3 (0.08–0.95)
	23:21	61	Ciprofloxacin + metronidazole	1000 mg p.o. then 750 mg p.o. b.d. × 6 + 500 mg i.v. t.d.s. × 9	44 (42)	38 (86)	4 (9)	0.5 (0.1–2.0)

*ERCP, endoscopic retrograde cholangiopancreatogram.

Table 15.1. (continued)

Reference/ specialty	Men:women	Age (mean or range) (years)	Agent	Dose regimen (loading) × number of doses	No. patients (no. evaluable)	Success (%)	Failure (%)	Odds ratio (95% CI)
	20:27	65	Gentamicin + metronidazole	120 mg i.v. × 1 then 80 mg t.d.s. × 2 + 500 mg i.v. t.d.s. × 3	47 (45)	32 (68)	13 (28)	
	21:23	57	Gentamicin + metronidazole	120 mg i.v. × 1 then 80 mg t.d.s. × 9 + 500 mg i.v. t.d.s. × 9	44 (42)	35 (80)	7 (16)	
20 Colorectal	23:11	–	Ciprofloxacin + metronidazole	200 mg i.v. b.d. × 2 + 500 mg i.v. t.d.s. × 3	34	31 (91)	3 (9)	0.6 (0.1–2.7)
	22:14	–	Cephazolin + metronidazole	2 g i.v. b.d. × 6 + 500 mg i.v. t.d.s. × 3	36	31 (86)	5 (14)	
21 Urological	55:0 55:0	68 71	Ciprofloxacin Placebo	500 mg p.o. × 1 × 1	55 55	49 (89) 33 (60)	6 (11) 22 (40)	0.18 (0.07–0.5)
22 Urological	50:0 51:0	68 68	Ciprofloxacin No prophylaxis	250 mg p.o. b.d. × 6	50 51	31 (62) 48 (94)	19 (38) 3 (6)	9.8 (2.7–36)
23 Urological	53:0 49:0	24–91 25–96	Ciprofloxacin Cefotaxime	300 mg i.v. × 1 1 g i.v. × 1	53 49	50 (94) 45 (92)	3 (6) 4 (8)	0.7 (0.1–3)
24 Urological	37:0 39:0	66 67	Ciprofloxacin Cefotaxime	300 mg i.v. × 1 1 g i.v. × 1	37 39	36 (97) 36 (92)	1 (3) 3 (8)	0.3 (0.03–3.4)
25 Urological	–	–	Ciprofloxacin Cefotaxime	Not stated	45 47	45 (100) 46 (98)	0 1 (2)	–

Table 15.1. (continued)

Reference/ specialty	Men:women	Age (mean or range) (years)	Agent	Dose regimen (loading) × number of doses	No. patient (no. evaluable)	Success (%)	Failure (%)	Odds ratio (95% CI)
26 Urological	28:0	67	Ciprofloxacin	500 mg p.o. b.d. × 2	28	28 (100)	0	–
	27:0	67	Gentamicin	1.5 mg/kg i.v. × 1 then 80 mg × 1, 8 hours later	27	21 (78)	6 (22)	
27 Urological	76:0	51–85	Ciprofloxacin	500 mg p.o. b.d. × 4	76	76 (100)	0	–
	75:0	57–89	Ciprofloxacin	500 mg p.o. b.d. × 16–18	75	75 (100)	0	
	71:0	56–83	No antibiotic		71	44 (62)	23 (32)	
28 Urological	84:0	–	Ciprofloxacin	500 mg p.o. × 1 500 mg p.o. × 1 then 250 mg p.o. b.d. × 6	84	79 (94)	5 (6)	0.95 (0.3–3.2)
	96:0	–	Ciprofloxacin		96	90 (94)	6 (6)	
29 Urinary catheter	6:60	31–91	Ciprofloxacin	250 mg p.o. once daily‡	66 (59)	57 (86)	2 (3)	5.8 (1.4–25)
	4:64	39–90	Ciprofloxacin	500 mg p.o. b.d.‡	68 (64)	60 (88)	4 (6)	3.2 (1.1–9.2)
	4:64	31–90	Placebo	–	68 (61)	49 (74)	12 (18)	
30 Urodynamic testing	18:0	53	Ciprofloxacin	500 mg p.o. b.d. × 6	18	18 (100)	0	–
	22:0	47	Placebo	3 days	22	19 (86)	3 (14)	
31 Gynaecological	0:42	30–75	Ciprofloxacin	300 mg i.v. × 1 (± 500 mg p.o. t.d.s. × 9)	42	41 (98)	1 (2)	–
	0:41	19–87	Placebo		41	41 (100)	0	
32 Gynaecological	0:54	29–81	Ciprofloxacin	200 mg i.v. × 1 1.5 g i.v. q.d.s. × 3 + 500 mg i.v. q.d.s. × 3	54	51	3	–
	0:58	32–80	Cefuroxime + metronidazole		58	58	0	

‡From second postoperative day until catheter removal.

of the patients, respectively. The regimens appeared similarly effective. A further comparison of oral ciprofloxacin, one or three doses of 500 mg, and intravenous cefuroxime, one dose of 1.5 g, in 288 elective cholecystectomies also showed no significant difference in efficacy between the regimens.[14]

Colorectal surgery

The risk of wound infections in colorectal surgery is high, particularly when faecal spillage occurs during the operation. The pathogens are part of the normal faecal flora and include Gram-negative aerobes, enterococci and anaerobes such as *Bacteroides fragilis*. A broad-spectrum antibiotic combination is, therefore, needed.

McArdle *et al.*[19] compared oral ciprofloxacin plus intravenous metronidazole with gentamicin plus metronidazole, given as either 1- or 3-day courses (Table 15.1).[17–20] Ciprofloxacin was significantly more effective in preventing wound infections than gentamicin when given as a 24-hour course (only 4 failures in 40 patients versus 13 in 45, $p < 0.02$). The two drug combinations given as 3-day courses were similar in efficacy and comparison of 1 versus 3 days for either antibiotic showed no clear difference. Another trial claimed a significant reduction in wound infections ($p = 0.002$) using ciprofloxacin (a single 750 mg oral dose) plus metronidazole (a single 500 mg intravenous dose) when compared with gentamicin (80 mg every 8 hours for 3 days, administered intravenously) plus metronidazole (a single 500 mg intravenous dose) (3/100 [3%] versus 96/718 [13%]), but this study was retrospective.[36] Gortz *et al.* compared ciprofloxacin with latamoxef in a double-blind study, using metronidazole in both regimens to improve anti-anaerobic activity.[17] There was no significant difference between the two with respect to wound infections or length of hospital stay.

In a trial carried out by Taylor *et al.*, ciprofloxacin was used as an oral agent to reduce the Gram-negative aerobic flora of the colon for the 24 hours before colorectal surgery.[18] All 327 patients were given a single

intravenous dose of piperacillin at the start of the operation, but were also randomised to receive oral ciprofloxacin or placebo with the preoperative cathartic. There were significantly fewer infections in patients who had been given ciprofloxacin (15% versus 33%, $p < 0.0002$), the difference being particularly marked in those having left hemicolectomies. Hospital stay was shortened, and no ciprofloxacin-resistant Gram-negative aerobic bacteria were isolated from blood or wound infections. The effect on the resistance patterns or the faecal flora was not studied.

Urological surgery

Antibiotic prophylaxis in transurethral resection of the prostate (TURP) is effective in preventing postoperative urinary infection and reducing the length of hospital stay.[3] The main pathogens are *Escherichia coli* and other Enterobacteriaceae, enterococci and staphylococci. High concentrations of ciprofloxacin, up to 2.3-fold higher than serum levels, are reached in the prostate following an oral dose of 500 mg.[37]

A double-blind, placebo-controlled trial examined the use of a single oral dose of ciprofloxacin, 500 mg, in patients undergoing TURP.[21] Unsuspected bacteriuria was present in 8 of 55 (15%) patients in the ciprofloxacin group and 13 of 55 (24%) patients in the placebo group before operation ($p = $ ns). Following operation, significantly fewer patients given ciprofloxacin developed bacteriuria (6/55 [11%] versus 22/55 [40%]) or required antibiotic treatment (8/55 [15%] versus 27/55 [49%], $p < 0.001$). Grabe *et al.* also observed significantly fewer cases of bacteriuria in patients undergoing TURP who were given prophylactic ciprofloxacin compared to those who received no antibiotic (0/76 versus 23/71, $p < 0.01$), but there was no significant difference between a 48-hour and an 8-day course.[27] Bijl *et al.* similarly found no significant difference between a single dose and a 3-day course of ciprofloxacin in transurethral surgery. However, the 3-day course was significantly more effective in eradicating preoperative bacteriuria (1/5 versus 10/12, $p = 0.05$).[28]

Several trials have compared ciprofloxacin and cefotaxime in the prevention of bacteriuria following prostatectomy. One double-blind trial showed no significant difference between success rates in 102 patients given a single intravenous dose of ciprofloxacin or cefotaxime preoperatively (50/53 [94%] versus 45/49 [92%], respectively).[23] Using a similar protocol, Christiansen et al. also found no significant difference between the same two antibiotics, and there were only 4 failures in 76 patients in the trial.[24] One patient in the ciprofloxacin group had bacteriuria within 1 week of surgery, while 3 in the cefotaxime group had positive urine cultures 4–6 weeks after surgery. In a further trial, Gombert et al. observed no infections in 45 patients given ciprofloxacin and only 1 infection in 47 patients given cefotaxime.[25]

In a study of 55 patients undergoing transrectal needle biopsy of the prostate, intravenous gentamicin was compared with oral ciprofloxacin.[26] Two doses of each antibiotic were given, but ciprofloxacin administration was started 12 hours before the procedure, whereas gentamicin was given only 2 hours before biopsy. However, ciprofloxacin appeared to be more effective. A total of 12 patients were found to have bacteraemia during the procedure, 10 in the gentamicin group and 2 in the ciprofloxacin group. Clinical signs of bacteraemia were observed in 6 patients, all of whom received gentamicin ($p = 0.02$, Fisher's test).

Antibiotic administration during catheter drainage of the bladder is usually avoided because of the potential risk of resistant pathogens emerging. However, a double-blind, placebo-controlled trial suggested that ciprofloxacin can reduce catheter-associated infections following surgery without such undesirable effects.[29] Oral ciprofloxacin, 250 mg every 24 hours or 500 mg every 12 hours, or placebo were given for 2–14 days while a urinary catheter was in place, irrespective of perioperative antibiotic prophylaxis. Bacteriuria developed in 40 of 57 patients in the placebo group but in only 6 of 113 in the ciprofloxacin group. Symptomatic infections occurred in 26% and 8%, respectively. In the placebo group, Enterobacteriaceae were the predominant isolate, but in those few patients given ciprofloxacin who developed bacteriuria, Staphylococcus epidermidis and Candida spp. were the usual isolates. No Gram-negative faecal flora resistant to ciprofloxacin were isolated as the result of prophylaxis. Aerobic Gram-positive bacteria in the faeces were resistant to ciprofloxacin in 8 of 23 cases following prophylaxis, though normal susceptibility had returned by the 6-week follow-up visit. In another double-blind, placebo-controlled trial, the incidence of urinary infection after urodynamic testing was not significantly affected by ciprofloxacin prophylaxis given 2 days before and during the procedure.[30] However, patient numbers were small.

Prolonged low-dose antibiotics, such as cotrimoxazole, can be used to prevent urinary tract infection following renal transplantation. Ciprofloxacin, 250 mg/day administered orally for 6 months, was compared with co-trimoxazole, 480 mg/day administered orally, in a double-blind trial.[38] After 6 months, 38 of 51 (75%) patients in the ciprofloxacin group and 37 of 52 (71%) in the co-trimoxazole group had not had a urinary tract infection (p = ns). Only 3 patients withdrew from ciprofloxacin treatment (all with adverse effects) compared with 13 who withdrew from co-trimoxazole treatment (9 with adverse events, 4 with resistant infections).

Gynaecological surgery

Pelvic or vaginal infection after gynaecological surgery is usually polymicrobial, including Enterobacteriaceae, staphylococci, streptococci and anaerobes. The pathogen causing an infection is often not known. A placebo-controlled trial of 83 patients undergoing hysterectomy used the area under the temperature curve as an indicator of postoperative morbidity.[31] Ciprofloxacin was given as a single intravenous dose of 300 mg, but some patients were also given a 3-day course of oral ciprofloxacin preoperatively.

There was no significant difference found in the temperature curves of the 28 patients undergoing abdominal hysterectomy, but there was a reduction in fever index in those given ciprofloxacin compared with those given placebo. There were no serious infections in either group. One patient in the ciprofloxacin group developed an abdominal wound infection.

Another trial compared the use of one or two doses of ciprofloxacin (200 mg administered intravenously) with a 7-day course of clindamycin (300 mg administered orally every 8 hours) in patients undergoing myomectomy, hysterectomy or excision of cervical lesions.[39] There was no significant difference between the groups in the number of postoperative infections (2/128 [2%] versus 4/127 [3%]), but the method of randomisation used was not clear.

A third randomised trial showed no significant difference in fever or urinary infection after hysterectomy in patients given a single preoperative dose of ciprofloxacin (200 mg administered intravenously) or three doses of cefuroxime (1.5 g administered intravenously every 6 hours) plus metronidazole (500 mg administered intravenously every 6 hours).[32]

Eradication of carriage of *Neisseria meningitidis*

Household contacts of patients with meningococcal disease have a greater than 50-fold increased risk of acquiring the disease over the general population. Vaccines are often ineffective in children and there is no vaccine available against *Neisseria meningitidis* group B. Eradication of nasopharyngeal carriage is the most effective method to prevent spread of the disease. Rifampicin is successful in only 60–90% of cases, resistance has emerged in some countries and administration is required over 2–4 days.[40] Ciprofloxacin is highly active against *Neisseria meningitidis*, and nasopharyngeal concentrations are sufficient to kill the organism. Several trials have demonstrated that ciprofloxacin is effective in eradicating persistent meningococcal carriage from the nasopharynx, even when given as a single dose.

A single oral dose of ciprofloxacin (750 mg in adults, 15 mg/kg in children) was shown to be as effective in eradication of nasopharyngeal carriage as a 2-day regimen of rifampicin (600 mg or 20 mg/kg administered orally every 12 hours) or a single intramuscular injection of ceftriaxone (2 g or 50 mg/kg).[41] Of those patients with positive initial cultures, eradication was achieved in 72 of 79 (91%) cases by ciprofloxacin, 86 of 88 (97.7%) cases by rifampicin and 40 of 41 (97.6%) cases by ceftriaxone. Less than 1% of the 711 contacts given ciprofloxacin (including 469 children aged 2–18 years) showed any drug-related adverse effects.

In a randomised, double-blind trial, 22 of 23 patients were culture negative 3 weeks after a single oral ciprofloxacin dose of 750 mg, compared with only 2 of 22 patients given placebo.[42] Tetracycline- and sulphonamide-resistant strains were eradicated. A larger, open trial using a single oral dose of 500 mg showed eradication to be successful in all but 10 of 336 (3%) of carriers.[40] Adverse effects were mild and were mostly headache (21 cases), diarrhoea (20 cases) and nausea (19 cases). A 5-day course of ciprofloxacin, 500 mg orally every 12 hours, had previously been shown to eradicate carriage in 21 of 21 (100%) of patients treated in a double-blind trial, compared with persistence in 14 of 21 (67%) of patients given placebo.[43] A 2-day course of oral ciprofloxacin, 250 mg every 12 hours, was also effective in 54 of 56 (96%) carriers in a further randomised trial, with persistence occurring in 46 of 53 (87%) of patients given placebo.[44]

Eradication of MRSA

Ciprofloxacin has been used in a small number of patients for the treatment and eradication of infections caused by MRSA. Ciprofloxacin resistance has been found likely to emerge whether or not the antibiotic is given with rifampicin.[45] Active infections of the urine and lungs can be treated successfully, but the treatment of soft tissue infections and osteomyelitis often fails following the development of resistance. Routine use cannot be advocated either prophylactically or therapeutically.

Of 32 patients treated for MRSA infections at various sites, 15 were cured, 14 improved, and treatment failed in 3 patients treated with ciprofloxacin (750 mg administered orally every 12 hours).[46] MRSA was eradicated in 60% of cases. Resistant strains emerged in 6 patients during treatment. Mulligan *et al.* also treated 14 patients colonised with MRSA (ciprofloxacin, 750 mg administered orally every 12 hours).[47] The organism was eradicated in 11 patients (79%), but 4 of these were again colonised within 1 month. In a further 21 patients infected with MRSA who were treated with ciprofloxacin plus rifampicin, 10 were found to be infected with strains resistant to ciprofloxacin, 5 of whom had not previously been exposed to ciprofloxacin.[48]

Other indications

In patients with cystic fibrosis, hospital admission is often necessary every few months for intravenous antibiotic treatment of pseudomonal infections. A course of ciprofloxacin, 500 mg administered orally every 8 hours, for 10 days every 3 months over 1 year was compared with placebo in 31 patients.[49] Patients given ciprofloxacin were found to have a significantly improved peak expiratory flow at the end of the study, whereas those given placebo showed no significant change. Ciprofloxacin-resistant *Pseudomonas aeruginosa* was isolated from 2 patients in the ciprofloxacin group and 4 in the placebo group at the start of the study, rising to 10 and 5 patients, respectively, by the end of the study.

Patients with spinal cord lesions and neurogenic bladder dysfunction commonly develop recurrent urinary tract infections. In a crossover study, long-term, low-dose ciprofloxacin was compared with placebo in the prevention of urinary infections in 21 patients.[50] Oral ciprofloxacin, 100 mg/day, or placebo were

given for consecutive 6-month periods. Urinary infections occurred on 5 occasions in patients given ciprofloxacin and in 59 cases in the placebo group ($p < 0.001$). Ciprofloxacin-resistant bacteria colonised the gut in only 1 patient, but the risk would probably have increased if the patients had been treated for longer periods.

In a double-blind, placebo-controlled study, a single oral dose of ciprofloxacin, 250 mg, was used in an attempt to prevent cholera developing in those who had come into contact with a confirmed case.[51] It was not found to be of benefit if only a few new cases were occurring. In patients with stool cultures negative for *Vibrio cholerae*, there was no difference between ciprofloxacin- and placebo-treated patients in the incidence of cholera (1 failure in 107 patients versus 2 in 104 patients, respectively). In those with positive stool cultures, however, there was a trend towards fewer clinical failures in the ciprofloxacin group (1/14 [7%] versus 6/16 [38%]).

Ciprofloxacin was reported to be effective in preventing spontaneous bacterial peritonitis in cirrhotic patients. A double-blind, placebo-controlled trial showed that oral ciprofloxacin, 750 mg once a week for 6 months, resulted in a reduction in the number of patients developing peritonitis.[52] However, the reduction was not statistically significant (1/28 [4%] versus 7/32 [22%], $p = 0.08$ Fisher's test).

Conclusions

Ciprofloxacin has been shown to be as effective as the current standard prophylactic regimens in several surgical specialties. It can be given as a single intravenous dose (200 mg) and the oral route (500–750 mg) has been used successfully, as in biliary surgery for example, allowing a saving in costs over parenteral regimens. For colorectal surgery, ciprofloxacin should be combined with metronidazole. Many of the trials have, however, been too small to demonstrate any but the most major differences between the regimens tested. The route of administration and the ecological impact of the use of ciprofloxacin have to be considered before using ciprofloxacin for routine prophylaxis. Selection of resistant mutants in Enterobacteriaceae is, however, extremely rare (frequency 10^{-7}).[53]

Ciprofloxacin is highly effective as a single dose in the eradication of pharyngeal carriage of *Neisseria meningitidis* (500 mg administered orally) and it is a drug of choice in adults. It cannot, however, be recommended for the eradication of carriage of MRSA. Long-term prophylactic use may be beneficial in patients with cystic fibrosis or a neurogenic bladder to reduce the incidence of respiratory or urinary pathogens. As with any antibiotic used in this way, however, there is a risk of resistant pathogens emerging.

References

1. Page CP, Bohnen JMA, Fletcher JR, McManus AT, Solomkin JS, Wittman DH. Antimicrobial prophylaxis for surgical wounds. Arch Surg 1993; 128: 79–88.

2. Burke JF. The effective period of preventive antibiotic action in experimental incisions and dermal lesions. Surgery 1961; 50: 161–8.

3. Dellamonica P, Bernard E. Fluoroquinolones and surgical prophylaxis. Drugs 1993; 45 (Suppl 3): 102–13.

4. Licitra CM, Brooks RG, Sieger BE. Clinical efficacy and levels of ciprofloxacin in tissue in patients with soft tissue infection. Antimicrob Agents Chemother 1987; 31: 805–7.

5. Vestweber K-H, Viell B, Schaaf S, Scholl H. Perioperative prophylaxis in colorectal surgery: is a single-shot with 200 mg ciprofloxacin sufficient to maintain therapeutic levels in gut tissues? 6th Mediterranean Congress of Chemotherapy, Taormina, Italy, 1988: 179–81.

6. Parry MF, Smego DA , Digiovanni MA. Hepatobiliary kinetics and excretion of ciprofloxacin. Antimicrob Agents Chemother 1988; 32: 982–5.

7. Morran C, McArdle C, Pettitt L, Sleigh D, Gemmell C, Hichens M *et al.* Brief report: pharmacokinetics of orally administered ciprofloxacin in abdominal surgery. Am J Med 1989; 87 (Suppl 5A): 86–8.

8. McArdle CS. Oral prophylaxis in biliary tract surgery. J Antimicrob Chemother 1994; 33: 200–2.

9. Landau Z, Pasik S, Mashih A, Reina A. Ciprofloxacin versus cefazolin for prevention of infection in vascular surgery. Eur J Clin Microbiol Infect Dis 1991; (Special Issue): 414–15.

10. Risberg B, Drott C, Dalman P, Holm J, Ivarsson L, Jivegard L *et al.* Oral ciprofloxacin versus intravenous cefuroxime as prophylaxis against postoperative infection in vascular surgery: a randomised double-blind, prospective multicentre study. Eur J Vasc Endovasc Surg 1995; 10: 346–51.

11. McArdle CS, Morran CG, Anderson JR, Pettit L, Gemmell CG, Sleigh JD *et al.* Oral ciprofloxacin as prophylaxis in gastroduodenal surgery. J Hosp Infect 1995; 30: 211–16.

12. Kujath P. Brief report: antibiotic prophylaxis in biliary tract surgery. Am J Med 1989; 87 (Suppl 5A): 255–7.

13. McArdle CS, Morran CG, Pettit L, Gemmell CG, Sleigh JD, Tillotson GS. The value of oral antibiotic prophylaxis in biliary tract surgery. J Hosp Infect 1991; 19 (Suppl C): 59–64.

14. Karran SJ, Karran SE, Brough P. Oral prophylaxis – a new approach in elective biliary surgery. 17th International Congress of Chemotherapy, Berlin, Germany, 1991: 1153.

15. Alveyn CG, Robertson DAF, Wright R, Lowes JA, Tillotson G. Prevention of sepsis following endoscopic retrograde cholangiopancreatography. J Hosp Infect 1991; 19 (Suppl C): 65–70.

16. Mehal WZ, Culshaw KD, Tillotson GS, Chapman RW. Antibiotic prophylaxis for ERCP: a randomized clinical trial comparing ciprofloxacin and cefuroxime in 200 patients at high risk of cholangitis. Eur J Gastroenterol Hepatol 1995; 7: 841–5.

17. Gortz G, Boese-Landgraf J, Hopfenmüller W. Ciprofloxacin as single-dose antibiotic prophylaxis in colorectal surgery. Results of a randomized double-blind trial. Diagn Microbiol Infect Dis 1990; 13: 181–5.

18. Taylor EW, Lindsay G, West of Scotland Surgical Infection Study Group. Selective decontamination of the colon before elective colorectal surgery. World J Surg 1994; 18: 926–32.

19. McArdle CS, Morran CG, Pettit L, Gemmell CG, Sleigh JD, Tillotson GS. Value of oral antibiotic prophylaxis in colorectal surgery. Br J Surg 1995; 82: 1046–8.

20. Offer C, Weuta H, Bodner E. Efficacy of perioperative prophylaxis with ciprofloxacin or cefazolin in colorectal surgery. Infection 1988; 16 (Suppl 1): S46–7.

21. Shearman CP, Silverman SH, Johnson M, Young CH, Farrar DJ, Keighley MRB *et al.* Single dose, oral antibiotic cover for transurethral prostatectomy. Br J Urol 1988; 62: 434–8.

22. Murdoch DA, Badenoch DF, Gatchalian ER. Oral ciprofloxacin as prophylaxis in transurethral resection of the prostate. Br J Urol 1987; 60: 153–6.

23. Cox CE. Comparison of intravenous ciprofloxacin and intravenous cefotaxime for antimicrobial prophylaxis in transurethral surgery. Am J Med 1989; 87 (Suppl 5A): 252–4.

24. Christiansen MS, Nielsen KT, Knes J, Madsen PO. Single-dose preoperative prophylaxis in transurethral surgery. Am J Med 1989; 87 (Suppl 5A): 258–60.

25. Gombert ME, du Bouchet L, Aulicino TM, Berkowitz LB, Macchia RJ. Intravenous ciprofloxacin versus cefotaxime prophylaxis during transurethral surgery. Am J Med 1989; 87 (Suppl 5A): 250–1.

26. Roach MB, Figueroa TE, McBride D, George WJ, Neal DE. Ciprofloxacin versus gentamicin in prophylaxis against bacteremia in transrectal needle prostate needle biopsy. Urology 1991; 38: 84–7.

27. Grabe M, Forsgren A, Bjork T, Hellsten S. Controlled trial of a short and a prolonged course with ciprofloxacin in patients undergoing transurethral prostatic surgery. Eur J Clin Microbiol 1987; 6: 11–17.

28. Bijl W, Janknegt RA. Single-dose versus 3-day prophylaxis with ciprofloxacin in transurethral surgery. A clinical trial. Urol Int 1993; 51: 73–8.

29. Van der Wall E, Verkooyen RP, Mintjes-De Groot J, Oostinga J, Van Dijk A, Hustinx WNM et al. Prophylactic ciprofloxacin for catheter associated urinary tract infection. Lancet 1992; 339: 946–51.

30. Darouiche RO, Smith MS, Markowski J. Antibiotic prophylaxis for urodynamic testing in patients with spinal cord injury: a preliminary study. J Hosp Infect 1994; 28: 57–61.

31. Gerstner GJ, Kronich W, Müller G. Ciprofloxacin prophylaxis for vaginal and abdominal hysterectomy – preliminary results. 6th Mediterranean Congress of Chemotherapy, Taormina, Italy, 1988: 175–8.

32. Brouwer WK, Hoogkamp-Korstanje JAA, Kuiper KM. Antibiotic prophylaxis in vaginal hysterectomy. Three doses of cefuroxime plus metronidazole versus one dose of ciprofloxacin. Pharm Weekbl (Sci) 1990; 12: 292–5.

33. Kasholm-Tengve B. Selective antibiotic prophylaxis in biliary tract operations. Surg Gynecol Obstet 1991; 173: 25–8.

34. Motte S, Deviere J, Dumonceau JM, Serruys E, Thys JP, Cremer M. Risk factors for septicaemia following endoscopic biliary stenting. Gastroenterology 1991; 101: 1374–81.

35. Chetlin SH, Elliott DW. Biliary bacteremia. Arch Surg 1971; 102: 303–6.

36. Rohwedder R, Bonadeo F, Benati M, Ojea Quintana G, Schlecker H, Vaccaro C. Single dose oral ciprofloxacin plus parenteral metronidazole for perioperative antibiotic prophylaxis in colorectal surgery. Chemotherapy 1993; 39: 218–24.

37. Waldron R, Arkell DG, Wise R, Andrews JM. The intraprostatic penetration of ciprofloxacin. J Antimicrob Chemother 1986; 17: 544–5.

38. Hibberd PL, Tolkoff Rubin NE, Doran M, Delvecchio A, Cosimi AB, Delmonico FL et al. Trimethoprim-sulfamethoxazole compared with ciprofloxacin for the prevention of urinary tract infection in renal transplant recipients. A double-blind, randomized controlled trial. Online J Curr Clin Trials 1992; Aug 11; Doc No 15.

39. Sianturi MHR. Short course of ciprofloxacin in myomectomies, hysterectomies and loop electrosurgical excision procedures (LEEP): a clinical investigation. 7th Congress on Clinical Microbiology and Infectious Diseases, Vienna, Austria, 1995: Abstract.

40. Gaunt PN, Lambert BE. Single dose ciprofloxacin for the eradication of pharyngeal carriage of Neisseria meningitidis. J Antimicrob Chemother 1988; 21: 489–96.

41. Cuevas LE, Kazembe P, Mughogho GK, Tillotson GS, Hart CA. Eradication of nasopharyngeal carriage of Neisseria meningitidis, in children and adults in rural Africa: a comparison of ciprofloxacin and rifampicin. J Infect Dis 1995; 171: 728–31.

42. Dworzack DL, Sanders CC, Horowitz EA, Allais JM, Sookpranee M, Sanders WE et al. Evaluation of single-dose ciprofloxacin in the eradication of Neisseria meningitidis from nasopharyngeal carriers. Antimicrob Agents Chemother 1988; 32: 1740–1.

43. Pugsley MP, Dworzack DL, Horowitz EA, Cuevas TA, Sanders WE, Sanders CC. Efficacy of ciprofloxacin in the treatment of nasopharyngeal carriers of Neisseria meningitidis. J Infect Dis 1987; 156: 211–13.

44. Renkonen O, Sivonen A, Visakorpi R. Effect of ciprofloxacin on carrier rate of Neisseria meningitidis in army recruits in Finland. Antimicrob Agents Chemother 1987; 31: 962–3.

45. Ball P. Emergent resistance to ciprofloxacin amongst Pseudomonas aeruginosa and Staphylococcus aureus: clinical significance and therapeutic approaches. J Antimicrob Chemother 1990; 26 (Suppl F): 165–79.

46. Piercy EA, Barbaro D, Luby JP, Mackowiak PA. Ciprofloxacin for methicillin-resistant Staphylococcus aureus infections. Antimicrob Agents Chemother 1989; 33: 128–30.

47. Mulligan ME, Ruane PJ, Johnson L, Wong P, Wheelock JP, MacDonald K et al. Ciprofloxacin for eradication of methicillin-resistant Staphylococcus aureus colonization. Am J Med 1987; 82 (Suppl 4A): 215–19.

48. Peterson L, Quick J, Jensen B, Homann S, Johnson S, Tenquist J et al. Emergence of ciprofloxacin resistance in nosocomial methicillin-resistant Staphylococcus aureus (MRSA) isolates during ciprofloxacin plus rifampicin therapy for MRSA colonization. 29th Interscience Conference on Antimicrobial Agents in Chemotherapy, Houston, USA, 1989: 1255.

49. Sheldon CD, Assoufi BK, Hodson ME. Regular three monthly oral ciprofloxacin in adult cystic fibrosis patients infected with Pseudomonas aeruginosa. Respir Med 1993; 87: 587–93.

50. Biering-Sorensen F, Hoiby N, Nordenbo A, Ravnborg M, Bruun B, Rahm V. Ciprofloxacin as prophylaxis for urinary tract infection: prospective, randomized, cross-over, placebo controlled study in patients with spinal cord lesion. J Urol 1994; 151: 105–8.

51. Echevarria J, Seas C, Carrillo C, Mostorino R, Ruiz R, Gotuzzo E. Efficacy and tolerability of ciprofloxacin prophylaxis in adult household contacts of patients with cholera. Clin Infect Dis 1995; 20: 1480–4.

52. Rolachon A, Cordier L, Bacq Y, Nousbaum JB, Franza A, Paris JC *et al*. Ciprofloxacin and long-term prevention of spontaneous bacterial peritonitis: results of a prospective controlled trial. Hepatology 1995; 22: 1171–4.

53. Wolfson JS, Hooper DC. Introduction to DNA gyrase, quinolones and quinolone resistance. In: Fernandez PB, ed. Quinolones. Princeton: JR Prous Science Publishers, 1989: 137–57.

Chapter 16

Safety and paediatric use

Clinical trials and postmarketing surveillance have contributed to an extensive literature on the safety of ciprofloxacin, given orally or intravenously. Some of the adverse effects reported are common to the other quinolones, such as upper gastrointestinal symptoms, central nervous system (CNS) reactions and phototoxicity, while others have been anticipated from animal models (arthropathy, renal damage from crystalluria) or from experience with nalidixic acid (benign intracranial hypertension, neurotoxicity).[1] Adverse effects present within 7–10 days of treatment with ciprofloxacin and are not increased by prolonged use of the drug.

Adverse effects

Estimates of the overall incidence of adverse events depend on the thoroughness of the surveillance and the regimens used. Adverse effects were observed in 5.5% of 13,081 patients treated with intravenous ciprofloxacin (2.5% gastrointestinal, 0.7% CNS, 1.1% skin, 1.2% miscellaneous).[1] Previously, Arcieri *et al.*[2] reported adverse effects in 295 of 1869 (16%) patients treated with intravenous ciprofloxacin, with treatment being discontinued in 45 of these patients because of adverse events. Another analysis included 690 patients given intravenous ciprofloxacin, 200 mg per day,

with a further 2282 patients given 400 mg per day and 683 patients given 600 mg per day, for an average duration of 7.3 days.[3] Adverse events were reported in 8.4% of patients receiving the 200 mg dose, 18.3% at 400 mg and 22.1% at 600 mg (Figure 16.1).[3] A total of 3 patients had convulsions at 600 mg per day and 4 patients at 400 mg per day, though there was no clear dose dependency.

High intravenous doses have not been consistently associated with a higher incidence of adverse reactions or crystalluria. At an intravenous dose of 800–1200 mg per day, adverse events occurred in 20–27% of patients in four trials (total 118/522), which was a similar incidence to the control regimens.[3] In 628 patients, the most common drug-related events were a local reaction at the injection site (6%), abnormal liver function tests (3%), and confusion or dizziness (1%).

Of 63,059 patients given oral ciprofloxacin, adverse effects occurred in 5.8% of patients, with 3.4% being gastrointestinal, 1.1% CNS related, 0.7% cutaneous and 0.6% miscellaneous.[1] The incidence of adverse effects was therefore similar to that found with intravenous ciprofloxacin (Figure 16.2).[1] CNS reactions were observed in 1.3% of patients compared with 0.6% of 10,094 patients given intravenous ciprofloxacin. Schacht, Arcieri and Hullmann reported adverse effects in 881 of 9473 (9%) patients, of which 55 reactions (0.6%) were serious (gastrointestinal 60%, CNS 15%, skin 13%).[4]

Severe adverse events resulting in a change of treatment occurred in 1%, 3.1% and 4.5% of

Wilson APR and Grüneberg RN.
Ciprofloxacin: 10 years of clinical experience
© 1997 Maxim Medical, Oxford.

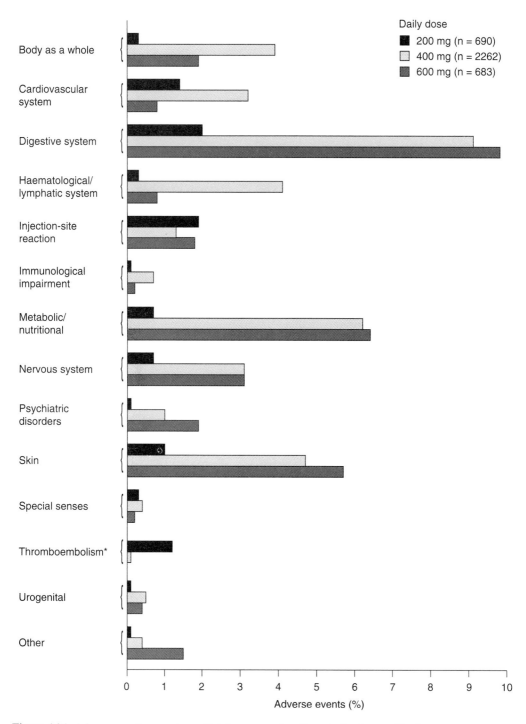

Figure 16.1. Adverse events occurring with intravenous ciprofloxacin, by dose and body system (COSTART).[3] Study with 200 mg dose does not include patients from the USA and Japan. Studies with 400 mg and 600 mg doses do not include patients from Japan. *Thromboembolism study without patients from the USA and Japan.

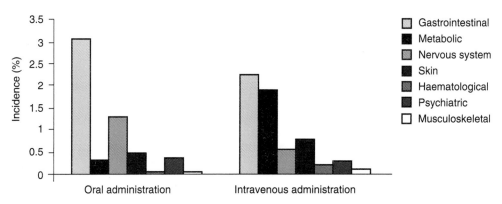

Figure 16.2. Comparison of adverse events following oral and intravenous doses of ciprofloxacin in phase IV clinical trials and postmarketing surveillance.[1]

patients given intravenous ciprofloxacin at a dose of 200 mg, 400 mg or 600 mg per day, respectively.[3] In 3635 patients, there were 4 cases of vomiting and of convulsions, 3 of confusion and of rash, and 2 each of hypotension, nausea, leucopenia, thrombocytopenia, oedema, somnolence, psychosis and urticaria.[3] There were single reports of fever, jaundice, abnormal liver function tests and liver damage, toxic megacolon, leucocytosis, purpura, anaphylactic shock, injection-site reaction, increased plasma creatinine, meningism and pruritus. Reports of serious reactions that were submitted to the USA Food and Drug Administration (FDA) within 120 days of the launch of ciprofloxacin, ofloxacin and norfloxacin were all within 3–6 cases per 100,000.[1] The UK Medicines Control Agency received 635 reports per million prescriptions of ciprofloxacin from launch in 1987 to 1995, compared with 755 for ofloxacin and 404 for norfloxacin (Figure 16.3).[1] Skin reactions were more common with ciprofloxacin (205 per million) than with ofloxacin (140 per million) or norfloxacin (102 per million), but psychiatric effects were less likely after treatment with ciprofloxacin than with ofloxacin (29 versus 96 per million).

Neutropenic patients
In neutropenic patients given ciprofloxacin as prophylaxis against febrile episodes, adverse events were much less common than in patients given co-trimoxazole (32/463 [7%] versus

34/103 [33%]).[5] In particular, rash and gastrointestinal effects were significantly less common (17/463 [3.7%] versus 32/257 [12.5%] and 12/463 [2.6%] versus 37/257 [14.4%], $p <$ 0.05). Ciprofloxacin used therapeutically was associated with adverse effects in 56 of 357 (15.7%) patients, with the most common reactions being gastrointestinal (7.0%), rash (4.8%), electrolyte disorders (1.7%) and nephrotoxicity (1.4%). However, ciprofloxacin treatment was only discontinued as a result of these effects in 2 patients.

Gastrointestinal symptoms
Gastrointestinal symptoms are the most common adverse effects of ciprofloxacin. When the drug is given orally, the incidence is 3.4%, and 2.5% when given intravenously, but the re-actions are usually mild.[1] Diarrhoea has been reported as an adverse event in 0.3–0.5% of clinical trials and surveillance reports. Cipro-floxacin has a limited effect on the anaerobic gut flora and is uncommon as a cause of anti-biotic-associated colitis. However, *Clostridium difficile* enterocolitis has been reported in several patients treated with ciprofloxacin.[6–8] This condition always resolved once ciprofloxacin treatment was stopped. Of 213 patients treated with oral ciprofloxacin in one study, 44 already had, or developed, diarrhoea, but neither *Clostridium difficile* nor its toxin were detected in any stool sample.[9] Of the remaining 169 patients, 73 were investigated

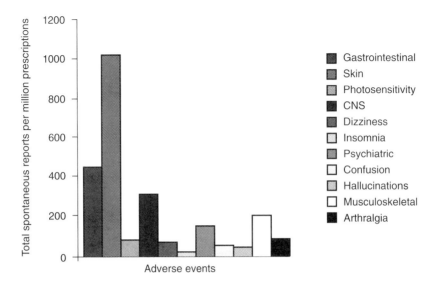

Figure 16.3. Reports to the UK Medicines Control Agency of serious reactions relating to ciprofloxacin from launch to 1995.[1]

for *Clostridium difficile* but results were negative. Cipro-floxacin has also been used to treat *Clostridium difficile*-associated colitis.[10,11]

Hepatitis and jaundice

These are rare adverse effects of ciprofloxacin, with only 10 cases being reported in 10,094 patients in the study by Ball and Tillotson.[1] In a postmarketing surveillance study, 3 of 37,233 patients were found to have liver dysfunction, but in only 1 case was ciprofloxacin implicated and the effect was transient.[12] Abnormalities of individual aspartate transaminase and alkaline phosphatase were observed in 32 (1.7%) and 26 (1.4%) of 1869 patients, respectively.[2]

Severe liver failure was observed in 4 patients.[13] One woman developed jaundice 2 weeks after completing a 1-week course of oral ciprofloxacin, 1 g per day. Although a liver biopsy showed severe hepatitis with necrosis, she recovered after several months. Two other patients (men, aged 66 and 92 years) developed fulminant hepatic failure within 2 days of starting ciprofloxacin treatment and both died. Another patient developed cholestatic jaundice but survived.

Convulsions

Theoretically, convulsions are a potential adverse effect following an overdose of ciprofloxacin or a drug interaction with theophylline or non-steroidal anti-inflammatory drugs. They are, however, rare in therapeutic use, with 7 cases recorded in 3635 patients[3] and only 1 case documented in 37,233 patients in a postmarketing survey.[12] The patient was also taking theophylline and had no further seizures. In critically ill patients, seizures were reported in 3 of 202 patients given ciprofloxacin, 400 mg every 8 hours, compared with 11 of 200 patients given intravenous imipenem, 1 g every 8 hours.[14]

As with other quinolones, ciprofloxacin may interact with benzodiazepine-binding sites in the brain, displacing γ-aminobutyric acid (GABA) from its receptors.[15] GABA is a major neurotransmitter, with its binding causing an inward flow of chloride ions into the neurons.[16] This stabilises the neurons' resting membrane potential and reduces the action of excitatory transmitters. Inhibition of the binding of GABA allows neuronal excitation. However, for all quinolones, the effect is weak and between 10- and 100-fold higher concentrations than are achievable in the blood are needed to produce 50% inhibition of GABA binding.[16]

CNS reactions

The most common CNS reactions to oral ciprofloxacin are dizziness (38/9743) and headaches (27/9743).[4] Hallucinations and psychoses occurred in only 0.02–0.05% of 63,059 patients given oral ciprofloxacin and 0.06% of 13,081 patients given intravenous ciprofloxacin.[1] Transient headache and shakiness were reported by two patients and hallucination in a third among 37,233 prescriptions.[12] Benign intracranial hypertension (cranial nerve palsy and papilloedema) was observed during the administration of ciprofloxacin, 250 mg every 12 hours, to a 14-year-old girl with cystic fibrosis.[17] However, no effect on the eye has been found in more than 800 patients studied.[4]

Skin reactions

Rash, commonly maculopapular or urticarial, was observed in 54 of 3635 (1.5%) patients given intravenous ciprofloxacin.[3] Pruritus was reported in 18 patients. In phase IV studies, skin reactions were reported in 0.5% of patients.[1] A total of 4 cases of rash, 3 extensive, were thought to be related to ciprofloxacin in 37,233 courses.[12] Phototoxicity (a reaction to sun exposure) is related to the dose of ciprofloxacin and length of exposure to ultraviolet light A (UVA). Quinolones can be degraded to produce free monovalent oxygen that may result in tissue damage.[18] Photosensitivity (transient erythema) has been observed in 50% of volunteers exposed to UVA or UVB wavelengths.[19] However, ciprofloxacin is seldom associated with phototoxicity or dermatitis, only 2 cases having been reported in 37,233 prescriptions.[12] Two further cases involved women with a history of psoriasis who developed a rash on sun exposure during treatment with oral ciprofloxacin, 500–750 mg every 12 hours.[20,21]

Local reactions to intravenous ciprofloxacin in volunteers were usually mild erythema and pruritus over the site of infusion, but these soon resolved.[22] Reactions are less likely when the drug is infused into a large vein and is given over 1 hour rather than 30 minutes. At high doses (300–400 mg), erythema was observed in 52% of the volunteers after a 30-minute infusion, but in only 27% after a 1-hour administration.[22] If ciprofloxacin is accidentally given subcutaneously, there is intense pain for 10 minutes with erythema.

Urinary tract infections

Crystalluria can develop in alkaline urine but this is usually prevented in humans by the low pH of urine. Of 6 volunteers on a normal diet, 1 experienced crystalluria following a dose of 1 g ciprofloxacin, while 22 of 36 urine samples from 5 patients given bicarbonate contained crystals.[23] A total of 2 cases were reported in the 63,059 patients given oral ciprofloxacin.[1]

Allergic interstitial nephritis has been reported and can be associated with fever, rash and eosinophilia.[24–27] It may be an inflammatory response to the presence of crystals in the kidney.[28] Oliguria can occur at high doses of ciprofloxacin (750 mg every 12 hours) in elderly patients with cancer, and renal failure may be precipitated in the presence of dehydration.[28,29]

Anaphylactoid reactions

Anaphylactoid reactions (hypotension, bronchospasm, fever and rash) are occasionally reported with ciprofloxacin treatment, but only at an incidence of 1 per 100,000 treatment courses.[30,31] A total of 15 cases were reported to the FDA in 1 year, each occurring between 5 minutes and 1 hour from ingestion, with most found in patients not previously given ciprofloxacin.[30] As with other agents, such reactions may be more common in patients who are HIV positive.[31] Vasculitis and serum sickness have also been reported, and both respond to withdrawal of the antibiotic or use of corticosteroids.[32–34]

Muscular reactions

Achilles tendinitis and rupture are rare effects with any quinolone, and have been reported with ciprofloxacin (1 g/day) in a patient with renal failure.[35] A total of 25 cases have occurred in association with various quinolones,[36] and are more common in men over the age of 60 years.[37] Tendinitis resolves when treatment is stopped.[1] Concomitant cortico-steroid administration is a risk factor and rupture may be caused by ischaemic necrosis. Ciprofloxacin has been suggested as a possible cause of exacerbation of myasthenia gravis on 2 occasions in 1 patient when the dosage was increased from 1 g per day to 1.5 g per day.[38] Subclinical myasthenia gravis became clinically apparent in another patient during treatment with ciprofloxacin.[39]

Haemolysis

Haemolysis did not occur in any of the 37,233 patients followed in the postmarketing surveillance study.[12] Of 10 patients reported to have had haemolysis, only 1 developed renal problems and thrombocytopenia.[40] This patient had probably developed haemolytic uraemic syndrome before ciprofloxacin was given. Ciprofloxacin at a dose of 1.5 g per day for 2 days had no significant effect on peripheral cell counts or on marrow-derived progenitor cells in 38 patients.[41]

There is little information concerning the effects of overdosing with ciprofloxacin.[42] In animals, salivation and tremors progress to reduced activity, breathlessness and convulsions. Induced vomiting or gastric lavage should be performed to remove the drug if taken orally, and fluids given to maintain hydration. Haemodialysis and peritoneal dialysis are not effective means of removal.

Antituberculosis therapy

Patients receiving ciprofloxacin as part of a multidrug regimen for tuberculosis (rifampicin, 600 mg/day, plus isoniazid, 300 mg/day, plus ciprofloxacin, 750 mg every 12 hours, for 4 months) experienced a similar number of adverse events to patients given a standard regimen of rifampicin, isoniazid, ethambutol plus pyrazinamide (32/75 versus 36/78).[43] The most common reactions in the ciprofloxacin group were arthralgia (7 cases) and pruritic rash (8 cases). Severe reactions (conjunctivitis, rash and convulsions) were reported in 3 patients given the regimen which included ciprofloxacin but the same number of severe events were reported in patients given the standard regimen without ciprofloxacin. The patient who developed convulsions during treatment with the regimen which included ciprofloxacin, continued to fit after treatment was withdrawn. HIV-related illness was the most likely cause and isoniazid can also cause fits.

Safety profile

Most clinical trials show no significant difference between ciprofloxacin and comparators with respect to safety. In one controlled study, adverse effects were reported more frequently following intravenous ciprofloxacin, 200 mg every 12 hours, than with intravenous ceftazidime, 1 g every 8 hours, with 16 of the 43 patients given ciprofloxacin developing a reaction compared with 4 of 43 patients given ceftazidime. There were 16 severe reactions in patients in the ciprofloxacin group (4 gastrointestinal, 3 CNS, 1 skin and 8 others).[44] This high incidence may have been related to the rapid rate of infusion. When 36 trials comparing ciprofloxacin and ceftazidime were pooled, adverse events were reported in 181 of 1047 (17%) patients given ciprofloxacin and in 140 of 1028 (14%) patients given ceftazidime, and this difference was not significant.[2]

Ball and Tillotson reported the comparative incidence of adverse reactions reported for various quinolones.[1] Between 1100 and 63,000 patients were included per drug. Overall the proportion of patients affected were 6.2% for enoxacin, 9.1% for norfloxacin, 8.0% for pefloxacin, 4.3% for ofloxacin, 3.3% for levofloxacin, 10–21% for fleroxacin and 22–32% for sparfloxacin, compared with 5–10% for ciprofloxacin. Gastrointestinal effects were observed in 2.5–5.0% of patients given ciprofloxacin compared with 1.2–11.0% of patients given other quinolones. Central nervous system complaints occurred in 0.7–1.6% of patients given ciprofloxacin and 0.9–9.0% of patients given other quinolones, and skin reactions occurred in 0.7–1.4% of those given ciprofloxacin versus 0.5–3.0% of those given other agents. In 16 trials of ciprofloxacin reviewed by Wolfson and Hooper, the median proportion of patients with reported adverse effects was 13% (range 2–82%) compared with 20% (range 5–63%, 9 trials) for norfloxacin and 14% (range 0–39%, 4 trials) for ofloxacin.[45] The median proportion of patients reporting adverse effects with the more common comparators was similar; ampicillin 11% (range 6–77%, 5 trials), cefotaxime 14% (range 12–39%, 3 trials), co-trimoxazole 15% (0–49%, 8 trials). Even those given placebo reported effects in 5% (range 0–20%, 8 trials). Prescription event monitoring has provided information on 11,477 patients given ciprofloxacin.[46] The number of events per 1000 patients in the first week were; rash 1.2, malaise 1.3, dizziness 1.0, headache 0.7, diarrhoea 1.8, nausea 4.7, and abdominal pain 1.9. For 11,033 patients given ofloxacin, events in each category varied from 0.6–4.9 and for 11,250 patients given cefixime the range was 0.6–9.2, diarrhoea being the most common event in the latter group. Two trials found significantly fewer adverse effects with ciprofloxacin than the comparator (co-trimoxazole, ampicillin) and one trial reported more effects with oral ciprofloxacin (750–1000 mg every 12 hours) than oral doxycycline (10 mg every 12 hours).

Drug interactions

Ciprofloxacin can interfere with theophylline methylation in the liver by inhibition of the specific cytochrome P450 enzymes. Patients treated with ciprofloxacin for chronic lung disease may retain theophylline if it is administered simultaneously.[47] There have been 39 reports to the FDA of theophylline-related adverse effects in patients given ciprofloxacin.[48] Convulsions occurred in 14 of these patients and 1 patient died. The rise in theophylline concentrations after starting treatment with ciprofloxacin, 0.5–2 g per day, was between 32% and 308%. Halving the dose of theophylline during treatment with

ciprofloxacin usually returns concentrations to the therapeutic range.

Non-steroidal anti-inflammatory drugs (e.g. fenbufen, indomethacin, and flurbiprofen) can increase the effect of ciprofloxacin on the binding of GABA to its receptors in the brain.[15] A single high dose of ciprofloxacin (200–400 mg/kg) administered following fenbufen caused convulsions in mice,[15] while biphenyl acetic acid, a metabolite of fenbufen, potentiated the inhibition of GABA binding 3000-fold in the rat dorsal root.[16] This potentiation would be sufficient to cause the effects that have been observed in humans.

Ciprofloxacin can inhibit the elimination of caffeine, so causing insomnia, and patients may therefore need to reduce their caffeine intake during treatment.[49]

Antacids taken before oral ciprofloxacin reduce its absorption through a chelating effect.[50] When volunteers were given an antacid but no food 24 hours before a 500 mg oral dose of ciprofloxacin, peak serum concentrations were reduced from a mean of 1.7 mg/litre to 0.1 mg/litre. Magnesium- and aluminium-containing compounds, calcium carbonate and sucralfate all reduce the absorption of ciprofloxacin.[51] Didanosine (ddI) tablets contain magnesium and aluminium buffers and reduce absorption by 90%.[52] Absorption of ciprofloxacin is also reduced by 65% by ferrous sulphate and 25% by zinc-containing multivitamins.[53] The reduction in absorption is more likely to be clinically significant in the treatment of severe pseudomonal infections (e.g. osteomyelitis) than in the treatment of urinary infections.

Other interactions have been reported occasionally.[42] Reports of an exaggerated hypoglycaemic effect of glibenclamide in the presence of ciprofloxacin were not substantiated in a prospective pharmacokinetic trial.[54] Case reports of a prolongation of prothrombin time in patients given warfarin[55] were not substantiated by a placebo-controlled trial.[56] Ciprofloxacin, 500 mg every 12 hours for 10 days, did not significantly affect the prothrombin time in 16 patients.[56] Another trial with a double-blind, crossover design also found no effect when patients were given ciprofloxacin, 750 mg every 12 hours for 12 days.[57] Case reports have also suggested that cyclosporin concentrations are affected by ciprofloxacin and that synergistic nephrotoxicity can occur.[58] However, this has not been confirmed in renal transplant patients given ciprofloxacin, 750 mg every 12 hours for 2 weeks.[59]

Paediatric use

Three potential adverse effects have limited the use of quinolones in children.[60] Arthralgia was observed occasionally in children and blisters or erosion of articular cartilage occurred in beagles following administration of very high doses, (100 mg/kg/day) (see Chapter 4). Metabolic acidosis can occur in infants as the result of immature liver function, and reduce the metabolism of the antibiotic. Finally, intracranial hypertension can follow the entry of quinolone into the CSF, or an overdose.

Arthritis may be caused by direct toxicity at high doses. Joint damage in immature beagles was found to be permanent, which has led to the avoidance of ciprofloxacin use in children. However, nalidixic acid has the same effect, and is freely used in children. No effects on joints were reported in two large retrospective studies of nalidixic acid or following its use in urinary infections.[60] In most animal models, the doses used were much higher than would be used in humans. Only in dogs did doses approach the level and duration used clinically. However, of the animals tested, dogs displayed the highest peaks and longest half-life for a given dose of ciprofloxacin.[61]

Chysky et al.[62] described 634 children who were treated with a mean dose of 25 mg/kg/day of ciprofloxacin. Of these, 80% were adolescent (10–17 years old) and 62% had respiratory infections, most commonly associated with cystic fibrosis. Oral doses were given in 548 patients (86%). A total of 31 patients (5%) experienced gastrointestinal symptoms, 21 (3%) rash and 8

(1.3%) transient arthralgia, with all the cases of arthralgia occurring in girls (Table 16.1).[62] Only 8 patients discontinued treatment prematurely. Arthralgia is less common in adults treated with ciprofloxacin (0.1%) and is common in patients with cystic fibrosis not receiving quinolones.[62]

Neither joint effusion nor cartilage changes were observed using nuclear magnetic resonance imaging in 18 children treated with ciprofloxacin, 30 mg/kg/day for 3 months.[63] There are 2 case reports of arthropathy in teenage girls, but there were no radiological signs of damage and the condition resolved.[64,65] The patients were not rechallenged. It is likely that there is a species difference with respect to articular damage.

A retrospective survey of 3341 children given ciprofloxacin in India found that adverse events occurred in only 104 (3%).[66] The events were gastrointestinal (50%), CNS-related (23%), cutaneous (19%), haematological (4%), cardiovascular (3%) and renal (1%). Only 9 patients required withdrawal of the drug.

Most prescriptions of ciprofloxacin in children are for the treatment of infective exacerbations of cystic fibrosis. Only 5 adverse effects were observed in 37 children with cystic fibrosis treated by Black et al.[67] These were diarrhoea (1 case), transient arthralgia (1 case) and photosensitivity/rash (3 cases). In another 202 children, adverse effects were recorded in 27%, but most resolved and only 4 were severe.[67] Five patients complained of joint pains, which required the drug to be discontinued in 2 cases. Four resolved and the other was lost to follow-up. Oral ciprofloxacin was used in a prospective trial to complete treatment after an intravenous course of the drug in 42 patients with cystic fibrosis, 25 of whom were children.[68] Transient arthralgia was reported in 2 cases. Two of the children who died from cystic fibrosis showed no histological changes in knee cartilage at post-mortem, despite previous repeated courses of ciprofloxacin.[69]

Anaphylactoid reactions have been associated with ciprofloxacin in 2 children,[70] renal failure secondary to interstitial nephritis in

Table 16.1. Adverse reactions thought to be related to ciprofloxacin in 634 treated children (under the age of 18 years).[62]

System	Adverse reaction	Number of patients
Gastrointestinal	Diarrhoea	12
	Nausea	10
	Vomiting	5
	Anorexia	2
	Jaundice	1
	Ulcerative stomatitis	1
Metabolic	Increased AST	4
	Increased ALT	4
	Alkaline phosphatase	1
	Lactic dehydrogenase	2
	Increased bilirubin	1
	Oedema	1
	Uraemia	1
	Weight loss	1
General	Fever	4
	Abdominal pain	2
	Back pain	1
	Asthenia	1
	Chills	1
	Malaise	1
	Headache	15
CNS	Dizziness	2
	Tremor	1
	Anxiety	1
	Hallucinations	1
	Tinnitus	1
	Taste changes	2
Skin	Rash	11
	Urticaria	2
	Photosensitivity	1
	Angioedema	1
	Pruritus	6
Haematological	Thrombocytopenia	1
	Leucopenia	1
	Eosinophilia	3
Cardiovascular	Thrombophlebitis	3
	Tachycardia	1
	Site reaction	4
Respiratory	Pulmonary haemorrhage	1
	Asthma	1
Urogenital	Dysuria	1
	Urinary retention	1
	Abnormal renal function	1
	Tubular nephritis	1
	Interstitial nephritis	1
	Pyuria	2
	Increased creatinine	1
Musculoskeletal	Arthralgia	8
Total number of patients with adverse events		80 (12.6%)
Total number of drug-related adverse events		122
Total number of patients treated		634

another,[71] and benign intracranial hypertension in a 14-year-old girl.[17] Two of 5 neonates treated for klebsiella infection with ciprofloxacin, 10–40 mg/kg/day for a period of 10–20 days, later developed green discoloration of the teeth.[72] Both had received several other drugs at the same time.

Efficacy in children

Ciprofloxacin has been shown to be effective in various infections in children, even in those with cystic fibrosis. Infections successfully treated include pseudomonal urinary infection and osteomyelitis.[73] Ciprofloxacin, 40 mg/kg/day for 30 days, produced a good clinical response in 24 children treated for infective exacerbations of cystic fibrosis.[74] The response to second or third courses of the drug was less marked. One girl complained of arthralgia, but no radiological changes were observed and the symptoms, which had preceded treatment, resolved when ciprofloxacin treatment was stopped. She developed juvenile rheumatoid arthritis 3 years later.[75] A double-blind trial in children with cystic fibrosis aged 5–17 years compared ciprofloxacin (10 mg/kg intravenously every 8 hours for 7 days, then 20 mg/kg orally every 12 hours) and ceftazidime (50 mg/kg intravenously every 8 hours, plus tobramycin, 3 mg/kg intravenously every 8 hours).[76] All patients showed a clinical response within 12–14 days of treatment.

Lang et al.[77] treated 21 children for chronic suppurative otitis media with ciprofloxacin, 15 mg/kg every 12 hours for 10–25 days, and observed a cure in 86% within 10 days. Treatment failed in 3 patients because of ciprofloxacin-resistant Pseudomonas aeruginosa and 7 other patients suffered a recurrence during follow-up. Ciprofloxacin has also been used in a few children with upper urinary tract infections.[78,79] Granulocytopenic children with fever have been treated with ciprofloxacin, 12 mg/kg/day administered intravenously for 3 days, then orally for up to 10 days, plus penicillin, 200,000 IU/kg/day, or ampicillin, 150 mg/kg/day. Of 56 episodes in 42 children, a cure was achieved in 90% with no super-

infections, and patients who had improved could go home on the fourth day with continuing treatment.[75]

Ciprofloxacin has been widely used for the treatment of salmonellosis and typhoid in children without severe adverse effects. A 2-year follow-up study of 173 children given oral ciprofloxacin (10 mg/kg/day for 7 days) and 153 given oral ofloxacin (10–15 mg/kg/day for 3–5 days) for the treatment of typhoid showed no significant difference in height or weight from untreated controls.[80] No child developed joint toxicity. Of 18 children with typhoid in another study, ciprofloxacin, 10 mg/kg/day, produced a clinical cure in 17, with fever resolving in 3 days.[81] Ciprofloxacin was given intravenously at first and then orally when appropriate. No adverse effects were observed. In 37 children with invasive salmonellosis (mostly non-typhi), all but 1 responded without a relapse.[82] Two children developed abnormal liver function and 1 a swollen knee, though no action was required. Four children have been treated successfully with oral ciprofloxacin (20 mg/kg/day for 28 days) for septic arthritis caused by Salmonella spp.[83] Finally, an unpublished study suggests a 90% response in 5 days in 189 children treated for suspected salmonellosis at an oral dose of 10 mg/kg every 12 hours.[84] Two patients developed joint swelling which resolved despite continued therapy.

Although effective in adult shigellosis, there are no controlled trials of ciprofloxacin for this disease in children.[85] Nalidixic acid, however, is widely used in children to treat shigellosis without reports of arthropathy, and the oral doses required to treat the shigellosis are low.[86] A non-randomised study from India reported cure in all 15 infants treated with intravenous ciprofloxacin (10 mg/kg/day) for persistent diarrhoea compared with only 6 of 15 others given ampicillin and chloramphenicol.[87] The risk of death in developing countries would outweigh any remote risk of arthropathy in a multi-resistant infection.

Ciprofloxacin, rifampicin and ceftriaxone have been used to eradicate nasopharyngeal carriage of Neisseria meningitidis in a large, randomised trial in Malawi.[88] Of the 711 contacts treated with ciprofloxacin, 470 were children. Meningococci were demonstrated to be present in 88 patients (10%) given oral rifampicin, 20 mg/kg every 12 hours for 2 days, 79 (11%) given a single oral dose of ciprofloxacin, 15 mg/kg, and 41 (13%) given a single intramuscular dose of ceftriaxone (pregnant women and infants only), 2 g or 50 mg/kg. Eradication was achieved in 91% of patients treated with ciprofloxacin, 97% of those treated with rifampicin and 95% of those treated with ceftriaxone. There were no significant differences between any of the antibiotics in adverse effects experienced, and no specific complaint affected more than 1% of patients.

In neonates, Aujard[89] reviewed five, small, uncontrolled studies that described the treatment of 25 patients, 23 of whom were cured. Treatment, usually ciprofloxacin, was given for compassionate reasons and the infections had usually been caused by Gram-negative bacteria resistant to other agents. A wide range of blood concentrations were observed and the doses given varied between 10 and 20 mg/kg/day. Adverse effects were reported only occasionally (e.g. metabolic acidosis, seizures). In another study, 6 neonates infected with *Enterobacter cloacae* were treated with ciprofloxacin at 10 mg/kg/day, with the CSF concentrations reaching 64% of the serum level.[90] The organism was eradicated in all 6 patients, 3 of whom subsequently died of other causes. No adverse effects were noted. Pneumonia caused by *Flavobacterium meningosepticum* in a 32-day-old child was cured by intravenous ciprofloxacin, 7.5 mg every 12 hours, plus intravenous clindamycin, (15 mg/kg/day) although the child later died of cardiac failure.[91]

Two neonates were treated with ciprofloxacin, 30–50 mg every 12 hours administered intravenously and then orally, for multi-resistant Gram-negative bacterial meningitis.[92] In each case, the response was slow but successful, with the CSF concentrations in one case reaching between 1.3 and 2.7 mg/litre. Another case of neonatal meningitis, caused by *Salmonella paratyphi* A, was cured by treatment with intravenous ciprofloxacin, 10 mg/kg every 12 hours for 3 weeks.[93] Chloramphenicol-resistant *Salmonella typhimurium* was eradicated from the CSF of another neonate by a course of ciprofloxacin, 25 mg every 12 hours for 13 days.[94] Ventriculitis caused by *Pseudomonas aeruginosa* in a newborn was treated successfully with intravenous ciprofloxacin, 4–6 mg/kg/day for 28 days, after failure with ceftazidime and intraventricular netilmicin.[95]

The low incidence of adverse effects in children suggests that ciprofloxacin can be used to treat severe infections, and a commission of the International Society of Chemotherapy has advised that quinolones should be used in children when clinically indicated and safe alternatives are not obtainable.[72,96] An oral suspension is in development, although controlled trials are needed to determine optimal dose regimens and appropriate combinations in children. Ciprofloxacin could be used to continue orally an intravenous course of antibiotics to treat urinary and septicaemic infections caused by multi-resistant pathogens, and systemic *Salmonella* infections.

Pregnancy and lactation

Ciprofloxacin is not recommended for use in pregnancy because of its potential effect on foetal joints, though no adverse effects have been demonstrated in animal models.[97] The pharmacokinetics of ciprofloxacin was studied in 20 pregnant women who were given a termination of pregnancy for β-thalassemia major. Two doses of intravenous ciprofloxacin, 200 mg, were given 12 hours apart.[98] Concentrations in the amniotic fluid were stable at 0.1 mg/litre between 2 and 12 hours postdose compared with serum levels, which fell from 0.3 mg/litre to 0.01 mg/litre in the same time. Berkovitch *et al.*[99] described 10 women given ciprofloxacin, 1 g/day for 8 days, and 28 given norfloxacin, 800 mg/day for 8 days, during pregnancy. Although foetal distress and Caesarean delivery were more likely in these women than in controls given other antibiotics, there were no foetal malformations and child development was not affected. A further 7 pregnant women were treated with intravenous ciprofloxacin, 200 mg every 12 hours for 4–5 days, then 500 mg orally every 12 hours for 2 weeks for multi-resistant typhoid.[100] Although two babies had physiological jaundice, there were no abnormalities, developmental effects or cartilage damage in any of the infants. Another three cases of maternal typhoid have been treated in this way, again without congenital abnormality.[101] The manufacturer of ciprofloxacin has been notified of 130 cases of ciprofloxacin administration during the first trimester of pregnancy, but no congenital abnormalities have been recorded.[100]

Ciprofloxacin is excreted in breast milk and its use is contraindicated in lactating women because of the potential risk of arthropathy in the infant. The pharmacokinetics have been assessed in 10 lactating women given two oral doses of ciprofloxacin, 750 mg, 12 hours apart.[98] The concentration of ciprofloxacin in breast milk was 3.8 mg/litre at 2 hours post-dose, falling to 0.2 mg/litre at 12 hours post-dose. At the same time, serum ciprofloxacin concentrations fell from 2.1 to 0.1 mg/litre.

Conclusions

Most adverse effects arising from the use of ciprofloxacin are related to the quinolones as a class rather than specifically to ciprofloxacin. Class effects include upper gastrointestinal symptoms, CNS reactions, phototoxicity and tendinitis. The incidence of these effects depends on the molecular configuration, CNS reactions, for example, depend on the C7 substituent. Ciprofloxacin has few adverse effects in clinical practice, and it is not as likely to cause CNS effects as ofloxacin, or to cause phototoxicity as lomefloxacin or sparfloxacin.

Despite early reservations concerning the safety of ciprofloxacin in children, serious adverse events are rare and articular damage has not been demonstrated. Ciprofloxacin is useful in the treatment of pseudomonal infections in children with cystic fibrosis and in invasive salmonellosis. The recommended daily dose is 5–10 mg/kg intravenously or two divided oral doses of 7.5–15 mg/kg. A single oral dose of 15 mg/kg will eradicate carriage of meningococci. The possibility of oral administration is an advantage over similar agents but no suspension is yet available, although this may soon change. As with children, use in pregnancy and lactation is still restricted to infections resistant to other agents.

References

1. Ball P, Tillotson G. Tolerability of fluoroquinolone antibiotics. Drug Safety 1995; 13: 343–58.
2. Arcieri GM, Becker N, Esposito B, Griffith E, Heyd A, Neumann C *et al*. Safety of intravenous ciprofloxacin. A review. Am J Med 1989; 87 (Suppl 5A): 92–7.
3. Reiter C, Pfeiffer M, Hullmann R, Schacht P. Integrated safety profile of intravenous ciprofloxacin. In: Garrard C, ed. Ciprofloxacin i.v. Defining its role in serious infections. Berlin: Springer, 1994: 131–46.
4. Schacht P, Arcieri G, Hullmann R. Safety of oral ciprofloxacin. Am J Med 1989; 87 (Suppl 5A): 98–102.
5. Rubinstein E, Potgieter P, Davey P, Norrby SR. The use of fluoroquinolones in neutropenic patients – analysis of adverse effects. J Antimicrob Chemother 1994; 34: 7–19.
6. Loge RV. Oral fluoroquinolone therapy for *Clostridium difficile* enterocolitis. JAMA 1989; 261: 2063–4.
7. Hillman RJ, Rao GG, Harris JRW, Taylor-Robinson DT. Ciprofloxacin as a cause of *Clostridium difficile*-associated diarrhoea in an HIV antibody-positive patient. J Infection 1990; 21: 205–7.
8. Bates CJ, Wilcox MH, Spencer RC, Harris DM. Ciprofloxacin and *Clostridium difficile* infection. Lancet 1990; 336: 1193.
9. Golledge CL, Carson CF, O'Neill GL, Bowman RA, Riley TV. Ciprofloxacin and *Clostridium difficile*-associated diarrhoea. J Antimicrob Chemother 1992; 30: 141–7.
10. Daniels J, Pristas A. Successful treatment of *Clostridium difficile* colitis with ciprofloxacin. J Clin Gastroenterol 1992; 15: 176–7.
11. Lettau LA. Oral fluoroquinolone therapy in *Clostridium difficile* enterocolitis. JAMA 1988; 260: 2216–17.
12. Jick SS, Jick H, Dean AD. A follow-up safety study of ciprofloxacin users. Pharmacotherapy 1993; 13: 461–4.

13. Villeneuve JP, Davies C, Cote J. Suspected ciprofloxacin induced hepatotoxicity. Ann Pharmacother 1995; 29: 257–9.

14. Fink MP, Snydman DR, Niederman MS, Leeper KV, Johnson RH, Heard SO *et al.* Treatment of severe pneumonia in hospitalized patients: results of a multi-center, randomized, double-blind trial comparing intravenous ciprofloxacin with imipenem-cilastatin. Antimicrob Agents Chemother 1994; 38: 547–57.

15. Christ W. Central nervous system toxicity of quinolones: human and animal findings. J Antimicrob Chemother 1990; 26 (Suppl B): 219–25.

16. Halliwell RF, Davey PG, Lambert JJ. Antagonism of GABA receptors by 4-quinolones. J Antimicrob Chemother 1993; 31: 457–62.

17. Winrow AP, Supramaniam G. Benign intracranial hypertension after ciprofloxacin administration. Arch Dis Child 1990; 65: 1165–6.

18. Domagala JM. Structure–activity and structure–side-effect relationships for the quinolone antibacterials. J Antimicrob Chemother 1994; 33: 685–706.

19. Ferguson J, Johnson BE. Ciprofloxacin-induced photosensitivity: in vitro and in vivo studies. Br J Dermatol 1990; 123: 9–20.

20. Granowitz EV. Photosensitivity rash in a patient being treated with ciprofloxacin. J Infect Dis 1989; 160: 910–11.

21. Nederost ST, Dijkstra JWE, Handel DW. Drug-induced photosensitivity reaction. Arch Dermatol 1989; 125: 433–4.

22. Thorsteinsson SB, Rahm V, Bergan T. Tolerance of intravenous ciprofloxacin. Scand J Infect Dis 1989; Suppl 60: 116–19.

23. Thorsteinsson SB, Bergan T, Oddsdottir S, Rohwedder R, Holm R. Crystalluria and ciprofloxacin, influence of urinary pH and hydration. Chemotherapy 1986; 32: 408–17.

24. Hootkins R, Fenves AZ, Stephens MK. Acute renal failure secondary to oral ciprofloxacin therapy: a presentation of three cases and a review of the literature. Clin Nephrol 1989; 32: 75–8.

25. Rippelmeyer DJ, Synhavsky A. Ciprofloxacin and allergic interstitial nephritis. Ann Intern Med 1988; 109: 170.

26. Rastogi S, Atkinson JLD, McCarthy JT. Allergic nephropathy associated with ciprofloxacin. Mayo Clin Proc 1990; 65: 987–9.

27. Allon M, Lopez EJ, Min KW. Acute renal failure due to ciprofloxacin. Arch Intern Med 1990; 150: 2187–9.

28. Lo WK, Rolston KVI, Rubenstein EB, Bodey GP. Ciprofloxacin-induced nephrotoxicity in patients with cancer. Arch Intern Med 1993; 153: 1258–62.

29. Gonski PN. Ciprofloxacin-induced renal failure in an elderly patient. Med J Aust 1991; 154: 638–9.

30. Davis H, McGoodwin E, Greene Reid T. Anaphylactoid reactions reported after treatment with ciprofloxacin. Ann Intern Med 1989; 111: 1041–3.

31. Wurtz RM, Abrams D, Beker S, Jacobson MA, Mass MM, Marks SH. Anaphylactoid drug reactions to ciprofloxacin and rifampicin in HIV-infected patients. Lancet 1989; i: 955–6.

32. Choe U, Rothschild BM, Laitman L. Ciprofloxacin-induced vasculitis. N Engl J Med 1989; 320: 257–8.

33. Stubbings J, Sheehan-Dare R, Walton S. Cutaneous vasculitis due to ciprofloxacin. BMJ 1992; 305: 29.

34. Slama TG. Serum sickness-like illness associated with ciprofloxacin. Antimicrob Agents Chemother 1990; 34: 904–5.

35. Lee WT, Collins JF. Ciprofloxacin-associated bilateral Achilles tendon rupture. Aust NZ J Med 1992; 22: 500.

36. Szarfman A, Chen M, Blum MD. More on fluoro-quinolone antibiotics and tendon rupture. N Engl J Med 1995; 332: 192–3.

37. Royer RJ, Pierfitte C, Netter P. Features of tendon disorders with fluoroquinolones. Therapie 1994; 49: 75–6.

38. Moore B, Safrani M, Keesey J. Possible exacerbation of myasthenia gravis by ciprofloxacin. Lancet 1988; i: 882.

39. Mumford CJ, Ginsberg L. Ciprofloxacin and myasthenia gravis. BMJ 1990; 301: 818.

40. Echols RM, Oliver MK. Ciprofloxacin safety relative to temafloxacin and lomefloxacin. 18th International Congress of Chemotherapy, Stockholm, Sweden, 1993: 349–50 (Abstract 27).

41. Broide E, Duer D, Shaked N, Yellin A, Lieberman Y, Rosen N *et al.* The effect of ciprofloxacin, ceftriaxone and placebo on peripheral WBC and marrow-derived-granulocytes-macrophage-progenitor cells in humans. 3rd International Symposium on New Quinolones, Vancouver, Canada, 1990: Abstract 437.

42. Adam D, von Rosentiel N. Adverse reactions to quinolones, potential toxicities, drug interactions and metabolic effects. Infect Dis Clin Pract 1994; 3 (Suppl 3): S177–84.

43. Kennedy N, Fox R, Uiso L, Ngowi FI, Gillespie SH. Safety profile of ciprofloxacin during long-term therapy for pulmonary tuberculosis. J Antimicrob Chemother 1993; 32: 897–902.

44. Gallis HA, Brennan RO, Goodwin SD, Swinney V, Rumbaugh MM, Drew RH. Comparison of the safety and efficacy of intravenous ceftazidime in the treatment of selected infections. Am J Med 1989; 87 (Suppl 5A): 76–80.

45. Wolfson JS, Hooper DC. Overview of fluoroquinolone safety. Am J Med 1991; 91 (Suppl 6A): 153–61.

46. Wilton LV, Pearce GL, Mann RD. A comparison of ciprofloxacin, norfloxacin, ofloxacin, azithromycin and cefixime examined by observational cohort studies. Br J Clin Pharmacol 1996; 41: 277–84.

47. Raoof S, Wollschlager C, Khan F. Serum theophylline levels are increased by ciprofloxacin (BAY 9867), a new quinolone antibiotic. Chest 1985; 88 (Suppl 1): Abstract 32S.

48. Grasela TH, Dreis MW. An evaluation of the quinolone–theophylline interaction using the FDA spontaneous reporting system. Arch Intern Med 1992; 152: 617–21.

49. Staib AH, Stille W, Dietlein G, Shah PM, Harder S, Mieke S *et al*. Interaction between quinolones and caffeine. Drugs 1987; 34 (Suppl 1): 170–4.

50. Höffken G, Borner K, Glatzel PD, Koeppe P, Lode H. Reduced enteral absorption of ciprofloxacin in the presence of antacids. Eur J Clin Microbiol 1985; 4: 345.

51. Polk RE. Drug interactions with fluoroquinolone antibiotics and patient education. Infect Dis Clin Pract 1994; 3 (Suppl 3): S185–94.

52. Sahai J, Gallicano K, Oliveras L, Khalig S, Hawley-Foss N, Gerber G. Cations in didanosine tablet reduce ciprofloxacin bioavailability. Clin Pharmacol Ther 1993; 53: 292–7.

53. Polk RE, Healy DP, Sahai J, Drwal L, Racht E. Effect of ferrous sulphate and multivitamins with zinc on absorption of ciprofloxacin in normal volunteers. Antimicrob Agents Chemother 1989; 33: 1841–4.

54. Ludwig E, Szekely E, Graber H, Csiba A. Study of interaction between oral ciprofloxacin and glibenclamide. Eur J Clin Microbiol Infect Dis 1991; Special issue: 378–9.

55. Jolson HM, Tanner A, Green L, Grasela TH. Adverse reaction reporting of interaction between warfarin and fluoroquinolones. Arch Intern Med 1991; 151: 1003–4.

56. Bianco TM, Bussey HI, Farnett LE, Linn WD, Roush MK, Wong YWJ. Potential warfarin–ciprofloxacin interaction in patients receiving long-term anticoagulation. Pharmacotherapy 1992; 12: 435–9.

57. Israel DS, Stotka JL, Rock WL, Polk RE, Rogge MC, Heller AH. Effect of ciprofloxacin administration on warfarin response in adult subjects. 31st Interscience Conference on Antimicrobial Agents and Chemotherapy, Chicago, USA, 1991: 199 (Abstract 599).

58. Avent CK, Krinsky D, Kirklin JK, Bourge RC, Figg WD. Synergistic nephrotoxicity due to ciprofloxacin and cyclosporin. Am J Med 1988; 85: 452–3.

59. Lang J, Finaz de Villaine J, Garaffo R, Touraine JL. Cyclosporin (cyclosporin A) pharmacokinetics in renal transplant patients receiving ciprofloxacin. Am J Med 1989; 87 (Suppl 5A): 82–5.

60. Adam D. Use of quinolones in pediatric patients. Rev Infect Dis 1989; 11 (Suppl 5): S1113–16.

61. Maggiolo F, Caprioli S, Suter F. Risk/benefit analysis of quinolone use in children: the effect of diarthrodial joints. J Antimicrob Chemother 1990; 26: 469–71.

62. Chysky V, Kapila K, Huilmann R, Arcieri G, Schacht P, Echols RR. Safety of ciprofloxacin in children: worldwide clinical experience based on compassionate use. Infection 1991; 19: 289–96.

63. Schaad UB, Stoupis C, Wedgwood J, Tschaeppeler H, Vock P. Clinical radiologic and magnetic resonance monitoring for skeletal toxicity in paediatric patients with cystic fibrosis receiving a three-month course of ciprofloxacin. Pediatr Inf Dis J 1991; 10: 723–9.

64. Alfaham M, Holt ME, Goodchild MC. Arthropathy in a patient taking ciprofloxacin. BMJ 1987; 295: 699.

65. Jawad ASM. Cystic fibrosis and drug-induced arthropathy. Br J Rheumatol 1989; 2: 179–80.

66. Karande SC, Kshirsagar NA. Adverse drug reaction monitoring of ciprofloxacin in pediatric practice. Indian Pediatr 1992; 25: 181–8.

67. Black A, Redmond AOB, Steen HJ, Oborska IT. Tolerance and safety of ciprofloxacin in paediatric patients. J Antimicrob Chemother 1990; 26 (Suppl F): 25–9.

68. Schaad UB, Wedgwood-Krucko J, Guenin K, Buehlmann U, Kraemer R. Antipseudomonal therapy in cystic fibrosis: aztreonam and amikacin versus ceftazidime and amikacin administered intravenously followed by oral ciprofloxacin. Eur J Clin Microbiol Infect Dis 1989; 10: 858–65.

69. Schaad UB, Sander E, Wedgwood J, Schaffner T. Morphologic studies for skeletal toxicity after prolonged ciprofloxacin therapy in two juvenile cystic fibrosis patients. Paediatr Infect Dis J 1992; 11: 1047–9.

70. Miller MS, Gaido E, Rourk MH, Spock A. Anaphylactoid reactions to ciprofloxacin in cystic fibrosis patients. Pediatr Infect Dis J 1991; 10: 164–5.

71. Simpson J, Watson AR, Mellersh A, Nelson CS, Dodd K. Typhoid fever, ciprofloxacin and renal failure. Arch Dis Child 1991; 66: 1083–4.

72. Lumbiganon P, Pengsaa K, Sookpranee T. Ciprofloxacin in neonates and its possible adverse effects on the teeth. Pediatr Infect Dis J 1991; 10: 619–20.

73. Aujard Y, Bingen E. Quinolones from a compassionate to a rational use in children. Curr Opin Pediatr 1992; 4: 291–8.

74. Rubio TT. Ciprofloxacin in the treatment of *Pseudomonas* infections in children with cystic fibrosis. Diagn Microbiol Infect Dis 1990; 13: 153–5.

75. Schaad UB, Salam MA, Aujard Y, Dagan R, Green SDR, Peltola H *et al*. Use of fluoroquinolones in pediatrics: consensus report of an International Society of Chemotherapy Commission. Pediatr Infect Dis J 1995; 14: 1–9.

76. Church D, Kanga J, Kuhn R, Rubio D, Haverstock R, Perroncel R. Prospective double-blind randomized comparison of ciprofloxacin vs ceftazidime/tobramycin in the treatment of pediatric cystic fibrosis patients. 35th Interscience Conference on Antimicrobial Agents and Chemotherapy, San Francisco, USA, 1995: 322 (Abstract LM30).

77. Lang R, Goshen S, Raas-Rothschild A. Oral ciprofloxacin in the management of chronic suppurative otitis media without cholesteatoma in children: preliminary experience in 21 children. Pediatr Infect Dis J 1992; 11: 925–9.

78. Martorana G, Giberti C, Pizzorno R, Bonamini A, Oneto F, Curotto A *et al*. Treatment of urinary tract infections with ciprofloxacin. Clin Ther 1988; 5: 516–20.

79. Lotti T, Mirone V, Imbimbo C, Russo A. Ciprofloxacin in the treatment of urinary tract infections. J Int Med Res 1987; 15: 240–4.

80. Bethell DB, Hien TT, Phi LT, Day NPJ, Vinh H, Duong NM *et al*. Effects on growth of single short courses of fluoroquinolones. Arch Dis Child 1996; 74: 44–6.

81. Dutta P, Rasaily R, Saha MR, Mitra U, Bhattacharya SK, Bhattacharya MK *et al*. Ciprofloxacin for treatment of severe typhoid fever in children. Antimicrob Agents Chemother 1993; 37: 1197–9.

82. Cheesbrough JS, Ilunga Mwema F, Green SDR, Tillotson GS. Quinolones in children with invasive salmonellosis. Lancet 1991; 338: 127.

83. Green SDR, Numbi A, Ilunga FM, Cheesbrough JS, Tillotson GS. Oral ciprofloxacin treatment of salmonella septic arthritis in children. 5th International Congress for Infectious Diseases, Nairobi, Kenya, 1992: Abstract 546.

84. Green SDR, Tillotson GS. Use of ciprofloxacin in developing countries. Pediatr Infect Dis J 1997; (Suppl). In press.

85. Bennish M. Quinolone therapy in childhood shigellosis: past experience and current dilemmas. FAC Adv Antimicrob Antineoplast Chemother 1992; 11–2 (Suppl): S191–201.

86. Fontaine O. Antibiotics in the management of shigellosis in children: what role for the quinolones? Rev Infect Dis 1989; 11 (Suppl 5): S1145–50.

87. Ghosh G, Chakraborty S, Ray J, Mukerjee SK. Parenteral ciprofloxacin in persistent diarrhoea in children. J Indian Med Assoc 1995; 93: 382–4.

88. Cuevas LE, Kazembe P, Mughogho GK, Tillotson GS, Hart CA. Eradication of nasopharyngeal carriage of *Neisseria meningitidis* in children and adults in rural Africa: a comparison of ciprofloxacin and rifampicin. J Infect Dis 1995; 171: 728–31.

89. Aujard Y. Quinolones in neonates. FAC Adv Antimicrob Antineoplast Chemother 1992; 11–2 (Suppl): S233–7.

90. Bannon MJ, Stutchfield PR, Weindling AM, Damjanovic V. Ciprofloxacin in neonatal

91. Humphreys H, Lovering A, White LO, Williams EW. *Flavobacterium meningosepticum* infection, in a 32-day-old child on acute peritoneal dialysis, treated with ciprofloxacin. J Antimicrob Chemother 1989; 23: 292–4.

92. Green SDR, Ilunga F, Cheesbrough JS, Tillotson GS, Hichens M, Felmingham D. The treatment of neonatal meningitis due to Gram-negative bacilli with ciprofloxacin: evidence of satisfactory penetration into the cerebrospinal fluid. J Infect 1993; 26: 253–6.

93. Bhutta ZA, Farooqui BJ, Sturm AW. Eradication of a multiple drug resistant *Salmonella paratyphi* A causing meningitis with ciprofloxacin. J Infect 1992; 25: 215–19.

94. Ragunathan PL, Potkins DV, Watson JG, Kearns AM, Carroll A. Neonatal meningitis due to *Salmonella typhimurium* treated with ciprofloxacin. J Antimicrob Chemother 1990; 26: 727–8.

95. Isaacs D, Slack PME, Wilkinson AR, Westwood AW. Successful treatment of *Pseudomonas* ventriculitis with ciprofloxacin. J Antimicrob Chemother 1986; 17: 535–8.

96. Schaad UB. Role of the new quinolones in pediatric practice. Pediatr Infect Dis J 1992; 11: 1043–6.

97. Schluter G. Ciprofloxacin: toxicologic evaluation of additional safety data. Am J Med 1989; 87 (Suppl 5A): 37–9.

98. Giamarellou H, Kolokythas E, Petrikkos G, Gazis J, Aravantinos D, Sfikakis P. Pharmacokinetics of three newer quinolones in pregnant and lactating women. Am J Med 1989; 87 (Suppl 5A): 49–51.

99. Berkovitch M, Pastuszak A, Gazarian M, Lewis M, Koren G. Safety of the new quinolones in pregnancy. Obstet Gynecol 1994; 84: 535–8.

100. Koul PA, Wani JI, Wahid A. Ciprofloxacin for multiresistant enteric fever in pregnancy. Lancet 1995; 346: 307–8.

101. Leung D, Venkatesan P, Boswell T, Innes JA, Wood MJ. Treatment of typhoid in pregnancy. Lancet 1995; 346: 648–9.

Enterobacter cloacae septicaemia. Arch Dis Childhood 1989; 64: 1388–91.

Chapter 17

Pharmacoeconomics

Peter Davey

From the Department of Clinical Pharmacology and Infectious Diseases,
University of Dundee, Scotland, UK

Pharmacoeconomic analysis may be required for two main reasons. The first is to establish whether the outcome with a new, less expensive treatment is as good as that with the current therapy. The second is to determine whether a new, costlier treatment is more effective than the current therapy and, if it is, the value of this improved effectiveness. A full pharmacoeconomic analysis always compares the costs and outcomes of two or more alternatives.[1] A less thorough examination is only a partial economic analysis. For example, a description of the cost, outcome or both of a single treatment is not a full economic analysis because it does not explicitly compare that therapy with any other.

The simplest form of full economic analysis is cost-minimisation analysis. Although this may appear to be simply a cost comparison, there are two important differences. Firstly, cost-minimisation analysis assumes that *at least one* outcome is achieved equally. For example, the clinical effectiveness of oral and intravenous quinolone therapy may be assumed to be the same in a cost-minimisation analysis, but it may still be necessary to include measurement of other outcomes that are not shared (for example, the phlebitis complicating intravenous therapy). Secondly, cost-minimisation analysis involves an explicit statement that the two treatments have similar

effectiveness, which must be justified with evidence.

A study comparing the costs and outcomes of two treatments has four possible results (Figure 17.1). For example, if a less expensive treatment gives a better outcome it is said to be dominant, and a financial value on the improvement in outcome is not needed. Conversely, a new treatment that is more expensive and less effective is obviously unjustifiable. Economic analysis is required when the more effective treatment is also the more expensive, to establish whether the increased effectiveness justifies its additional cost.

In most healthcare systems, the drug budget is separated from other costs. A drug with a higher acquisition cost may have a lower total cost if, for example, it is easier to administer or requires less therapeutic monitoring. A pharmacoeconomic analysis can be used to determine the total healthcare cost of the most effective treatment.

Both costs and outcomes are valued differently by hospital practitioners, community health-

Figure 17.1. Potential results of a full economic analysis of two treatments.

Wilson APR and Grüneberg RN.
Ciprofloxacin: 10 years of clinical experience
© 1997 Maxim Medical, Oxford.

care workers and patients. For example, the use of oral switch therapy to achieve early discharge may be perceived by the hospital as an improvement in patient outcome at a lower cost to the health service. However, primary-care doctors may view this as an attempt by the hospital to offload their work on to the community. Patients or their relatives may also be worried, particularly if the early discharge coincides with media reports of cuts in health services.

Cost models

Classification of costs

'Bottom-up' cost models are based on prospective collections of data from individual patients. Any model aims both to quantify costs and to allocate them to the appropriate person(s) or budget(s). In health economics, it is usual to separate costs into three broad categories: healthcare costs, other financial costs and intangible costs.

'Healthcare costs' are the financial costs of the health services (e.g. drug acquisition costs or the cost of days spent in hospital). They are usually subdivided into variable and fixed categories. Variable costs change according to the number of patients treated, and include money spent on drug acquisition and other consumables, such as needles and syringes. Fixed costs do not vary with the number of patients treated, at least in the short term (usually 1 year), and include, for example, the capital costs of the building or equipment and staff salaries.

'Other financial costs' fall outside the health services, including prescription charges or other treatment expenses incurred by the patient, the cost of the patient's or carer's travel to and from hospital, the costs of providing social services, and loss of productivity.

'Intangible costs' are those that are difficult to assess financially (e.g. pain, anxiety and loss of energy, and the time given up by voluntary carers).

Overheads

To avoid confusion, the classification above does not use the terms 'direct' or 'indirect' costs. To an accountant, indirect costs are those not arising directly from a single treatment, investigation or service. These are essentially overhead costs, such as those incurred from heating or lighting a building, training staff or renewing or servicing equipment. Various systems have been used for allocating these costs, with the principal aim of ensuring that the organisation recovers all of its operating costs.[2] Accurate allocation of costs to individual patients or treatments is not necessarily a priority, and these systems inevitably involve some cross-subsidisation.[2] For example, the pharmacy delivers drugs that are bought from a wholesaler and passed on to the patient. This process includes a number of additional costs (e.g. storage, reconstitution or preparation, dispensing in a form safe for administration, patient education and therapeutic drug monitoring). Some additional costs are easy to allocate to particular drugs (e.g. those involved in the preparation of intravenous injections and the therapeutic monitoring of aminoglycosides). Some general overhead costs, however, do not arise directly from one agent. These sums are usually recovered by calculating a surcharge or dispensing fee for each drug. This is a fixed amount and it inevitably involves some averaging across patients. For example, the time needed to take a full history of penicillin allergy is unlikely to be charged directly to patients prescribed this drug. Moreover, this time inevitably varies, depending on the complexity of the history and the actions that have to be taken (i.e. telephoning the doctor to question the decision to prescribe penicillin to an allergic patient). Inevitably, patients prescribed drugs requiring no special instructions or history-taking are effectively subsidising others. The important point to understand is that a non-profit organisation must recover all of its operating costs, which inevitably involves the addition of an overhead to the actual cost of a particular treatment.

In contrast, for an economist, indirect costs are social costs, such as loss of productivity, which are only indirectly related to healthcare.[3]

These indirect costs, however, are not synonymous with non-medical financial costs, because economists also describe a category of 'direct, non-medical costs'.[3] This includes out-of-pocket expenses for the patient or carers which arise directly from healthcare (e.g. travel expenses and co-payment for drugs).

Hence, the terms direct and indirect costs are potentially confusing and imprecise; it is often unclear whether they are used to distinguish costs arising directly or indirectly from a particular treatment or costs directly or indirectly related to healthcare. If these terms are used in an economic analysis, their meaning must be precisely defined. Alternatively, the information may be conveyed by distinguishing between healthcare costs and other financial costs, and further defining variable and fixed costs.

Planning a cost model

The perspective of the pharmacoeconomic analysis must be decided before a cost model is constructed. Analysis from the viewpoint of a hospital budget-holder might be restricted to the costs incurred by the hospital, and is likely to yield different results to one from the perspective of community health services. For example, early discharge may lead to financial costs for the patient, particularly if the healthcare system reimburses a lower proportion of costs incurred outside the hospital.[4]

The process of costing should be divided into three clear stages: identification, measurement and valuation (Table 17.1). The separation should be maintained throughout the analysis up to and including reporting the results. This allows the reader to understand fully the elements in the model and, if necessary, to adjust it to suit their own perspective.

The classification used for the costs of drug administration is straightforward and is equally applicable to the costs of adverse drug effects or treatment failure (Table 17.1) Treatment failure costs need to be identified (e.g. additional drug therapy, visits to the doctor). Once identified, these costs can be measured and

valued in the same way as other costs. The requirements for data collection should be clear if the stages of identification, measurement and valuation are separated.

The most difficult step is the valuation of intangible costs. Implied valuation is a crude, but simple, method of doing this. Suppose, for example, that a non-ototoxic drug was compared with gentamicin. After a thorough analysis of healthcare costs, including the therapeutic drug monitoring of gentamicin, the non-ototoxic drug was found to cost US$50 more per patient treated. If the incidence of symptomatic deafness caused by gentamicin is 1%, a decision to use the non-ototoxic drug implies that the decision-maker believes it is worth investing at least US$5000 to prevent a case of deafness (as one case will be avoided per 100 patients treated, at a total cost of US$50 × 100). Sometimes the implied value generated may be compared with resources already committed by society to the prevention of a similar disability in another setting. In this example, it would be relevant to obtain data on the costs of preventing noise-induced[5] hearing loss in industry or on compensation awards for industrial or other cases of established hearing loss.[5] Unfortunately, no such comparative data are readily available in most cases. Nonetheless, implied valuation still serves as a crude first step to making decisions based on intangible costs.

The financial valuation of short-term intangible costs is achieved by measuring patients' willingness to pay to avoid them.[3] The same technique can be applied to long-term problems. Long-term disability may also be quantified by measurements of utility or quality of life.

Sources of variation in healthcare costs

Genuine variations exist in the costs of treatments both within and between countries. It is important to be aware of this when interpreting economic analyses and when planning the sensitivity analysis for new economic analyses. A sensitivity analysis means identification of any assumptions that underlie the analysis, and an

Table 17.1. Examples of cost identification, measurement and valuation (these are illustrative rather than exhaustive). LRTI, lower respiratory tract infection.

Stage	Hospital intravenous drug administration	Community-acquired LRTI
Identification	Healthcare financial costs – drug acquisition – consumables – staff time – laboratory tests	Healthcare financial costs Variable: – drug acquisition – consumables Fixed: – primary-care doctor's time – primary-care nurse's time – hospital out-patient visits – hospital in-patient admissions
	Other financial costs – travel costs of patient's visitors	Other financial costs – travel costs of patient or visitors – time off work of patient or carers
	Intangible costs – discomfort from intravenous cannula	Intangible costs – symptoms of pneumonia – concerns of carers or relatives
Measurement	Number of consumables Hours of staff time Number of tests Number of hospital visits by family Visual analogue scale for pain measurement	Drug doses and duration Number of tests Hours of staff time Extra days in hospital Working days affected for patient or carers Travel time and method of transport for patient or carers Symptom score Number of days to return to full health
Valuation	Obtain financial values for all healthcare costs Obtain financial values for all other costs (e.g. transportation costs or transportation time from the Ministry of Transport) Depending on the reimbursement system, calculate implied value of reducing any or all fixed direct costs, indirect costs or intangible costs Consider other methods for valuation of intangible costs – willingness to pay to avoid intangible costs – standard gamble or other measures of risk averseness – quality of life or other utility measures	

analysis of whether or not the conclusions of the analysis are sensitive to these assumptions. In this case, the range of costs of treatments in other countries would need to be defined and the analysis repeated to ensure that conclusions are not sensitive to treatment cost variation.

The sources of variation in costs associated with drug treatment include those found in accounting methods, reimbursement systems, and economies of scale and medical practice.

Fixed costs (those of staff salaries and buildings or other capital equipment) comprise the greatest proportion of any healthcare budget. Accounting practice for the allocation of these costs varies considerably. In the UK, quoted hospital drug costs equate with the acquisition costs of these agents. The costs are usually derived from sources such as the *British National Formulary*, and are usually higher than most hospitals currently pay because discounts are negotiated with suppliers. However, no allowance is made for pharmacy services provided by the hospital for dispensing, preparation or clinical monitoring. In contrast, in the USA some fixed costs are often allocated to drug utilisation, though the practice varies between hospitals. In a survey of 71 hospitals across the USA, it was found that 93% charged a preparation fee, 63% charged a dispensing fee and 68% charged an additional variable mark-up, particularly for drugs such as gentamicin which require intensive monitoring by clinical pharmacy services.[6] This mark-up often exceeded the acquisition cost of the drug, and the maximum was a 961% mark-up on the acquisition cost of gentamicin. The scale of other charges also varied considerably; for example, preparation fees ranged from US$0.80 to US$31.50. [6] Similar variations in accounting practice have been reported for other consumables, such as intravenous lines and minibags.[7,8]

Drug wastage is another potential source of accounting variation. Wastage occurs because drugs cannot be used due to incorrect preparation, breach of sterility or lapsed expiry date, or because a drug is prepared for one particular patient and the presentation size is greater than the required dose.[9,10] Wastage rates vary between hospitals and are lowest in establishments using a centralised intravenous additive service.[11] In addition to genuine variation, there are differences in abilities to track and record wastage rates accurately.[12] The accounting method used to recover the costs of drug wastage is also a source of variation between hospitals.

Reimbursement systems that pay 'per patient treated' make it easy to allocate fixed costs to individual patients or treatments administered. For example, in the USA, a decrease in the length of hospital stay allows more patients to be treated and increases revenue, as charges may be made for each individual receiving therapy. In other healthcare systems, hospitals receive a total annual budget or a fixed-block contract for treating a specified number of patients. Under these systems, it is more difficult to achieve savings through earlier discharge of patients. In fact, reducing hospital stay is likely to increase the average cost per day in the hospital (Figure 17.2).[13] This paradox occurs because treatment costs are not distributed evenly throughout the time a patient spends in hospital; they are usually higher early on, when investigation and treatment are often more intense.[13] Programmes such as home intravenous drug administration result in the earlier discharge of patients whose diagnosis has been established, and they may be replaced by others who require intensive investigation and treatment. In an ideal world, hospitals would be reimbursed per patient successfully treated, which would discourage inappropriate early discharge. However, as yet, no healthcare system has achieved this.

The term 'marginal cost' is used to describe the cost of producing additional units of output. Most production processes have a mixture of fixed costs (buildings, equipment and staff salaries) and variable costs (consumables). The marginal cost of producing one more unit is generally just the cost of consumables. At some point, however, the marginal cost of producing additional units inevitably includes fixed costs, such as more staff or equipment.

The relationship between throughput and marginal cost was illustrated by a survey of laboratory costs associated with serum aminoglycoside assays.[14] The marginal cost of performing one additional assay is basically the cost of the reagents used. The staff time and

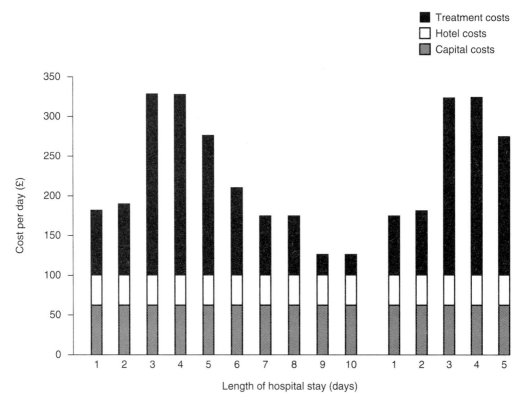

Figure 17.2. Impact of shortening hospital stay on the total costs of care and on the mean cost per day in hospital. Due to the different intensities of treatment needed over time, discharge of a patient after 5 days instead of 10 reduces the total cost per patient treated (from £2090 to £1280) but increases the average cost per patient day (from £209 to £256).[13]

capital equipment involved are fixed costs that will not vary if one additional assay is performed. In this survey, the reagent cost per assay was estimated for each laboratory by dividing the total annual expenditure on reagents required by the number of assays performed. In this case, there was an exponential relationship between the throughput and reagent costs per assay of paired peak and trough samples (Figure 17.3).[14] Throughput influences the marginal assay cost in two ways. Firstly, there is a discount on assay reagents for bulk purchasers. Secondly, the assay technique requires consumption of a fixed amount of reagent to calibrate the equipment. Therefore, the more assays that can be performed at one time, the lower the amount of reagent used per sample assayed. Another source of cost

variation identified in this study was the method of payment for capital equipment.[14] Laboratories that bought their equipment could negotiate lower reagent costs than those that leased it from reagent manufacturers (Figure 17.3).[14]

Economies of scale also affect the costs of consumables used for drug preparation and administration[7] and the costs of the agents themselves. Awareness of economies of scale by healthcare purchasers may make it difficult for small departments to survive. However, the importance of a local, personal service should not be forgotten, and this will probably result in small hospitals continuing to maintain their own laboratories or pharmacies. There will, therefore, continue to be genuine variation in healthcare costs produced by economies of scale in the foreseeable future.

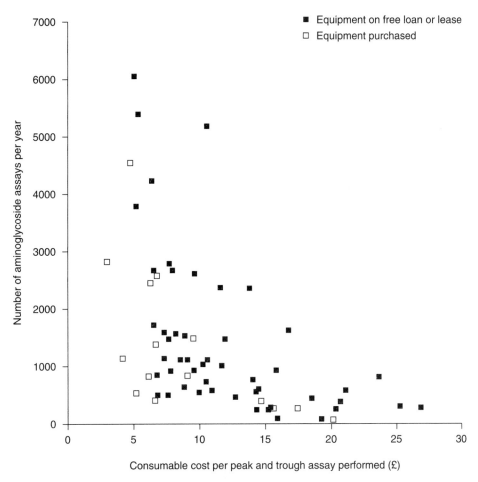

Figure 17.3. Relationship between laboratory throughput and cost of laboratory reagents used for the assay of serum gentamicin concentrations by method of purchase of assay equipment. An exponential relationship exists between the number of samples assayed per year and the consumable cost per peak and trough assay performed. The cost of consumables is lower in the laboratories that bought assay equipment compared with those loaning or leasing it from reagent manufacturers. Reproduced with permission.[14]

There are many examples of systematic variation in medical practice, that is, consistent variation between the work of doctors located in different institutions or geographical areas.[15,16] Some variations in practice may be due to genuine differences in the epidemiology of disease. However, this seldom explains the existing marked systematic variations in medical practice. Much of the research in this area relates to elective surgery,[15,16] but a few examples involving antibiotic therapy in hospitals will illustrate the potential impact of medical practice variation on pharmacoeconomic analysis.

Intravenous formulations of drugs are almost always more expensive than their oral counterparts, often by a factor of ten.[9] The proportion of antibiotic doses administered intravenously varies markedly between countries in Europe (Figure 17.4).[17] The prescribing of antibiotics in the UK is predominantly by the oral route, even in hospitals, and the duration of treatment and hospital stay is shorter than in France,

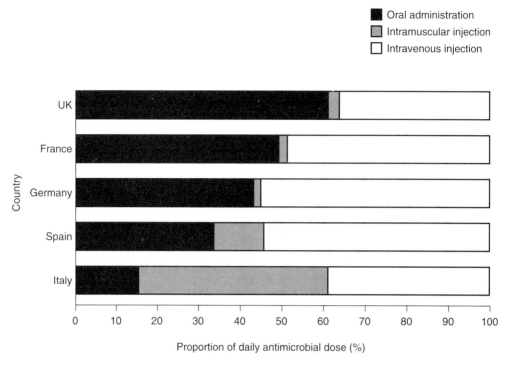

Figure 17.4. Proportion of daily doses of antimicrobial agents administered via the oral, intravenous and intramuscular route, by European country. Reproduced with permission.[17]

Germany, Spain or Italy. Preventing an infection in a hospital in the UK will, therefore, save fewer resources than preventing one in Germany.

There are many other examples of systematic variation in antibiotic prescription.[18] The impact of medical practice variation on pharmacoeconomic studies can be illustrated by comparing the costs of antibiotics administered to treat infections occurring after caesarean section in UK hospitals with reported costs from the USA (Table 17.2).[19,20] The published figures for the USA are sometimes 100-fold higher than those for the UK. This discrepancy is, to some extent, due to the effect of a different accounting system: the costs of drugs reported in the USA often include those for pharmacy services, whereas costs quoted in the UK are solely for acquisition. The major source of discrepancy, however, is that practitioners in the USA routinely prescribe 7 days of intravenous drug treatment, whereas most infections

in the UK are managed with oral therapy. Oral treatment is generally ten-fold less expensive than the equivalent intravenous formulation.[9]

Oral versus intravenous quinolone therapy

The costs of defined daily doses of oral formulations of any antibiotic are usually two- to ten-fold lower than those of their intravenous counterparts (Table 17.3).[21] Quinolones are relatively expensive oral antimicrobial drugs, yet oral regimens of these agents are still less expensive than all but the cheapest intravenous antibiotic (Table 17.3). Administration costs are also incurred with intravenous therapy (consumables, staff time required for preparation or administration, and wastage resulting from needing less than the full dose contained

Table 17.2. Comparison of costs of the management of a woman with postoperative fever following caesarean section in a study reporting experience in the USA[20] and an audit of practice in the UK.[19]

Source of cost	USA study (cost in US$)	UK study (cost in £)
Isolation of mother	447×5 days = 2235	Not practised
Isolation of baby	614×5 days = 3070	Not practised
Investigations	570	6–10
Drug acquisition costs	1251	14
Additional costs of preparation, administration and monitoring of i.v. drugs	316	Almost all doses prescribed orally
Total cost per woman with suspected infection	7442	20–34

in a vial). These costs have been well described in a number of studies,[7,8,11,22–31] and the oral administration of antibiotics would reduce them. As the cost of oral quinolone therapy is almost always lower than that of intravenous therapy, an economic analysis to prove this is the case would be of little value to the decision-maker. An economic analysis in this setting should set out to prove that savings in drug costs can be made in clinical practice using oral

therapy, and to reassure the decision-maker that no hidden additional costs are involved, for example arising from reduced efficacy.

The clinical efficacy of oral quinolones has been established in a wide range of indications (Table 17.4).[26,32–48] These articles do not all include a comprehensive description of the comparative costs, but the quinolone regimen is always likely to be less expensive than the comparative intravenous therapies mentioned,

Table 17.3. Comparative daily costs of intravenous and oral antibiotics in the UK.[21] These costs are for branded products; generic and contract prices are likely to be lower in practice.

Intravenous			Oral		
Drug	**Daily dose (g)**	**Cost (£)**	**Drug**	**Daily dose (g)**	**Cost (£)**
Benzyl penicillin	4.80	3.60	Trimethoprim	0.40	0.18
Co-trimoxazole:		6.36	Co-trimoxazole		0.50
trimethoprim	0.30		trimethoprim	0.30	
sulphamethoxazole	1.60		sulphamethoxazole	1.60	
Amoxycillin	3.00	3.93	Amoxycillin	1.50	1.05
Gentamicin	0.40	8.00	Chloramphenicol	2.00	0.64
Cefuroxime	2.25	7.91	Cefuroxime axetil	2.00	3.60
Amoxycillin clavulanate	3.60	8.10	Amoxycillin clavulanate	1.90	1.70
Ciprofloxacin	0.80	58.00	Ciprofloxacin	1.00	2.75
Ofloxacin	0.80	88.04	Ofloxacin	0.80	4.10
Cefotaxime	4.00	19.80	Cefixime	0.40	2.74
Imipenem	2.00	60.00	Azithromycin	0.50	5.00

Table 17.4. Examples of clinical indications in which oral quinolone therapy has been compared with standard intravenous antibiotic treatment. In general, the results showed that oral quinolone therapy appeared to be as effective as intravenous therapy.

Clinical indication	Reference
Cystic fibrosis	32–34
Other lower respiratory tract infections	35, 36
Skin and soft tissue infection	37, 38
Bone and joint infections	38–44
Infections complicating peritoneal dialysis	45
Mixed infections	26, 46
Urinary tract infections	26, 47, 48

particularly when the preparation and administration costs of intravenous drugs are considered. The efficacy and safety of oral quinolone therapy are reviewed elsewhere in this volume. The following discussion highlights the issues of particular importance to economic analysis.

Factors influencing the cost of quinolone regimens

There are many potential alternatives to quinolone treatment (Figure 17.5).[47] Although some oral antimicrobial agents are less expensive than the quinolones, all intravenous regimens compared in this study cost more than norfloxacin, sometimes by hundreds of dollars per day.[47] The costs for preparation, administration and therapeutic drug monitoring of intravenous regimens have also been quantified in a number of studies.[4,7–10,12,14,22,23,25,27,29] In clinical practice, these vary considerably, depending on: the number of daily doses; the administration method (infusion is more expensive than bolus injection); the equipment required to establish intravenous access (many patients already have an intravenous line in place when antibiotics are prescribed); the financial value attached to staff time (depending on the grade of staff involved and on the total amount of time required to prepare and administer intravenous drugs); and the number

of assays performed. Observed variations in all these factors may lead to ten-fold differences in the daily cost of drug preparation and administration (Table 17.5).[49]

The potential for shortening the length of a patient's hospital stay with quinolone therapy depends on the infection being treated (Figure 17.6).[50] In a large, multicentre study,[50] 766 patients receiving intravenous antibacterial drugs were switched to oral ciprofloxacin therapy. A total of 496 (65%) of these patients were discharged before completion of the ciprofloxacin treatment. If the patients had not been switched to oral ciprofloxacin, most would have continued on intravenous therapy, either as in-patients or out-patients. Only 82 (11%) patients were considered to be suitable for other oral antibacterial treatment. It was estimated that switching to oral ciprofloxacin resulted in the earlier discharge of 427 (56%) of the patients. The most common reasons for patients remaining in hospital despite changing to oral ciprofloxacin were concurrent medical conditions (303 of 339; 89%) and difficulty in placing them into a nursing home or other chronic-care institution (62 of 339; 18%). A poor response to oral ciprofloxacin delayed discharge in only 24 (7%) patients. In addition, the longer the planned duration of antibacterial treatment, the greater the potential for

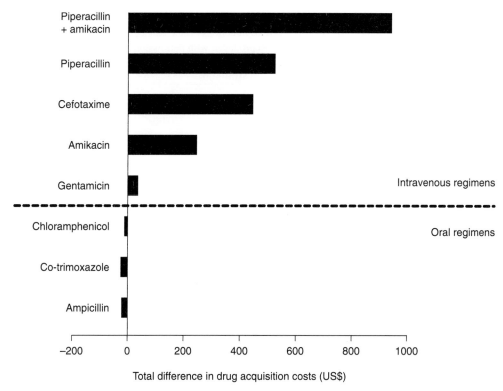

Figure 17.5. Comparison of drug acquisition cost of norfloxacin with alternative regimens for the treatment of complicated urinary tract infections.[47]

improving concurrent medical problems and resolving social requirements. This study[50] showed that the potential for early discharge was greatest for patients with bone and joint infections. This is likely to be the result of prolonged treatment, together with a lower probability of concurrent medical conditions influencing hospitalisation (Figure 17.6).

Oral and intravenous quinolone regimens in clinical practice

In clinical studies, patients may be randomised to receive either oral quinolone treatment or the clinician's choice of an alternative regimen. Although this inevitably results in a range of comparator drugs, dosages and durations of treatment, it gives greater insight into usual practice than a rigid protocol. The latter is required in the early clinical evaluation of the safety and efficacy of quinolones, but a

pragmatic protocol provides more information on the potential cost and outcome of alternative treatments as they are actually used.

Scheife et al.[48] randomised patients with multi-resistant nosocomial urinary tract infections (UTI) to receive either oral norfloxacin (n = 46) or the clinician's choice of regimen (n = 45). The most common regimen used in the latter group was cefotaxime, 4000 mg per day (n = 19; 42%). The remaining 26 patients received five different single intravenous drugs, six different combinations of intravenous drugs or seven different combinations of intravenous and oral agents. The cost of norfloxacin was significantly lower (p < 0.001) than the mean cost of the alternative regimens, even when the analysis was restricted to drug acquisition costs (Table 17.6).[48]

All comparator regimens required consumables for preparation and administration;

Table 17.5. Range of costs for the daily preparation, administration and monitoring of vancomycin observed in 59 patients receiving treatment for prosthetic device infections. The mean and 95% CI were calculated from individual data obtained from all 59 patients. Reproduced with permission.[49]

Item	Unit cost (£)	Minimum		Maximum	
		n	£	n	£
Intravenous line	1.77	0	0.00	2	3.54
Syringe	0.07	1	0.07	2	0.14
Needle	0.01	1	0.01	2	0.02
Water for injections	0.10	1	0.10	2	0.20
Heparin	0.28	0	0.00	2	0.56
Wipe	0.01	2	0.02	2	0.02
Minibag	0.86	1	0.86	2	1.73
Assay	19.60	0	0.00	0.75	14.70
Staff time	8.50 per hour	0.10 hours	0.85	0.50 hours	4.25
Total			1.91		25.16
Mean (95% CI) of observed daily costs in 59 patients			**£8.96 (£7.03–8.99)**		

inclusion of these removed any overlap between the daily cost of norfloxacin (US$3.00) and the least expensive comparator regimen (US$10.63). The analysis did not include the cost of staff time required for preparation or administration. Of the 45 patients treated with parenteral antibiotics, 19 (42%) remained in hospital specifically to continue intravenous treatment. There was no difference in clinical cure rates between norfloxacin and the comparators, but the trend was towards a higher odds ratio (better results) for norfloxacin, with a marked trend towards a lower risk of adverse reaction.[48]

Randomisation is the best method for ensuring internal validity and removing bias; however, it inevitably introduces an artificial element into the study. Purely observational studies provide accurate information about usual practice which may be used to supplement the results from more formal clinical trials. Cooke et al.[46] studied 485 adult patients receiving antibiotics for UTI, respiratory tract infection (RTI) or suspected septicaemia in five UK teaching hospitals over an 18-month period. Of these, 148 (31%) patients were treated with oral ciprofloxacin. The remaining 337 (69%) received intravenous therapy with a range of antimicrobial agents, including cefotaxime, gentamicin, ampicillin, cefuroxime, piperacillin and ceftazidime. All patients in the study were assessed by a clinical pharmacist and were either receiving other drugs orally or were judged to be capable of taking oral medication. In addition to recording the site of infection, a scoring system was used to measure its severity (sepsis score). Patients receiving oral ciprofloxacin had significantly lower sepsis scores (less severe infection) overall than those given other treatments ($p < 0.05$), and the scores were generally smaller in each of the three main categories of infection treated (Figure 17.7a).[46] A total of 94 patients who received oral ciprofloxacin were matched by site of infection and sepsis score to others receiving parenteral therapy: the outcomes in these two groups were similar (Figure 17.7b).[46]

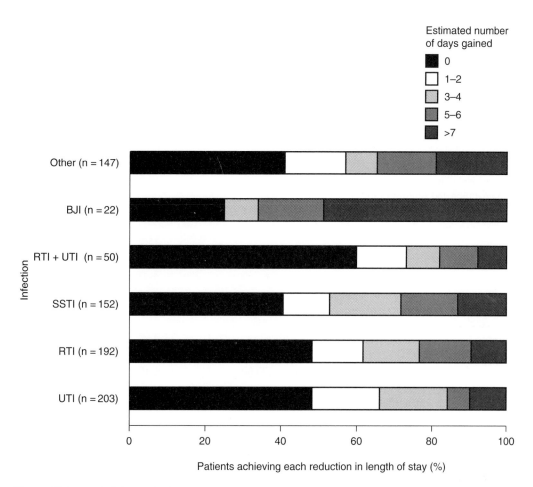

Figure 17.6. Hospital days gained by switching to oral ciprofloxacin by diagnosis. BJI, bone and joint infections; RTI + UTI, combined respiratory and urinary tract infections; SSTI, skin and soft tissue infections; RTI, respiratory tract infections; UTI, urinary tract infections.[50]

Patients given parenteral therapy had more changes in antimicrobial regimen (usually a switch to another oral antibiotic) than those in the oral ciprofloxacin group. However, in only 2 of 94 (2%) patients receiving parenteral therapy was treatment judged to have failed, compared with 4 of 94 (4%) taking oral ciprofloxacin. The total cost of therapy was compared in the same matched pairs and was ($p < 0.001$) lower in the ciprofloxacin group, though the standard deviations of mean costs were wide (Figure 17.8).[46]

The same sepsis score was used to assess outcome in patients with Gram-negative bacteraemia and in others receiving gentamicin.

There was a clear relationship between sepsis score and mortality (Figure 17.9a)[51] or other adverse outcomes, such as recurrence of infection in hospital or readmission with infection within 2 weeks of discharge (Figure 17.9b).[51] Analysis of variance showed a weak relationship between sepsis scores and treatment cost in the aminoglycoside group (sepsis score only accounting for a maximum of 2.6% of the variance in treatment costs).

Of the 215 non-bacteraemic, aminoglycoside patients, 22 (10%) had sepsis scores of 0, indicating little clinical evidence of infection. None of these patients died, yet the average treatment

Table 17.6. A pharmacoeconomic analysis of oral norfloxacin compared with parenteral therapy in the treatment of nosocomial urinary tract infections. Patients were randomised to receive either norfloxacin or the clinician's choice of empirical intravenous treatment, followed by oral therapy based on the results of culture and bacterial sensitivity. Clinicians selected a total of 13 different empirical intravenous regimens; the oral therapy following initial intravenous treatment was co-trimoxazole, amoxycillin or cephradine.[48]

	Norfloxacin	Parenteral therapy
Daily drug cost (US$)	3.00	0.37–44.29
Daily cost including consumables for preparation and administration (US$)	3.00	10.63–54.55
Duration of treatment (days)		
Mean	14	11
95% CI	10–18	10–12
Range	7–90	3–19
Cost (US$, drugs only) for entire course of therapy		
Mean	43.30	244.71
95% CI	31.26–55.34	220.21–269.21
Range	21.00–270.00	1.10–643.36

Odds ratio for cure with norfloxacin (95% CI) = 1.59 (0.64–3.93)

Odds ratio for adverse event with norfloxacin (95% CI) = 0.35 (0.11–1.04)

costs in this group were £209 per patient (range: £23–701). The diagnostic group with the lowest sepsis score was that containing patients with epididymo-orchitis (median 0; range: 0–5). There were no deaths in this group, yet the average treatment cost was £168 per patient (range: £51–651). Many patients with little or no evidence of infection, therefore, continue to receive expensive intravenous antimicrobial treatment and should be prime targets for conversion to oral therapy.

Shulkin *et al.* documented the high costs incurred by patients with suspected infection.[52] In this study, patients with cancer and confirmed postsurgical infection had a mean increase in costs of US$12,542 per patient compared with patients who had no evidence of infection and received no anti-infective treatment.[52] However, only 16% of patients with

postoperative fever had confirmed bacterial infection, and the additional management costs of febrile patients without confirmed infection were US$9145 per patient higher than patients with no evidence of infection. The increased costs were attributable to drugs, investigations and extended hospital stay. If patients with suspected infection outnumber those with confirmed infection by 6 to 1, the management of the former group costs the hospital more than that of the infected individuals. The extensive use of intravenous antibiotics may have detrimental effects in addition to healthcare costs arising from treatment. Anecdotal evidence suggests that during a 3-month visit to three UK teaching hospitals, no cases of antibiotic-associated colitis were seen, whereas in the USA, incidences as high as 7.8 cases per 100 admissions were described.[53]

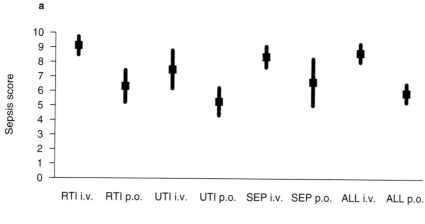

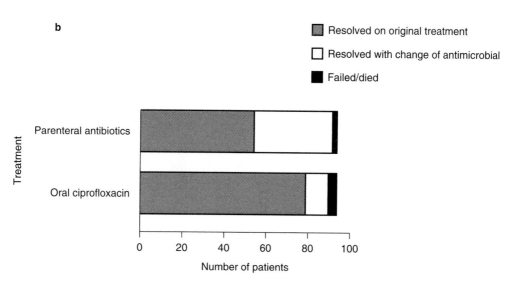

Figure 17.7. (a) Means and 95% CIs of sepsis scores for patients receiving parenteral antibiotics (intravenous, n = 333) or oral ciprofloxacin (oral, n = 148) by site of infection. Patients were treated for respiratory tract infection (RTI), urinary tract infection (UTI) or suspected septicaemia (SEP). Data are also shown for all infections combined (ALL).[46] (b) Outcome of 94 pairs of patients matched for site of infection and sepsis score.[46]

The costs of failure of antibiotic treatment in hospital were quantified in a study of patients treated with gentamicin.[51] Compared with patients having a successful outcome, treatment costs were an average of £357 per patient higher among those who died (95% CI = £31–682) and an average of £418 greater in those who failed to respond to initial therapy (95% CI = £89–747). The removal of patients with Gram-negative bacteraemia had little

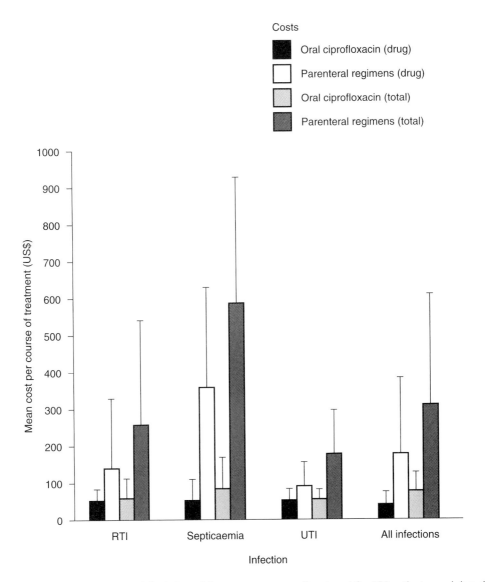

Figure 17.8. Mean and standard deviation of the cost per course of treatment for 188 patients receiving either oral ciprofloxacin (n = 94) or parenteral antibiotics (n = 94). Patients were case-matched for site of infection and severity of illness (by sepsis score). The urinary tract infection (UTI) group contained 25 matched pairs (50 patients), the respiratory tract infection (RTI) group contained 47 pairs and there were 22 pairs in the septicaemia (SEP) group. Costs are shown as those for drug acquisition (drug) or the total cost of treatment including the consumables and labour required for preparation and administration (total).[46]

impact on these results: the treatment costs were £431 per patient higher in non-bacteraemic individuals who did not respond to initial therapy (95% CI = £61–802).

The potential costs of inadequate treatment were graphically illustrated by one patient who received 6 days of therapy for a wound infection and was discharged from hospital with no

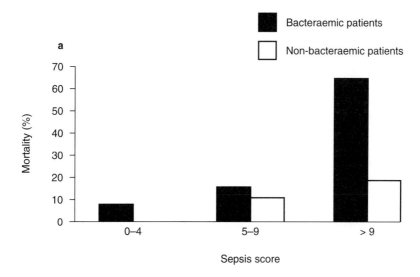

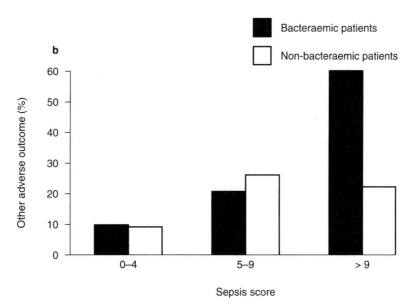

Figure 17.9. The relationship between sepsis score and outcome in patients with Gram-negative bacteraemia and others treated with aminoglycoside regimens. (a) Mortality by sepsis score in all bacteraemic patients (n = 85) and non-bacteraemic patients receiving aminoglycosides (n = 215). (b) Rate of other adverse outcomes by sepsis score for all surviving bacteraemic patients (n = 68) and for surviving, non-bacteraemic patients administered aminoglycosides (n = 194). 'Other adverse outcomes' were recurrence of infection in hospital or readmission with recurrent infection within 2 weeks of discharge. Reproduced with permission.[51]

further antibacterial drugs.[51] The total treatment cost for the first admission was £186. The patient was readmitted after 2 days with gross wound suppuration, and the total treatment cost for the second admission was £1757 (antibiotics, equipment and staff time).

Simple scoring systems may be written into guidelines to help junior staff to assess the need for intravenous drugs at the initiation of treatment, and for continuous review of requirements on each day of therapy. The information gathered could include whether symptoms of infection are present, the patient's vital signs, the date antibiotic therapy started and the reason for it, drug(s) given and their dose and route of administration, the planned duration of therapy and whether blood cultures were taken. The collection of a standard set of clinical data also facilitates subsequent audits of process or outcome.

Residual doubt always remains in a trial that fails to show a difference between two treatments, particularly if clinicians believe that the new or 'test' regimen may actually be less effective than standard therapy. Many doctors believe that intravenous therapy is inherently superior to oral treatment. It is, therefore, reassuring that evidence is emerging that oral quinolone therapy may actually be superior to its intravenous counterpart.[54] In an open, randomised trial, ofloxacin, 200 mg every 12 hours, given orally for 5 days, was compared with ceftriaxone, 3000 mg once daily, given intravenously for 3 days in the treatment of uncomplicated enteric fever. For culture-confirmed cases, complete cure was the outcome for all 22 (100%) patients receiving ofloxacin and 18 of 25 (72%) of those treated with ceftriaxone ($p < 0.01$). There were six acute treatment failures and one relapse in the ceftriaxone group. The mean (± standard deviation) fever clearance times were 81 (± 25) hours for ofloxacin and 196 (± 87) hours for ceftriaxone ($p < 0.0001$). The UK costs for the regimens used would be £108.00 for ceftriaxone compared with £10.26 for ofloxacin. In this trial,[54] the oral quinolone was clearly dominant (less expensive and significantly more effective than parenteral treatment).

Oral quinolone therapy in hospitals

It is important to show that the potential benefits of oral switch therapy shown in research studies can be reproduced in clinical practice. The key to implementing a successful alteration in practice is to set up a multidisciplinary team which includes all of the disciplines involved with the assessment and management of patients with suspected infections. The members of the team will vary, but should include specialists in infection (medical, nursing or pharmacy) and representatives (medical, nursing or pharmacy) from the clinical units which are the target for the policy, in order to understand potential barriers to change.[55,56] Studies have shown that efforts to increase oral antimicrobial use are successful, and cost savings arising from a reduction in the use of intravenous antibiotics have been demonstrated. The results of a recent meta-analysis of 26 published studies examining the effects of different interventions on physicians' prescribing found significant changes in prescribing compared with control groups.[57] The interventions ranged from mailed information to personal interviews and education of individual clinicians. One-to-one meetings had the greatest effect on influencing prescribing behaviour, whereas group meetings had the smallest impact.

In the hospitals described above, there were no disincentives to pharmacists to encourage the prescription of oral antimicrobial agents. Some USA hospital pharmacies do have financial disincentives as they are still revenue–profit centres. USA hospitals have a mix of patients (private-pay, company insured or Medicare). In 1987, the revenue generated from pharmacy operations in some institutions accounted for 15% of total hospital income.[58] This situation is changing rapidly with the introduction of managed care because hospitals now tend to be paid a fixed fee for treating a patient. However, reimbursement systems may still inadvertently encourage the use of intravenous antibiotics, because this effectively increases income to the hospital.[59]

Some studies document the inappropriate use of oral quinolone therapy.[60–63] A review of all patients receiving antibiotics in seven selected wards during a 10-week period, for example, identified 14 who were administered oral ciprofloxacin; however, only 5 (36%) of these prescriptions conformed with the local policy.[61] The 9 courses inconsistent with the hospital guidelines included 5 cases where no pathogen was isolated, 2 where a microbiology test report was not cited, and 2 in which ciprofloxacin was used as a single agent to treat methicillin-resistant *Staphylococcus aureus* infection. The authors also identified 36 patients for whom oral ciprofloxacin was indicated as an alternative to intravenous antibiotics according to the guidelines; however, it was prescribed to only 5 (14%) of those eligible. If ciprofloxacin had been prescribed to the remaining 31 eligible patients, the hospital would have saved US$5426 over the 10-week study period.

A review of ciprofloxacin prescribing in the long-term care setting also concluded that there was considerable room for improvement and identified less expensive, alternative drugs in 49 of 100 patients.

Which oral quinolone?

Hospitals may wish to select a single quinolone for their formulary. It is unlikely, however, that one quinolone is always superior to another across the entire range of indications. The choice depends on the cost of equivalent doses, which is influenced by the susceptibility of the bacteria responsible for infection. Forrest *et al*.[64,65] developed a population model relating serum concentrations of ciprofloxacin to bacterial and clinical outcomes for patients with pneumonia. The area under the inhibition curve (AUIC) (the area under the time–concentration curve, AUC, divided by the mean inhibitory concentration, MIC) was the best predictor of outcome, being superior to both time/MIC and the peak concentration:MIC ratio. The dose response was sigmoidal and the end of the steep, linear portion of the curve occurred at an AUIC of 125 mg/litre. There was some evidence, however, that the E_{max} (maximum effect) did not occur at an AUIC of 125 mg/litre. There appeared to be a continuing,

albeit much shallower, dose response for greater AUICs, and the authors concluded that an AUIC of 250–500 mg/litre would be ideal, whilst acknowledging that 125–250 mg/litre may be acceptable. This model provides a basis for comparing the pharmacodynamics of ciprofloxacin and ofloxacin after oral or intravenous administration, by linking data from kinetic studies with data on *in vitro* antimicrobial potency.

A literature search was carried out for papers documenting the kinetics or *in vitro* susceptibility of ciprofloxacin and ofloxacin.[66] The data showed that the AUC per 100 mg of ofloxacin administered was higher than for ciprofloxacin (also 100 mg) after dosing orally (7.5 versus 1.9 mg.hour/litre) or intravenously (6.3 versus 2.9 mg.hour/litre). As Gram-negative bacteria are two- to eight-fold more susceptible to ciprofloxacin than to ofloxacin, however, the AUIC ratio (ciprofloxacin:ofloxacin) after oral or intravenous administration ranges from 0.5 to 3.5, suggesting that the ofloxacin dose should sometimes be the same or higher than that of ciprofloxacin. In contrast, for the control of Gram-positive and anaerobic bacteria, the dose of ofloxacin required is consistently lower than that of ciprofloxacin. Taking 400 mg as the standard dose of ofloxacin, the equivalent daily amount of ciprofloxacin needed is consistently less than both 1000 mg orally and 400 mg intravenously for Gram-negative bacteria. For Gram-positive and anaerobic bacteria, the equivalent ciprofloxacin doses are 1000–1500 mg daily.

Having established equivalent doses for particular infections, the costs of the two drugs may be compared. However, the relative costs are likely to show substantial differences between countries (Table 17.7).[67] Even within countries there may be considerable variation because of local contract negotiation. The method is easily adapted to local data, and hospitals may use it to compare the daily costs of the two drugs based on the identity and susceptibility of bacteria for which quinolones are recommended on the formulary. However, it is impossible to say which is the less expensive of

Table 17.7. Relative costs of ciprofloxacin and ofloxacin in different countries.[67] Note that the relative cost of the drugs varies between countries and that the relative costs of intravenous and oral formulations are also highly variable. For example, in the UK, 800 mg of intravenous ciprofloxacin or ofloxacin is over 20-fold more expensive than an equivalent dose of the oral formulation, whereas in Germany, 800 mg of intravenous ciprofloxacin is only seven-fold more expensive than 1000 mg of oral ciprofloxacin. NA, formulations or doses not available.

Country (currency)	Ciprofloxacin, 1000 mg p.o.	Ofloxacin, 800 mg p.o.	Ciprofloxacin, 800 mg i.v.	Ofloxacin, 800 mg i.v.	Cost ratio p.o. ciprofloxacin:p.o. ofloxacin	Cost ratio i.v. ciprofloxacin: i.v. ofloxacin
Italy (lire)	9,533.00	9,633.00	109,200.00	NA	1.0	NA
Spain (pesetas)	904.00	800.00	16,434.00	22,232.00	1.1	0.7
France (francs)	34.70	58.60	NA	NA	0.6	NA
Germany (marks)	18.70	19.00	134.40	184.60	1.0	0.7
UK (pounds sterling)	2.75	4.08	58.00	88.04	0.7	0.7

the two quinolones; this depends on what are judged to be equivalent doses and then on the relative cost per 100 mg of each drug.

Future research on oral quinolone regimens for hospital use

Abundant information is available on the effectiveness of quinolones in a variety of infections. The serum concentrations of drug likely to provide successful treatment are also established. Concerns remain about the potential effect of concomitant disease or sepsis on quinolone absorption, and these are probably best addressed by kinetic studies in patients. Trials comparing the clinical outcome of oral quinolone therapy with parenteral treatment indirectly examine whether patients with infection absorb them reliably. However, clinical outcome is affected by many factors besides quinolone absorption. Moreover, it is difficult to design a protocol that avoids the need to fix the duration of oral and intravenous therapy. It is preferable to define groups of patients in whom absorption of quinolones might be impaired (e.g. those with postoperative ileus, diarrhoea or signs of sepsis). The absorption of quinolones or other oral antimicrobial agents could then be studied by measuring serum concentrations while giving intravenous treatment with an alternative drug if necessary.

These points are well illustrated by the results of a large (n = 691), randomised, double-blind, controlled clinical trial[68] and a small (n = 9) kinetic study.[69] In the former, patients with intra-abdominal sepsis were randomised into two groups. Individuals in the first group received intravenously either imipenem or ciprofloxacin–metronidazole. Patients in the second group were given intravenous ciprofloxacin–metronidazole, converting to the same drugs by mouth when oral feeding was resumed. In the first group, patients were switched to oral placebos while maintaining intravenous therapy. In the oral switch group, patients remained on intravenous placebos while receiving active oral therapy. Of the original 691 patients, 341 could not be evaluated for efficacy, mainly because of the

absence of documented infection, and 20 patients were not evaluable due to protocol violations. Of the 330 valid cases, 155 (47%) received oral therapy as part of the study protocol, usually after about 4 days of intravenous therapy, but only 46 (14%) received active oral antibiotics rather than oral placebo. There was no statistically significant difference in outcome between these patient groups. As in the study by Cooke et al.,[46] patients receiving oral therapy were less severely ill than those who received only intravenous treatment, with significantly lower acute physiology and chronic health evaluation (APACHE) scores, and 40% of them had appendicitis compared with 17% of those not given oral therapy. From a starting population of 691, therefore, this trial provides information on the clinical outcome in 46 patients with well-documented infection who received oral therapy at least 4 days postoperatively. They had infections such as appendicitis, which may well have been cured by the initial intravenous therapy. As a result, this trial does not provide information about the reliability of absorption of ciprofloxacin, although it is an excellent study of decision-making by surgeons with respect to switching patients from intravenous to oral therapy and their assessment of patients receiving oral therapy.

In contrast, the kinetic study[69] enrolled nine patients who received 750 mg of ciprofloxacin via nasogastric tubes every 12 hours for 48 hours after major abdominal surgery. Ciprofloxacin concentrations were measured after the first and fourth doses. After the first dose, there was minimal absorption (mean peak concentration = 0.6 mg/litre; mean AUC = 3.5 mg.hour/litre). After the fourth dose, absorption was significantly better than this (mean peak concentration = 2.1 mg/litre; AUC = 17.7 mg.hour/litre), but three patients still had peak concentrations below 1 mg/litre (range: 0.19–0.74 mg/litre) and AUCs below 10 mg.hour/litre (range: 1.4–6.1 mg.hour/litre). This study shows that major surgery impairs the absorption of ciprofloxacin. Further studies are needed to establish clear criteria for selecting patients for oral quinolone therapy and for assisting with drug use reviews. A kinetic design would also be applicable to comparative studies between different quinolones or between quinolones and other oral antibacterial drugs.

Further reviews are also required to document how quinolones are used in practice. The study by Adu *et al.*[61] serves as a useful precedent for a drug use review of oral quinolone therapy. These authors documented three patient groups. The first group comprised patients who switched to oral quinolones as recommended by local guidelines. Patients in the second group could take oral quinolones but continued to receive parenteral antibiotics. Individuals in the third group received oral quinolones when less expensive oral drugs were also appropriate. Using such information, the net cost saving achieved through maintaining oral quinolones as part of the hospital formulary can be calculated and the additional benefits realised by compliance with policy may be quantified. This, in turn, should assist decisions as to the effort needed to improve compliance with policies. It may also be used in designing studies of the drug use review's cost-effectiveness, which could be modelled on several successful investigations in the ambulatory care setting.[70]

Ideally, hospitals should monitor indicators of the outcome of antibacterial treatment. These include death in hospital, escalation or reintroduction of antibacterial treatment and readmission within 2 weeks of discharge. Unfortunately, this information is not readily available in most hospitals, and it will probably remain necessary to examine individual cases even where computerised records are available. For example, though most readmissions to hospital for infection occur in the 2 weeks after discharge, this accounts for only half the total number in that period, with the other half being non-infectious problems.[50] Finally, outcome data should be adjusted for risk if possible. The sepsis score referred to previously provides one method for achieving this.[46,51] However, further multivariate analysis is required to refine the weighting of the information collected and, if possible, to reduce the amount of data required.

The outcome of infection depends on a number of factors: its site; the infecting organism; concomitant disease; whether there is evidence of systemic inflammatory response syndrome; and the speed of initiating appropriate antimicrobial treatment together with fluid replacement and other resuscitative measures. These other factors should be considered when assessing the contribution of antimicrobial treatment to outcome.

Quinolones as oral switch therapy in hospitals and chronic-care settings

The advantages of oral quinolone therapy include potential financial savings through lower drug acquisition costs, a reduction in the consumables needed for intravenous preparation or administration and earlier hospital patient discharge. There is growing consensus about the relationship between serum levels of quinolones and outcome. It should, therefore, be possible to design studies documenting quinolone absorption in patients and then comparing different ones with each other and with other antibacterial treatments. The introduction of quinolones onto a hospital formulary will improve efficiency only if the hospital ensures that patients receive them according to carefully written guidelines. Further studies on the successful implementation and monitoring of oral quinolones in hospital are required. The placing of quinolones within an overall plan for managing infections in hospital is illustrated in the following section.

Intravenous ciprofloxacin versus imipenem in severe pneumonia

Ciprofloxacin was compared with imipenem in a large, double-blind, multicentre trial of the treatment of severe pneumonia.[71] The costs of the two regimens were analysed separately.[72] The doses administered depended on the patients' clinical condition and renal function, and the organism causing infection.

The protocol recommended starting treatment at doses of ciprofloxacin, 400 mg every 8 hours, or imipenem, 1000 mg every 8 hours. However, doses could be reduced in patients with renal impairment. Furthermore, clinicians were allowed to select a low-dose regimen (ciprofloxacin, 400 mg every 12 hours, or imipenem, 500 mg every 6 hours) based on evaluation of clinical severity or of the susceptibility of the causative organism. Two patients were excluded because of missing dose information in the final analysis. Of the 201 evaluable patients given ciprofloxacin, 5 (3%) received the low-dose regimen, 161 (80%) received the high-dose regimen and 35 (17%) received both regimens. The proportions were similar in the 199 patients in the imipenem group: 1 (0.5%) received the low dose only, 163 (82%) the high dose only and 35 (18%) both high- and low-dose regimens. The drug costs were lower in patients treated with ciprofloxacin than in those receiving imipenem (Table 17.8).[71]

There was a marked trend towards better outcome among patients in the ciprofloxacin group. Clinical resolution occurred without a change in therapy in 68 of 98 (69%) evaluable ciprofloxacin patients compared with 58 of 104 (56%) evaluable imipenem patients, giving an odds ratio for successful outcome with ciprofloxacin of 1.8 (95% CI = 1.1–2.9). The four factors independently predicting clinical response, identified by a multivariate analysis, were: no mechanical ventilation required; low APACHE II score; absence of *Pseudomonas aeruginosa*; and treatment with ciprofloxacin.[71]

These are essentially examples of the criteria predicting outcome. The need for mechanical ventilation illustrates the influence of underlying disease. The APACHE score gives further information on underlying disease and includes all elements of the systemic inflammatory response. The fact that treatment with ciprofloxacin had an additional, statistically significant impact on outcome ($p = 0.04$) over and above these factors is strong evidence of the regimen's efficacy for treating severe pneumonia.

The costs of treatment failure were not documented in the report of the main trial, but one participating centre conducted a detailed analysis.[73] This centre contributed 14 evaluable patients to both the ciprofloxacin and imipenem regimens. A total of 3 (21%) of the ciprofloxacin patients required additional antibiotic therapy compared with 7 (50%) in the imipenem group. The total cost of post-trial antimicrobial treatment was US$744 in the ciprofloxacin group compared with US$3386 in the patients given imipenem. Additional antimicrobial therapy would, therefore, be expected to add US$53 (US$744/14) versus US$242 (US$3386/14) to the average antibiotic costs for a patient treated with ciprofloxacin or imipenem, respectively. In addition to lower drug costs, patients in the ciprofloxacin group stayed for a lower total number of days in hospital (398) than those in the imipenem group (532). Overall, the estimated mean total treatment costs (including duration of admission) were lower by US$15,000 per patient in the ciprofloxacin group compared with those who received imipenem (ciprofloxacin: US$636,800 total, mean US$45,486 per patient; imipenem: US$851,200 total, mean US$60,800 per patient).

Seizures were significantly less common in the ciprofloxacin group (3 of 202 [1.5%] patients) compared with the imipenem group (11 of 200 [5.5%] patients). The odds ratio of having a seizure while receiving ciprofloxacin versus imipenem was 0.26 (95% CI = 0.07–0.94).[71] The resource costs associated with seizures were documented in a separate analysis (Table 17.9). Other adverse events occurred with similar incidences in the two groups: 129 of 202 (64%) patients receiving ciprofloxacin versus 137 of 200 (69%) patients given imipenem.[72]

In this trial,[71] the ciprofloxacin regimen was dominant (i.e. it had lower resource costs with a better outcome). The purpose of the trial was to demonstrate the efficacy of intravenous ciprofloxacin as monotherapy in the management of severe pneumonia. The comparator (imipenem) and its regimen were chosen after consultation with clinical experts because it was regarded as being the best monotherapy available when the study was undertaken. The

Table 17.8. Comparison of drug acquisition costs for ciprofloxacin and imipenem at the doses administered in a randomised, double-blind, controlled clinical trial.[71]

	Ciprofloxacin	Imipenem
Average wholesale price (US$)	28.81 per 400 mg dose	22.40 per 500 mg dose
Low-dose regimen	400 mg b.d.	500 mg q.d.s.
Number of patients	40	36
Total regimen days	266	257
Cost per day (US$)	57.62	89.60
Total regimen cost (US$)	15,326.92	23,027.20
High-dose regimen	400 mg t.d.s.	1000 mg t.d.s.
Number of patients	196	198
Total regimen days	1476	1577
Cost per day (US$)	86.43	134.40
Total regimen cost	127,570.68	211,948.80
Total treatment costs (US$)	142,897.60	234,976.00
Average cost per patient (US$)	605.50	1004.17

Table 17.9. Resource utilisation associated with seizures in a clinical trial comparing intravenous ciprofloxacin and imipenem. Seizures occurred in 3 of 202 (1.5%) patients in the ciprofloxacin group compared with 11 of 200 (5.5%) in the imipenem group. The odds ratio for a patient having a seizure while receiving ciprofloxacin versus imipenem was 0.26 (95% CI = 0.07–0.94). Reproduced with permission.[72]

Type of resource	Examples	Number of patients (%)
Additional medication	KCl i.v. $MgSO_4$ i.v. Anticonvulsants (phenytoin, diazepam, lorazepam, phenobarbitone) Dexamethasone	14/14 (100%)
Additional investigation	Computed tomography scan Electroencephalogram Lumbar puncture Magnetic resonance imaging scan	10/14 (71%)
Staff time	Additional time spent with patient by medical or nursing personnel	9/14 (64%)
	Specialist referral	7/14 (50%)
Hospitalisation	Change in setting (transfer to intensive care unit because of seizure)	2/5 (40%) (9 patients already on intensive care unit at time of seizure)
	Increased length of hospital stay	1/14 (7%)

need to demonstrate the efficacy of ciprofloxacin monotherapy arose primarily from the requirements of the United States Food and Drug Administration. In clinical practice, neither intravenous ciprofloxacin nor intravenous imipenem are likely to be used as monotherapy for nosocomial pneumonia, which accounted for 78% of the cases in the trial. Recently published guidelines stress the importance of combination therapy for nosocomial pneumonia caused by *Pseudomonas aeruginosa*.[74] Most patients will, therefore, probably receive empirical combination treatment until the results of microbiology cultures become available.

Although the trial described above was not designed primarily as an economic evaluation, some analysis was carried out after its completion.[73] The trial, however, did not reflect usual clinical practice. Indeed, the authors went to considerable lengths to restrict entry to a selected group of patients, and to make the design double blind to minimise the risk of confounding variables and bias. As well as providing evidence of the efficacy of ciprofloxacin, however, this trial documents the consequences of failure of antibiotic treatment, along with their resource costs. Most importantly, the demonstration of differences in both clinical outcome (efficacy and safety) and resource costs in a randomised, double-blind clinical trial provides solid evidence of cause and effect.

Previous studies have documented the additional resource costs associated with nosocomial pneumonia. For example, an estimated US$8800 per patient of additional costs have been demonstrated to be incurred with ventilator-associated pneumonia.[75] In this study, the costs of pneumonia cases were compared with those in up to five matched control patients. The possibility remains, however, that the association between pneumonia and excess cost is due to additional confounding variable(s). For example, obesity may increase the risk of pneumonia and raise hospital costs. Randomised, double-blind, controlled trials are the best methods of equalising the effect of confounding variables and minimising observer bias.[76]

The trial by Fink *et al.*[71] provides important evidence that both failure of antibiotic treatment and adverse events are directly linked to healthcare resource costs.

Modelling costs and consequences of nosocomial pneumonia treatment regimens

Recently published guidelines recommend combination therapy for pneumonia caused by *Pseudomonas aeruginosa*.[74] The data from Fink *et al.*[71] may be used to model the potential costs of treatment failure and adverse events. This will help the decision-maker to understand the impact of these factors on the expected average cost per patient treated, which is calculated as follows:

Expected average cost per patient treated = drug acquisition cost + (risk of treatment failure × cost of treatment failure) + (risk of adverse event × cost of adverse event).

The costs of a range of ciprofloxacin regimens have been calculated (Table 17.10),[71–73,77] including those used in the published trial of nosocomial pneumonia.[71] The cost of failed antibiotic treatment for pneumonia has been set at US$15,000. This was the difference in average cost per patient receiving ciprofloxacin compared with imipenem in the analysis by Caldwell *et al.*[73] This may underestimate the additional costs generated by failed treatment for severe pneumonia. The total cost generated by the 14 patients receiving ciprofloxacin was US$636,800, of which 3 experienced subsequent infection requiring additional antimicrobial therapy. The total cost generated by the 14 patients receiving imipenem was US$851,200, of which 7 had subsequent infection. If the difference in total cost (US$214,400) was generated purely by the four extra patients in the imipenem group needing further therapy for pneumonia, the cost of the additional therapy was US$53,600 per patient. The cost of managing seizures has been set at US$4000, based on information concerning additional resource utilisation (Table 17.9).[72]

Table 17.10. Costs and consequences of a range of regimens for treatment of Gram-negative pneumonia.[71-73,77]

Regimen	Drug acquisition cost (US$)	Efficacy (clinical response rate)* (%)	Convulsions (%)
A: High-dose imipenem (1000 mg i.v. t.d.s.) and high-dose ciprofloxacin (400 mg i.v. t.d.s.) for 14 days	3092	73	7**
B: High-dose imipenem (i.v.) and high-dose ciprofloxacin (i.v.) for 4 days; continued for a further 10 days if *Pseudomonas aeruginosa* isolated (23% of patients), otherwise stop imipenem	2256	73	2.8
C: As for B, but switching to high-dose ciprofloxacin (750 mg p.o. b.d.) after 7 days in patients without *Pseudomonas aeruginosa*	1803	73	2.8
D: High-dose ciprofloxacin (i.v.) for 14 days	1210	69	1.5
E: High-dose ciprofloxacin (i.v.) for 7 days; low-dose ciprofloxacin (400 mg i.v. b.d.) for 7 days	1008	69	1.5
F: Low-dose ciprofloxacin (i.v.) for 14 days	807	64	1.5
G: High-dose ciprofloxacin (i.v.) for 7 days; high-dose ciprofloxacin (p.o.) for 7 days	757	69	1.5
H: Low-dose ciprofloxacin (i.v.) for 5 days; high-dose ciprofloxacin (p.o.) for 9 days	378	66	1.0
I: High-dose ciprofloxacin (p.o.) for 14 days	305	60	1.0
J: Low-dose ciprofloxacin (250 mg p.o. b.d.) for 14 days	102	40	0.5

*Clinical response is the percentage of patients responding to antibiotic regimen without modification.
**Assumes that the risk of seizures is the sum of the risk with imipenem alone (5.5%) plus the risk with ciprofloxacin alone (1.5%).

It was assumed that combination therapy was more effective than ciprofloxacin monotherapy for pneumonia caused by *Pseudomonas aeruginosa* and that low-dose, intravenous treatment was less effective than high doses of the drug given by the same route against Gram-negative pneumonia. It was also assumed that high-dose, oral ciprofloxacin was as effective as high-dose, intravenous forms of the drug provided absorption was reliable; however, this may not be the case during the first few days of severe pneu-

monia treatment, particularly in postoperative patients.[69] Hence, it was assumed that a regimen of high-dose, oral ciprofloxacin from day 1 (regimen I; see regimens A–J in Table 17.10) was less effective than high-dose, intravenous ciprofloxacin followed by high-dose, oral ciprofloxacin (regimen G), but that the latter was as effective as high-dose, intravenous ciprofloxacin throughout (regimen D).

The importance of accurate diagnosis is illustrated by comparing the expected costs of the regimens, assuming that either 100% or 25% of patients treated have Gram-negative pneumonia. Only half the patients entered into the trial were fully evaluable, and the proportion of those with confirmed clinical pneumonia would probably be lower in clinical practice.[71] For example, in a study of patients treated with antibiotics for post-operative fever, only 16% had evidence of bacterial infection,[53] and an audit of those receiving antibacterial drugs for lower RTI (LRTI) in a UK hospital showed that most had little or no objective evidence of infection.[78] If only 25% of patients treated have pneumonia, the other 75% incur the costs and risks of antibiotic treatment without any benefit.

If 100% of the patients treated have pneumonia, the analysis is relatively straightforward. A regimen of low-dose, oral ciprofloxacin for 14 days (regimen J) has the lowest drug acquisition costs (US$102), but the consequences of poor effectiveness are clear. This regimen also has the highest expected average total cost (US$9127 compared with US$7492 for a regimen of high-dose, intravenous imipenem and high-dose, intravenous ciprofloxacin for 14 days (regimen A), which has a drug acquisition cost of US$3092). Consequently, when the regimens in Table 17.10 are arranged in ascending order of drug acquisition cost, the expected average total cost per patient shows a distinct U-shape (Figure 17.10).[72,73] Regimen G (high-dose, intravenous ciprofloxacin for 7 days followed by high-dose, oral ciprofloxacin for 7 days) has the lowest expected average cost per patient treated and is dominant (i.e. has a lower cost with equal or greater effectiveness) over all other regimens except A–C. The question arises as to the value of increasing effectiveness from 69% to 73% by selecting regimens A–C instead of G. In contrast, if only 25% of patients have pneumonia, regimen H (low-dose, intravenous ciprofloxacin for 5 days followed by high-dose, oral ciprofloxacin for 9 days) has the lowest expected average total cost, and the decision-maker must consider the value of six alternative regimens (A–E and G) which have higher costs but greater effectiveness. The costs of

regimens A–C are driven both by drug acquisition and the risk of seizures, which are assumed to be dose related and which occur whether or not the patient has pneumonia. As the proportion of patients treated who have pneumonia reduces to 0%, the expected average total cost of less expensive, less effective regimens declines to drug acquisition cost alone, whereas for high-dose regimens the expected average cost always includes the cost of adverse effects.

Having identified the regimen with the lowest expected cost, the final part of the economic analysis requires the calculation of incremental cost-effectiveness (cost per additional case cured) for regimens that are both more effective and more expensive than others (Table 17.11). Regimens that are more effective than others should not be rejected simply because they have higher expected healthcare resource costs; this should be the start of the economic analysis, not the end. If a new treatment improves outcome and reduces healthcare costs it is dominant, and the decision should be straightforward. If the new treatment is more effective but requires additional resources, the decision-maker must consider other consequences of treatment failure, including financial costs outside the health service, intangible costs to the patient and potential costs of litigation arising from unsuccessful therapy. The final decision depends on whether the value of preventing treatment failure exceeds the incremental cost-effectiveness (Table 17.11). Once again, the economic analysis emphasises the importance of accurate diagnosis: the incremental cost per additional patient cured by regimen C versus regimen G is US$97,500 if only 25% of the patients treated have pneumonia, but only US$14,225 if all the patients have pneumonia (Table 17.11).

This model illustrates a number of key points. Firstly, if the costs of treatment failure are high, they can easily remove the savings made from reduced drug costs. Secondly, the cost-effectiveness of any treatment is dependent on the accuracy of diagnosis, particularly for regimens with both high drug acquisition costs and a risk of serious adverse events. Thirdly, efficient disease

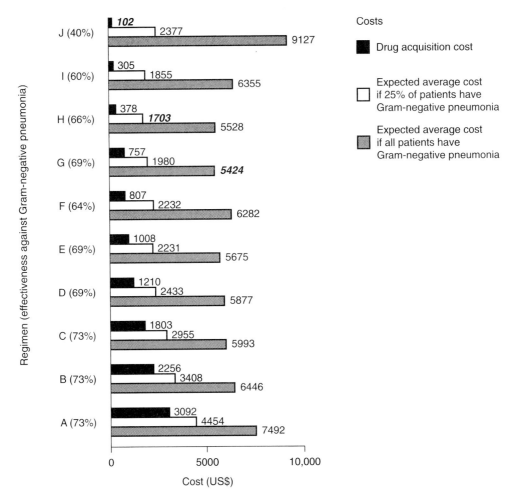

Figure 17.10. Drug cost and expected average total cost per patient treated for suspected Gram-negative pneumonia with 10 different antibiotic regimens. The regimens are arranged in ascending order of drug acquisition cost with the efficacy of each regimen shown in parentheses. Further details of the drug regimens, their efficacy and adverse events are given in Table 17.10. The expected average costs per patient treated have been calculated under the assumption that either 25% or 100% of patients treated have Gram-negative pneumonia. The costs of treatment failure (US$15,000) and convulsions (US$4000) were based on information in references 72 and 73. The lowest cost regimen in each category is shown in bold italics.

management requires that all patients with confirmed serious infection receive effective empirical treatment. This inevitably means that some patients receive unnecessary treatment. Modifying or stopping unnecessary treatment as soon as possible[79] is a crucial component of disease management. Fourthly, in deciding between treatments that are both more expensive and more effective than others, it is essential to consider incremental costs.

The following questions must be considered. (i) What is the incremental cost of the more effective regimen (the cost of the more effective regimen minus that of the alternative regimen)? (ii) What is the incremental effectiveness of the more effective regimen (the effectiveness of the more effective regimen minus that of the alternative regimen)? (iii) What is the incremental cost-effectiveness of the more effective regimen (the cost per

Table 17.11. Incremental cost-effectiveness (cost per additional patient cured) for selected regimens for nosocomial pneumonia from Figure 17.10. In each case the regimen with the lowest expected average cost is compared with regimens that are both more expensive and more effective.

	Additional cost per patient treated (US$)	Additional patients cured (%)	Incremental cost per additional patient cured (US$)
Probability of pneumonia 100%; lowest expected cost regimen G (US$5424 per patient treated)			
Regimen C	569 (5993–5424)	4	14,225
Regimen B	1022	4	25,500
Regimen A	2068	4	51,700
Probability of pneumonia 25%; lowest expected cost regimen H (US$1703 per patient treated); regimens compared with H unless otherwise stated			
Regimen G	277 (1980–1703)	0.75 (3% of 25%)	36,933
Regimen C	1252	1.75 (7% of 25%)	71,543
Regimen C versus regimen G	975	1.0 (4% of 25%)	97,500

additional patient cured by the more effective regimen), which is (i) divided by (ii)? (iv) What are the resource consequences of treatment failure and what value will the decision-maker attach to curing one additional patient? An economic analysis makes the consequences of decision-making transparent, but the ultimate decision usually rests on value judgements.

Quinolones and the management of community-acquired infection

Cost-effectiveness of quinolones compared with less expensive regimens

Quinolones are generally more expensive than other antibacterial regimens used for the empirical treatment of infections in the community. The elements required for decision analysis have been stated clearly in a comparison of the cost-effectiveness of chloramphenicol and ciprofloxacin for the treatment of enteric fever in India.[80] The results of the analysis were expressed as a two-way sensitivity analysis (Figure 17.11).[80] The authors assumed that chloramphenicol resistance always resulted in treatment failure and that the bacteria resistant to this antibiotic would respond to ciprofloxacin. These are reasonable assumptions because enteric fever is one of the few infections for which a direct relationship exists between drug resistance and clinical response.

There is also good evidence to support the efficacy of quinolones for enteric fever caused by pathogens resistant to other oral antimicrobial agents. In a trial conducted in Vietnam, 63% of 47 isolates (6 *Salmonella paratyphi* and 41 *Salmonella typhi*) were resistant to ampicillin, chloramphenicol, co-trimoxazole and tetracycline.[54] All 22 patients randomised to receive oral ofloxacin, 200 mg every 12 hours, were cured. In the sensitivity analysis (Figure 17.11),[80] the decision to prescribe a quinolone

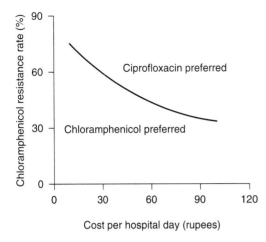

Figure 17.11. Two-way sensitivity analysis, showing the point at which the costs of ciprofloxacin and chloramphenicol are equal according to the prevalence of chloramphenicol resistance and the cost per day in hospital.[80]

then depends on the value attached to the other healthcare resources consumed when chloramphenicol treatment fails (it was assumed that patients would require additional hospitalisation and treatment with ciprofloxacin). The cost of additional ciprofloxacin was known, but the cost of a day in hospital varied throughout India and, as discussed earlier (Figure 17.2), the resource savings arising from early discharge are debatable. Presentation of the results as a sensitivity analysis allows the decision-maker to identify critical values for shortening hospital stay. For example, at the chloramphenicol resistance rate observed by Smith *et al.* (60%),[54] the decision-maker must believe that it is worth spending at least 30 rupees on ciprofloxacin to gain one hospital bed day through early patient discharge (Figure 17.11).[80] Finally, the authors assumed that a 14-day course of quinolone treatment was required to cure enteric fever,[80] whereas more recent trials have documented the effectiveness of shorter (5-day) regimens.[54] However, the model could easily be adapted to vary the cost of quinolone treatment.

This model (Figure 17.11) is simple, but still encompasses all the elements required to discuss the value of ciprofloxacin in the management of community-acquired infection. Hospitalisation is a rare outcome in the treatment of community-acquired infection, even for LRTI. In a study of 1140 patients presenting to primary-care doctors with symptoms of RTI, only two admissions to hospital occurred following failure of antibacterial therapy in the community.[81]

It will be difficult to show that antibiotic treatment reduces hospitalisation in a randomised, controlled clinical trial. Other experimental designs are possible, and one epidemiological study suggests that a restriction on ciprofloxacin prescription may have increased hospital admissions in Saskatchewan. Unfortunately, this study has not been published except in abstract form, but it is worth summarising. Ciprofloxacin was introduced in Quebec in February 1989. From this time onwards, a decrease in hospitalisation was seen for pyelonephritis (by 21%) and bronchitis (by 25%), but there was no concomitant reduction in hospital admissions for these diagnoses in Saskatchewan, where ciprofloxacin was not introduced. The authors checked for confounding variables (smoking, use of other antibiotics and changes in admission rates for other diagnoses), as these are observational data. Nonetheless, there are precedents for connecting attempts to control drug costs with impaired patient outcomes.[82,83] It is also unlikely that any randomised trial could include enough patients to detect a reduction in hospitalisation rates through improved antibiotic management of community-acquired infections. Observational studies in large databases may, therefore, be the only way this question can be addressed.

The consequences of antibiotic treatment failure in the community are usually limited to effects on health services and the patient. Before these consequences can be explored, information is needed on the effectiveness of community antibiotic treatment. An observational study of the efficacy and use of resources over a 3-year period was conducted in a cohort of 917 patients who received at least one prescription for an antibiotic between January and March 1989.[84] A 'first success' for antimicrobial treatment was defined as a patient who received no antibiotic within the 28 days before the infection was diagnosed and did not return with further symptoms in the 28 days after receiving a prescription.

First success rates were lower in patients over 65 years old, particularly for those with UTI. First success rates for upper respiratory tract infection (URTI) were 80–90%, and the overall first success rate for penicillin V (prescribed mainly for URTI) was 92%. It is difficult to believe that a role for quinolones exists for infections which are treated satisfactorily with such inexpensive alternatives. A 10-day course of penicillin V costs £0.57, compared with £19.25 for a 7-day course of ciprofloxacin, 500 mg every 12 hours. Even if ciprofloxacin is 100% effective, the decision-maker must believe that the value of one additional successful outcome is at least £233 (£18.68/0.08) to justify the prescription of ciprofloxacin (Table 17.12).[81] Even with generous estimates of costs to primary-care doctors and patients, it is unlikely that anyone would agree with such a valuation.[81,84]

Unfortunately, most studies comparing quinolones with other antimicrobial drugs are designed to show equivalence. For example, in three trials comparing ciprofloxacin with co-trimoxazole, 128 of 140 (91%) patients treated with co-trimoxazole were cured.[85] If co-trimoxazole cures 91% of patients, what role do quinolones have? Fortunately, more pragmatic trial designs reveal potentially important differences between antibacterial treatments (Figure 17.12).[77] The striking differences between success rates for regimens for simple cystitis are due both to recurrence of cystitis and to vaginal candidiasis occurring in the 6 weeks following antibacterial treatment. Patients taking cefadroxil had both the highest rate of relapse of cystitis (34%) and the highest rate of candidiasis (38%), so that only 28% of episodes were successfully treated (Figure 17.12). The authors compared the results of this trial[77] with an earlier study comparing co-trimoxazole with a 3-day ofloxacin regimen.[86] Although this is a historical control, it provides an interesting basis for comparing the cost-effectiveness of regimens for community-acquired infection.

Are the rates of recurrent cystitis and candidiasis credible? The overall rate of recurrent cystitis is 20%, giving an 80% rate of successful treatment. This is similar to the first success rate observed by MacDonald et al. in patients aged 13–65 years (Figure 17.13).[84] The poor performance of cefadroxil is also consistent with the results of five other published, randomised, controlled trials comparing cephalexin (a similar drug to cefadroxil) with either trimethoprim,[87,88] co-trimoxazole[89,90] or both trimethoprim and co-trimoxazole.[91] These trials consistently showed that recurrence of cystitis is more likely to occur after cephalosporin treatment. The odds ratio for individual trials ranges from 1.52[90] to 19.36,[89] because the response rates range from 53%[89] to 83%[90] for cephalexin, whereas they range from 82%[77] to 96%[89] for trimethoprim or co-trimoxazole.

All of the comparative trials consistently report higher rates of adverse effects after treatment with cephalosporins compared with trimethoprim or co-trimoxazole. Much of this difference is accounted for by vaginitis, though not all trials document the presence of *Candida*. These data are consistent with an observational study by MacDonald et al., which used the prescription of antifungal preparations as a surrogate measure of vaginal candidiasis.[92] The study used a database that recorded all prescriptions written by a group of doctors serving a population of 10,000 citizens in Tayside, Scotland from March 1985 to December 1989. A cohort of women taking antibiotics had a higher incidence of vaginal candidiasis after exposure to such agents than before treatment.[92] The data were analysed by calculation of attributable risk. This compares the proportion of women who received antifungal treatment in the 28 days before antibiotic treatment versus the 28 days after antibiotic treatment. The difference between these proportions is the risk of receiving antifungal treatment which is attributable to the prescription of an antibiotic. The attributable risk of the prescription of vaginal antifungal drugs was age related, being significantly greater than one in women aged 21–40 years (Figure 17.14a) ($p < 0.05$).[92] Moreover, the attributable risk

Table 17.12. Critical values of avoiding one repeat consultation by using more expensive, more effective treatment than other therapy. Reproduced with permission.[81] The critical value is the minimum value which the decision-maker must attach to preventing one repeat consultation to justify the more expensive, more effective treatment. Example 1: if a drug costs £5.00 per patient more and has an increased effectiveness of 12%, they must believe that it is worth spending at least £42.00 to avoid one repeat prescription. Example 2: if a doctor will spend no more than £40.00 to prevent a repeat consultation, then a drug which costs £7.50 more than standard treatment must be at least 20% more effective.

Difference in efficacy* (%)	Critical value of avoiding repeat consultation (£) by difference in drug cost**												
	2.00	2.50	3.00	3.50	4.00	4.50	5.00	7.50	10.00	12.50	15.00	17.50	20.00
2	100	125	150	175	200	225	250	375	500	625	750	875	1000
4	50	63	75	88	100	113	125	188	250	313	375	438	500
6	33	42	50	58	67	75	83	125	167	208	250	292	333
8	25	31	38	44	50	56	63	94	125	156	188	209	250
10	20	25	30	35	40	45	50	75	100	125	150	175	200
12	17	21	25	29	33	38	42	63	83	104	125	146	167
14	14	18	21	25	29	32	36	54	71	89	107	125	143
16	13	16	19	22	25	28	31	47	63	78	94	109	125
18	11	14	17	19	22	25	28	42	56	69	83	97	111
20	10	13	15	18	20	23	25	38	50	63	75	88	100
22	9	11	14	16	18	20	23	34	45	57	68	80	91
24	8	10	13	15	17	19	21	31	42	52	63	73	83
26	8	10	12	13	15	17	19	29	38	48	58	67	77
28	7	9	11	13	14	16	18	27	36	45	54	63	71
30	7	8	10	12	13	15	17	25	33	42	50	58	67

*Difference in efficacy between more expensive drug and current treatment.
**Difference in cost between more expensive drug and current treatment.

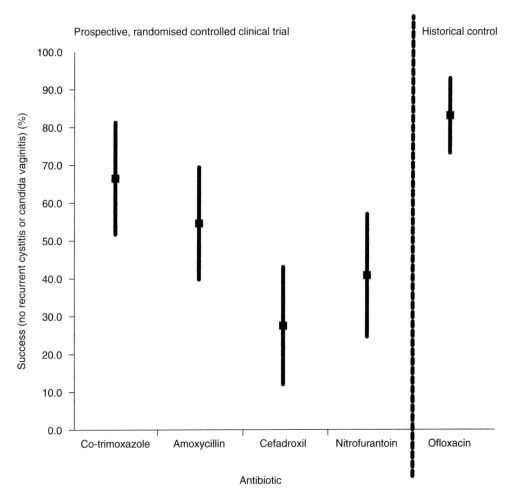

Figure 17.12. Probability of successful outcome (with 95% CIs) for treatment of simple cystitis in young women.[77]

varied between antibiotics, being markedly higher for cephalosporins than for co-trimoxazole or trimethoprim (Figure 17.14b).[92] These observational results are consistent with those of Hooton *et al.*,[77] who identified a markedly increased risk of candidiasis after cephalosporin treatment in a study population from a student health centre (mean age 24 years) likely to be at high risk of vaginal candidiasis (Figure 17.14a). The study by MacDonald *et al.*[92] was completed before vaginal antifungal drugs were available over the counter without prescription in UK pharmacies.

Costs and consequences of failed antibiotic treatment in the community: a comparison between the USA and the UK

The study by Hooton *et al.*[77] contains an analysis of the healthcare costs arising from the treatment of cystitis. It also includes the costs of managing recurrent cystitis and vaginal candidiasis. The paper follows the recommended practice of identifying all costs clearly in a way that makes it easy for the reader to relate them to local practice. Applying UK costs, it rapidly

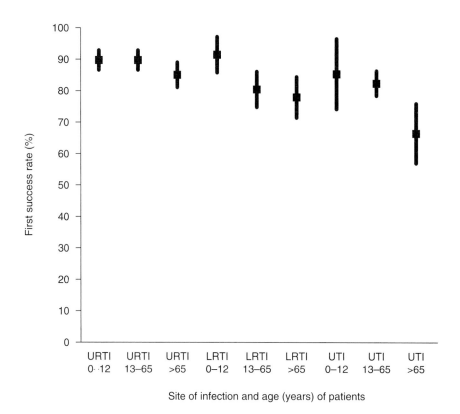

Figure 17.13. First success rates with 95% CIs for antibiotics prescribed in primary care by site of infection and patient age. A first success was defined as a patient who received no antibacterial therapy within the 28 days before the infection was diagnosed and did not return with further symptoms in the 28 days after receiving an antibiotic prescription. URTI, upper respiratory tract infection (n = 1502); LRTI, lower respiratory tract infection (n = 419); UTI, urinary tract infection (n = 441). For each site of infection, the patients were grouped by age (0–12 years; 13–65 years and > 65 years).[84]

becomes apparent that they are substantially different (usually lower) from those in the USA (Tables 17.13[77] and 17.14[77,81]). The drug acquisition costs quoted in the paper include a pharmacist's fee, but this is presented clearly and may be deducted to calculate the actual drug cost. Even after subtracting the pharmacist's fee, the cost of drugs in the USA is usually substantially higher than in the UK (by over four-fold for cefadroxil). Exceptions include co-trimoxazole and amoxycillin; these were costed as generic formulations in the USA study, whereas the UK costs in Table 17.13 were obtained from an index of branded products.[21]

The other healthcare costs included in the analysis are also generally higher in the USA. The conservative estimate of UK laboratory costs was obtained from the microbiology laboratory at Ninewells Hospital, Dundee, where bacterial culture and sensitivity testing attract the same charge as the processing of a vaginal swab for the identification of yeasts (£5, Table 17.14[77,81]). In contrast, the USA charge for urine culture and sensitivity is more than twice as high as that for the analysis of vaginal fluid. A wider survey of either USA or UK microbiology costs would probably reveal substantial local variations. For example, a survey of gentamicin assay costs in the UK found that

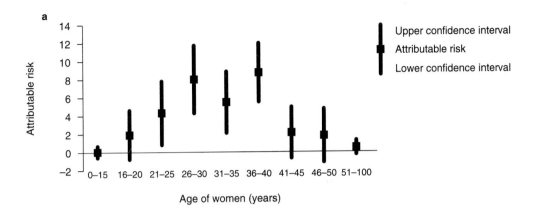

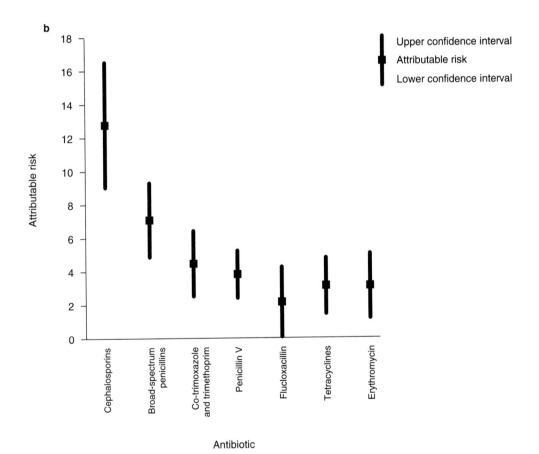

Figure 17.14. Risk of prescribing vaginal antifungal agents after a course of antibiotics. (a) Attributable risk by age group; (b) attributable risk by antibacterial drug.[92]

Table 17.13. Comparison of drug costs in the UK and USA for the regimens used in the study by Hooton *et al.*[77] The UK equivalent of the USA drug acquisition cost was calculated by deducting the pharmacist fee and dividing by 1.5 to convert US$ to £. The UK cost of the study dosage has been calculated from MIMS.[21]

Regimen	Costs quoted in USA paper (US$)	UK equivalent* (£)	UK cost of study dosage (£)
Trimethoprim–sulphamethoxazole, 160 mg/800 mg b.d. × 3 days	4.73	0.60	1.50
Nitrofurantoin, 100 mg q.d.s. × 3 days	19.20	8.64	2.28
Cefadroxil, 500 mg b.d. × 3 days	16.97	7.40	1.68
Amoxycillin, 500 mg t.d.s. × 3 days	6.35	1.50	3.42
Ofloxacin, 200 mg b.d. × 3 days	22.95	10.72	6.16
Ciprofloxacin, 250 mg b.d. × 3 days	21.77	10.07	4.50
Clotrimazole vaginal cream applied daily × 7 days	20.45	9.33	5.09**

*Pharmacy fee deducted (US$3.65 fixed fee plus 20% of the costs of the drug) and converted to £ by dividing by 1.5.
**UK formulation is for six applications, not seven.

variations were more than ten-fold.[14] In the USA, the costs of laboratory tests vary strikingly, depending on whether they are carried out in-house or externally. For example, the cost of diagnostic tests is crucial to discussion about the relative virtues of empirical antibiotic treatment of pharyngitis versus therapy based on bacteriological diagnosis.[93,94] A group paediatric infectious diseases practice with in-house laboratory facilities estimated the cost of culture to be US$2–5 and the cost of a test for streptococcal antigen to be US$3.[94] In contrast, for an emergency room that sent samples out to a commercial laboratory the costs were US$42 for culture and US$39 for the antigen test. Any economic analysis must be presented in a form that can be adapted to local variations in medical practice (e.g. the number of tests performed and drug dosing regimens) and healthcare costs.

Carrying out a cost-effectiveness analysis of the four regimens compared directly by Hooton *et al.* (co-trimoxazole, amoxycillin, cefadroxil and nitrofurantoin; see Figure 17.12[77]) presents

no problems. Co-trimoxazole was less expensive and more effective than amoxycillin, cefadroxil or nitrofurantoin. The expected average total cost for co-trimoxazole is therefore the lowest, irrespective of the healthcare costs used in the analysis (Figure 17.15).[77,81] Inclusion of the data for ofloxacin indicates that a quinolone may be as cost-effective as co-trimoxazole when all costs are considered (Figure 17.15). However, this study is based on two separate trials and the cost-effectiveness of quinolones is sensitive to other aspects of patient management, including the laboratory tests performed. Nonetheless, some firm conclusions may be drawn from this study. The first is that drug costs make up only a fraction of the total cost of healthcare, even for the management of simple infections in the community. The second is that the results of *in vitro* sensitivity testing of bacteria isolated from urine samples should not be interpreted too literally. For first-generation cephalosporins in particular, clinical outcomes are consistently poorer than would be predicted from *in vitro*

Table 17.14. Comparison of healthcare costs in the USA and the UK relevant to the management of cystitis. Data from the USA were taken from reference 77 and divided by 1.5 to convert US$ to £. The ranges of costs in the UK were taken from reference 81. The conservative estimate of a visit to the doctor in the UK is based on an analysis of the marginal cost of seeing one extra patient in a health centre. The maximum estimated cost of a visit to the doctor in the UK is based on the British Medical Association scale of hourly rates for physicians' time in primary care, and assumes that 20% of patients are seen in their own home, rather than the health centre.

Cost	USA cost (£)	Conservative estimate of UK cost (£)	Maximum estimate of UK cost (£)
Office visit/consultation with general practitioner	44.83	7.50	33.00
Urine culture and sensitivity testing	21.83	5.00	20.00
Wet-mount and potassium hydroxide evaluation of vaginal fluid/vaginal swab	9.33	5.00	20.00
Urine dipstick	4.33	No equivalent	
Cost of ciprofloxacin for recurrent cystitis (250 mg b.d. × 3 days for USA and conservative UK; 500 mg b.d. × 7 days for maximum UK)	10.07	4.50	19.25
Cost of first visit (excluding cost of antibiotic prescribed)	49.20	7.50	33.00
Cost of recurrent cystitis (including treatment with ciprofloxacin)	81.17	17.00	72.25
Cost of vaginal candidiasis	67.79	12.64	60.12

tests, even when these include identification and substrate characterisation of β-lactamases.[90] In the trial by Hooton *et al.*,[77] the initial results of cefadroxil therapy were good: none of the 37 patients treated had persistent symptoms or bacteriuria 1–3 days after completing treatment, whereas early treatment failure was common with nitrofurantoin (6 of 38 patients; 16%) and amoxycillin (6 of 43 patients; 14%). Problems with cefadroxil only emerged at 2- and 6-week follow-up visits, when 11 women had a recurrence of cystitis and 12 had vaginal candidiasis. Co-trimoxazole treatment significantly reduced vaginal colonisation by *Escherichia coli* compared with the other drugs ($p < 0.001$), and the authors speculated that this may be an important factor in determining the treatment outcome of cystitis.[77]

Whatever the mechanism, the response to rising rates of trimethoprim resistance should not necessarily be a rush to prescribe cephalosporins or nitrofurantoin. More trials are needed to define the relationship between *in vitro* susceptibility testing and clinical outcome. Most trials performed for drug registration do not help to address this issue because they exclude patients with drug-resistant bacteria.

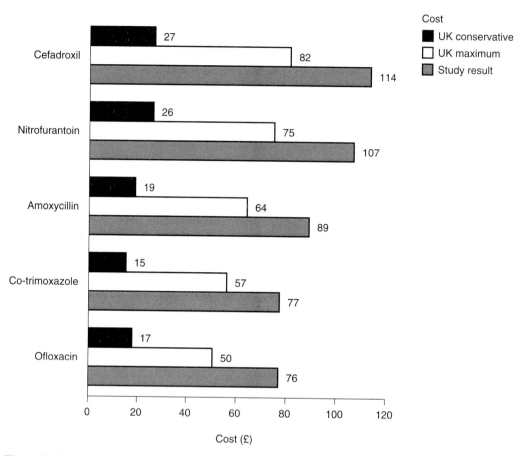

Figure 17.15. Expected average total healthcare cost per woman treated for cystitis.[77,81]

Prophylaxis of infections with oral quinolones

Oral quinolone prophylaxis has been used in two different strategies: short-term (often single-dose) regimens for the prevention of post-operative infection and long-term prevention of Gram-negative infections, for example in neutropenic patients or in individuals with indwelling catheters.

Short-term surgical prophylaxis

In a review of prophylactic quinolone use in 1993, Dellamonica and Bernard[95] commented that the role of these drugs remained undefined because there were few randomised, controlled trials, the numbers of patients in each trial were low, and the cost-effectiveness of prophylaxis had not been measured. Most of the published trials at that time involved intravenous quinolone formulations. More recent trials with oral ciprofloxacin have addressed these deficiencies.

Oral ciprofloxacin has been used as prophylaxis for colorectal surgery. One trial[96] compared ciprofloxacin, 750 mg at 1, 2 and 3 hours preoperatively in addition to intravenous metronidazole, 500 mg every 8 hours for 3 days. There were no differences in outcome between patients on the ciprofloxacin regimens. In addition, a lower wound infection rate was found with oral ciprofloxacin compared with historical controls who received gentamicin.

Table 17.15. Trials of surgical prophylaxis with ciprofloxacin that have shown a difference in outcome versus the comparator and that allow cost-effectiveness analysis. Odds ratios have been calculated for ciprofloxacin and its comparator.

Study	Regimen		Regimen costs (£)		Outcomes	Odds ratio (95% CI)	Cost-effectiveness
	Ciprofloxacin	Comparator	Ciprofloxacin	Comparator			
Colorectal surgery[97]	Piperacillin, 4000 mg i.v.; ciprofloxacin, 1000 mg p.o. (n = 159)	Piperacillin, 4000 mg i.v. (n = 168)	13.68	10.93	Wound infection Total infective morbidity Death	0.55 (0.29–1.04) 0.35 (0.20–0.60) 0.21 (0.02–1.79)	£15 per major infection prevented by ciprofloxacin
Colorectal surgery[98]	Ciprofloxacin, 1000 mg p.o. + metronidazole, 1500 mg i.v. (n = 41) or Ciprofloxacin, 4000 mg p.o. + metronidazole, 4500 mg i.v. (n = 44)	Gentamicin, 280 mg i.v. + metronidazole, 1500 mg i.v. (n = 47) or Gentamicin, 760 mg i.v. + metronidazole, 4500 mg i.v. (n = 44)	1 day 4.24 3 days 21.28	1 day 7.76 3 days 20.12	Wound infection Respiratory infection 30-day mortality (Results for 1- and 3-day regimens have been combined)	0.37 (0.15–0.89) 0.22 (0.08–0.62) 0.25 (0.05–1.21)	Ciprofloxacin dominant for 1-day regimen; £9 per wound infection prevented for 3-day regimen
Prostatic biopsy[99]	Ciprofloxacin, 500 mg p.o. (n = 28)	Gentamicin, 1.5 mg/kg i.v. (120 mg assumed; n = 27)	1.40	2.37	Bacteraemia	0.13 (0.03–0.67)	Ciprofloxacin dominant

These preliminary results are consistent with those of two prospective, randomised, controlled clinical trials (Table 17.15).[97–99] In one trial, oral ciprofloxacin was given in addition to intravenous piperacillin,[97] whereas in the other it was substituted for intravenous gentamicin.[98] In both trials, the odds ratio for wound/intra-abdominal infection was significantly reduced by the ciprofloxacin regimen. Moreover, both trials showed a marked trend towards reduced mortality in the ciprofloxacin group. This result is consistent with earlier placebo-controlled trials in which prophylaxis reduced mortality as well as wound infection.[100]

There is continuing debate about the relative merits of systemic antibiotic prophylaxis versus oral non-absorbable antibiotics versus both for preventing infection after colorectal surgery. The results of these two trials[97,98] suggest that administration of oral ciprofloxacin enhances systemic prophylaxis with piperacillin and is more effective than systemic prophylaxis with gentamicin. It is conceivable that oral ciprofloxacin achieves both selective decontamination of the colon and effective systemic prophylaxis. Whatever the mechanism, ciprofloxacin is likely to be dominant over existing regimens or highly cost-effective (infections after colorectal surgery increase hospital costs by thousands of pounds).[101–104]

Roach et al.[99] showed that oral ciprofloxacin was more effective and less expensive than intravenous gentamicin in preventing bacteraemia after prostatic biopsy, and was therefore dominant (Table 17.15). Other trials suggest that oral ciprofloxacin is as effective and less expensive than intravenous cefuroxime for prophylaxis in patients undergoing gastroduodenal surgery[105] or endoscopic retrograde cholangio-pancreatography.[106]

Overall, these results suggest a promising role for oral quinolones in surgical prophylaxis. They are likely to be less expensive than most intravenous prophylactic regimens and the possibility that they combine the features of systemic prophylaxis with selective decontamination of the colon merits further investigation.

Long-term prophylaxis with quinolones

Despite the large number of comparative clinical trials that have been conducted in neutropenic patients, the use of prophylactic quinolones remains controversial.[107] Few placebo-controlled trials have taken place and the optimal regimens for prophylaxis remain to be demonstrated. Prevention of Gram-negative bacteraemia is the most commonly used endpoint, and some evidence from comparative trials indicates that quinolones achieve this more effectively than either co-trimoxazole or colistin.[107] Moreover, quinolones are generally better tolerated than co-trimoxazole or colistin.[108] However, there is evidence that co-trimoxazole and colistin may be superior in other respects. In a large, randomised prospective trial, 230 leukaemic patients received either ciprofloxacin or co-trimoxazole plus colistin.[109] Bacteraemia caused by resistant, Gram-negative rods occurred only in the co-trimoxazole–colistin group. However, patients in the ciprofloxacin group fared less well according to a number of other potentially important outcome measures. For example, compared with the ciprofloxacin group, the co-trimoxazole–colistin group contained more patients without infective complications (31% versus 18%, $p = 0.02$), with fewer febrile days (mean 5.9 versus 8.2, $p = 0.02$) and with a lower proportion of infective events (0.9 versus 1.2, $p = 0.005$), and fever occurred later (median 19 days versus 14 days, $p < 0.05$). The authors concluded that the choice of prophylaxis depended on whether patients required protection against Gram-negative infection or better systemic prophylaxis overall.

From the perspective of this review, the major problem with all trials of prophylaxis in neutropenic patients is that they rely on intermediate or surrogate outcome measures. Inclusion of information on healthcare resource utilisation, mortality and morbidity (quality of life) might clarify the relative merits of alternative regimens and the overall benefits of prophylaxis.

There has always been concern that prophylaxis might select drug-resistant bacteria. One recent report suggests that this may be occurring.[110] Among 35 episodes of *Escherichia coli* bacteraemia, 13 (37%) strains were found to be resistant to ciprofloxacin and norfloxacin. These were all isolated from patients who had been administered prophylactic norfloxacin, whereas only 1 of 22 (5%) patients with bacteraemia due to quinolone-susceptible strains had received norfloxacin. This is further evidence that patients who have received quinolones are at greater risk of infection with quinolone-resistant strains.[111] The problem is greatest in areas with a high prevalence of quinolone-resistant strains in the community; patients probably arrive in hospital with these strains that are then selected by prophylaxis.[112] Strains may also spread between patients in hospital.[111] Whatever the mechanism, this problem adds further complexity to the use of prophylaxis in neutropenic patients. It is astonishing that after decades of trials, the overall benefits and limitations of prophylaxis remain unclear.[112]

Quinolones have been used for prophylaxis in patients with catheter-associated UTI. In a placebo-controlled trial, surgical patients scheduled to have urinary catheters in place for 3–14 days postoperatively were randomised to receive either placebo or ciprofloxacin, 250 mg daily or 1000 mg daily. There was no difference in outcome for patients receiving ciprofloxacin regimens. Patients receiving placebo had a higher prevalence of symptomatic UTI (20% compared with 5% for those given ciprofloxacin), and Van der Wall *et al.* concluded that only 7 patients needed to be treated to prevent 1 from having infectious morbidity.[113] However, they provided little information to help the reader understand the potential economic consequences of 'infectious morbidity'. For example, only 8 of 12 (67%) patients with symptomatic UTI in the placebo group were treated with antibiotics, so the economic consequences of the remaining four, unrelated infections may have been minimal. The reduction in risk of receiving treatment for UTI was more modest (14.0 to 5.5%). The median duration of catheterisation was 7 days. Assuming a cost of £0.70 per day for the 250

mg ciprofloxacin regimen, the median cost of ciprofloxacin would be £4.90. Therefore, for every 100 patients treated, the cost is £490 and eight UTIs may be prevented at a cost of £61 per infection prevented (£490/8). This is above the cost of antibiotics that would be prescribed in Ninewells Hospital, Dundee, to treat such an infection.

The benefits of preventing catheter-associated UTI depend on the costs of managing the condition, which may be high (> US$500) in some USA hospitals.[114] As with prophylaxis in neutropenic patients, it is hard to assess the economic benefit of prevention of catheter-associated UTI without information on the consequences of infection and the overall impact of prophylaxis on healthcare costs and patient well-being.

Conclusions

In conclusion, there is good evidence that oral quinolones are highly effective antimicrobials which are less expensive than most intravenous regimens, particularly when the additional costs of preparation and administration of intravenous drugs are included. A study which documents savings on drugs and consumables made by switching from intravenous to oral therapy, however, is a cost comparison and not a full economic analysis. A full economic analysis must include measurement of both costs and outcomes.

The ideal of a full economic analysis has been achieved by some of the studies reviewed in this chapter. The challenge for future research is to show how quinolones can be used to improve the cost-effectiveness of management of infections in day-to-day practice, both in the community and in hospitals.

References

1. Davey PG, Malek M. Defining criteria for the pharma-co-economic evaluation of new oral cephalosporins. PharmacoEconomics 1994; 5 (Suppl 2): 11–19.

2. Finkler SA. The distinction between cost and charges. Ann Intern Med 1982; 96: 102–9.
3. Drummond MF, Stoddart GL, Torrance GW. Methods for the economic evaluation of health care programmes. Oxford: Oxford University Press, 1987.
4. Poretz DM, Woolard D, Eron LJ, Goldenberg RI, Rising J, Sparks S. Outpatient use of ceftriaxone: a cost–benefit analysis. Am J Med 1984; 77 (Suppl 4C): 77–83.
5. Davey P, Hernanz C, Lynch W, Malek M, Byrne D. Human and non-financial costs of hospital-acquired infection. J Hosp Infect 1991; 18 (Suppl A): 79–84.
6. McCue JD, Hansen C, Gal P. Hospital charges for antibiotics. Rev Infect Dis 1985; 7: 643–5.
7. Tanner DJ, Nazarian MQ. Cost containment associated with decreased parenteral antibiotic administration frequencies. Am J Med 1984; 77 (Suppl 4C): 104–10.
8. Knodel LC, Goldspiel BR, Gibbs RS. Prospective cost analysis of moxalactam versus clindamycin plus gentamicin for endomyometritis after cesarean section. Antimicrob Agents Chemother 1988; 32: 853–7.
9. Parker SE, Davey PG. Pharmacoeconomics of intravenous drug administration. PharmacoEconomics 1992; 1: 103–15.
10. Birdwell SW. Direct costs of intravenous delivery systems. PharmacoEconomics 1993; 4: 8–13.
11. Newhouse JG, Paul VM, Waugh NA, Frye CB. Reducing i.v. waste to under 2.25%. Hosp Pharm 1988; 23: 241–7.
12. Birdwell SW, Meyer GE, Scheckelhoff DJ, Giambrone CS, Iteen SA. Survey of wastage from intravenous admixture in US hospitals. PharmacoEconomics 1993; 4: 271–7.
13. Lowson K. Health economics for clinician managers. Clinician Management 1993; 2: 8–10.
14. Vacani PF, Malek MMH, Davey PG. Cost of gentamicin assays carried out by microbiology laboratories. J Clin Pathol 1993; 46: 890–5.
15. Andersen TF, Mooney G. Medical practice variations: where are we? In: Anderson TF, Mooney G, eds. The challenges of medical practice variations. Basingstoke: Macmillan, 1990: 1–15.
16. McPherson K. Why do variations occur? In: Andersen TF, Mooney G, eds. The challenges of medical practice variations. Basingstoke: Macmillan, 1990: 16–35.
17. Halls GA. The management of infections and antibiotic therapy: a European survey. J Antimicrob Chemother 1993; 31: 985–1000.
18. Davey PG, Parker SE, Malek MM. Pharmacoeconomics of antibacterial treatment. PharmacoEconomics 1992; 1: 409–37.
19. Keane D, James D. Prophylactic antibiotics at caesarean section do not reduce costs. Health Trends 1993; 25: 84–7.
20. Ford LC, Hammil HA, Lebherz TB. Cost-effective use of antibiotic prophylaxis for cesarean section. Am J Obstet Gynecol 1987; 157: 506–10.
21. Monthly Index of Medical Specialties (MIMS). London: Haymarket, Feb 1995.
22. Malek M, Lynch W, Wells N, Elliott T, Bint A, Sanderson P et al. A comparison of the costs of ceftazidime therapy and gentamicin combinations in three UK hospitals. J Antimicrob Chemother 1992; 29: 207–17.
23. Davey P, Dodd T, Kerr S, Malek M. Audit of i.v. antibiotic administration. Pharm J 1990; 30 June: 793–6.
24. Baldwin DR. Workload management system for i.v. therapy. JIN 1988; 11: 308–14.
25. Plumridge RJ. Cost comparison of intravenous antibiotic administration. Med J Aust 1990; 153: 516–18.
26. Powers T, Bingham DH. Clinical and economic effect of ciprofloxacin as an alternative to injectable antimicrobial therapy. Am J Public Health 1990; 47: 1781–4.
27. Kerr JR, Barr JG, Smyth ETM. Computerised calculation of the true costs of antibiotic therapy. Eur J Microbiol Infect Dis 1993; 12: 622–5.
28. Kumana CR, Kou M, Wong BCY, Lee PW, Li KY. Drug audit in Hong Kong with special reference to antibiotics. J Hong Kong Med Assoc 1993; 45: 177–80.
29. Kerr JR, Barr JG, Smyth ETM, O'Hare J. Technique for calculation of the true costs of antibiotic therapy. Eur J Clin Microbiol Infect Dis 1992; 11: 823–7.
30. Rapp RP, Bannon CL, Bivins BA. The influence of dose frequency and agent toxicity on the cost of parenteral antibiotic therapy. Drug intelligence and clinical pharmacy. Ann Pharmacother 1982; 16: 935–8.
31. Quintilliani R, Cooper BW, Briceland LL, Nightingale CH. Economic impact of streamlining antibiotic administration. Am J Med 1987; 82 (Suppl 4A): 391–4.
32. Hodson ME, Roberts CM, Butland RJA, Smith MJ, Batten JC. Oral ciprofloxacin compared with conventional intravenous treatment for *Pseudomonas aeruginosa* infection in adults with cystic fibrosis. Lancet 1987; I(8527): 235–7.
33. Bosso JA, Black PG, Matsen JM. Ciprofloxacin versus tobramycin plus azlocillin in pulmonary exacerbations in adult patients with cystic fibrosis. Am J Med 1987; 82 (Suppl 4A): 180–4.
34. Strandvik B, Hjelte L, Lindblad A, Ljungberg B, Malmborg A, Nilsson-Ehle I. Comparison of efficacy and tolerance of intravenously and orally administered ciprofloxacin in cystic fibrosis patients with acute exacerbations of lung infection. Scand J Infect Dis 1989; 60: 84–8.
35. Fass RJ. Efficacy and safety of oral ciprofloxacin in the treatment of serious respiratory infections. Am J Med 1987; 82 (Suppl 4A): 202–7.
36. Sanders WE, Alessi P, Morris JF, Makris AT, McCloskey RV, Trenholme GM et al. Oral ofloxacin for the treatment of acute bacterial pneumonia: use of a nontraditional protocol to compare experimental therapy with 'usual care' in a multicenter clinical trial. Am J Med 1991; 91: 261–6.

37. Peloquin CA, Cumbo TJ, Schentag JJ. Kinetics and dynamics of tobramycin action in patients with bacteriuria given single doses. Antimicrob Agents Chemother 1991; 35: 1191–5.

38. Nix DE, Cumbo TJ, Kuritzky P, Devito JM, Schentag JJ. Oral ciprofloxacin in the treatment of serious soft tissue and bone infections. Am J Med 1987; 82 (Suppl 4A): 146–53.

39. Greenberg RN, Tice AD, Marsh PK, Craven PC, Reilly PM, Bollinger M et al. Randomised trial of ciprofloxacin compared with other antimicrobial therapy in the treatment of osteomyelitis. Am J Med 1987; 82 (Suppl 4A): 266–9.

40. Gentry LO, Rodriguez GG. Oral ciprofloxacin compared with parenteral antibiotics in the treatment of osteomyelitis. Antimicrob Agents Chemother 1990; 34: 40–3.

41. Mader JT, Cantrell JS, Calhoun J, Texas G. Oral ciprofloxacin compared with standard parenteral antibiotic therapy for chronic osteomyelitis in adults. J Bone Joint Surg 1990; 72A: 104–10.

42. Dan M, Siegman-Igra Y, Pitlik S, Raz R. Oral ciprofloxacin treatment of Pseudomonas aeruginosa osteomyelitis. Antimicrob Agents Chemother 1990; 34: 849–52.

43. Gentry LO, Rodriguez G. Ofloxacin versus parenteral therapy for chronic osteomyelitis. Antimicrob Agents Chemother 1991; 35: 538–41.

44. Drancourt M, Stein A, Argenson JN, Zannier A, Curvale G, Raoult D. Oral rifampin plus ofloxacin for treatment of Staphylococcus-infected orthopedic implants. Antimicrob Agents Chemother 1993; 37: 1214–18.

45. Fleming LW, Moreland TA, Scott AC, Stewart WK, White LD. Ciprofloxacin in plasma and peritoneal dialysate after oral therapy in patients on continuous ambulatory peritoneal dialysis. J Antimicrob Chemother 1987; 19: 493–503.

46. Cooke J, Cairns CJ, Tillotson GS, Conner S, Lewin SKM, Nicholls J et al. Comparative clinical, microbiologic, and economic audit of the use of oral ciprofloxacin and parenteral antimicrobials. Ann Pharmacother 1993; 27: 785–9.

47. Ramirez-Ronda C, Colon M, Saavedra S, Sabbaj J, Corrado ML. Treatment of urinary tract infection with norfloxacin: analysis of cost. Am J Med 1987; 82 (Suppl 6B): 75–87.

48. Scheife RT, Cox CE, McCabe RE, Grad C. Norfloxacin versus best parenteral therapy in treatment of moderate to serious, multiply-resistant, nosocomial urinary tract infections: a pharmacoeconomic analysis. Urology 1988; XXXII (Suppl 3): 24–30.

49. Davey PG, South R, Malek M. Impact of glycopeptide therapy after hospital discharge on inpatient costs: a comparison of teicoplanin and vancomycin. J Antimicrob Chemother 1996; 37: 623–34.

50. Grasela TH, Paladino JA, Schentag JJ, Huepenbecker D, Rybacki J, Purcell JB et al.

51. Davey PG, Parker SE, Orange G, Malek M, Dodd T. Prospective audit of costs and outcome of aminoglycoside treatment and of therapy for Gram-negative bacteraemia. J Antimicrob Chemother 1995; 36: 561–75.

52. Shulkin DJ, Kinosian B, Glick H, Glen-Puschett C, Daly J, Eisenberg JM. The economic impact of infections: an analysis of hospital costs and charges in surgical patients with cancer. Arch Surg 1993; 128: 449–52.

53. Gorbach SL. A funny thing happened... Infect Dis Clin Pract 1994; 3: 49–51.

54. Smith MD, Duong NM, Hoa NTT, Wain J, Ha HD, Diep TS et al. Comparison of ofloxacin and ceftriaxone for short-course treatment of enteric fever. Antimicrob Agents Chemother 1994; 38: 1716–20.

55. Allen B, Naismith NW, Manser AJ, Moulds RFW. A campaign to improve the timing of conversion from intravenous to oral administration of antibiotics. Aust J Hosp Pharm 1992; 22: 434–9.

56. Frighetto L, Nickoloff D, Martinusen SM, Jewesson PJ, Mamdani FS. Intravenous-to-oral stepdown program: four years of experience in a large teaching hospital. Ann Pharmacother 1992; 26: 1447–51.

57. Wachter RM, Luce JM, Safrin S, Berrios DC, Charlebois E, Scitovsky AA. Cost and outcome of intensive care for patients with AIDS, Pneumocystis carinii pneumonia, and severe respiratory failure. J Am Med Assoc 1995; 273: 230–5.

58. Barriere SL. Economic impact of oral ciprofloxacin: a pharmacist's perspective. Am J Med 1987; 82 (Suppl 4A): 387–90.

59. Pilley G. Cost comparison of ciprofloxacin versus cefamandole. Ann Pharmacother 1989; 23: 92–3.

60. Frieden TR, Mangi RJ. Inappropriate use of oral ciprofloxacin. J Am Med Assoc 1990; 264: 1438–40.

61. Adu A, Donovan B, Newgham C, Armour C. Ciprofloxacin usage in a community hospital. Aust J Hosp Pharm 1994; 24: 318–22.

62. Pickering T, Gurwitz JH, Zaleznik D, Noonan JP, Avorn J. The appropriateness of oral fluoroquinolone-prescribing in the long-term care setting. Am Geriatr Soc 1994; 42: 28–32.

63. Speirs GE, Fenelon LE, Reeves DS, Speller DCE, Smyth EG, Wilcox MH et al. An audit of ciprofloxacin use in a district general hospital. J Antimicrob Chemother 1995; 36: 201–7.

64. Forrest A, Ballow CH, Nix DE, Birmingham MC, Schentag JJ. Development of a population pharmacokinetic model and optimal sampling strategies for intravenous ciprofloxacin. Antimicrob Agents Chemother 1993; 37: 1065–72.

65. Forrest A, Nix DE, Ballow CH, Goss TF, Birmingham MC, Schentag JJ. Pharmacodynamics of intravenous

ciprofloxacin in seriously ill patients. Antimicrob Agents Chemother 1993; 37: 1073–81.

66. Xue I, Davey PG. Comparative pharmacodynamics of ciprofloxacin and ofloxacin; a method for estimating equivalent doses. 2nd Biennial Conference of Federation of Infection Societies, Manchester, UK, 1995: Abstract P11.8.

67. From official published prices in national drug lists. Data on file, Bayer AG.

68. Solomkin JS, Reinhart HH, Dellinger EP, Bohnen JM, Rotstein OD, Vogel SB et al. Results of a randomized trial comparing sequential intravenous oral treatment with ciprofloxacin plus metronidazole to imipenem/cilastatin for intra-abdominal infections. Ann Surg 1996; 223: 303–15.

69. Cohn SM, Cohn KA, Rafferty MJ, Smith AH, Degutis LC, Kowalsky SF et al. Enteric absorption of ciprofloxacin during the immediate postoperative period. J Antimicrob Chemother 1995; 36: 717–21.

70. Kreling DH, Mott DA. The cost effectiveness of drug utilisation review in an outpatient setting. PharmacoEconomics 1993; 4: 414–36.

71. Fink MP, Snydman DR, Niederman MS, Leeper KV, Johnson RH, Heard SO et al. Treatment of severe pneumonia in hospitalised patients: results of a multicenter, randomized, double-blind trial comparing intravenous ciprofloxacin with imipenem-cilastatin. Antimicrob Agents Chemother 1995; 38: 547–57.

72. Graham E, Whalen E, Smith EM, Block AL, Schentag JJ. Comparison of the costs between ciprofloxacin and imipenem for the treatment of severe pneumonia in hospitalized patients. Pharmacother 1994; 14: 370–1.

73. Caldwell J, Singh S, Johnson R. Pattern of subsequent infection and antibiotic use following initial treatment with ciprofloxacin versus imipenem for nosocomial pneumonia. 34th Interscience Congress of Antimicrobial Agents and Chemotherapy, Orlando, USA, 1994; Abstract M49.

74. American Thoracic Society. A consensus statement. Hospital-acquired pneumonia in adults: diagnosis, assessment of severity, initial antimicrobial therapy, and preventative strategies. Am J Respir Crit Care Med 1995; 153: 1711–25.

75. Kappstein I, Schulgen G, Beyer U, Geiger K, Schumacher M, Daschner FD. Prolongation of hospital stay and extra costs due to ventilator-associated pneumonia in an intensive care unit. Eur J Clin Microbiol Infect Dis 1992; 11: 504–8.

76. Brennan P, Croft P. Interpreting the results of observational research: chance is not such a fine thing. BMJ 1994; 309: 727–30.

77. Hooton TM, Winter C, Tiu F, Stamm WE. Randomized comparative trial and cost analysis of 3-day antimicrobial regimens for treatment of acute cystitis in women. J Am Med Assoc 1995; 273: 41–5.

78. Moss F, McNicol MW, McSwiggan DA, Miller DL. Survey of antibiotic prescribing in a district general

hospital II. Lower respiratory tract infection. Lancet 1981; ii: 407–9.

79. Isaacs D, Wilkinson AR, Moxon ER. Duration of antibiotic courses for neonates. Arch Dis Child 1987; 62: 727–8.

80. Narendranathan M, Geroge TP. Chloramphenicol and ciprofloxacin in enteric fever cost-effectiveness. J Assoc Physicians India 1992; 40: 176–8.

81. Davey P, Rutherford D, Graham B, Lynch W, Malek M. Repeat consultations after antibiotic prescribing for respiratory infection in one general practice. Br J Gen Pract 1994; 44: 509–13.

82. Soumerai SB, Ross-Degnan D, Avorn J, McLaughlin TJ, Choodnovskiy I. Effects of Medicaid drug-payment limits on admission to hospitals and nursing homes. N Engl J Med 1991; 325: 1072–7.

83. Soumerai SB, McLaughlin TJ, Ross-Degnan D. Effects of limiting Medicaid drug-reimbursement benefits on the use of psychotropic agents and acute mental health services by patients with schizophrenia. N Engl J Med 1994; 331: 650–5.

84. MacDonald TM, Collins D, McGilchrist MM, Stevens J, McKendrick AD, McDevitt DG et al. The utilisation and economic evaluation of antibiotics prescribed in primary care. J Antimicrob Chemother 1995; 35: 191–204.

85. Sanders WE. Efficacy, safety and potential economic benefits of oral ciprofloxacin in the treatment of infections. Rev Infect Dis 1988; 10: 528–42.

86. Hooton TM, Johnson C, Winter C, Kuwamura L, Rogers ME, Roberts PL et al. Single-dose and three-day regimens of ofloxacin versus trimethoprim–sulfamethoxazole for acute cystitis in women. Antimicrob Agents Chemother 1991; 35: 1479–83.

87. Cheung R, Sullens CM, Seal D, Dickins J, Nicholson PW, Desmukh AA et al. The paradox of using a 7 day antibacterial course to treat urinary tract infections in the community. Br J Clin Pharmacol 1988; 26: 391–8.

88. Kasanen A, Hajba A, Junnila SYT, Sundquist H. Comparative study of trimethoprim and cephalexin in urinary tract infection. Curr Ther Res 1981; 29: 477–85.

89. Bradley C. Learning to say no to requests for prescriptions. Prescriber 1995; 6: 53–5.

90. Brauner A, Dornbursch K, Hallander HO. Beta-lactamase production by strains of Escherichia coli of intermediate susceptibility to beta-lactam antibiotics – a study of their clinical significance in urinary tract infection. Scand J Infect Dis 1978; Suppl 13: 67–72.

91. Mayon-White RT. The clinical impact of pneumococcal disease and strategies for its prevention. Internat Congr Symp Series 1995; 210: 1–72.

92. MacDonald TM, Beardon PHG, McGilchrist MM, Duncan ID, McKendrick AD, McDevitt DG. The risks of symptomatic vaginal candidiasis after oral antibiotic therapy. Q J Med 1993; 86: 419–24.

93. Green SM. Acute pharyngitis: the case for empiric antimicrobial therapy. Ann Emerg Med 1995; 25: 404–6.

94. Pichichero ME. Group A streptococcal tonsillopharyngitis: cost-effective diagnosis and treatment. Ann Emerg Med 1995; 25: 390–403.

95. Dellamonica P, Bernard E. Fluoroquinolones and surgical prophylaxis. Drugs 1993; 45 (Suppl 3):102–13.

96. Rohwedder R, Bonadeo F, Benati M, Quintana GO, Schlecker H, Vaccaro C. Single dose oral ciprofloxacin plus parenteral metronidazole for perioperative antibiotic prophylaxis in colorectal surgery. Chemotherapy 1993; 39: 218–24.

97. Taylor EW, Lindsay G. Selective decontamination of the colon before elective colorectal surgery. World J Surg 1994; 18: 926–32.

98. McArdle CS, Morran CG, Pettit L, Gemmell CG, Sleigh JD, Tillotson GS. Value of oral antibiotic prophylaxis in colorectal surgery. Br J Surg 1995; 82: 1046–8.

99. Roach MB, George WJ, Figueroa TE, Neal DE, McBride D. Ciprofloxacin versus gentamicin in prophylaxis against bacteremia in transrectal prostate needle biopsy. Urology 1991; 38: 84–7.

100. Baum ML, Anish DS, Chalmer TC, Sacks HS, Smith H, Fagerstrom RM. A survey of clinical trials of antibiotic prophylaxis in colon surgery: evidence against further use of no-treatment controls. N Engl J Med 1981; 305: 795–9.

101. Edwards LD. The epidemiology of 2056 remote site infections and 1966 surgical wound infections occurring in 1865 patients: a four year study of 40,923 operations at Rush-Presbyterian-St Luke's Hospital, Chicago. Ann Surg 1976; 184: 758–66.

102. Lynch W, Malek M, Davey PG, Byrne DJ, Napier A. Costing wound infection in a Scottish hospital. PharmacoEconomics 1992; 2: 163–70.

103. Davey PG, Lynch W, Malek MM, Byrne DJ, Thomas, P. Cost-effectiveness of single dose cefotaxime plus metronidazole compared with three doses each of cefuroxime plus metronidazole for the prevention of wound infection after colorectal surgery. J Antimicrob Chemother 1992; 30: 855–64.

104. Coello R, Glenister H, Fereres J, Bartlett C, Leigh D, Sedgwick J et al. The cost of infection in surgical patients: a case-control study. J Hosp Infect 1993; 25: 239–50.

105. McArdle CS, Morran CG, Anderson JR, Pettit L, Gemmell CG, Sleigh JD et al. Oral ciprofloxacin as prophylaxis in gastroduodenal surgery. J Hosp Infect 1995; 30: 211–16.

106. Mehal WZ, Culshaw KD, Tillotson GS, Chapman RW. Antibiotic prophylaxis for ERCP: a randomised clinical trial comparing ciprofloxacin and cefuroxime in 200 patients at high risk of cholangitis. Eur J Gastroenterol Hepatol 1995; 7: 841–5.

107. Zinner SH. Prophylactic uses of fluoroquinolone antibiotics. Infect Dis Clin Pract 1995; 3 (Suppl 3): S203–10.

108. Rubinstein E, Potgieter P, Davey P, Norrby SR. Review. The use of fluoroquinolones in neutropenic patients – analysis of adverse effects. J Antimicrob Chemother 1994; 34: 7–19.

109. Donnelly JP, Maschmeyer G, Daenen S, and EORTC-Gnotobiotic Project Group. Selective oral antimicrobial prophylaxis for the prevention of infection in acute leukaemia – ciprofloxacin versus co-trimoxazole plus colistin. Eur J Cancer 1992; 28A: 873–8.

110. Carratala J, Fernandez-Sevilla A, Tubau F, Callis M, Gudiol F. Emergence of quinolone-resistant *Escherichia coli* bacteremia in neutropenic patients with cancer who have received prophylactic norfloxacin. Clin Infect Dis 1995; 20: 557–60.

111. Richard P, Delangle M, Merrien D, Barille S, Reynaud A, Minozzi C et al. Fluoroquinolone use and fluoroquinolone resistance: is there an association? Clin Infect Dis 1994; 19: 54–9.

112. Ball P. Editorial response: is resistant *Escherichia coli* bacteremia an inevitable outcome for neutropenic patients receiving a fluoroquinolone as prophylaxis? Clin Infect Dis 1995; 20: 561–3.

113. Van der Wall E, Verkooyen RP, Mintjes-de Groot J, Ostinga J, Van Dijk A, Hustinx WNM et al. Prophylactic ciprofloxacin for catheter-associated urinary-tract infection. Lancet 1992; 339: 946–51.

114. Platt R, Polk BF, Murdock B, Rosner B. Prevention of catheter-associated urinary tract infection: a cost–benefit analysis. Infect Control Hosp Epidemiol 1989; 10: 60–4.

Chapter 18

Intracellular infections

Quinolones penetrate easily into cells and their concentrations within phagocytes correlate with those in the extracellular space. The ratio between intracellular and extracellular concentrations of quinolones varies *in vitro*, being 6.9–8.1 in human alveolar macrophages, 2.0–4.6 in human polymorphonuclear leucocytes and 5.0–11.9 in guinea-pig peritoneal macrophages.[1] Intracellular concentrations of ciprofloxacin are 6–7 times greater than the corresponding extracellular concentrations.[2] The intracellular bactericidal activity of quinolones has been reported for *Staphylococcus aureus*, *Legionella* spp., *Mycobacterium fortuitum* and *Salmonella* spp.[3] These penetration, concentration and distribution characteristics have confirmed the usefulness of ciprofloxacin in some infections, for example, tuberculosis, *Mycobacterium avium–intracellulare* complex infection, enteric fever and legionellosis (see Chapters 8 and 13), and its potential efficacy in others, such as Q fever. Ciprofloxacin is not reliably effective in the treatment of chlamydial urethritis.

Respiratory pathogens

Three intracellular pathogens, *Legionella* spp., *Chlamydia pneumoniae* and *Mycoplasma pneumoniae*, are responsible for 15% of cases of community-acquired pneumonia.[1] *Legionella* spp. are often susceptible to ciprofloxacin at low concentrations (minimum inhibitory concentration, MIC 0.06–0.5 mg/litre),[4] but the drug is less active against *Mycoplasma* spp. (MIC 2.0–8.0 mg/litre).[5] The activity of ciprofloxacin against *Chlamydia pneumoniae* falls between these values (MIC 1.0 mg/litre).[6] Penetration into the lung is sufficient to exceed the MIC for *Legionella* spp. and *Chlamydia pneumoniae*. At an oral dose of 500 mg every 12 hours, the concentration of ciprofloxacin in the bronchial mucosa is 4.4 mg/kg.[7] The minimum extracellular concentration of ciprofloxacin able to inhibit the intracellular multiplication of *Legionella pneumophila* is between 0.001 and 0.03 mg/litre, 3.8-fold less than the MIC.[8,9] In clinical studies, ciprofloxacin eradicated effectively *Legionella* infection in 8 of 10 patients[10] and cured all 50 patients with atypical pneumonia caused by *Mycoplasma pneumoniae* or *Chlamydia psittaci*[11] (see Chapter 8).

Another intracellular respiratory pathogen, *Coxiella burnetii*, is effectively inhibited by ciprofloxacin. In fibroblast culture exposed to the organism, 5 mg/litre of ciprofloxacin reduced the proportion of infected cells from 92% to 2% over 10 days.[12] Isolates implicated in both acute and chronic forms of *Coxiella burnetii* infection (*Nine Mile* and *Priscilla* strains) are inhibited by ciprofloxacin (5 mg/litre), the number of infected cells being reduced from 92% to 1% and from 88% to 23%, respectively. If rifampicin is given with ciprofloxacin, synergy between the drugs reduces the infected cell count by 91%.[13] Clinical assessment of ciprofloxacin alone is awaited.

Wilson APR and Grüneberg RN.
Ciprofloxacin: 10 years of clinical experience
© 1997 Maxim Medical, Oxford.

Intracellular activity is an important indicator for the use of ciprofloxacin in mycobacterial disease (see Chapter 8).

Brucellosis

Brucella spp. are facultative intracellular parasites. They are susceptible to ciprofloxacin. In a study, 16 patients with brucellosis were treated with oral ciprofloxacin (750 mg every 8 hours) for 6–12 weeks.[14] All patients responded clinically but bacteraemia continued in one individual. Another four patients had a recurrence of symptoms in 8–32 weeks, suggesting that ciprofloxacin needs to be used in combination with other antibiotics.

Tularaemia

Tularaemia is a disease of protracted fever, chills, malaise and painful lymphadenopathy at the site of infection. There may be a skin ulcer, purulent conjunctivitis or tonsillitis. The causative organism, *Francisella tularensis*, is a small, Gram-negative bacterium and an intracellular parasite, being taken up by macrophages. Rabbits, hares, ticks and muskrats are its usual reservoir, and infection is acquired by bites, aerosol inhalation, contact with body fluids or ingestion of contaminated food or water. The drug of choice is usually streptomycin.

In one study, five patients with acute tularaemia were treated with 400–750 mg of ciprofloxacin every 12 hours for 10 days.[15] In each case, fever resolved within 2 days, and after 1 week most symptoms had settled. The speed of response was similar to that seen after streptomycin treatment, but ciprofloxacin could be administered at home. Ciprofloxacin has also been used in a veterinary surgeon who acquired tularaemia from a cat.[16] Fever recurred, despite a month of treatment with amoxycillin followed by doxycycline. After a 2-week course of ciprofloxacin (750 mg every

12 hours) the patient recovered completely without relapse.

Conclusions

Unlike many antibiotics, ciprofloxacin is effective in eradicating intracellular pathogens. This property explains its efficacy in diseases such as legionellosis and tuberculosis. Brucellosis responds to treatment with ciprofloxacin (750 mg every 8 hours for 6–12 weeks) but combination regimens are advisable. Tularaemia can be treated with an oral course (750 mg every 12 hours) for 10 days. Ciprofloxacin has not, however, been adequately assessed in many of the less common intracellular infections in which it is likely to be active.

References

1. Chidiac C, Mouton Y. Quinolones in the treatment of lower respiratory tract infections caused by intracellular pathogens. Infection 1991; 19 (Suppl 7): S365–71.
2. Easmon CSF, Crane JP. Uptake of ciprofloxacin by human neutrophils. J Antimicrob Chemother 1985; 16: 67–73.
3. Easmon CSF, Crane JP, Blowers A. Effect of ciprofloxacin on intracellular organisms: *in vitro* and *in vivo* studies. J Antimicrob Chemother 1986; 18 (Suppl D); 43–8.
4. Ruckdeschel G, Ehret W, Ahl A. Susceptibility of *Legionella* spp. to quinolone derivatives and related organic acids. Eur J Clin Microbiol 1984; 3: 373.
5. Cassell GH, Waites KB, Pate MS, Canupp KC, Duffy LB. Comparative susceptibility of *Mycoplasma pneumoniae* to erythromycin, ciprofloxacin and lomefloxacin. Diagn Microbiol Infect Dis 1989; 12: 433–5.
6. Chirgwin K, Roblin PM, Hammerschlag MR. *In vitro* susceptibilities of *Chlamydia pneumoniae* (*Chlamydia* sp. strain TWAR). Antimicrob Agents Chemother 1989; 33: 1634–5.
7. Honeybourne D, Lodwick R, Andrews JM, Ashby JP, Wise R. Assessment of the penetration of amoxycillin and ciprofloxacin into the bronchial mucosa. Thorax 1988; 43: 223P.
8. Kitsukawa K, Hara J, Saito A. Inhibition of *Legionella pneumophila* in guinea pig peritoneal macrophages by new quinolone, macrolide and other antimicrobial agents. J Antimicrob Chemother 1991; 27: 343–53.

9. Fitzgeorge RB, Featherstone ASR, Baskerville A. The effect of ofloxacin on the intracellular growth of *Legionella pneumophila* in guinea pig alveolar phagocytes. J Antimicrob Chemother 1988; 22 (Suppl C): 53–7.

10. Unertl KE, Lenhart FP, Forst H, Volger G, Wilm Y, Ehret W *et al.* Brief report: ciprofloxacin in the treatment of legionellosis in critically ill patients including those cases unresponsive to erythromycin. Am J Med 1989; 87 (Suppl 5A): 128–31.

11. Schönwald S, Petričević V, Soldo I, Škerk V. Ciprofloxacin applied in treatment of interstitial pneumonias of infectious etiology. In: Berkard B, Huemmerle HP, eds. 15th International Congress of Chemotherapy, Istanbul, Turkey, 1987: 1148–50.

12. Yeaman MR, Mitscher LA, Baca OG. *In vitro* susceptibility of *Coxiella burnetii* to antibiotics, including several quinolones. Antimicrob Agents Chemother 1987; 31: 1079–84.

13. Yeaman MR, Roman MJ, Baca OG. Antibiotic susceptibilities of two *Coxiella burnetii* isolates implicated in distinct clinical syndromes. Antimicrob Agents Chemother 1989; 33: 1052–7.

14. Al-Sibai MB, Halim MA, El-Shaker MM, Khan BA, Qadri SM. Efficacy of ciprofloxacin for treatment of *Brucella melitensis* infections. Antimicrob Agents Chemother 1992; 36: 150–2.

15. Syrjala H, Schildt R, Raisainen S. *In vitro* susceptibility of *Francisella tularensis* to fluoroquinolones and treatment of tularemia with norfloxacin and ciprofloxacin. Eur J Clin Microbiol Infect Dis 1991; 10: 68–70.

16. Scheel O, Reiersen R, Hoel T. Treatment of tularaemia with ciprofloxacin. Eur J Clin Microbiol Infect Dis 1992; 11: 447–8.

Chapter 19

Current recommended dosage regimens

For all indications, the dosage of ciprofloxacin administered should be determined by the age and weight of the patient and the severity of the infection. In most countries, ciprofloxacin is usually administered every 12 hours, though the standard regimen in Japan is 200 mg every 8 hours. While a course of treatment lasting 5–7 days is sufficient to eradicate most infections, 7–14 days of therapy are commonly given. Patients with deep-seated sepsis or prosthetic infections receive longer courses. Osteomyelitis is treated for 4–6 weeks and malignant otitis for 3 months. Uncomplicated urinary infections need not be treated for more than 3 days.

Ciprofloxacin for intravenous use is supplied in 50 ml, 100 ml or 200 ml bottles containing 100 mg, 200 mg and 400 mg, respectively, in 0.01% weight/volume lactic acid plus 0.9% weight/volume sodium chloride (15.4 mmol sodium/100 ml bottle). The infusion is administered over 30–60 minutes. Intravenous ciprofloxacin is incompatible with other solutions that are not stable at pH 3.9–4.5, penicillins and heparin, for example. It may be diluted in 0.9% sodium chloride, Ringer's solution, glucose solution (5% or 10%), glucose/saline and fructose solution (10%). Ciprofloxacin should be stored in its cardboard container as it is sensitive to light, and should not be refrigerated as crystals may form. Tablets containing 250 mg, 500 mg and 750 mg of the drug are available.

Wilson APR and Grüneberg RN.
Ciprofloxacin: 10 years of clinical experience
© 1997 Maxim Medical, Oxford.

Treatment of specific infections and prophylaxis

In the treatment of urinary tract infections, 250–500 mg, administered orally every 12 hours (or 100 mg given intravenously every 12 hours) are recommended, the higher dose being required for the treatment of complicated infections. For gonorrhoea, a single oral dose of 250–500 mg (or 100 mg given intravenously) is sufficient. Upper respiratory tract infections may be treated with a dose of 250 mg orally every 12 hours, but 750 mg every 12 hours is usual in malignant otitis externa. For lower respiratory tract infections, 250–750 mg orally every 12 hours may be used. If ciprofloxacin is used to treat pneumococcal infections, 750 mg orally every 12 hours is recommended. Parenteral treatment at 200–400 mg every 12 hours is usually adequate, and the dose needed depends on the severity of infection. In ventilated patients with proven or suspected pseudomonal pneumonia, 400 mg are given every 8 hours in the USA, but the dose interval is every 12 hours in the UK. For patients with cystic fibrosis, an oral dose of 750 mg every 12 hours (or 400 mg given intravenously every 12 hours) is administered to adults, depending on body weight. Osteomyelitis is treated with 750 mg, administered orally every 12 hours (or 200 mg given intravenously every 12 hours). Other severe staphylococcal, streptococcal or pseudomonal infections are treated with 200–400 mg, given intravenously every 12 hours (or 750 mg orally every 12 hours). Oral treatment can follow intravenous administration as the patient's condition improves.

Ciprofloxacin may be used for surgical prophylaxis as an oral dose of 750 mg 1 hour before surgery (but not within 1 hour of opiate administration) or as 200 mg, given intravenously at induction. It has been shown to be effective in colorectal, gastroduodenal, biliary (including endoscopic retrograde cholangio-pancreatography, ERCP) vascular, gynaecological and prostate surgery, metronidazole being added if infection with anaerobic organisms is likely.

Ciprofloxacin is highly effective in the eradication of pharyngeal carriage of *Neisseria meningitidis*. A single oral dose of 500 mg is sufficient therapy.[1]

Specific patient groups

Recently, clinicians have been advised not to reduce the ciprofloxacin dosage in patients with severe renal failure to avoid serum concentrations reaching subtherapeutic levels.[2] Ciprofloxacin is eliminated by the transintestinal route in these patients. The manufacturer recommends that the dose may be halved if necessary, but that the results of serum assay provide the most rational basis for any alteration in dosage. No changes in dosage are necessary in elderly patients or in those with hepatic failure.

Ciprofloxacin should not be administered to pregnant women. There is no evidence from animal studies of an effect on foetal development or abortion, but the risk from ciprofloxacin use in this group has not been formally assessed.[3] Ciprofloxacin is secreted in breast milk. It is contraindicated in patients with a history of hypersensitivity to quinolones. Caution is advised if it is used in people with a history of epilepsy and all patients should be well hydrated to avoid crystalluria. Haemolytic reactions may occur in patients with glucose-6-phosphate dehydrogenase deficiency.

Ciprofloxacin has been used with caution in children because of effects on growing cartilage in weight-bearing joints in animals. However, it appears to be well tolerated and may be given in severe infections when alternative treatment is not available (see Chapter 16).[4] The recommended dose is 5–10 mg/kg/day given intravenously or 7.5–15 mg/kg/day taken orally in two divided doses. Salmonellosis and infective exacerbation of cystic fibrosis are common indications. No paediatric oral suspension is available and further trials are needed to determine optimal dose regimens.

References

1. Gaunt PN, Lambert BE. Single dose ciprofloxacin for the eradication of pharyngeal carriage of *Neisseria meningitidis*. J Antimicrob Chemother 1988; 21: 489–96.
2. MacGowan AP, White LO, Brown NM, Lovering AM, McMullin CM, Reeves DS. Serum ciprofloxacin concentrations in patients with severe sepsis being treated with ciprofloxacin 200 mg iv bd irrespective of renal function. J Antimicrob Chemother 1994; 33: 1051–4.
3. Schluter G. Ciprofloxacin: toxicologic evaluation of additional safety data. Am J Med 1989; 87 (Suppl 5A): 37–9.
4. Schaad UB, Salam MA, Aujard Y, Dagan R, Green SDR, Peltola H *et al.* Use of fluoroquinolones in pediatrics: consensus report of an International Society of Chemotherapy commission. Pediatr Infect Dis J 1995; 14: 1–9.

Chapter 20

Stop press

Despite entering its second decade, ciprofloxacin is still the focus of a considerable research effort. During 1996, there were four major congresses at which new ciprofloxacin data were presented: 1st European Congress of Chemotherapy (Glasgow, UK), 7th International Congress of Infectious Diseases (Hong Kong), 36th Interscience Congress for Antimicrobial Agents and Chemotherapy (New Orleans, USA), and the 34th Conference of the Infectious Disease Society of America (New Orleans, USA). New relevant laboratory and clinical findings are initially presented at such conferences with the full report being published at a later date.

Laboratory and susceptibility data

Resistance

Some countries have particular problems due to a large number of companies manufacturing and marketing the agent, largely in an uncontrolled manner, or from the widespread use of the drug in the food/veterinary arena. Less controlled use of ciprofloxacin leads to the development of resistance. Rodriguez *et al*. reported a rate of 15.6% ciprofloxacin resistance (MIC ≥ 4 mg/litre) in *Escherichia coli* isolated during 1994 in Spain compared with 4.1% in 1990.[1] *Escherichia coli* causing bacteraemia were resistant to ciprofloxacin in 41 of 382 (11%) cases. Analysis of risk factors suggested that prior exposure to fluoroquinolones in patients with recurrent urinary tract infection or neutropenic patients receiving fluoroquinolone prophylaxis heightened the rate of development of resistance.

Although less dramatic, there has been an upward shift in the median MICs among some enterobacteria in the UK. Murphy *et al*. reported that 1.8% of 455 aerobic Gram-negative isolates had an MIC ≥ 4 mg/litre to ciprofloxacin, while 7.4% had an MIC ≥ 0.25– ≤ 1 mg/litre, and 88.7% of strains had an MIC < 0.25 mg/litre.[2]

Salmonella typhi isolated in India has been noted to be developing resistance to ciprofloxacin in addition to other antimicrobials, probably as the result of antibiotic misuse or poor control. Jesudason and co-workers noted that during 2 months in 1995, 14 isolates had an MIC of 0.25 mg/litre whereas in 1993, all isolates in the same 2 months were sensitive to 0.03 mg/litre ciprofloxacin.[3] The authors are requesting that a more judicious use of the drug should be encouraged.

Susceptibility data

Tillotson and Dorrian presented contrasting susceptibility data from a multicentre longitudinal survey.[4] They observed little change in susceptibility among *Escherichia coli* (99.8%), *Klebsiella* spp. (99.1%), *Proteus* spp. (99.5%), *Haemophilus influenzae*

Wilson APR and Grüneberg RN.
Ciprofloxacin: 10 years of clinical experience
© 1997 Maxim Medical, Oxford.

(99.5%), or *Moraxella catarrhalis* (100%). The activity of ciprofloxacin against *Pseudomonas aeruginosa*, however, has fallen from 98.2% in 1987 to 93.1% in 1995 (number of isolates was not stated). Similarly in Sweden, Hanberger *et al.* reported that 99% of *Escherichia coli* isolated from intensive care units were sensitive to ciprofloxacin.[5] Susceptibility rates among *Klebsiella pneumoniae* (91%) and *Pseudomonas aeruginosa* (87%) were noted in a total of 759 isolates of Gram-negative bacteria. Brown and colleagues observed no resistance to ciprofloxacin or cefuroxime among 200 isolates of *Haemophilus influenzae*.[6] However, resistance to amoxycillin was noted in 17% of isolates and to co-amoxiclav in 3.7%. Further susceptibility data from nursing homes for the elderly in the UK showed that overall, ciprofloxacin resistance was 6.1%, compared with 26.1% for co-amoxiclav, 38.9% for trimethoprim and 52.9% for amoxycillin (number of isolates was not stated).[7] Several reports from Canada showed high levels of ciprofloxacin susceptibility among Gram-negative species (Table 20.1).[8,9] In Argentina, prevalence of ciprofloxacin resistance in urinary isolates from the community has increased from 'extremely rare' to 2.3% (9/385) in 5 years.[10] In Brazil, however, prevalence of resistance in *Enterobacter* spp. and *Klebsiella* spp. has risen from 7.4% in 1989 to 16.5% in 1994.[11]

The incidence of multi-resistant *Streptococcus pneumoniae* has increased greatly in many countries. In Europe, Spain appears to have the highest prevalence. In Barcelona, for example, Linares *et al.* found 102 of 434 (24%) clinical strains to be multi-resistant.[12] Of the 102 strains, 100% were erythromycin resistant, 88% were penicillin resistant, 94% tetracycline resistant, 67% chloramphenicol resistant and 17% cefuroxime resistant. However, 97% of multi-resistant strains were susceptible to ciprofloxacin or ofloxacin.

Bacterial gastroenteritis is common and difficult to manage in developing countries because antibiotic resistance is common and many drugs are not easily available; thus, susceptibility data is of value to both local clinicians and doctors in the developed world who may treat returning travellers. Pitman and co-workers in Malawi examined 124 strains of *Shigella* spp. and found none to be resistant to ciprofloxacin.[13] A similar picture was seen in Jamaica by Bodonaik.[14]

Table 20.1. Susceptibility of pathogens to ciprofloxacin in Canada.[8,9]

Pathogen	No. of isolates	Forward *et al.*[8]	Blondeau *et al.*[9]*
		Susceptible strains (%)	
Escherichia coli	805	98	–
Klebsiella pneumoniae	152	99	–
Klebsiella oxytoca	48	199	–
Enterobacter cloacae	77	96	–
Acinetobacter spp.	25	88	78
Pseudomonas aeruginosa	111	97	85
Enterobacteriaceae	1440	98	97
Staphylococcus aureus	–	–	96
Coagulase-negative staphylococci	–	–	68
Enterococcus spp.	–	–	63

*Number of isolates not stated

Pharmacokinetics and pharmacodynamics

A group of patients who have difficulty absorbing drugs are AIDS/HIV-positive patients. Owens *et al.* showed that the bioavailability of a 500 mg oral dose of ciprofloxacin was 82% (± 13%) of a 400 mg intravenous dose.[15] The authors concluded that ciprofloxacin is reliably absorbed from the gut in AIDS patients.

Penetration of an antibiotic to the site of infection is clearly essential for optimal therapy. Takahashi and colleagues used a skin chamber model to evaluate whether ciprofloxacin accumulated in skin chambers as well as in white blood cells.[16] Ciprofloxacin levels were always higher in the chamber fluid than in the circulating white blood cells, reaching 0.15 mg/litre 18 hours after a single oral dose of 500 mg. Serum concentration at that time was 0.02 mg/litre.

The elderly patient tends to receive antibiotics more often than most other age groups, but dosage often has to be adjusted. Shi *et al.* investigated the handling of penicillins, cephalosporins, aminoglycosides and quinolones in the elderly compared with that in young volunteers.[17] They found that ciprofloxacin was the only agent which did not require dosage reduction in the elderly.

Critically ill patients treated for pseudomonal pneumonia may be given a high intravenous dose of 400 mg every 8 hours. Lipman *et al.* showed that this dose results in serum trough concentrations of 0.5–0.7 mg/litre and peak concentrations of 6.0–6.9 mg/litre.[18] If critically ill patients are also treated with sucralfate, there is no deleterious effect on the pharmacokinetics of ciprofloxacin.[19]

Clinical data

Community-acquired pneumonia

The emergence of multi-resistant respiratory pathogens in different parts of the world has led clinicians to consider alternative empirical therapies for community-acquired pneumonia. Rizzato and colleagues evaluated ciprofloxacin and teicoplanin compared with ceftriaxone for the treatment of the elderly immunocompromised patients hospitalised with community-acquired pneumonia.[20] A total of 150 patients were enrolled, of whom 74 received teicoplanin (a single 400 mg intravenous dose, then 400 mg once daily), plus oral ciprofloxacin (500 mg every 12 hours) for at least 10 days. Another 76 patients received intravenous ceftriaxone (2 g) for 10 days. In the teicoplanin–ciprofloxacin group, 65 of 69 patients were cured or improved compared with 54 of 74 in the ceftriaxone group ($p < 0.01$). Both regimens were equally well tolerated. The authors concluded that the teicoplanin–ciprofloxacin regimen might be suitable for treating community-acquired pneumonia.

Ciprofloxacin as a comparator

In some trials, ciprofloxacin is now being used as the comparator for new agents. An Argentinian skin and soft tissue infection study compared ciprofloxacin (500 mg every 12 hours for 10 days) with levofloxacin (500 mg every 12 hours for 7 days). The safety and efficacy profile of the two drugs was similar.[21] Clinical success was reported in 116 of 124 (94%) patients and 124 of 129 (96%) patients, respectively, and the overall bacteriological eradication rates were 92% and 93%.

Another new quinolone, sparfloxacin, was compared with ciprofloxacin in a double-blind trial by Iravani for the treatment of uncomplicated urinary tract infections.[22] Ciprofloxacin (250 mg every 12 hours) was given as a 7-day course, whereas sparfloxacin was administered as a single dose of 400 mg with or without two following daily doses of 200 mg. There was no significant difference in efficacy (233/263 [89%] versus 335/360 [93%] versus 328/355 [92%]). Another double-blind trial compared the two antibiotics in the treatment of soft tissue infections. Clinical response was achieved in 87% of patients given oral ciprofloxacin (750 mg every 12 hours for 10 days) and in 90% of patients given oral sparfloxacin (400 mg as a single dose then 200 mg daily for 10 days) out of a total of 475 patients.[23] The treatment of orthopaedic device-related staphylococcal infections with ciprofloxacin and rifampicin was compared to ciprofloxacin alone by Blatter and colleagues.[24] All patients received flucloxacillin or vancomycin for the first 2 weeks, with or without rifampicin. The success rate for the combination therapy was 100% (12/12), compared with 58% (7/12) for the ciprofloxacin monotherapy. Ciprofloxacin resistance developed in the ciprofloxacin monotherapy group in two strains of *Staphylococcus aureus* and one strain of *Staphylococcus epidermidis*.

Gastrointestinal infections

Ciprofloxacin's role in the treatment of a variety of gastrointestinal infections was examined by a number of investigators. In Peru, Gotuzzo now regards ciprofloxacin and other quinolones as the treatment of choice for typhoid fever.[25] In Hungary, Tusnádi and Bényei showed that 5 days' treatment with 500 mg of ciprofloxacin (given every 12 hours) led to 94% bacteriological eradication among 100 patients.[26]

Agalar observed an 84% cure rate in 25 patients with typhoid given a 7-day course of oral ciprofloxacin (500 mg every 12 hours).[27] In a smaller study from Texas, Girgis *et al.* also showed that a 7-day course of oral ciprofloxacin (500 mg every 12 hours) was similar in efficacy to oral azithromycin (1g as a single dose then 500 mg once daily for 6 days) (17/17 versus 16/16).[28] In a controlled trial of 74 patients with cholera, Usubütün *et al.* showed that a single oral dose of 1g of ciprofloxacin shortened the duration of diarrhoea from 4 days to 1.9 days, whereas two oral doses of ciprofloxacin (500 mg once daily) shortened the duration of diarrhoea to 2.5 days and oral doxycycline (100 mg every 12 hours for 3 days) to 2.7 days.[29]

Treating infections in the elderly

Zhong *et al.* showed clinical efficacy of 86.6% in 45 elderly patients with respiratory infections.[30] Chodosh *et al.* compared ciprofloxacin with clarithromycin for the treatment of acute exacerbations of chronic bronchitis.[31] A total of 376 patients were enrolled in a double-blind trial and received 500 mg (every 12 hours for 14 days) of one or other drug. Clinical success rates were 88% (147/167) and 84% (139/165) for ciprofloxacin and clarithromycin, respectively. The bacteriological eradication rates were 91% and 76% (95% CI for 0.052–0.26) showing superiority for ciprofloxacin, probably related to infections caused by *Haemophilus influenzae*. The incidence of adverse events was similar in both antibiotic groups. Cvjetkovic *et al.* compared oral ciprofloxacin (500 mg daily) in 32 patients with intravenous penicillin (12 mega units/day) plus oral co-trimoxazole (160 mg/800 mg per day) in 20 patients for the treatment of erysipelas in elderly patients.[32] The signs and symptoms of infection resolved 6 days sooner among the ciprofloxacin-treated patients.

Preventing and locating infection

Ciprofloxacin can be used in the prevention of infection in colorectal surgery, and to prevent blockage of biliary stents. Rohwedder and co-workers showed that the combination of a single dose of oral ciprofloxacin (750 mg) and a single dose of oral ornidazole (1g) was significantly better than a single dose of intravenous gentamicin (80 mg) plus a single dose of intravenous ornidazole (1g) for the prevention of wound infection following colorectal surgery (4/120 versus 14/120, $p < 0.01$).[33] Lam *et al.* showed that ciprofloxacin could play a significant role in preventing bacterial colonisation and blockage of stents used for biliary drainage and ciprofloxacin may be able to maintain the patency of such palliative approaches.[34] Perfusion of a stent for 30 days *in vitro* with bile containing ciprofloxacin (4 mg/litre) resulted in growth of only 50 cfu/cm^2 of a piece of stent compared with 2.5×10^5 cfu/cm^2 using bile alone.

Ciprofloxacin can even be used to locate deep-seated infections accurately. Hall and colleagues labelled the antibiotic with $^m99$ Technetium, and showed in 51 patients that this hybrid binds only to live bacteria.[35] It locates accurately deep-seated sepsis, showing a sensitivity of 84% and specificity of 96% when compared to radio-labelled leukocyte imaging.

During 1994, the imminent spread of possible pneumonic plague in southern India prompted new research into the optimal approach to treatment and prevention of plague. Russell and colleagues showed that ciprofloxacin, unlike doxycycline, was effective in preventing the disease in mice exposed to an aerosol of *Yersinia pestis*.[36] Treatment of infected mice with ciprofloxacin (40 mg/kg) raised the median lethal dose from 23 cfu to 2×10^5 cfu.[37]

Conclusions

Research activity continues to extend the recognised applications of ciprofloxacin. Therapeutic use is threatened by the development of bacterial resistance when prescription of the antibiotic is poorly controlled. Nevertheless, when assessed clinically, ciprofloxacin remains effective in a wide variety of indications.

References

1. Rodriguez CM, Gomez L, Xercavins M, Freixas N, Garau J. Bacteremias caused by ciprofloxacin-resistant *Escherichia coli*. 1st European Congress of Chemotherapy, Glasgow, UK, 1996: Abstract 002.
2. Murphy O, Stewart S, Fairbairn C, Freeman R. Ciprofloxacin-resistant enterobacteriaceae – an increasing problem? 1st European Congress of Chemotherapy, Glasgow, UK, 1996: Abstract T103.
3. Jesudason MV, Malathy J, Jacob JT. Increasing levels of minimum inhibitory concentration of ciprofloxacin to *Salmonella typhi*. 1st European Congress of Chemotherapy, Glasgow, UK, 1996: Abstract T133.
4. Tillotson GS, Dorrian I. Longitudinal UK survey of the activity of ciprofloxacin against Gram-negative bacteria since 1987. 1st European Congress of Chemotherapy, Glasgow, UK, 1996: Abstract T104.
5. Hanberger H, Nilsson LE and the Swedish Study Group. Antibiotic susceptibility of Gram-negative isolates in intensive care units at ten hospitals in Sweden. 1st European Congress of Chemotherapy, Glasgow, UK, 1996: Abstract T109.
6. Brown S, Amyes SGB, Thomson CJ. Antibiotic resistance in *Haemophilus influenzae* isolated in England and Wales. 1st European Congress of Chemotherapy, Glasgow, UK, 1996: Abstract T135.
7. Bowman C, Mitchell J, Tillotson G, Lane K. Elderly nursing homes, are they the source of antibiotic resistance? 1st European Congress of Chemotherapy, Glasgow, UK, 1996: Abstract T186.
8. Forward KR, Franks P, Low DE, Laverdiere M, Rennie R, Simor AE. A cross Canada survey of resistance to piperacillin–tazobactam (PT) and other antibiotics against 2,747 aerobic blood culture isolates. 36th Interscience Congress for Antimicrobial Agents and Chemotherapy, New Orleans, USA, 1996: Abstract E14.
9. Blondeau JM, Yaschuk Y, Shiplett M and the Ciprofloxacin Study Group. Static ciprofloxacin resistance rates: a cumulative Canadian multicentre study. 36th Interscience Congress for Antimicrobial Agents and Chemotherapy, New Orleans, USA, 1996: Abstract E16.
10. Farinati AE, Villar H, Jugo M, Roca A, Mendez E, Nardin ME *et al*. Ciprofloxacin (CIP) susceptibility in successive clinical isolates obtained from urine samples from outpatients. 7th International Congress for Infectious Diseases, Hong Kong, 1996: Abstract 111.023.
11. Rocha H, Lopes AA, Salgado K, Martinelli R. Increase in the frequency of norfloxacin and ciprofloxacin resistance among bacteria isolated from positive urine cultures. 7th International Congress for Infectious Diseases, Hong Kong, 1996: Abstract 111.012.
12. Liñares J, Tubau F, Ardanuy C, de Abadal M, Dominguez MA, Alcaide F *et al*. Comparative in vitro activities of sparfloxacin and nine antimicrobials against 102 multidrug-resistant *Streptococcus pneumoniae* strains. 7th International Congress for Infectious Diseases, Hong Kong, 1996: Abstract 71.009.
13. Pitman C, Amali R, Kanyere H, Siyasiya A, Phiri S, Phiri A *et al*. Adults with bloody diarrhoea in Malawi: a controlled study of clinical features, infectious agents, and antimicrobial sensitivities. 7th International Congress for Infectious Diseases, Hong Kong, 1996: Abstract 124.009.

14. Bodonaik NC, Chen WN. Antibiotic resistance in strains of shigella encountered in Jamaica. 7th International Congress for Infectious Diseases, Hong Kong, 1996: Abstract 63.017.

15. Owens RC, Patel KB, Nightingale CH, Quintiliani R, Banevicius MA, Nicolau DP. Oral bioavailability of ciprofloxacin in patients with acquired immun-deficiency syndrome. 36th Interscience Congress for Antimicrobial Agents and Chemotherapy, New Orleans, USA, 1996: Abstract A8.

16. Takahashi K, Duchateau V, Husson M, Bourguignon AM, Crokaert F. A human model of local abscess using skin chambers: penetration of azithromycin (AZ) and ciprofloxacin (CIP). 36th Interscience Congress for Antimicrobial Agents and Chemotherapy, New Orleans, USA, 1996: Abstract A81.

17. Shi YG, Zhang YY, Chen YJ, Wang ZP, Wang F. Pharmacokinetic study of antimicrobial agents in the elderly. 7th International Congress for Infectious Diseases, Hong Kong, 1996: Abstract 112.005.

18. Lipman J, Scribante J, Pinder M, Tshukutsoane S, Gous A, Hogendoorn CYA et al. Serum levels of ciprofloxacin (400 mg IVI Q8H) in severe sepsis. 7th International Congress for Infectious Diseases, Hong Kong, 1996: Abstract 25.006.

19. Krüger, WA, Ruckdeschel G, Unertl K. Transintestinal secretion of ciprofloxacin after iv application: fecal drug levels and impact on enterobacteriaceae are not altered by a combined therapy with sucralfate. 7th International Congress for Infectious Diseases, Hong Kong, 1996: Abstract 69.007.

20. Rizzato G, Montemurro L, Mosconi G and Multicentre Study Group. The teicoplanin–ciprofloxacin combina-tion versus ceftriaxone in community-acquired pneu-monia of elderly and patients with underlying diseases. 1st European Congress of Chemotherapy, Glasgow, UK, 1996: Abstract W174.

21. Nicodemo AC, Robledo JA, Jasovich A, Neto W. A multicentre randomised study comparing the efficacy and safety or oral levofloxacin (LVFX) versus ciprofloxacin (CIP) in the treatment of skin and skin structure infections. 36th Interscience Congress for Antimicrobial Agents and Chemotherapy, New Orleans, USA, 1996: Abstract LM4.

22. Iravani A for the SPAR Multicentre UUTI Study Group. Treatment of community-acquired acute uncomplicated urinary tract infections (UUTI) with sparfloxacin (SPAR) and ciprofloxacin. 36th Interscience Congress for Antimicrobial Agents and Chemotherapy, New Orleans, USA, 1996: Abstract LM6.

23. Lipsky BA, SPAR Multicenter SSSI Study Group. Treatment of community-acquired complicated skin and skin structure infections with sparfloxacin and ciprofloxacin. 36th Interscience Congress for Antimicrobial Agents and Chemotherapy, New Orleans, USA, 1996: Abstract LM20.

24. Blatter M, Widmer AF, Frei R, Zimmerli W and the ODRI Study Group. Treatment of orthopedic device-related staphylococcal infections (ODRI) with oral ciprofloxacin plus rifampicin: a double-blind, ran-domised, clinical trial. 36th Interscience Congress for Antimicrobial Agents and Chemotherapy, New Orleans, USA, 1996: Abstract LM20.

25. Gotuzzo E. Treatment of typhoid fever. 7th International Congress for Infectious Diseases, Hong Kong, 1996: Abstract 94.001.

26. Tusnádi A, Bènyei M. Efficacy of ciprofloxacin in patients with salmonella gastroenteritis. 7th International Congress for Infectious Diseases, Hong Kong, 1996: Abstract 63.009.

27. Agalar S, Usubütün E, Tütüncü E, Gürbüz Y, Türkyilmaz R. Ciprofloxacin treatment in enteric fever. 7th International Congress for Infectious Diseases, Hong Kong, 1996: Abstract 25.018.

28. Girgis NI, Brown FM, Butler T, Tribble D. Randomized trial of azithromycin (AZM) vs. ciprofloxacin (CIP) for treatment of typhoid fever. 7th International Congress for Infectious Diseases, Hong Kong, 1996: Abstract 12.001.

29. Usubütün E, Agalar C, Diri C, Türkyilmaz R. Single dose ciprofloxacin in cholera. 7th International Congress for Infectious Diseases, Hong Kong, 1996: Abstract 25.019.

30. Zhong SQ, Chen SP, Chen SM, Chen SC. Ciprofloxacin (Termaril®) in elderly lower respiratory tract infection. 7th International Congress for Infectious Diseases, Hong Kong, 1996: Abstract 25.024.

31. Chodosh S, Schreurs AJM, Shan M, Moesker HL, Kowalsky S and the Bronchitis Study Group. The effi-cacy of oral ciprofloxacin (CIP) vs. clarithromycin (CLR) for the treatment of acute bacterial exacer-bations of chronic bronchitis (AECB). The 34th Annual Meeting of Infectious Disease Society of America, New Orleans, USA, 1996: Abstract 289.

32. Cvjetkovic D, Jovanovic J, Hrnjakovic-Cvjetkovic I, Bogdanovic M. Ciprofloxacin versus penicillin + trimethoprim/sulfamethoxasole combination in the treatment of erysipelas of elderly adults. 7th International Congress for Infectious Diseases, Hong Kong, 1996: Abstract 25.032.

33. Rohwedder R, Bonadeo F, Benati M, Ojea Quintana G, Schlecker H, Vaccaro C. Single dose intravenous genta-micin plus intravenous ornidazole compared to single dose oral ciprofloxacin plus oral ornidazole for peri-operative antibiotic prophylaxis in colorectal surgery. 7th International Congress for Infectious Diseases, Hong Kong, 1996: Abstract 27.008.

34. Lam K, Destra T, Leung JW. Long term ciprofloxacin in the prevention of stent blockage. 7th International Congress for Infectious Diseases, Hong Kong, 1996: Abstract 70.012.

35. Hall AV, Solanki KK, Bomanji JJ, Britton KA, Das SS. 99MTc-Infection. In vitro binding to bacteria and clinical efficacy in imaging sites of infection. 36th Interscience Congress for Antimicrobial Agents and Chemotherapy, New Orleans, USA, 1996: Abstract D9.

36. Russell P, Eley SM, Titball RW. Ciprofloxacin and doxycycline prophylaxis against experimental pneumonic plague infection. 36th Interscience Congress for Antimicrobial Agents and Chemotherapy, New Orleans, USA, 1996: Abstract B57.

37. Russell P, Eley SM, Manchee RJ, Titball RW. The treatment of severe bacterial disease with ciprofloxacin. 36th Interscience Congress for Antimicrobial Agents and Chemotherapy, New Orleans, USA, 1996: Abstract B58.

Index